Lian Malai Madsen, Martha Sif Karrebæk, Janus Spindler Møller (Eds.)

Everyday Languaging

Trends in Applied Linguistics

Edited by
Ulrike Jessner
Claire Kramsch

Volume 15

Everyday Languaging

Collaborative Research on the Language Use of Children and Youth

Edited by
Lian Malai Madsen
Martha Sif Karrebæk
and Janus Spindler Møller

DE GRUYTER
MOUTON

ISBN 978-1-5015-1629-0
e-ISBN (ePub) 978-1-61451-480-0
e-ISBN (PDF) 978-1-5015-0093-0
ISSN 1868-6362

Library of Congress Cataloging-in-Publication Data
A CIP catalog record for this book has been applied for at the Library of Congress.

Bibliographic information published by the Deutsche Nationalbibliothek
The Deutsche Nationalbibliothek lists this publication in the Deutsche Nationalbibliografie; detailed bibliographic data are available in the Internet at http://dnb.dnb.de.

This volume is text- and page-identical with the hardback published in 2016.
Typesetting: PTP-Berlin, Protago-TEX-Production GmbH, Berlin
Printing and binding: CPI books GmbH, Leck

♾ Printed on acid-free paper
Printed in Germany

www.degruyter.com

Contents

Martha Sif Karrebæk, Lian Malai Madsen and
Janus Spindler Møller

Introduction
Everyday Languaging: Collaborative research on the language use of children and youth

1 Introduction

Increased mobility and new technological affordances have changed the contemporary sociolinguistic landscape dramatically not the least in a European context. Individuals navigate between many and highly varied linguistic possibilities and constraints, and the situation is characterised not only by the inevitable variation and change but also by emergent norms and by meetings between new and old normativities. All of this poses significant empirical and theoretical challenges for sociolinguistics (in the broad sense) (Arnaut 2012; Blommaert and Rampton 2011), and these challenges are at the heart of the studies presented in this book. The volume offers a theoretical perspective on empirically based descriptions and understandings of sociolinguistic practices and processes, and most central is the inquiry into (young) people's practice of using language. Language use is referred to as *languaging* (Jørgensen 2008, 2010) in order to avoid a principled, a priori and naturalised division of linguistic resources into distinct language. Instead this enables us to treat what is usually regarded as hybridity on a par with non-hybridity, in accordance with recent theoretical deconstructions of the concept of 'a language' (Blackledge and Creese 2010; García and Wei 2014; Heller 2007; Harris 2009; Jørgensen 2010; Pennycook 2010; Pennycook and Otsuji 2015).

The book presents insights reached by a team of scholars, through collaborative research, with a shared over-arching aim, a shared epistemological foundation, and in particular a shared empirical starting-point in a school in Copenhagen, the capital of Denmark. Our contribution to current theory building consists in the investigation of the role of language in the lived everyday lives, realities and understandings of real children and youth. We also add reflections on the fact that the language of children and youth not only reflects current and new conditions, but also creates and points toward future developments and changes. This constitutes the basis for the claim that our studies of everyday languaging in Copenhagen provide perspectives on language as a social phenomenon far beyond this specific setting – today as well as in the near future.

It is a basic assumption of the book that language is an everyday phenomenon which is used, constructed, and ascribed meaning in the local realities and encounters of people. In addition, constructed meanings, practices and norms continue to contribute to further developments and communicative encounters. Thus, we seek to understand the participants' languaging as part of their everyday lives, we want to understand the social goals that actors pursue with and through language, and we aim to identify the connections between isolated moments in time, and between different individuals' trajectories of socialisation. We attempt to make this leap by combining the snapshots of the individual case-studies in what in effect becomes a "moving picture" going across cohorts. The collaborative research involving a shared, ethnographic focus on a single setting has enabled a comprehensive and unique account of the linguistic everyday life of a relatively large, and at the same time relatively limited, group of children and young people. Through this account we are able to reach generally applicable and relevant conclusions with regard to language as well as to the social uses of language. The following chapters will show how the young individuals construct, reactivate, negotiate, contest, and navigate between different linguistic and socio-cultural norms and resources, simultaneously or alternately, how they do this linguistically, and how they do it while challenging or validating otherwise hegemonic discourses and norms.

In the remainder of this introduction we will elaborate on the common methodological and theoretical underpinnings of the chapters. First, we situate our work within the sociolinguistic perspective on diversity. In particular we discuss recent uptakes of the concept of superdiversity. After this, we describe the setting, the fieldwork and data collection in more detail, then we unpack the key theoretical concepts of languaging, polylanguaging and enregisterment, and finally we present the outline of the volume with a brief introduction of each chapter.

2 A critical sociolinguistics of diversity

The school in relation to which our fieldwork was organised affords a particular focus on linguistic and cultural diversity. It is located in a traditional working class area, now characterised by great ethnic and social diversity. Although there have been, and still are, institutional attempts at reducing the diversity at the school, the pupils currently (2014) comprise individuals associated with more than 20 different linguistic backgrounds in addition to a large number of national, cultural (including religious) and ethnic backgrounds. Such diversity means that the young people, and the participating adults, bring very different linguistic and cultural understandings and repertoires to school, and we have found Vertovec's theoretical notion *superdiversity* (Vertovec 2006, 2007b, 2010a) of relevance. Vertovec originally approached superdiversity as a social and societal phenomenon. He focused on the increasing ethnic and socio-cultural heterogeneity of societies, in particular European nation-states, resulting from individuals' increased mobility and new technological affordances (see Nørreby's chapter). Vertovec also compared the 'diversification of diversity' and individuals' multiple and simultaneous demonstrations of belonging (Vertovec 2007b) to a prior socio-political landscape coloured by ideologies of multiculturalism (Vertovec 2010b). The sociolinguistic and linguistic ethnographic uptake of the notion has focused on how individuals' language use, expressions of identity and affiliation with socio-cultural values have become less uniform, more individualised, and from a traditional and academic point of view less predictable (Blommaert and Rampton 2011).

The notion of superdiversity, its novelty, general applicability and relevance, has been contested (Makoni 2012; Orman 2012; Reyes 2014), and rightly so. Surely it does not explain much in itself. We regard superdiversity as a 'perspective' in Arnaut's (2012) sense, that is, a declaration of intent for looking at practices that may previously have been disregarded, neglected, negatively evaluated, and considered marginal, and for re-considering their ontological status and function for the individual language user, the communities of users (or non-users), and for the larger (socio)linguistic landscape. This interest is of course not inherent to the notion of superdiversity, nor is it unique to research that takes 'superdiversity as a perspective', but that does not make it less important. As Coupland states "we can only critique what we can theorise, only theorise what we can understand, only understand what we see, and only see what we look at." (Coupland 2003: 470), and it surely has become necessary to develop strategies to deal with diversity, with the relation between 'diversity' and 'variation', and with unpredictability, for language users as for researchers.

Whatever the reason and the causal relations, and regardless of whether superdiversity is something new in essence or as a theoretical perspective, the matter of the fact is that today we are ready to see and thereby document new complexity in the combination of linguistic and cultural resources deployed by individuals, as well as in their expectations and preferences within situations. In addition, as it has been pointed out on several occasions, such variation, hybridity and diversity (or even superdiversity) is really in some senses the normal, unmarked and unremarkable everyday state of affairs (e.g., Blommaert 2013; Pennycook 2010). This is certainly the case in the studies presented in this book, as in all of our work in and around this school, and it ties in very well with the languaging approach.

At the same time we have a strong commitment to demonstrate how labelled languages, traditional ethnicities, as well as other more or less well-established social categories and formations are presupposed and exploited. In fact, ideologies insisting on the moral necessity of regarding and treating ethno-linguistic groups and national identities as bounded phenomena continue to have very strong currency in societies built on modernist ideas and on the idea of stability as a fundamental (and desired) life condition; this regardless of commonly observed linguistic hybridity in practice, and of the prevalent (super)diversity. Such ideologies have linguistic counterparts (Jørgensen 2010). For instance, a preference for monolingual (rather than *polylingual*) language use seems to apply rather generally across Europe. Also, more or less institutionally orchestrated language standardisation constitutes an important part of the general sociolinguistic context and development in most places (Kristiansen and Coupland (eds.) 2011), but it is argued to have been particularly powerful in Denmark (Kristiansen 2009; Pedersen 2009: 51). In short, linguistic hegemony, a conservative standard language ideology, and a refusal, ignorance and dismissal of hybrid linguistic practices have firmly governed linguistic attitudes and policies in Denmark, and we see evidence of it in public discourse and education (e.g. Holmen and Jørgensen 2010; Karrebæk 2012a, 2013b; Kristiansen and Jørgensen (eds.) 2003). It is interesting to consider the fact that the composition of the pupil population of our focus school has changed over the last few years in this light. In 2007 62 % of pupils had ethnic and linguistic minority background. In 2011, according to the school administration, this percentage had decreased to 30 % which corresponds to the average for schools in the area. The change resulted from strategic work by a new school principal who aimed at transforming the school's ethnic composition in order to reflect the neighbourhood demography, as he repeatedly reported in interviews conducted by us as well as by journalists. Despite this general trend there continue to be large differences in the composition of different classrooms, in particular between the school-beginners and the school-leavers. In the two classes we followed through 7th to 9th grade, 75 % and 82 % of pupils had ethnic minority background (see Møller this volume for a discussion of this categorisation), at the same time a 3rd grade class we had followed for some time had two thirds ethnic minority background children, and in the new cohorts of school-starters which we meet in this book (the chapters by Karrebæk and Nassri) it was about fifty percent. We cannot know for sure if this has any impact, or which impact it has, on the type of meaning constructions, language and linguistic negotiations that we observe. But we do see the attempt at diminishing diversity in the classrooms as nicely reflecting the general standard-oriented, monolingual preference that we observe in society at large. Our focus children are thereby situated right in the middle of a larger scale societal struggle.

In contrast to the societal approaches to the diverse, or superdiverse, settings, focused on linguistic hegemony, sociolinguists have demonstrated creativity, innovation and linguistic ingenuity among speakers who draw on the wealth of linguistic and cultural resources available (Blackledge and Creese 2010; Blommaert 2010, 2014; Jaspers 2011a; Pennycook and Otsuji 2015; Rampton 1995, 2006). At a closer look, the creativity and individuality often consists in no more than re-assemblage of available resources, but it is re-assemblage *regardless* of traditional associations between linguistic and cultural resources and named languages or groups. The new – and creative – combinations may reaffirm traditionally recognised and institutionalised centres of normativity, such as family, school, the language academy, or introduce alternative ones, such as the peer group, the hip hop community, popular culture subgroups, and it may challenge the institutionalised centres that refuse certain (linguistic and other) behaviour and license others. In a Bakhtinian understanding, language in use embeds two forces operating simultaneously: A centripetal force drawing features, structures, and norms towards a central unified point, and a centrifugal force working in the opposite direction drawing away from the central unified point towards variation in all directions (Bakhtin 1981: 667–68). This can be understood at different levels, e.g. at a level of linguistic processes at large, centripetal forces can result in language standardisation (and register formation in Agha's sense which we return to), and centrifugal forces result in language variation. But the forces also work within the single utterance. Language in use is multi-voiced, incorporating prior utterances, perspectives and understandings, and points to such prior uses incorporating these perspectives, either accepting them, or challenging them (Bakhtin 1984). When considered in this way it is not surprising that hybridity is seen as messy, transgressive and counter-hegemonic, and that it is taken to destabilise the established systems, or regimes, of difference (cf. Arnaut 2012: 12). This perspective is important to underline.

The previous paragraphs point to diversity's close relation to a societal enforcement of hegemony and to counter-forces. We see it as part of our obligation not only to celebrate sociolinguistically exciting developments and discoveries, but also to raise socially and societally relevant and pertinent questions. Thereby this book (in particular the chapters by Madsen, Nørreby and Møller), and our work in general (e.g. Karrebæk 2012b, 2013a, 2013c; Karrebæk and Ghandchi 2015; Madsen 2013a, 2012; Møller forthc b.; Ag and Jørgensen 2012; Stæhr 2014a), represents a socio-politically engaged type of sociolinguistics, or what Arnaut (2012) labels a *critical sociolinguistics of diversity*, which "takes concrete encounters or events as sites where diversity is being articulated, experienced and made sense of with communicative and discursive resources that circulate locally or more broadly, reluctantly or more powerfully." (Arnaut 2012: 8; see also Kroskrity 2000: 5).

3 Copenhagen studies of everyday languaging: Methodological and theoretical underpinnings

The Copenhagen studies of everyday languaging have been carried out by a team of researchers who have done fieldwork alone, in pairs, and teams from 2009 until 2014, and the work continues. During the first phase of the project the studies focused on pupils in their final three years of school (grade 7–9; age 13–16) and school starters (grade 0–1; age 5–7). Several of the chapters in this book focus on data from the adolescents from this first phase (Stæhr, Ag, Madsen, Nørreby, Møller); the everyday life of the school starters have been documented elsewhere (e.g. Karrebæk 2012a, 2012b, 2013a, 2013b, forthc.). When the oldest pupils left grade school, some of us continued to follow some of them on Facebook and met with them on a regular basis (Stæhr, Nørreby). The second phase of the project aims to follow a cohort of children, divided into three so-called parallel classes, from school start in grade 0 (2010) throughout their entire school trajectory, that is, until the end of grade 9. In addition to these main strands, some team members have focused on middle school pupils (grade 4–6; 2010–14; Hyttel-Sørensen), and a recent partly overlapping project takes a methodological starting point in complementary classrooms in which Arabic, Turkish, Farsi and Polish are taught to minority pupils for whom these languages are recognised as mother tongues. This type of non-compulsory, institutionalised language instruction is labelled Mother Tongue Education in the legislative documents that regulate it, and the name (Mother Tongue Education) has become the conventional term, in Denmark, for instruction in minority languages for minority pupils, regardless of whether or not they have actual, practical competences and a wide repertoire in the language. Two of the contributions in the volume draw on data from the Arabic classrooms, and from the corridors outside them (Lundqvist, Nassri), and one contribution focuses on one of the boys who attends Arabic (Karrebæk). All participants are anonymised and the same name refers to the same person across the chapters.

Although our work is school-based, our research agenda necessitates that we go beyond the school-context and remember to consider the everyday life and activities of the participants. In order to cover just some of this, the Copenhagen studies on everyday languaging draw on a range of data types such as audio and video recordings of encounters, self-recordings, group-recordings, audio-recordings from homes, diaries from participant observation, ethnographic interviews, written texts, drawings, and computer mediated communication. By now, the corpus consists of more than 1000 hours of conversational data, and in addition many hours of recorded interviews and thousands of pages of field diaries. Also, although we have spent much time in school, and outside of it, with the young participants doing ethnographic fieldwork, some studies have supplemented this method with others, such as online ethnography (Androutsopoulos 2013; Stæhr), guise experiments (Hyttel-Sørensen), and the yearly group conversations (Karrebæk). The group conversations involve a quasi-experimental method which constitutes the back-bone of our longitudinal study. The participants are recorded in groups and given a task such as 'make a birthday drawing together' or 'describe what you do in your spare time'. Although we are most interested in the recordings of interaction and speech and not in the results of the creative tasks, it is important to us that our recordings point to lived lives. In addition, language use occurs in the moment but the processes of enregisterment and socialization extend over time. The moments that are represented in the transcripts discussed here are plucked from what is in fact a continuous process. Organizing our work among the children as both ethnographic fieldwork and yearly group recordings present us with the opportunity to compare similar situations over time, and to contextualize these as well as other less easily comparable encounters in the social and linguistic trajectories of the different children. Neither of these types of data have primacy, we see both as necessary and we aim to describe and understand their interconnections. Underlying the work is our commitment to the principle that if we do not seek to understand the children's language as part of their lives, and to identify the connections between these isolated moments in time – and between different individuals' trajectories of socialization – we will fail utterly in the project of understanding the intentions and social goals that actors pursue with and through language.

The studies in this volume are fundamentally indebted to the work and theoretical suggestions of Normann Jørgensen (2008, 2010, and numerous other publications). Among other things, this means that we put emphasis on language as a social phenomenon and on the ideological aspects of language, and we prefer to look at languaging, rather than language. In addition, our work draws extensively on Asif Agha's insights which are concerned with how human beings use language to organise social space, and how different cultural and social models are implied in and constructed while doing it (Agha 2005a, 2007a, 2007b, and others). Agha taught us not to differentiate between 'languages' and 'styles', but to view both as cultural codifications, labelled 'registers', enacted in everyday communication, and marking differences in social space. Agha also made us acutely aware of the ever emergent character of such registers, and that our object of study is not material and stable, but consists in is the processes through which single signs are grouped, re-grouped, and assigned with meaning. Finally, a significant theoretical source of inspiration is Silverstein's concept of the *total linguistic fact* (Silverstein 1985). Accordingly we regard language as a tri-part phenomenon consisting of form, use and ideology. Although we realise that the word 'total' may suggest an understanding of capturing 'everything' within this perspective, this is not the intention. Rather, the concept invites a holistic approach to language and it refutes the erroneous belief that each aspect of language is self-reliant and socially meaningful in isolation from the other two.

Methodologically our work falls within the framework of Linguistic Ethnography (e.g. Blackledge and Creese 2010; Creese 2008; Maybin and Tusting 2011; Rampton 2007). This implies that we believe that the contexts for communication should be investigated rather than assumed, and that this investigation should be ethnographic. Also, we assume the need to connect data (and case-studies) to the wider social world, and last we consider the internal organization of data (linguistic or other) to be essential to the understanding of the observed semiotic phenomena's significance and position in the world (see also Rampton 2007: 585). All of our studies have adopted these fundamental methodological tenets. Also, we see the development of language use as language socialisation (Kulick and Schieffelin 2004; Ochs and Schieffelin 2012), that is, socialisation to the use of language through the use of language (see particularly Ag's and Karrebæk's chapters). However, language is also only one among a number of semiotic resources that are important for understanding and explaining linguistic regimes, registers and individual development. It follows from this that we incorporate a range of other semiotic types in our analyses.

Linguistic ethnography, language socialisation, Normann Jørgensen's and Agha's approaches all regard language and social life as mutually shaping. They combine micro-analysis with considerations of locally prevalent ideologies and with larger scale social issues, and they consider the concept of indexicality (e.g. Silverstein 2003) as central for the understanding of the meaning and significance of situated language use. Last, it is fundamental to our work that we consider the metalinguistic level of data analysis essential. By this we mean that it is through meta-pragmatic activities on various scale-levels (Blommaert 2010), and manifested through more or less self-reflexive usage and linguistic commentary, that semiotic, including linguistic, resources become associated with particular values and social stereotypes as part of enregisterment. We investigate such metalinguistic levels through micro-analysis of interactional data, but also through orchestrating and analysing metalinguistic activities (Agha 2007a; Karrebæk forthc.; Madsen, Møller, and Jørgensen 2010; Madsen 2013a; Møller and Jørgensen 2011; Stæhr 2014b).

4 Languaging, polylanguaging and enregisterment

4.1 The Køge project: From code switching to polylanguaging

Our work has grown largely from the legacy of the Køge project (e.g. Jørgensen 2010; Møller 2009; Møller, Jørgensen and Holmen 2014). This was a unique longitudinal study of the linguistic development among a cohort of children of Turkish descent who attended a public school in the provincial Danish town Køge in Denmark. The central part of the data was collected once a year from 1989 to 1998, and it was subsequently supplemented with data from the participants when they were in their 20s (2006–2007; Møller 2009). The yearly data-collections (1989–1998) consisted of group conversations of groups of four: mixed boys and girls, boys only, girls only, Turkish-Danish speakers only, mixed Danish and Turkish-Danish. The data also included matched guise tests, official school results, language evaluation tests, interviews, etc., and the corpus has been explored from a number of linguistic and educational perspectives, e.g. second language acquisition, code choice in interaction, language attitudes among teachers and pupils (see overview in Jørgensen 2010).

In the Køge project we observed how linguistic features generally associated with different languages were increasingly juxtaposed in the children's conversations during the first part of the data collection. In particular several of the participants with a Turkish-Danish background developed linguistic practices involving frequent and fluent juxtaposition of features generally associated with Danish and Turkish, but also of features associated with other languages. Often the participants did not treat these linguistic features as 'not belonging together' nor as 'inauthentic' elements in their linguistic repertoires, and we therefore found that this way of speaking – deploying features associated with different languages – could not in a satisfactory way be described as 'bi-lingual', 'multilingual' or in other terms that rely on the separability of 'languages'. In other words, in a research field otherwise focused on code switching (e.g. Auer 1984; Auer 1998; Gumperz 1982; Heller 1992; Myers-Scotton 1993; Sebba 1993) we experienced an increasing discomfort with counting codes.

Against this background Jørgensen suggested describing language users as *languagers* (Jørgensen 2003: 146) and with Møller further developed the notion of *languaging* which designates the use of language by human beings, directed with an intention to other human beings (Jørgensen and Møller 2014). From this perspective 'language' refers to the practice of using linguistic features or resources rather than using languages, as coherent, bounded and distinct entities. Describing languaging as 'intentional' involves the central assumption that every time human beings use language in contact with other human beings they do so in order to have an impact (Jørgensen 2008, 2010: 13; Jørgensen et. al. 2011). Linguistic production is designed to influence one's interlocutors, and this of course presupposes that the interlocutors can make sense of it. In other words, language is always used for a reason, many times this reason is of a social kind, and language users, or languagers, are aware that languaging can have all kinds of consequences. Naturally, such consequences may be large or small, trivial or pathbreaking, and they may take place on several discursive levels. Yet, the important point is that language is used in interaction to grasp, influence, and shape the world (Jørgensen 2004: 13), and the studies in this book all address how languaging relates to understandings of the world, organisation of social life, constructions of interpersonal relationships, identifications etc.

Languaging covers all types of everyday linguistic communication. The observed linguistic practices carried out by (especially) young people in ethnically and linguistically heterogeneous settings, however, suggest that rather than orienting to a monolingual or bilingual norm, these languagers orient to a norm that Jørgensen (2010) baptised *polylingual* and defined as:

> language users employ whatever linguistic features are at their disposal to achieve their communicative aims as best they can, regardless of how well they know the involved languages; this entails that the language users may know – and use – the fact that some of the features are perceived by some speakers as not belonging together. (Jørgensen 2010: 145)

This means that in interaction speakers use linguistic resources, or features, and not 'languages' understood as coherent and bounded linguistic packages. Languages may be understood as bounded and natural categories, but these categories are socio-cultural and socio-historical constructions (Gal and Irvine 1995; Heller 2007; Jørgensen 2008; Makoni and Pennycook 2006; Møller 2008). Languaging in contemporary urban contexts is often characterised by a mix of linguistic resources usually associated with different named languages. But more generally, and in accordance with a Bakhtinian view, linguistic variation is the basic linguistic reality everywhere; there is never complete unity, similarity or homogeneity – although this is somehow always posited – instead there are forces operating towards unity, homogeneity and similarity as well as to the opposite. Speakers may use phrases and expressions from foreign languages taught in school (e.g. Jørgensen 2003; Rampton 1999, 2006), linguistic fragments or features encountered in media or travelling activities (e.g. Møller 2010; Lytra 2007; Rampton 2006), or selected features from styles of speaking generally thought to belong to a particular groups to which the speaker is not regarded as belonging, e.g. peer-group members' ethno-linguistic categories. This last example is what Rampton (1995) has termed *crossing* (see also Quist and Jørgensen 2007; Rampton and Charalambous 2010). Human beings can use multi-layered combinations of linguistic forms, and single forms do not necessarily carry clear distinct connections to specific codes or languages (e.g. Blackledge and Creese 2010; Jørgensen 2010; Jørgensen et al. 2011; Møller 2009; Pennycook 2010). In effect, there are no linguistic constraints on the combination of linguistic features, or resources, and when individuals refrain from drawing on parts of their entire linguistic repertoire, complex and heterogeneous as it will be, it also has a social motivation (Jørgensen 2010). To refer to these linguistically hybrid practices rather than linguistic norm orientation, Jørgensen suggested the concept of *polylanguaging* (Jørgensen 2010; Møller 2009).

The prefix 'poly' in polylingual and polylanguaging has been inspired by Hewitt's notion of 'poly-culture'. This refers to a "collection of cultural entities that are not (a) discrete and complete in themselves; (b) that are not in any sense 'intrinsically' 'equal' and (c) are active together and hence bound up with change" (Hewitt 1992: 30). Our findings focusing on language were similar to Hewitt's concerning culture in the sense that the speakers did not treat linguistic codes as coherent entities used one at a time. We have seen how it is often impossible to decide where one 'language' begins and another 'language' ends on an empirical basis. Emphasising that 'languages' are ideological constructions also entails that widely used notions such as 'monolingualism', 'bilingualism' and 'multilingualism' are inadequate as *descriptive* tools. Rather, they are norms of behaviour and build on the normative and ideological presuppositions such that a) languages may be separated and counted, and b) it is possible to establish when speakers 'possess' languages. We take the contrasting position that the relation between linguistic features and 'languages', as well as the relation between 'languages' and speakers, should be put forward as empirical questions rather than being taken for granted in analytical work. Speakers can choose to orient to a monolingual norm in their interaction, but they can also choose not to do so, and none of the ways of speaking are more 'natural' for human beings than the other.

This does not mean that named languages (English, Greenlandic, Serbian, Arabic etc.) do not exist. They do. Language users associate linguistic resources with 'languages' on a normative and ideological level, and these constructions are based in well-established national-romantic ideologies. They are, as such, also forceful and often consequential. But we insist that the understanding of language as divided into countable and separable languages refers to socio-cultural constructions, and it is from this vantage point that we use terms such as Arabic, Danish, etc. We also insist that on an analytic level, rather than positing and presupposing particular meanings associated with named languages, we look at how features and named categories (languages for instance) are associated, what meanings linguistic features, and languages, have, how these meanings are brought forward, how they impact the lived lives of participants, and how they are (made) relevant.

In this sense, research based on the Køge Project has participated in a paradigm shift in the approach to multilingualism as well as to language, and what we refer to as polylanguaging have been observed and described with other labels in recent sociolinguistic work. Some examples are translanguaging (García 2009, García and Wei 2014), metrolingualism, (Otsuji and Pennycook 2010, 2015) and transidiomatic practices (Jacquemet 2005). *Translanguaging* in García's understanding is "the act performed by bilinguals of accessing different linguistic features or various modes of what are described as autonomous languages, in order to maximize communicative potential" (García 2009: 140). The *trans-* prefix underlines a particular interest in what "goes between and beyond socially constructed language and educational systems" (García and Wei 2014). García's view of languages as dynamic and her focus on linguistic practices as they are carried out by human beings is entirely compatible with our view of languaging and polylanguaging. A difference is that translanguaging is often evoked in analyses of the space that is created when participants go between languages, but positing the existence of these languages first (Pennycook and Otsuji 2014) which polylanguaging tries not to do.

With the concept of *metrolingualism* (Pennycook 2009; Otsuji and Pennycook 2010) the main focus is on the interplay between the modern metropolis' affordances and linguistic resources viewed as products of personal life trajectories. Metrolingualism describes how:

> people of different and mixed backgrounds use, play with and negotiate identities through language; it does not assume connections between language, culture, ethnicity, nationality or geography but rather seeks to explore how such relations are produced, resisted, defied or rearranged. (Otsuji and Pennycook 2010: 246)

In this sense the empirical approach linked to the concept of metrolingualism addresses how bits and pieces of language become associated with (similarly fluent and dynamic) categories such as ethnicity and nationality. The prefix *metro-* should be understood as "the productive space provided by, though not limited to, the contemporary city to produce new language identities" (Otsuji and Pennycook 2010: 247). In this sense the concept of metrolingualism deals with the linguistic outcomes of human mobility, individual linguistic repertoires, and the space of the modern metropolis. Jacquemet (2005) takes a similar point of departure, with his *transidiomatic* practices, to describe the interactions involving transnational groups using different languages through different communicative channels including digital platforms for communication (Jacquemet 2005: 264–265). With call centres in India as his point of departure Jacquemet argues that:

> the world is now full of locales where speakers use a mixture of languages in interacting with friends and co-workers, read English and other "global" languages on their computer screens, watch local, regional, and global broadcasts, and listen to pop music in various languages. (Jacquemet 2005: 266)

Jacquemet's broad description of *transidiomatic environments* in fact describes almost perfectly what takes place linguistically in the classrooms among especially the older participants in our project. Only the list of electronic devices now includes smart phones and tablets as well.

As it should be clear by now, the concepts of translanguaging, metrolingualism, and transidiomatic practices are more similar than different both in terms of epistemology and ontology. They all take a starting point in the undeniable fact that individuals' language use is not necessarily limited by common associations of certain linguistic resources belonging to certain 'varieties' or 'languages'. They all re-examine the traditional conception of a 'language' or a 'variety' as bounded and separable sets of linguistic features. And they all problematise the normative aspects of this conception.

Our recent studies, reported in this volume and elsewhere, have taken up the exploration of languaging and polylanguaging, and of the forces driving language use more generally, but now with the important inclusion of ethnography as an essential basis.

4.2 Enregisterment

Agha's theory of enregisterment appeals to this kind of approach to language with attention to how linguistic signs over time become associated with wider cultural formations and how these wider formations interact with everyday communication. The concept of enregisterment has been widely employed and discussed within the past years of sociolinguistic research (e.g. Johnstone, Andrus, and Danielson 2006; Newell 2009; Madsen, Møller, and Jørgensen 2010) with its focus on "processes and practices whereby performable signs become recognized (and regrouped) as belonging to distinct, differentially valorized semiotic registers by a population" (Agha 2007a: 81). The theory of enregisterment takes into consideration meta-pragmatic activities on various levels ranging from circulating media stereotypes to local speaker practices. Enregisterment is the process through which human beings display and enact social functions of language. It concerns how we associate linguistic forms with particular ways of being and acting by talking about and using linguistic resources in particular ways. Language users label language use, for instance, as 'upper-class speech', 'polite language' or 'scientific term', and such labels relate certain ways of speaking to social relations, social practice, and identity categories of the speakers:

> Metalinguistic labels of this kind link speech repertoires to enactable pragmatic effects, including images of the person speaking (woman, upper-class person), the relationship of speaker to interlocutor (formality, politeness), the conduct of social practices (religious, literary, or scientific activity). (Agha 2007a: 145)

It is the situated semiotic activities of language users which over time shape the broader socio-historical development of language as social practice. Ways of speaking come to point to, or index, ways of being and acting, because they are repeatedly used in certain types of situations by certain types or speakers, and they are talked about or parodied in certain ways (Agha 2003; Silverstein 2003). From an enregisterment perspective, speakers' interactional use of different linguistic forms (re)creates and sometimes challenges the stereotypic indexical values of the used forms. Hence, in interactional use of resources associated with different registers, the stereotypic indexical values of the registers can be said to be brought into play and used for situational purposes. At the same time, the employment of linguistic resources continuously contributes to their enregisterment through ratified usage, and in this sense the indexical values of the linguistic features used are also (re)created. The ascriptions of values to linguistic styles can be more or less explicit. Mass media, of course, plays a significant part in the general uptake of value ascriptions to linguistic styles such as 'street-', 'gangster-' or 'perker language' (Hyttel-Sørensen's chapter; Madsen 2012), and linguists' descriptions and naming of linguistic practice e.g. as 'ethnolects' or 'Rinkeby Swedish' (sometimes re-circulated in media) are equally of importance (Jaspers 2008; Stroud 2004).

Enregisterment may also include the type of languaging we refer to as polylanguaging (that is, "the use of linguistic features associated with different 'languages', even when speakers know only few features associated with these 'languages'" (Jørgensen et al. 2011: 33)). This is the case when our participants juxtapose linguistic resources conventionally associated with for example Arabic, Turkish, or Kurdish with words associated with Danish (Hyttel-Sørensen and Karrebæk this volume). Some of the participants describe this practice as a central performable sign indexing what they refer to as street language (Madsen 2013a).

This exemplifies how the practice of polylanguaging itself may become enregistered and even labelled as part of new speech styles. Furthermore, it underlines the need to carry out analyses at the level of features rather than at the level of languages and to pay careful attention to new indexes of speech, entire registers and single linguistic resources. If we just viewed polylanguaging as hybridity or a mix of 'languages' we would miss that this can be enregisterment of a new way of speaking, and if we on the other hand just treated Street language as a coherent package of features we would overlook the dynamic aspects of the way of speaking including the indexical potentials of the individual features associated with Arabic, Turkish, Hip-Hop-language, Danish-as-a-second-language, etc., respectively.

It is clear that the ideological constructions of separate languages are not irrelevant to the practices of the young participants. On the contrary, they are highly metalinguistically aware of different ways of speaking and the values and norms associated with these. The adolescents organise their sociolinguistic environment with respect to dimensions of different ways of speaking understood as existing sets of linguistic resources usually described as 'languages' or 'varieties' (e.g. English, Urdu, street language, integrated etc.), with respect to a stylistic dimension of more or less formal/academic/respectful versus informal/peer-related/relaxed, and finally, with respect to ownership and rights to certain ways of speaking (Møller and Jørgensen 2013). Language norms are not only school instigated, they are also brought about in all communicative contexts we study, including family settings (Ag and Jørgensen 2012) and CMC interactions (Stæhr 2014a).

In fact, a striking contrast exists between the language use and norms among the adolescents, on the one hand, and the school beginners, on the other. Among the school beginners, Danish dominates talk in both institutional and informal contexts despite their diverse linguistic backgrounds. We also witness very little polylanguaging. In order to uncover the official understandings of the absence of minority language resources (and polylanguaging) we talked to the principal and the teachers. These institutional adults are responsible for the official approach to and understanding of pedagogy and classroom morality, as well as for the ways in which it is carried out in classrooms. In addition, we interviewed the other important authorities in children's lives, namely their parents. Together with interactional classroom data such interviews contribute to the understanding of the particular cultural environment in which the children strive to carve out places for themselves. From our different types of data it was clear that the linguistic hegemony with Danish as a dominant language is understood and exercised differently by different adult authorities. However, the school is clearly not conducive to the use of languages and cultural resources associated with minority backgrounds. Minority language repertoires are, at best, treated as irrelevant in school, and it is characterised as the best choice within the school area that the children use linguistic resources associated with Danish and not resources associated with minority languages. During everyday school life this attitude is left implicit – as there are no explicit restrictions of the use of minority languages – but very present and clear. The primary school children show little resistance to the monolingual order and linguistic hegemony in school, despite their diverse linguistic backgrounds. Thereby they are active participants in the process of socialization into a norm of institutional monolingualism and Danish dominance (see also Knoop- Henriksen 2013).

In contrast to these pictures of an almost all-encompassing Danish hegemony we have explored language practices in the minority family (Ag and Jørgensen 2012) with a particular focus on literacy in the home setting in a pilot study. It is clear that the hegemony of Danish is not exclusive here. Children may be socialised to the use of linguistic resources which are associated with a heritage language. The children draw on their knowledge of the different indexicalities of the linguistic resources available in the social context, and the adult caretakers' implicit and explicit evaluations of linguistic resources get reflected by their language use, with adults and with peers.

5 Outline of the book

The volume consists of eleven chapters including this introduction, nine empirical studies and a final commentary by Professor Asif Agha. The chapters all in different ways interrogate existing understandings of social categories, cultural diversity and language in the light of the everyday languaging and interaction of the children and adolescents. Most chapters investigate how urban children and youth construct, reactivate, negotiate, contest, and navigate between different linguistic and socio-cultural norms and resources. Some also treat the interplay between the educational system, parents', and the young participants' resources, aspirations and identifications.

Chapter 2, 3 and 4 discuss metapragmatic activities and enregisterment and they involve the peer register of the participants, a contemporary urban vernacular (Rampton 2011). Karrebæk's contribution, chapter 2, treats incipient enregisterment of the peer register referred to as Arabic among the children she studies. She focuses on a boy with Arabic and a boy with Danish linguistic family background and she illustrates that social regularities known as registers are permeable, locally constructed, and only partly shared by users. In chapter 3

Hyttel-Sørensen discusses different media representations of the contemporary urban vernacular, which subsumes (some understandings of) Arabic discussed in chapter 2, or Street language as was a recurrent term among the adolescents. Hyttel-Sørensen investigates the reactions to a media performance by the children, while Stæhr's chapter 4 investigates the adolescent Facebook users and how they orient towards different norms of language use by means of self- and other-corrections. He argues that corrections of language use are about more than mere orientation towards linguistic correctness and he suggests that correction practices on Facebook provide information about social relations among the adolescents.

In chapter 5, Ag discusses aspects of family belonging and identity positioning in relation to different normative centres and authorities. Lundqvist, chapter 6, shows that one child's trajectory of social identification increasingly points towards a metapragmatic model of the 'smart student'. Moreover, she points out that students, whom teachers assign favored positions, become socially vulnerable to peer group exclusion and their learning chances may be reduced. Nassri's chapter 7 shows how popular culture (the boy band One Direction) is used by a girl with Arabic background to position herself and to create alliances, and she demonstrates how issues of gender, homosocial behavior, transnational youth culture and social hierarchies are much more relevant than presupposed identities of 'Arabic' and 'Danish' in this girl's social life.

Chapter 8, 9 and 10 in different ways engage with stereotypical discourses of ethnic otherness and integration. Madsen (chapter 8) relates participation in rap cultural leisure activities and value ascription to linguistic practice to prevalent understandings of integration through club membership. Madsen argues that it is essential to attend to participants' stakes and skills in relation to the practiced activities whenever such activities are viewed as potential sites for social development. Nørreby (chapter 9) discusses the common essentialist understanding of ethnicity in relation to everyday ethnic positioning through linguistic practice of an adolescent boy, and Møller's chapter (10) emphasises the local, situated functions of more or less playful reinterpretations of racist discourses.

Finally Asif Agha whose work has had a major influence on all of us, discusses the wider aspects of the studies in chapter 11. In his commentary, Agha focuses, in particular, on how several of the contributions to this volume describe the social-semiotic processes through which enregistered emblems of social differences are formulated under conditions of immigration-based multilingualism. These include enregisterment of linguistic signs as well as other perceivable behaviours. He observes how some features of these models are formulated by mediatized processes and made available to a national imaginary while others are formulated and negotiated by young people in peer group activities.

6 Acknowledgements

It was Professor Jens Normann Jørgensen who came up with the idea that we should compile different studies from our collaborative research and publish them as a book. He had many irreverent and visionary ideas, and we would never have dared sending a book proposal on our own. Sadly, Jens, or Normann (he went under both names among us), was not able to carry through the work. In the summer of 2012 he was diagnosed with cancer and he passed away the following summer. It took us some time to take over from him; it took some time to accept that we had to, that he was no longer around. This book, and the work that led to it, is inspired by our teacher, supervisor, colleague, and very very dear friend, a remarkable man, a man who was hard to overlook, and who left an impression on people he met. This book is dedicated to him.

Jens Normann Jørgensen was responsible for bringing our Copenhagen team in close contact with what eventually became the InCoLaS, or, as it is also known, the International Consortium on Language and Superdiversity. Through InCoLaS we have made new friends, received tremendous support and inspiration, and constructive feedback, on this book manuscript as well as in general. Without our world-class international colleagues the time after Jens would have been even more impossible to get through – and this book may not have become a reality. For their invaluable engagement in us, as well as in the book process, we thank Asif Agha, Karel Arnaut, Adrian Blackledge, Jan Blommaert, Angela Creese, Sirpa Leppänen, Robert Moore, Ben Rampton, Max Spotti, Stanton Wortham, and other occasional participants in meetings and affiliated members.

In addition to the InCoLaS other colleagues have helped out by reading and giving valuable advice on manuscripts and work at some stage. We thank Jürgen Jaspers, Rickard Jonsson, Marie Maegaard, Janus Mortensen, Jakob Steensig and an anonymous reviewer for valuable inputs and Birte Dreier for editorial assistance.

Last, but not least, we thank all the children, parents, teachers and the school principal that have taken part in these studies over the years. We are grateful for the cooperation and engagement that made this work possible, worthwhile and extremely exciting.

Martha Sif Karrebæk

Arabs, Arabic and urban languaging: Polycentricity and incipient enregisterment among primary school children in Copenhagen

1 Introduction

All trajectories of socialization and all semiotic repertoires are unique. At the same time individuals participate in collective social processes which seem to go in particular directions into what may eventually emerge as socially recognized 'ways of speaking'. Following Agha (2005, 2007a) I identify this as processes of *enregisterment*, and in this contribution I discuss the permeability, local construction, and only partly shared nature of the social regularities known as registers. I will treat what we may term incipient enregisterment through an analysis of the use of resources associated with a non-standard, contemporary urban, maybe even youth, vernacular, occasionally referred to as 'Arabic', among a group of primary school children in Copenhagen, Denmark.

With its focus on young children and their socio-linguistic development, the study covers ground akin to the framework of Language Socialization. This was originally defined as the study of the role of language in children's socio-cultural development (Ochs and Schieffelin 2012: 1), as well as of language as an important target for socialization (Schieffelin 1990: 14).[1] It was formulated as an epistemological alternative to a Chomskyan approach to language acquisition, which focussed on the individual child's development of an idealized, abstract linguistic competence, embodied in a decontextualized speaker. Language Socialization countered this with accounts of the formation of communicatively competent language users and culturally competent participants who were situated in time and space (Heath 1983; Hymes 1972; Ochs and Schieffelin 1994). Also, it has been pointed out repeatedly that a co-existence of different norms and registers characterise all social communities (e.g., Duranti 1994; Kyratzis, Reynolds and Evaldsson 2010; Ochs 1988). Thus, language socialization, as a process, is not

1 Over the years the Language Socialization framework has expanded its area. Today its central research foci include children as socializing agents (e.g., Kyratzis 2004; Goodwin and Kyratzis 2007), adult novices, trajectories of socialization into non-standard or deviant subjects and subject behaviour (e.g., Capps and Ochs 1995; Karrebæk 2011a; Kulick and Schieffelin 2004, Ochs and Schieffelin 2012).

teleological and does not mean the gradual approximation towards a – or *the* – linguistic Standard, but involves a constant, and creative, struggle between continuity and transformation (cf. Garrett and Baquedano-López 2002). However, in fact, the ontological understanding of language has been little discussed within the Language Socialization framework, apart from the intrinsic and fundamental relation between language and the social world, and between language and other communicative modalities (although see Garrett and Baquedano-López 2002: 344). This constitutes a striking contrast to its thorough treatment within critical sociolinguistics where increasingly loud voices have argued that language has no boundaries outside of the discursive construction of these, that boundaries are created through ideological processes, and that they may be non-shared, poorly (or un-) defined, variable, negotiable, contested (Bauman and Briggs 2003; Heller 2007; Gal and Irvine 1995; Makoni and Pennycook 2007, and many others). So, norms are inherently unstable, and in fact language users' normative understandings, and linguistic practices, may differ, even though they participate in the same communities. Accordingly, social actors need to work to establish the mutual orientation which facilitates and ensures the progression of communicative processes (Hanks 1996), and the process of language socialization may result in emergent linguistic norms, developed in interactional sequences and consolidated over time.

All of this is highly relevant for studies of language socialization in contemporary urban settings. Semiotic, including linguistic, resources have spread far beyond the localities with which they are traditionally associated during processes of migration and globalization. At any locale today, resources with ties to many places are deployed in hybrid linguistic practices (referred to as *crossing, poly-languaging, translanguaging, metro-linguistic* and *transidiomatic*; Creese and Blackledge 2010; García 2009; Jacquemet 2005; Jørgensen et al. 2011; Otsuji and Pennycook 2010; Rampton 2006) and this points to new, and sometimes unexpected, types of alignments between speakers, personae, linguistic features, activities, labels, and participation frameworks. In addition, hybrid practices are part of processes through which speakers create new ways of speaking that get to be recognized as exactly 'ways of speaking.' 'Hybridity' may be a misnomer, or at least may be in need of serious re-conceptualization. For sure, many previously dominant *a priori* assumptions within sociolinguistics need revision, as argued by Blommaert and Rampton (2011).

In this contribution I combine the epistemologies and methodologies of Language Socialization and newer critical studies of sociolinguistics, including the sociolinguistics of super-diversity, and I complement these with a theoretical approach to language as a social semiotic phenomenon based on Asif Agha's theory of *enregisterment* (Agha 2007a). The empirical main focus lies on two boys, one with Arabic and one with Danish language family background, who are part of a pan-ethnic group of young children. I will demonstrate how language ideologies are performed in everyday life among young children, and how such social actors orient to multiple different norms and ideologies within one and the same encounter, sometimes even within single utterances. On a more theoretical level I wish to suggest the role and experience of single individuals in larger linguistic processes. Everyday life presents actors with a range of linguistic and normative possibilities, and in order to understand enregisterment processes it is important to know which normative possibilities people are orienting to, and exactly how they perform these orientations.

To contextualize the following analyses I will briefly summarize two prior observations regarding language choice and linguistic ideologies which we have made in the same school setting. The striking contrast between them motivated the research questions pursued here. Our fieldwork in two classes of (ethnically mixed) adolescents (age 13–16) resulted in descriptions of the use of different registers of language, some of which were rather local. Some of the young participants labelled these local registers 'Street language' and 'Integrated' (Madsen, Møller and Jørgensen 2010; Madsen 2013a; Møller and Jørgensen 2012; see also Hyttel-Sørensen's, Madsen's and Stæhr's contributions to this vol.). 'Street language' recalls the more general phenomenon of contemporary urban youth vernaculars or even (avoiding the 'youth' element) contemporary urban vernacular (Rampton 2011), which – whatever the label – refers to a 'deviant' register of language from a standard perspective; 'slang' in Agha's (forthc.) sense. Concurrently with this empirical work we followed an ethnolinguistically very similar class of school-starters (5–6 years). Here the sociolinguistic situation was very different as we hardly ever witnessed an orientation to other registers than (Standard) Danish.[2] Among the few situations (23 in more than 300 hours of recordings), 13 involved Turkish and 6 involved Arabic. The semiotic and linguistic resources (lexical, interactional, participation formats, and genres) deployed in these encounters, and the stereotypes, or in Agha's terminology 'characterological figures' (Agha 2007a: 165, 177), evoked were highly different from those associated with urban youth vernaculars (see Karrebæk (2012a, b, 2013a, b, c) for more detailed analyses of the school-starters). The reasons for the absence of Street language or other types of urban youth vernaculars, on the level of use, among the school-starters remain to be uncovered, but it certainly does not presuppose that the children had no knowledge of an urban youth register or no access to it. It

2 Many of the children spoke what is routinely recognized as 'accented Danish'. It is far from trivial to determine when they oriented to the Standard language, and when they did not. However, this topic is not the focus of the present chapter so I shall leave it for another occasion.

was deployed by peers from parallel streams who spend time with ‘our’ children in the afterschool centre and during breaks[3]. Yet, my present point is that that the striking differences between classes, cohorts and age groups at this one school need to be explored further. My contribution presents one such attempt.

2 Enregisterment, variation and change

Enregisterment is the basic social process through which elements such as lexical items, sounds, discourses, food items and other material objects become grouped together, into cultural models, i.e. *registers*, and associated with stereotypical actors, conduct, social and cultural values. Human beings constantly create, re-create and organize their social life through reflexive models and to a large extent they do it linguistically (Agha 2007a: 2, 2011). For instance, the deployment of a lexical item such as *wallah*, the (implicit or explicit) claim to know Arabic, or a refined wine-vocabulary, are stances, practices and orientations that enable social actors to demonstrate that they belong to particular social groups and to orient to particular social models (Karrebæk 2012b; Madsen, Møller and Jørgensen 2010; Silverstein 2003). At the same time, signs only emerge as social regularities, that is, as enregistered signs, when recognized and confirmed as such by other social actors. The population of speakers that recognize a register constitutes its social domain (Agha 2007a: 124). Some registers have names (Danish), some remain nameless (‘the way we speak in our family’), and others are referred to by means of several labels (‘RP’/ ‘posh’). Some registers are well-known and highly mediatized, some are recognized only by a single friendship group or family. Some registers are highly standardized, others not. Regardless of the size of their social domain and of the degree of standardization all registers are in a constant state of emergence; they are ‘open’, permeable, and unstable. New signs may become enregistered, old signs may no longer be recognized or become objects of re-interpretation. Registers may even go out of use. Changes result from different types of processes and from processes on different scales (Wortham 2012), and an important source of divergence, and potentially of change, is that individuals’ different trajectories of socialization may influence the understanding and re-enactment of a register (Wortham 2005, 2012). Individuals also exhibit

3 When in their third grade a team member (Narges Ghandchi) and I carried out a group discussion with the class. This focused on the children’s metalinguistic knowledge and usage patterns. At that moment the children had very specific understandings of urban youth style. They described it as characterised by the use of the lexical items ew and koran, associated it with street smart teenagers, and with the use of hand signs and particular ways of walking.

different degrees of competence and legitimacy in register usage. Some are recognized as expert-authorities, others as legitimate novice users, and some are illegitimate and inauthentic users altogether. In sum, one register label may be associated with quite different elements when studied over time or from the perspective of different individuals, and it is an empirical question if, how, and to what degree social actors share understandings, knowledge of, competence and legitimacy in the use of signs indexing registers. Agha refers to such part-overlaps as *fractional congruency* (Agha 2007a: 97). Fractional congruency opens for the creation of social boundaries within society, and people's continuous assessments of interactional conduct in social encounters draws on the *meta-pragmatic* knowledge of such divisions. Thereby uses of semiotic signs in situated encounters "form a sketch of the social occasion in which they occur" (Agha 2007a: 15) and we construe social relations and social groups as effects of their occurrence. The metapragmatic classification of discourse types links linguistic registers to typifications of actors ('boy', 'good student', 'street-wise', Arabic), role relationships (peer group, student-teacher), participation frameworks, genres and types conduct (play, transgression, school). Thereby the individual's register range equips him or her with portable emblems of identity (Agha 2007a: 146).

3 Language and urban youth – in Copenhagen and beyond

Numerous studies in Europe have pointed to new and relatively stable ways of speaking, often referred to as (multi-)ethnolects, which have emerged in culturally, linguistically, and ethnically heterogeneous settings. The studies describe the linguistic phenomena in very similar ways, as characteristic of youth (though see Rampton 2011 who argues that this way of speaking should no longer be associated uniquely with young people) and as involving linguistic features associated with immigrant languages and slang, a noticeable prosodic pattern, and grammatical reductions compared to the standard languages (e.g., Androutsopoulos and Scholz 1998; Auer 2003; Jaspers 2008; Kotsinas 1988; Madsen 2013a; Quist and Svendsen 2010). In Copenhagen such an urban youth register was first described more than a decade ago (Quist 2000). It has nation-wide recognizability (Hyttel-Sørensen 2009) and is deployed in other big cities than the capital (Christensen 2010). The register is circulated by the public media (Madsen 2013b) in discourses of educational failure and societal decline (compare Milani 2010 on the Swedish situation) as well as in satires mocking both ethnic majority and minority citizens (Hyttel-Sørensen this vol.; see also Madsen 2015: chapt. 4). The linguistic features (most relevant for this study) highlighted in the Copenhagen context comprise affricated and palatalized t-pronunciation [t^{j}], unvoiced uvular r [ʁ̥], alveolar s [ʃ], absence of glottal stop, a non-standard prosodic pattern, slang, swearing, lexical features associated with minority languages (e.g., *wallah (billah), ew, koran* etc.), and occasional common instead of neuter gender (e.g., Hansen and Pharao 2010; Madsen 2013a; Maegaard 2007; Quist 2000). Yet, as Agha (forthc.) points out, it has little explanatory value to list such structural properties. We do not get closer to understanding the register as a phenomenon, its composing elements, or groups of speakers' motivation for adopting or rejecting them. Neither does a list, in itself, explain why the features are used the way they are. We need to complement the structural description with a description of the metapragmatic and ideological qualities associated with the features.

Quist's (2000) study initiated a series of engagements with new ways of speaking that had emerged in ethnically and linguistically heterogeneous urban settings. She described a range of phonological, lexical and (morpho-)syntactic resources (including the aforementioned), demonstrated that the users of the resources associated them with a (positively defined) identity, and discussed if this variety of Danish could be considered a dialect, a sociolect or a register. She baptised it 'multi-ethnolect' (because it was associated with a multitude of ethnic minority groups, and because it drew on different 'languages') and concluded that all the traditional sociolinguistic categories were inadequate; the phenomenon was of an entirely new character. Quist concurred with Kotsinas' (1985) conclusion with regard to 'Rinkebysvensk' in Sweden that it was highly likely that 'multiethnolect' would influence the standard language (here Standard Danish) in the long run, on both a linguistic and sociological level. This could happen through 'low Copenhagen speech', from individuals' mutual social engagement, and in interactions, between young people with and without immigrant backgrounds. In a later study Quist (2005) put 'multiethnolect' into a different context. Inspired by Eckert (1989, 2000) Quist (2005) looked at linguistic variation in two high-school classes, and on language users' attributions of social meaning to linguistic variation. She identified 'Cool' as a style cluster which was associated with dark skin, masculinity, 'foreigner' status, specific clothing practices, lack of school orientation, among other things; linguistically 'Cool' was characterized by the use of 'multiethnolectal' resources which comprised the particular prosodic pattern mentioned earlier and the lexical items *wallah, eow, inshallah, jalla.*

On the basis of an ethnographic study of two 9th grade classes (a 'community of practice'; Lave and Wenger 1998), Maegaard (2007) established (emically) the social category of foreigner which was performed through a range of linguistic features. Maegaard found large differences between the language use of boys and girls, and most notably between the foreigner girls and foreigner boys. Linguistically foreigner girls were most and foreigner boys least close to the standard. Maegaard pointed out that the variables studied (t͡s, t͡ʃ, ʁ̥, raised e before nasal, and ʃ) were, in fact, sociolinguistically well-described and had been attributed to 'younger Copenhagen speech', 'low Copenhagen speech' or even 'high Copenhagen speech'. The foreigner boys took the lead over their female and non-foreigner classmates in the use of , t͡ʃ, ʁ̥, e and ʃ. Maegaard complemented the linguistic study with considerations of how other social practices were central for the construction and maintenance of the social categories. These practices comprised clothing, lunch-break activities (and food), afterschool activities, future aspirations, attitude to smoking and heterosexual behaviour, alcohol, and classroom behaviour. In this approach language was thus a stylistic resource on a par with other stylistic resources.

Based on data from the same school as my study Madsen (2013a; building on Ag 2010; Madsen et al. 2010; Møller and Jørgensen 2012; Stæhr 2010) described how one youth language register known as *gadesprog* 'street language' was associated with street culture rather than school success, and with tough, masculine, and emotional behaviour. She suggested that the meaning potential of Street language was related to the existence of another register named *integreret* 'integrated;' Integrated and Street somehow constituted a binary opposition (see also Madsen et al. 2010). The young people treated Street language as only legitimately accessible to 'perkers', a category of people with immigrant background (see Stæhr, Nørreby and Hyttel-Sørensen, this vol., on *perker*), or to Danes who had grown up in ethnically diverse neighbourhoods (Møller and Jørgensen 2012; Stæhr this volume). Madsen's analysis of Street language contains an additional point. Due to its specific indexicalities it can be exploited to "achieve school competent identities in a nonnerdy way" (Madsen 2013a: 134), i.e., speaking Street and orienting positively to school achievements. This is somehow reminiscent of Rampton's (2006: 298f) description of a young boy of Bangladeshi descent using stylized Cockney to combine displays of being on-task with signs that show him not to be a nerd.[4]

In relation to this contribution it is important to remind ourselves that the urban youth registers are 'slang' and in extension they are less codified and standardized than (Standard) Danish. They are still subject to different types of normativity of course (Stæhr this vol.), but the register is more prone to change than the standard, and the outcomes and trajectories of socialization are probably more open than socialization into standard registers.

4 Thanks to Robert Moore for pointing this out.

4 Indexicality and centres of authority

The social models involved in processes of enregisterment are normative understandings of patterns of behaviour, linked to (articulated or at least articulable) judgments of appropriateness, correctness, and value schemes of 'good' and 'bad' (Agha 2007a: 97; Silverstein 1998: 406). The relation between signs, models, and evaluative behaviours is *indexical* (Ochs 1992; Silverstein 2003), that is, based on perceptions of contiguity and pointing to the immediate linguistic context. Some signs may even be (indexical and iconic) emblems. At the same time, indexical meanings depend on specific socio-cultural domains and spaces. Consider, for instance, that some words are regarded as appropriate for use in certain contexts but not in others: *shit* is less likely to be appreciated in a classroom setting than *subtraction*, and the indexical meanings of the two words therefore differ according to the over-all framing. Individuals orient to specific ritual centres of authority (Silverstein 1998) when they evaluate semiotic behaviour. Such normative centres differ ontologically. They may be purely discursive constructions they may be embodied in specific persons, or codified in books such as dictionaries or religious texts. School (or: the teacher) may be one such normative centre, the (or: a specific) peer group another, and the family (or: the parents) a third. Authority centres are hierarchically ordered within ideological, moral schemes and with regard to particular spaces (Blommaert 2010; Silverstein 2003), and evaluations of registers or isolated signs reflect such hierarchies. For instance, in Denmark, Danish is the only legitimate choice in official institutions and settings, and immigrant languages are treated as out-of-place and of lesser value (Daryai-Hansen 2014; Holmen and Jørgensen 2000, 2010; Karrebæk 2013a; Møller forthc.). We find places that organize language use and language hierarchies differently embedded within larger official institutions as well as alongside them (Blommaert, Collins and Slembrouck 2005; Blommaert 2013; Madsen and Karrebæk 2015). Participants in all situated encounters may evoke (draw on or gesture towards) multiple normative centres – even if it is not always obviously the case (Blommaert 2010: 40). This multiplicity of potential sources of indexical authorization is called polycentricity (Blommaert, Collins and Slembrouck 2005; Silverstein 1998: 405). Thus, the relation between lexical items such as *shit* and *subtraction* is (almost) sure to change when moving from the classroom to the playground; or inside the classroom, when used in unofficial exchanges among peers in comparison to when used in official classroom discourse. As will be clear from the following extracts, the children we have followed are attentive to and exploit their understanding of different normative centres, and the existence of such different centres gives meaning to linguistic signs.

5 Method and data

This chapter draws on data from the on-going longitudinal study of a cohort of children's school career. At the moment of writing (April 2014) the children are in their 3rd grade / 4th school year (age 9/10). The cohort under study comprises approximately 75 children divided into three different classes or streams, and I focus particularly on two boys, Hossein and Tommy, who attend the same class. This narrower focus enables me to demonstrate in more detail differences between individuals' sociolinguistic experiences and processes of socialization. Tommy has a linguistic and ethnic Danish background; Hossein's parents are Palestinian immigrants from Syria and Lebanon and he may be regarded as of linguistic and ethnic Arabic background. (I will say more about my choice of main participants below). The chapter includes examples from recordings of yearly group conversations from grade 0–3 (ages 5/6–9/10) and from a fieldtrip (grade 2). The group conversations have a comparative character, whereas the fieldtrip occasioned a metalinguistically (and socially) unique encounter in terms of the light it throws on the relations between language use, linguistic registers, and linguistic authority. Overall, the analysis depends on our year-long engagement with these boys, the familiarity with other data on these boys, including insight into Hossein's attendance of so-called Arabic 'mother-tongue' classes, and the experience with this school as a cultural institution.

For the children the social side to the socialization process usually takes precedence over the linguistic, and it is a starting assumption of this contribution that language only exists in conjunction with human beings who use it to pursue social goals; what we refer to as *languaging* (Jørgensen 2010; see Introduction). As I analyse language use through situated activities, I engage with much wider ranging issues than the selection of specific linguistic resources, including identification processes and the production of social groups in relation to the development of ways of speaking and normativity. The triadic relation the *total linguistic fact* (Silverstein 1985) is a central analytic guideline. This implies that I study recordings of interactional conduct with specific attention to linguistic features, their interactional use and ideological association to larger models of personhood, morality, and belonging.

As a preliminary note on terminology I will not deploy the label Street language in my analysis. Street was one among a number of other labels (e.g., (in translation) *styled language, perker language, slang, gangsta language*) in use at the school that characterized similar form-meaning-stereotype relationships. Some children recognized and drew on the register but did not have a label for it, and to the extent that the young participants whom we meet in this contribution labelled it at all, they referred to it as Arabic. The relation between Standard

Arabic and this Arabic register is worth a paper in itself; I will not speculate on it here. However, the ambiguity of the term Arabic certainly underlines some of the difficulties with register labels. As mentioned, the non-standard registers associated with groups of young people of various ethnic backgrounds, with streetwise attitude etc. carry a number of names in the media as well as in academia, but it is not entirely clear to what extent the registers are congruent. Not to label the linguistic practices has the advantage of not suggesting the register to be a bounded, fixed and homogeneous entity, and it does not presuppose similarity with previous findings. The cover term I use most often is urban youth language / style (Jaspers 2008; Madsen 2015: chapt. 4; Milani 2010, on problems associated with labelling registers).

6 Primary school students' development over three years: Arabs and Arabic

Our longitudinal study covers a cohort of children divided into three classes, and from their school-start we observed rather clear differences between the classes. In one class a group of six boys tended to use lexical items associated with Arabic and slang, in particular *wallah, koran, eow* (a summoning interjection), affricated and palatalised t-pronunciation, and a noticeable prosodic pattern. This was highly recognizable to us from earlier work on Street. Six boys were particularly active participants. One had Somali background (Abdi[5]), one Eritrean background (Aleksandros), three had (different kinds of) Arabic backgrounds (Hossein, Abdollah, Abbas[6]), and one had majority Danish background (Tommy). In the following examples we meet all these six boys, as well as some of their classmates, but I focus on Tommy and Hossein. In this way the contribution is a portrait of the relation between two specific boys, and an attempt to place the two individuals socially within the larger group, and the larger group within the (local but) larger community of the school. I selected the two boys because they were both strikingly different and equally strikingly similar in their orientations and in their performances of semiotic relations. Their main teacher (in grade 1–3) characterized Tommy as a not too socially confident child, and his school performance as rather weak. According to our observations he was not the central figure in the group, and linguistically he used urban youth style, referred to as

5 All names are pseudonyms, except when I occasionally refer to myself (MSK) or other researchers.

6 Abbas left the school after second grade.

Arabic, sometimes with great success but at other occasions his use was treated as illegitimate *crossing* (Rampton 1995). In contrast, when Hossein used this linguistic style (which he often did) his authenticity and legitimacy was never disputed. The other boys regularly treated Hossein as an authority in both linguistic and social matters, and their teacher described him as strong on a physical, psychological and academic level, although with occasional behavioural issues. He also said that a weaker boy such as Tommy would naturally seek the attention of a boy like Hossein.

6.1 Group conversations grade 0: Tommy

In grade 0 Tommy participated in a group recording with three other majority Danish background children (one boy, two girls). The conversation was joyful with lots of laughter. Teasing and transgression were central social actions, and social identification became important, too. All of this is illustrated in example 1.

Example 1: "I am an Arab"; Spring 2011; audio-recording.
Participants: Tommy (b), Konstantin (b), Michelle (g), Ella (g).

Speaker	Original	*Translation*
Mih:	fuck (.) ☺undskyld☺	*fuck (.) ☺sorry☺*
	(.)	*(.)*
Kon:	NÅ NU KA NU KA DEN HØRE	*WELL NOW IT ((the recorder))*
	DET (.) den har lige hørt	*CAN NOW IT CAN HEAR IT ((the*
	det	*utterance)) (.) it ((the*
		recorder)) has just heard it
		((Michelle's exclamation))
Tmy:	nu har den optaget det	*now it has recorded it*
Kon:	hehe[he	*hehe[he*
Mih:	[(håhå)und↑skyld (.)	*[so(hoho)↑rry (.) hh*
	hh det var ik min mening	*it wasn't my intention that*
	det der	*(thing)*
Tmy:	å: fucking l:ort (.)	*o:h fucking sh:it (.) IH[III*
	IH[IIII (.) hi]hihi	*(.) hihihi*
Mih:	[Tommy (.) hva lav:er	*[Tommy*
	[law:er] du]	*what are you do:ing*
Mih:	har du din øh kx[xx	*have you your eh kh[xxx*
Kon:	[ER DU	*[ARE YOU*
	ARABER?	*AN ARAB*

20		(.)	(.)
21	Mih:	nej:h	*no:h*
22	Kon:	jahahaha[ha	jahahaha[ha
23	Tmy:	[mjeg er araber	*[mI am an Arab*
24		(.)	(.)
25	Kon:	nhihi	nhihi
26	Mih:	hva rager det dig	*it's none of your business*

Michelle initially exclaims *fuck* (l. 01). She shows to be aware of this as a linguistic transgression of institutionally recognized norms ('don't swear') as she apologizes. Michelle performs the excuse in a smiling voice which makes both the transgression and her excuse open to multiple interpretations, but surely it is to be taken as playful. The rest of the example continues within the same frame and keying (Goffman 1986). Konstantin points out very loudly that Michelle's utterance (and therefore her transgressive act) has been recorded (or: 'heard'), Tommy confirms this and Konstantin's laughter underlines the light-hearted atmosphere. The transgressions are just (for) fun. Michelle excuses herself once more and adds that she did not act deliberately (l. 10–12). The small break before the excuse may be inserted to make the transgression appear as an unintentional and unexpected act that Michelle did not perceive as problematic until after she said it. Her excuse is done while giggling which partly cancels out the sincerity (and credibility) of the speech act. Tommy takes the same transgressive line but one-ups Michelle's action: He expands on the same linguistic item in "fucking lort" 'fucking shit', said in an expressive and self-conscious way while laughing loudly. In a part-overlap Michelle asks Tommy what he is doing, and by that she points out that he also transgressed a norm; again she demonstrates her knowledge of institutionally ratified norms of speaking (which 'fucking shit' is certainly not part of) and at least pretends to demonstrate respect for these; it is hard to believe that she endorses them whole-heartedly. Subsequently, Konstantin asks Michelle if she is an Arab. This is probably just for fun, maybe motivated by her transgressive languaging and (possibly) non-standard pronunciation of *laver* [law:er] 'do(ing)' (l. 15–16). Michelle denies the attempt at othering and now an important change in the role alignment happens, as Tommy self-identifies as exactly an Arab (l. 23). The conversation continues in excerpt 2 where Tommy performs the new identity linguistically:

Excerpt 2: "I say khabakhalæ"

	Speaker	Original	Translation
27	Tmy:	♪demundisundi:♪	*♪demundisundi:♪*
28	Kon:	i arabere [de	*you / in Arab [they*
29	Tmy:	[KHABAKHALÆ	*[KHABAKHALÆ*
30		[xɑbɑxɑle̝] (.) jeg sir	*[xɑbɑxɑle̝] (.) I say kha-*
31		khabakhalæ [xɑbɑxɑle̝]	*bakhalæ [xɑbɑxɑle̝] that means*
32		det betyder ☺de:n lh:	*☺tha:t shh: [(.) s: it] means*
33		[(.) l: det] betyder det	*that >s h i t<☺*
34		>l o r t<☺	
35	Mih:	[hehe]	*[hehe]*
36	Mih:	aj Tommy [xxx	*noh Tommy [xxx*
37	Kon:	[khalæi	*[khalæi* [[xɑle̝i]]
		[[xɑle̝i]]	
38	Tmy:	SHÆDA:M [[sʰe̝dam]]	SHÆDA:M [[sʰe̝dam]]
39	Mih:	SHÆIDAMA (.) jeg ved ik	*SHÆDAMA (.) I don't know what*
40		hva det betyder	*it means*
41	Tmy:	hende der hun ved ik	*that girl she doesn't even*
42		engang hva shæidam det	*know what shæidam means (.)*
43		betyder (.) hehe (.) BUH	*hehe (.) BUH ((to Kon))*
44	Ell:	det betyder sikkert shit	*it probably means shit*
45	Tmy:	nej!	*no!*
46	Mih:	Haha	*Haha*
47	Tmy:	SHÆIDAM tror du det- (.)	*SHÆIDAM do you think so- (.)*
48		hende der hun er helt	*that girl she is totally fin-*
49		færdig	*ished* ((referring to Michelle
50			who is laughing heartedly))
51	Mih:	hihi[hi (.)] jeg ska lige	*hihi[hi (.)] I need to use the*
52		bruge den lillae Ella	*purple one Ella*
53			
54	Ell:	[hehe	*[hehe*
55	Tmy:	shæ:dam	*shæ:dam*

Tommy initially sings a small (self-composed?) tune of nonsense words, but then in his next turn he presents the other children with the sign form *khabakhalæ* [xɑbɑxɑle̝]. Tommy most likely associates it with Arabic, an assumption I build on his self-identification (as an Arab) and on the resemblance between [xɑbɑxɑle̝] and the institutionally enregistered Arabic lexical item *khara* [xara] 'shit.' Besides Tommy translates [xɑbɑxɑle̝] as *S H I T* (l. 33–34). 'Shit' can be regarded as an equivalent to Michelle's *fuck* on a metapragmatic level, and so Tommy stays within the same frame (transgression and fun) but self-identifies as a new kind of persona, an Arab, both explicitly and through his choice of linguistic resources. This is well appreciated, and Tommy continues with a second Arabic linguistic item: *shæidam* (l. 38), probably a version of the Arabic word for Satan (*shaytân*). Michelle claims to be unaware of the word's meaning and Tommy ridicules her for the lack of allegedly very basic insight ('she doesn't *even* know'; l. 41–43). Instead he seems to address a group of (imagined) overhearers who will agree with his categorization of her as ignorant, possibly a group of (other) Arabs. During the entire excerpt Tommy and Michelle demonstrate awareness of the different norm centres at play and the transgressive potential of selected items within the school's regime. Tommy shows this by shifting between use (l. 29, 38, 55) and mention (l. 30–31, 42, 47) of the dangerous-and-therefore-attractive word forms. The mentioning of the graphemic form of the English translation of 'shit', broken up into meaningless parts (letters), demonstrates Tommy's distancing of self-as-animator from the strong indexicality of the 'unmentionable' (Fleming and Lempert 2011). Michelle, too, plays with the thrilling experience of tasting the dangerous words in a way that minimizes the social risks of breaking a taboo when she only claims her lack of understanding of *shæidam(a)* subsequently to saying (mentioning) it (l. 39–40), again simultaneously claiming innocence *and* aligning with Tommy and the play-frame.

Examples 1 and 2 illustrate the use of linguistic resources associated with other languages and registers than Danish (Arabic), their exploitation in processes of identification, here with the group of 'Arabs', the construction of a cool persona, and of all of this being appreciated in the peer group encounter. They also illustrate the co-existence and simultaneous relevance of different norm centres. One centre is located with the institutional adults and the school regime, another with the peer group community, and one specifically with 'Arabs'. The children's laughter is evidence of their understanding of a clash between the use of specific signs and the institutional setting usually associated with another normative order. Unmentionables project participation frameworks, communicative events, and actors to inhabit them (Fleming and Lempert 2011: 7). It is not a far cry to see the use of taboo expressions as the direct motivation for Konrad's introduction of the category 'Arab', it suggests that 'Arabs' in this context are associated with norm transgressions, and this in turn motivated Tommy's introduction of 'Arab' sign forms.

6.2 Group conversations grade 0: Hossein

In grade 0 Hossein participated in a group recording with the boys Danilo (Roma background) and Aleksandros (Eritrean background). The conversation was keyed rather differently than the previous, and the example illustrates one of the many exchanges of challenges between Aleksandros and Hossein; Danilo was generally marginalized interactionally. The example falls after Hossein has told Aleksandros not to *spille smart* 'play smart'.

Example 3: sixandahalf years; Spring 2011; audio-recording
Participants: Hossein (b), Danilos (b), Aleksandros (b)

01	Ale:	du tror du er noget du bare	*you think you are someone*
02		en lille kvaj'	*you're just a small fool*
03	Hos:	du bare en lille lort	*you're just a small shit*
		[ɭoɐ̯ˀd]	
04	Ale:	du bare en lille (.) en	*you're just a small (.) a*
		lille lort oss	*small shit too*
05	Hos:	bare en [lille prut]	*just a [small fart]*
06	Dan:	[Hossein]	*[Hossein]*
07			
08	Ale:	[jeg mener jeg sir det] jeg	*[I mean I am going to tell] I*
09		er ligeglad [jeg sir det til	*don't care [I am going to tell*
10		Louise	*Louise]*
11	Dan:	[Hossein] (.) [Hossein	*[Hossein] (.) [Hossein*
12			
13	Hos:	jeg [sir det oss] Louise du	*I [am also going to tell*
14		sagde jeg er en lort	*Louise you said I'm a shit*
15	Dan:	Hosse[in	*Hosse[in*
16	Ale:	[du begyndte	*[you started*
19	Hos:	[koran du gjorde	*[koran you did*
20	Dan:	[Hossein	*[Hossein*
21	Dan:	Hossein	*Hossein*
22	Hos:	mm	*mm*
23	Dan:	hvor mange år er du?	*how many years are you?*
24	Ale:	koran	*koran*
25	Hos:	HVA	*WHAT*
26	Dan:	hvor mange år er du	*how many years are you*
27			((almost beggingly))
28	Hos:	åhr jeg er seks	*orh I am six*

29		(.)	(.)
30	Dan:	seks?	*six?*
31	Hos	jaeh	*yeah*
32	Ale:	årh du sagde det [der ord	*orh you said [that word*
33	Dan:	[jeg	*[I*
34	Hos:	[sexy: (.)	*[sexy: (.) [sexy*
		[sexy	
35	Dan:	[er du seks år	*[are*
36			*you six years*
37	Dan:	er du [seks år?	*are you [six years?*
38	Hos:	[det ik for små børn	*[it isn't for small*
39		(.) eller ta:r det hele (.)	*kids (.) or take it all (.)*
40		seksetha:lvt ((rapping))	*sixandahalf* ((rapping))
41		(.)	*(.)*
42	Dan:	er du seks år	*are you six years*
43	Hos:	<u>SEKSETHALVT</u> sagde jeg	*<u>SIXANDAHALF</u> I said*

In his response (to Hossein) Aleksandros draws on an idiomatic and demeaning formulation (*at tro man er noget* 'to believe to be something') which constructs Hossein as making unwarranted claims of superior status ('you're something'; l. 01). Aleksandros points out that it is *Hossein* who holds the understanding (suggesting that it is not shared by others), and that it is a *belief* (which presupposes an epistemic stance of uncertainty). Instead Aleksandros claims with no markers of uncertainty or modification that Hossein is an example of the type 'fool': "du bare en kvaj" (l. 02); this phrase contains the use of common instead of neuter gender (*en* rather than standard *et*) described as typical for urban youth language (Quist 2000). Hossein initiates a sequence of format-tying (Goodwin 1990: 177–88) turns when he calls Aleksandros a small shit ("du bare en lille lort"), an upgrade from the more harmless *kvaj* 'fool'. Aleksandros appears to have run out of good ideas for insults as he pauses and then repeats Hossein's *shit* ("du bare en lille (.) en lille lort oss"; l. 04), one additional example of format-tying where the essential difference is the change of referent of 'you' (*du*) from Aleksandros to Hossein. Hossein substitutes 'a shit' for 'a fart', again building on the same phrase structure, but Aleksandros withdraws from the exchange of insults and threatens Hossein with telling on him to the teacher (*Louise*): 'I mean it I'm going to tell I don't care I am going to tell Louise' (l. 08–10); 'I don't care' may index a peer norm of social behaviour according to which one does not involve the teacher in conflicts. The implicit message is that Hossein has transgressed an institutional behavioural norm which the teacher will respond negatively to, should Aleksandros choose to tell on him. The part of the utterance 'I mean I say it' is pronounced with the remarkable prosodic pattern, and the formulation 'I mean it', an intensifier, is also widely used in urban youth language. Hossein responds to the threat and explicitly refers to a transgressive act committed by Aleksandros (he allegedly called Hossein a shit). Aleksandros remarks that it was Hossein who started the name-calling routine which may free Aleksandros from some responsibility. Hossein contests Aleksandros by positioning him as the instigator; *koran* is used to emphasize the truth-value of the proposition. *Koran* is conventionally attributed to Arabic but more relevant here it is highly emblematic of urban youth speech, as one of two shibboleths, the other one being *wallah*. Simultaneously with Hossein and Aleksandros' sequence of insults and threats Danilo attempts to attract Hossein's attention and when he finally succeeds he asks Hossein about his age, possibly to use this to establish a social hierarchy, possibly just to make him pronounce the word *seks* 'six'. In Danish the numeral *seks* and the common noun *sex* 'sex' are homophones, and the similarity is made relevant by Aleksandros' reaction to Hossein's turn. Speakers may avoid signs that are phonetically similar to taboos and transgressive expressions (Fleming and Lempert 2011: 9), and Aleksandros treats 'that word' (six / *seks*) as an unmentionable – which has now been said loud. The keying changes from insults / threats, on one side, and neutral informational exchange, on the other, into fun and play. Hossein exploits the newly introduced theme to say "sexy sexy" which is transgressive – and tempting – in itself. Subsequently Hossein creatively builds on his knowledge of (the institutional approach to) sex and related topics as he launches himself into a rap which includes the phrase 'this is not for small children'. Sex and related matters are not for children, and six year old Hossein does not identify with this group. Instead he orients towards youth culture associated with rap. Hossein has presented (parts of) this rap song earlier in the conversation but it fits perfectly into the local context. He adjusts it when he finishes off by adding a specification of his age: 'sixandahalf'. Danilo asks if he is six years old, and Hossein shouts out 'SIXANDAHALF I said', thereby treating Danilo as either inattentive or dumb, and in any case of so much lower status than Hossein that he is allowed to discipline him with an exaggerated correction.

To sum up, this extract shows how three boys deploy performable signs well-known from studies of urban language use, including a special prosodic pattern, lexical resources, formulaic phrases, rap song, (ritual) insults. Two of the boys (who are six (andahalf) and seven years old) construct confrontational, tough, (maybe even) masculine personae, and one tops this up with a demonstration of competence in pop culture and an interest in sex. The boys orient to a peer group norm centre, but the existence of an additional one (the teachers) is alluded to several times.

6.3 Non-standard Danish in the longitudinal study

We have much more evidence of the use of non-standard Danish features in Hossein and Tommy's friendship group than the sequences in the above. I will now show a few additional examples, from the group recordings. I have no space for discussing them thoroughly in this contribution, and the section is merely meant to give a picture of the linguistic (form- and usage-) types we find and some of their social consequences. Some initial methodological comments are necessary. In the selection process I considered prior studies' associations of linguistic features with urban youth, as referred to earlier in the paper, including: pronunciation (affricated and palatalized t-pronunciation [t^j], unvoiced uvular r [ʁ̥], alveolar s [ʃ], absence of glottal constriction), a marked prosody, slang, swearing, hybrid language use (including lexical features such as *wallah (billah), eow, koran* etc.), common instead of neuter gender (e.g., Hansen and Pharao 2010; Madsen 2013a; Maegaard 2007; Quist 2000). I focused mostly on lexical items and slang, but other features co-occur with these. This is unsurprising. As pointed out repeatedly by Agha (2005, 2007a, 2011), enregistered style is really a co-occurrence pattern, and it also involves different types of semiotic material. In the following the focal linguistic items are in bold. A full linguistic analysis of the data material and the children's development over the three years remains to be made; for this contribution I have picked out some of the most salient examples.

A second methodological issue concerns the basis for the classification of the features. Although we have evidence that *other* children and adolescents have associated some linguistic features with a specific persona, style, sociocultural model etc., i.e. with a (urban youth) register, we have no guarantee that the children in the cohort here agree with prior categorizations, or with my categorization, that they do it all the time, or that they did at the time of recording. However, the considerable overlap between previous descriptions, including the co-occurrence of several earlier described features, does give a certain degree of certainty that here we meet the performance of an urban youth register.

Example 4:
(grade 0)

01	Kon:	jeg vil klippe ham her på	*I will cut him on*
02		(.)	(.)
03	Tmy:	nej (.) ham klipper du ik	*no (.) you are not cutting him*
04		på	*on*
05	Kon:	Hehe	hehe

06 Tmy:	**WALLAH BI**	**WALLAH BI**
07 Kon:	Hehe	hehe

Tommy and Konstantin are disagreeing, in a friendly way, about what to glue on a large cardboard illustration. Very loudly Tommy says “wallah bi”, a truncated form of *wallah billah*, to emphasize his prior contestation of Konstantin. Both are expressing that they find the exchange engaging and fun.

Example 5:
(grade 0)

01 Ale:	hva tegner du	*what are you drawing?*
02 Hos:	ved jeg ik	*don't know*
03 Ale:	haha (.) **ornli sjov ornli**	*haha (.)* ***proper fun proper fun***
04	**sjov**	
05 Kon:	Hehe	hehe

Hossein claims not to know what he is drawing, but Aleksandros characterizes his drawing as ‘proper fun’. Aleksandros often uses *ornli* ‘proper’. This is a non-standard modifier (‘slang’) that at some point was taken up by the media in (humorous) representations of gangsta personas from ethnically heterogeneous environments (Madsen 2015: chapt. 4). Of course, it is not sure at all that this lexical item index ethnically heterogeneous youth groups, nor even *gangstas*, in this situation, to Aleksandros or to any of the young children we have studied. It may belong to a broader register of Danish youth slang.

Example 6:
(grade 0)

Hos: kig nu ik han tegner **grimt** (.) **koran han tegner grimt** kig *look now right is drawing* ***ugly (.) koran he is drawing ugly*** *look*

Hossein is referring to Danilo’s drawing as ‘ugly’. He emphasizes his stance through the intensifier *koran* and pronounces *r-* in *grimt* as [ʁ̥]. A similar pronunciation is presented by Tommy and Abdi when they evaluate the physical appearance of women represented on postcards provided by the research team:

Example 7:
(1st grade)

01 Tmy:	ska jeg sige dig hvem der	*do you want me do you want me*
02	er g**r**im g**r**im g**r**im g**r**im g**r**im	*to tell you who is* ***ugly ugly***
03	lidt pæn men: mest pæn (.)	***ugly ugly ugly*** *a little nice*
04	hende der	*bu:t most nice (.) that one*
05 Adi:	jeg synes hende der er mest	*I think that one (femininum;*
06	pæn	*MSK) is most nice*
07 Tmy:	er du gal mand hende der er	*are you mad man that one (fem-*
08	fucking g**r**im	*ininum; MSK) is fucking* ***ugly***
09 Abl:	hvem hvem	*who who*
10 Adi:	hende der hun er fucking g**r**im	*that one (femininum; MSK) she is fucking* ***ugly***

Later in the same conversation the third participant Victor, a boy of Danish majority background, comments indirectly on Aleksandros and Abdi's way of speaking. Abdi demands that Victor says *wallah* (meaning that Victor should swear) but Victor refuses on the grounds that he does not want to use 'that language':

Example 8:
(1st grade)

01 Adi:	sig **wallah**	*say* ***wallah***
02	(.)	*(.)*
03 Vct:	jeg sir ik det der sprog	*I don't say that language*

Victor distances himself from the use of *wallah* which he refers to as "det der sprog" 'that language', probably in lack of a better word. I believe that it is not a far cry to see *wallah* used here as an emblem of a range of resources associated with a stereotypical speaker with which Victor does not wish to identify.

Examples 4–8 illustrate the general deployment of linguistic features that index urban youth style. Some of them are traditionally associated with Arabic (*wallah, Koran*), some of them are not (prosody, [ʁ̥], *ornli*). The boys we have met all have different ethnic and linguistic backgrounds (Danish, Arabic, Eritrean, Somali) and it does not make sense to motivate the languaging with specific background characteristics. It is more likely to be motivated by the role relationships, identifications, genres and keyings that they perform. The interactions are often keyed as fun, some as confrontational, many include negative evaluations and negotiations of the relative positions in a social hierarchy. There is an emerging relation between these types of social acts and linguistic choices, and given the similarity between the uses, such relation gets strengthened over encounters and time. There are also differences in the boys' understandings, use and legitimacy of certain of the resources; this is the point of the paper's last part. Again I focus on Tommy and Hossein in order to show how these two boys go through different processes of socialization.

6.4 Tommy and Hossein: Metalinguistic discussions of *wallah* in 2nd grade

At the time of writing our last series of group recordings dated from 2nd grade; here Hossein and Tommy participated in the same group conversation. They were both avid users of linguistic features associated with urban youth style, and so was Abdi, the third participant. The example illustrates how a polycentric potential gets activated through the boys' language use and their normative behaviour, including metapragmatic comments. In addition it presents fractional congruency (Agha 2007a: 97) between the boys' understanding of linguistic signs.

Example 9: *wallah* isn't a swear word
Participants: Hossein, Abdi, Tommy

Hos:	eh wallah tænk hvis de havde	*eh wallah imagine that they*
	denne der med indenfor	*had that one with them inside*
Adi:	ko[ran jeg] er ligeglad gør	*ko[ran I] don't care do what*
	hvad I vil	*you want*
Tmy:	[fuck]	*[fuck]*
Tmy:	eow wa[llah jeg ME:NER jeg ik	*eow wa[llah I MEA:N it I say*
	sir et grimt [kʁ̥] ord mer	*no ugly word anymore*
Hos:	[eow la nu vær med og	*[eow stop saying it*
	sig det	
	(.)	*(.)*
Hos:	ja det gjorde jeg heller ik	*yes I didn't even do it*
Tmy:	det gør jeg heller ik	*I don't do it either*
Hos:	bare la: (.) Abdi sige det	*just le:t (.) Abdi say it*
	hva rager det os	*what do we care*
Tmy:	ja (.) du sagde xxx	*yes (.) xxx*
Hos:	hva ska vi tegne	*what should we draw*
Tmy:	det sagde du	*you said it*
Hos:	hvad	*what*

19	Tmy:	du sagde wallah oss	*you said too wallah*
20	Hos:	ja hva rager det os (.) de:t	*yes what do we care (.) i:t*
21		det ik et bandeord	*it isn't a swear word*

Hossein suggests that the boys consider the consequences if 'they', i.e., the team of researchers, had access to 'this one', i.e., the audio-recorder, at the particular moment (l. 01). This type of utterance recurs in the recordings and usually points to the violation of institutional norms by some prior action. Hossein uses *wallah* to underline the seriousness of the transgression or of the potential repercussions. Abdi responds as if Hossein has threatened him when he claims to be indifferent to Hossein and Tommy's future actions; *koran* underlines the claim of indifference. In overlap Tommy exclaims *fuck* (l. 05) and thereby stays within the same linguistic (institutionally) transgressive line but he re-orients and (re-) aligns with Hossein's implied message that they should speak 'nicely' (l. 06–07). To do this Tommy deploys non-standard performable signs: the lexical items *eow* and *wallah*, the prosodic pattern, the use of [ʁ̥] i *grimt*, and the formulaic phrase *jeg mener* 'I mean'. Hossein overlaps and polices Tommy or Abdi (or both), and he demands their attention, using *eow* (l. 08–9). He claims that he didn't do 'it' (probably that he did not use foul language), and Tommy aligns as he claims not to do it either (l. 12). By then Abdi is positioned as the sole transgressor of institutional linguistic norms but Tommy shows to have qualms. He reacts to Hossein's use of *wallah* as not in accordance with the institutional norms for appropriate linguistic behaviour. Hossein dismisses this understanding; *wallah* 'isn't a swear word' (l. 20–21). Tommy's (not-included) response is implicit; he seems to accept (tacitly) and thereby he agrees with Hossein's positioning as the authority on the meaning of *wallah* as well as of 'speaking nicely'.

The example illustrates that the boys have access to resources not associated with the Standard (Danish), that they engage in confrontational sequences when using them, that there exist different metapragmatic understandings of some of these resources, and that not all are treated as transgressions of institutional linguistic norms – at least not all the time and by everybody. In this example, the line between standard and non-standard language does not coincide neatly with the line between transgression and non-transgression.

Explicit metalinguistic discussions and the association of performable signs with stereotypes and cultural models are at the core of my last example, too. Once more *wallah* is the linguistic point of attention. The recording was made during an overnight fieldtrip at the end of 2nd grade. Tommy and Hossein are hanging out with Abbas, Abdulla and Aleksandros. Hossein and Abbas are engaged in a game of table football, the others are waiting for their turn, and the boys' primary attention is on the game (which explains some of the slightly odd formulations and poor turn-coordination).

Example 10: "wallah I didn't spin"
Participants: Abdi, Hossein, Abdullah, Tommy, Abbas, Aleksandros

01	Hos:	DU SNURREDE KORAN du snurrede dér	*YOU SPUN KORAN you spun there*
02	Abb:	NEJ wallah je[g ik snurrede	*NO wallah I [didn't spin*
03	Hos:	[WALLAH du	*[WALLAH you did*
04		gjorde	
05	NN:	[xxx	*[xxx*
06	Abb:	[jeg gjorde sådan her	*[I did like this*
07	Hos:	wallah nej wallah du	*wallah no wallah >you spun*
08		>snurrede en gang hurtigt<	*once fast<*
09	Ale:	du du du [har snurret	*you you you [have spun*
10	Hos:	[du SNURREDE	*[you SPUN*
11		(4)	*(4)*
12	Abb:	jeg snurrede ik	*i didn't spin*
13	Hos:	°jo du gjorde°	*°yes you did°*
14	Abb:	nej jeg gjorde xxx	*no I didn't xxx*
15	Hos:	lige før gjorde du	*a minute ago you did*
16	Abb:	ja	*yes*
17	Hos:	ja ik så indrøm det [lige	*yes right then just ad[mit it*
18	Ale:	[han	*[he*
19		sagde wallah han ik snurrede	*said wallah he didn't spin*
20	Abb:	nej jeg gjorde ej (.) jeg	*no I didn't (.) I didn't even*
21		sagde ikke engang wallah	*say wallah*
22	Hos:	der er nogen der ved hvad	*there are some people who know*
23		det betyder Abbas	*what it means Abbas*

Hossein has previously stipulated that you are not allowed to 'spin' the handles. Suddenly he claims that this is what Abbas just did, and when repeating the accusation he adds a *koran* which intensifies the epistemic value and seriousness (l. 03–4). Abbas refuses and stresses the truth-value of his statement with *wallah* (l. 02). An energetic exchange of accusations and counter-accusations follows, several of which incorporate *wallah*, when suddenly Abbas appears to admit to have spun the handles (l. 16). Hossein responds triumphantly, confident of winning the argument, while Aleksandros claims, in overlap, that Abbas actually 'said wallah he didn't spin' (l. 18–19). This takes the conversation to a new level as the topic becomes the linguistic rather than play rule transgression. Abbas refuses to have said *wallah* upon which Hossein comments 'there are some people who know what it means Abbas' (l. 22–23). The linguistic focus is probably occasioned by *wallah*'s religiously associated meaning; (some) Arabic speaking parents admonish their children not to use it in vain. It appears to be one type of transgression if you spin when you are not allowed to, another one if you lie about it, but the transgressive act belongs to an entirely different moral level if *wallah* is included in an untrue statement. Now Abbas is both accused of abusing a sacred word and of breaking the rules of the game, surely an uncomfortable position. Nevertheless the game continues, and as Abbas responds that he too knows the meaning of *wallah*, the discussion jumps from a metapragmatic to a metasemantic level.

Example 11: "What does wallah actually mean?"
(NN = nonidentifiable speaker)

Abb:	jeg ved godt hvad det betyder	*I do know what it means*
	(.)	*(.)*
Ale:	er det ik han sværger eller sådan noget	*isn't it he swears or some-thing*
Abl:	jeg [sværger det betyder ik jeg mener det	*I [swear it doesn't mean I mean it*
NN	[xxx ((jo?))	*[xxx ((yes?))*
Tmy:	jamen (.) hvad betyder wallah egentlig	*but (.) what does wallah actually mean*
Abl:	det betyder jeg sværger	*it means I swear*
Tmy:	hm	*hm*
Abb:	[NE:J	*NO:*
Tmy:	[bare på arabisk bare på arab[isk	*[just in Arabic just in Arab[ic*
Abb:	[NO	*[NO*
Tmy:	bare på arabisk (.) det betyder wallah (.) på arabisk	*just in Arabic (.) it means ↑wallah (.) in Arabic*
Ale:	JA:	*YE:S*
NN:	xxx	*xxx*
Abb:	JEG MENER DET det betyder wallah (.) arabisk	*I MEAN IT it means wallah (.) Arabic*
Tmy:	xxx	*xxx*

Aleksandros hedges his suggested translation of *wallah* with markers of uncertainty (l. 27–28): he formulates it as a question, suggesting that some of the other children present may have more expertise in the area, and he ends the turn with a 'or something', that is, he does not take full responsibility for the truth-value of his suggestion. Abdullah confirms that it means 'I swear' rather than 'I mean it', which I suppose is another often suggested candidate translation; there is certainly a degree of overlap between the pragmatic meanings of the two. Tommy is still unsure and asks for yet another translation (l. 32), Abbas repeats that *wallah* means I swear, and Tommy asks if that is the meaning in Arabic. This response suggests that Tommy associates *wallah* with the linguistic register Arabic, but in addition to this he may also associate *wallah* with other types of language use where it may not have the same meaning. So, 'I swear' is the meaning in Arabic in contrast to the meaning it may have in other registers. The meaning clarification is of paramount importance to Tommy, and he does not leave the topic until an issue of more immediate urgency arises, namely whether the teacher has initiated the roasting of marsh-mellows over the bonfire. In order to find out, the boys leave the room. (The energetic and loud no's and yes's during the sequence are referring to the game rather than Tommy's metalinguistic inquiry.)

Examples 9 and 10 invite us to consider the relation between the different associations, uses and meanings of *wallah*. On the one hand it is associated with Arabic, maybe even both with something we may call Standard Arabic and a religious Arabic register, on the other, it is part of an urban youth register, which for this group of children is also referred to as Arabic, at least on some occasions. The different registers of Arabic represent different norm centres and they assign different pragmatic meanings to the sign form. This may confuse users who are only acquainted with one of the registers, which here seems to include Aleksandros and Tommy. So, despite the fact that all boys have deployed *wallah* in accordance with the peer group usage ('youth language') for several years, Hossein, Abbas and Abdullah have a different level of authority with regard to the Arabic register(s) and norm centre(s).

7 Concluding comments: Enregisterment over time, speakers and encounters

All trajectories of socialization are unique, and yet individuals participate in collective processes of enregisterment that seem to go in particular directions. My contribution has been an illustration and a discussion of this intriguing fact. During fieldwork in an urban school we found differences in the children's' linguistic practices, norms and registers. For instance, Arabic, in its various meanings, held a privileged space in Tommy and Hossein's classroom, whereas resources associated with immigrant languages and cultures were relegated to the margins of other classrooms (see also Møller forthc.). Whatever the reasons for this, it is remarkable, and it shows that institutional settings, such as a school, are not constituted by coherent social communities where norms are shared by all social actors and where all social actors orient to the same norm centres at all times. The existence and range of similar and compatible patterns of semiotic behaviour inside institutions is an empirical question, and so is what type of social formation an institution such as a school is, an insight explored in great detail by Rampton (e.g., 1995, 2006).

I have focused on the use and understanding of lexical items occasionally referred to as Arabic in conjunction with other non-Standard Danish resources. The acquisition of language has been treated as a social phenomenon inseparable from other social and cultural aspects of human life, and language socialization as a mutual accomplishment in which both novices and expert-authorities participate and which takes place in social encounters. As a matter of fact, what counts as authority depends on the situation. Whereas other (mainstream, ethnic majority Danish) children affirmed Tommy as an authority on Arabic in one situation, he (was) positioned as a novice in others. Whereas he introduced new language use in one situation, in others he was subject to instruction. The mutual orientation to patterns of language use and forms of speech is part of the emergence, establishment, and affirmation of social groups, and forms of language use have the power to create the feeling of continuity. I have depicted enregisterment of a form of speech from what may be regarded as its embryonic stages in a particular group. Hossein and Tommy – and their friends – oriented to a (partly) shared understanding of Arabs and Arabic. This included performable signs (*wallah, koran* etc.), social stereotypes (masculine assertive persona), interactional type (peer group conversation), genre and keying (fun, confrontation, challenge, transgression). Besides this Arabic was – or were – not the only register(s) in use, and peer norms were not hegemonic. The children oriented to several other centres of authority that licensed other types of language use and participation, and through their simultaneous orientations in different directions the children created several social groups; of (imagined) Arabs, of themselves, of adults, and of peers with different practices and orientations. In effect, polycentricity is a key notion to the understanding of the social interactions I have analysed.

A related point concerns the nature of language. The examples have illustrated how language is not divided into stable, fixed and uniform categories by nature, and this despite the fact that the whole regime of Standard Danish which schools are designed to inculcate (and protect), rests completely on the assumption that it is, or should be (if not by "nature," at least by "culture" and by force of the State). Even young children seem to be aware of this at some level. Rather, language participates in social regularities here referred to as registers. These registers are only partly shared by language users, they are permeable and locally constructed. So, is *khabakhalæ* Arabic or isn't it? When and in what sense may it be Arabic? And to whom? Also, *wallah* was widely used but it received an additional meaning potential when interpreted as part of a register of (Standard) Arabic. In this way, the systems of enregisterment in which *wallah* as a sign-form participates were multi-layered. The introduction of this register affiliation simultaneously introduced a new normative centre, with a different type of morality, in the boys' social encounter. It was never given in advance but depended on local needs, wants, participants etc. what was and what was not Arabic, and which understanding of Arabic was relevant. As an implication of this, the locally relevant meaning of any enregistered sign differed. As Wortham (2012: 130) points out, all signs are polysemous and their disambiguation occurs in situations where participants presuppose widely circulating models; to this I will add that such work of disambiguation also implies that social actors take into account locally relevant contexts. Despite the fluidity and open nature of registers and the ambiguity of sign forms, languages are generally treated as having clear and fixed social affiliations, and form, participation and metadiscourses are all important. Arabs use Arabic words, and those individuals positioned as Arabs are taken to have privileged insight into such Arabic word forms. The subject for negotiation is, of course, who counts as an Arab and what counts as Arabic, when, why and for what purpose. As illustrated, this may change from one encounter to the next, even in a small group.

Processes of identification have a special affinity to languaging and socialization. We have seen how Tommy identified explicitly (and with appreciation from his peers) as an Arab during his first school year. This identification was accomplished through language use and social participation: Tommy's Arab identity was performed through linguistic signs which indexed specific (streetwise, audacious) stances, pragmatic functions and personas, and he used this Arab identity to claim the centre stage. As Agha (2005: 1) says, all signs-in-use point both backwards and forwards, to previous experiences and imagined and possible futures. Tommy's situational performance at this one event points back by showing what linguistic resources and identities Tommy had had access to, but its significance increases when we know how it anticipated Tommy's orientation towards to the group dominated by Hossein with Arabic background and towards languaging recognized as Arabic. Hossein did not identify as an Arab in any of the sequences shown (although he occasionally did in other recordings).

He probably did not feel the need to do so, as his authority, on the use of Arabic as on appropriate behaviour, was never contested. Hossein performed identifications implicitly through the use of performable signs associated with urban youth style, and he constructed a confrontational, tough, maybe even masculine persona. This social model and its relation to urban languaging, and Arabic, is already circulating, a point that I will return to shortly. For now it is important to make it clear that Tommy and Hossein defined each other's positions reciprocally, and the repeated performance of their relation constituted a process of socialization, including the socialization into identities, authorities, language use and ideologies.

The linguistic and cultural practices of Tommy and Hossein (and Abbas, Abdi, Aleksandros etc.) were not unique but nationally and internationally recognisable and well-described for other children in other contexts. On the local level, we have documented patterns of linguistic conduct similar to those of Tommy and Hossein but carried out by previous cohorts of students from the same school, students who had left school before Tommy *et al.* even entered. Thereby Tommy, Hossein and their friends participated in inter-generational and societally wide-spread processes of language socialization, and the degree of continuity, rather than change and transformation, is remarkable. Nevertheless the relations between Tommy *et al.*'s use and understanding of an urban youth register, between this class and larger scale social processes, and between this study of linguistic development over *la courte durée* compared to the sociolinguistic development over *la (plus) longue durée* certainly need further discussion, as does the regimentation of actions and events by larger scale ideas, institutions and practices (Wortham 2012: 129). I cannot predict the enduring effects of the illustrated languaging and identifications. With regard to Hossein and Tommy and, on the other side, to the larger sociolinguistic development, such effects will manifest only in future encounters, but some do seem more likely. For instance, shibboleths of an urban language register such as *eow, koran* and *wallah* may change their meaning and become re-enregistered over time. The wide currency and emblematic status of such lexical items make them prone to re-interpretation into an nth order indexical meaning (Silverstein 2003) where they could be associated with coolness, or late modernity, instead of pan-ethnic, street-wise, urban youth. I will save the in-depth discussion of this for another (future) paper. In this I have discussed the early stages of a process where perceptible sign-forms become linked to a reflexive (metapragmatic) model (of what kind of person uses sign-form X in what kind(s) of situations, with what kind(s) of effects). This is, in effect, a process of incipient enregisterment, enregisterment in childhood where the social meanings are in the making, and groupings and re-groupings are negotiated. I have argued that Tommy *et al.* were not free-floating in time and space.

Their access to the urban youth style had many sources, and they participated in the strengthening of a particular, already established, association, between linguistic forms, genres, social and cultural models.

Liva Hyttel-Sørensen

Gangster talk on the phone – analyses of a mass media parody of a contemporary urban vernacular in Copenhagen and its reception

1 Introduction

This chapter treats different media representations of an enregistered way of speaking, which is common among Copenhagen youth. It examines how the use of this register (in Agha's 2007 sense) in a comedy sketch is perceived by a group of speakers who know and use linguistic features associated with this register in their everyday interaction. Recent studies (Ag 2010; Madsen 2013a; Nørreby 2012; Stæhr 2010) have shown that Copenhagen youth organize language they meet in their everyday in several different ways of speaking. Among these is a clustering of features labelled as (among other labels) *street language* ("gadesprog") by the school leavers, while the pupils in this study refer to it rather as *slang* ("slangsprog") or *gangster language* ("gangstersprog"). Studies have shown that different features associated with this way of speaking are recognized and valorised similarly among pupils in different parts of Denmark (Hyttel-Sørensen 2009, 2011), and the register can be categorized as what Rampton (2011) coins a contemporary urban vernacular. A crucial factor in the enregisterment of the contemporary urban vernacular seems to be its opposition to a more conservative standard register (Madsen 2013a), which is referred to by the school leavers as *integrated speech*.

Agha (2007: 170) argues that mass media can play an important role in processes of enregisterment and he names youth slang as an example where popular culture has made possible the existence of similar registers across different geographic locations. The role of popular culture in enregisterment is even more complex, as Androutsopoulos (2001) shows, when he argues that media representations have influenced a particular German youth slang, which has gone "from the streets to the screens and back again". This chapter focuses on a comedy sketch from Danish national TV and its reception. The sketch is called *Gangster talk on the phone* ("Gangstersnak i telefonen") and in it a girl switches from using features associated with a more conservative standard register (using highly academic vocabulary) to using features associated with the contemporary urban vernacular. Thereby this sketch is an example of a particular kind of languaging that has gone from the streets to the screens. I played the sketch for the middle school pupils, the idea being that providing them with stimulus that they knew beforehand and hopefully found interesting, was a means to extract metalinguistic knowledge from them.

The very existence of a sketch featuring a speaker switching between a more conservative standard and a contemporary urban vernacular shows that by displaying and emphasising particular connections between speech forms and social types and values, mass media does indeed play a role in the enregisterment of these two ways of speaking. That speakers associate different ways of speaking with different values and stereotypes is one thing, but when this typification takes place in mass media it becomes another matter with potentially greater consequences because the typification circulates on a wider social scale. In order to investigate how mass media has influenced the enregisterment of the contemporary urban vernacular I will introduce different media representations and show how they have portrayed both this way of speaking and the stereotypes associated with it.

Jaffe (2011: 563, 30–32) cites the existing research literature on the ideological aspects of representations of language and language variation in the media and highlights that "media productions about language simultaneously produce (or constitute) ideologies about the nature of language as well as about the people who produce, consume and/or are represented by" a given media text. While I find it important to note that there is no clearly delineated group of people, who are represented by a certain media text, certainly the reception of any representation of language in the media will depend on what relationship the viewers have with the language being portrayed. In the case of the gangster talk sketch, the reception by the middle school pupils does indeed involve processes of identification (Brubaker 2002), as the two ways of speaking used by the girl in the sketch correspond to a similar organization of languages in their everyday linguistic practices. The fact that all of them knew the sketch show and that most of them had seen the sketch before, reveals that whether or not they belong to the audience imagined by the producers they are also consumers of this media text. As the sketch is an example of languaging going from the streets to the screens, how then, do these pupils as consumers of this particular media text react to the stereotypes used in this sketch? How does the sketch participate in the enregisterment of the contemporary urban vernacular by typifying and positioning its speakers, and how do the pupils respond to this? And finally, what do these reactions say about the relationship between media representations on the one hand and authenticity and ownership of linguistic resources on the other?

In the current chapter I will first introduce my method, my ethnographic fieldwork among the preadolescent pupils and the class session where I played the sketch for the pupils. After this I present an overview of how the involved speech styles have been characterized in previous research. I will then briefly discuss two older media representations of this way of speaking before I analyse the sketch *Gangster talk on the phone* and discuss the sketch show it is part of ("Det slører stadig", i.e. *It's still veiling*). After these introductory sections I will present some excerpts from the class session and analyse the pupils' comments in order to show how they respond to the portrayal of both the contemporary urban vernacular and the stereotypes associated with it.

2 Data collection

My data collection has been conducted among the preadolescents at the focus school. They started school in the summer of 2007, and I first met them at the end of the third grade in June of 2011 where I conducted a guise experiment in their class. Since then I and two of my colleagues have followed the pupils on and off and collected a wide range of data including ethnographic observations, audio and video recordings, social media data, and finally the class session concerning the gangster talk sketch.

In February 2013 I noticed that one of the girls in the class, Nada, posted a video clip of the gangster talk sketch on Facebook. The sketch caught my attention because it featured the girl switching from the conservative standard code to the contemporary urban vernacular and back again. After talking to some of the pupils I realized that many of them knew the sketch show, which gave me the idea to play the sketch for them as a way to get them to talk about language, language ideologies, and norms for language use. The session with the pupils where the sketch was played took place in their classroom and was video-recorded.

We had asked the teachers for permission to conduct a session with these pupils, explaining that we would be playing a sketch and discussing it with them. The middle school pupils often all have class together, although there are in fact two different classes. On this day both classes were present as were a teacher from each class. In total there were 27 pupils present, facing the black board, while the two teachers were sitting in the back of the class out of sight of the pupils (see Figure 1). We were three researchers, of whom I was the only one who knew the pupils beforehand. The session was carried out by Janus Spindler Møller (JSM), while I was sitting in the corner observing, and the third researcher was sitting at the back. We started by playing the sketch for the pupils and then proceeded to ask them open-ended questions about the sketch, the language in the sketch, and language in their everyday lives in general. They were first asked to discuss these questions in groups with their page buddies before discussing them with the rest of the class and JSM. The questions were:

> Can you describe how she speaks on the phone and how she speaks with the other girl on the lawn?
> What can you call these ways of speaking?
> Do you know anyone who speaks like the ways we see in the video?
> Do you know other ways of speaking?

We placed two cameras next to the blackboard, facing the class, enabling us to clearly see all the pupils in the video recordings. Furthermore, we placed audio recorders on each of the groups' tables to make sure that we would catch as much of the interaction as possible. Given the nature of the recordings and the structure of the session, there are at all times discourse on different scales at play in the recordings. For example, there is the official classroom discourse, which is moderated by JSM, and which can be heard more or less at all times on the video recordings. Then there is the group discourse, which can be heard on the individual recordings, and which is sometimes taking place simultaneously with the classroom discourse. There are also examples of discourse aimed at the recorder, as when a pupil picks up the recorder and talks into the microphone, commenting on what is going on in the classroom discourse.

3 "Gangster" and "nerd" – examples of enregisterment

Earlier studies among the school-leavers at the focus school (Madsen, Møller, and Jørgensen 2010; Møller and Jørgensen 2011b; Madsen 2013a) have documented an ongoing enregisterment (Agha 2007) of two distinct and contrasting ways of speaking, of which one can be categorized as a contemporary urban vernacular, while the other, at least with regard to the values and privileges it envokes, is enregistered as a more conservative standard code (Madsen 2013a: 135). We know from these studies that the two registers are given a range of emic labels by the students. The more standard code is primarily referred to as *integrated speech* ("integreret"), while the contemporary urban vernacular is given a range of different labels such as *street language* ("gadesprog"), *gangster language* ("gangstersprog"), *slang* ("slang") or *"perker" language* ("perker" is in the mainstream understanding as represented in e.g. mainstream media and dictionaries a pejorative term for immigrants, but in in-group use it is a common term used to refer to people of ethnic minority status). These two registers are associated with very different indexical values, and each register is characterized by a range of semiotic resources. Of the two, the contemporary urban vernacular has received the most attention from researchers and is thus relatively well described. Different studies of the contemporary urban vernacular have observed, that a range of different linguistic resources can be associated with this way of speaking, and among them are grammatical, phonetic, prosodic, and lexical resources alike (Maegaard 2007; Madsen 2013a; Pharao and Foget Hansen 2005; Pharao et al. 2014; Quist 2008, see also Karrebæk this volume). Examples of grammatical resources associated with this register are lack of inversion and a more frequent use of common gender (where the Copenhagen standard has neuter gender). Examples of the phonetic resources that can be associated with the contemporary urban vernacular are palatalized t-pronunciation, voiceless pronunciation of initial uvular r, and fronted s-pronunciation, while the supra-segmental resources are connected to the contrast between long and short vowels and the relation between stressed and unstressed syllables. Notable among the supra-segmental resources is a less frequent use of the Danish glottal constriction known as 'stød'. The lexical resources consist primarily of the use of words and phrases that are otherwise associated with other national languages such as Turkish (e.g. *eow*, which means "hey") and Arabic (e.g. *wallah*, which means "(I swear) by God").

The abovementioned characteristics of the contemporary urban vernacular are what researchers have observed through a range of different analyses of everything from ethnographic observations and microanalysis of interaction to guise experiments involving a single phonetic feature. However, when the older pupils at the school are asked to describe the register, which they refer to as eg. *street language*, they only refer to a few of these resources. In general the students often give examples of some of the lexical resources such as slang words, swearing, and the use of words not typically associated with Danish. Of the other resources the students explicitly mention the palatalized t-pronunciation as an example of a typical feature of street language, while some also comment that street language is associated with a so-called "strange accent".

Regarding the conservative standard code, Madsen (2013a: 127) based on the adolescents' own accounts lists some of the resources associated with this way of speaking: distinct pronunciation, abstract and academic vocabulary, high pitch, quiet and calm attitude, and ritual politeness phrases.

The two registers are associated with very different indexical values. Where the contemporary urban vernacular is associated with toughness, masculinity, youth, academic non-prestige, and what Madsen (2013a) refers to as panethnic minority "street" culture, the conservative standard is associated with higher class culture and wealth, sophistication, authority, emotional control and aversion to rudeness, academic skills, politeness and respect, and finally Danishness (see also Madsen 2014; Madsen, Møller, and Jørgensen 2010; Møller and Jørgensen 2013).

4 Media representations of the contemporary urban vernacular

It's still veiling is merely one of several current media representations that feature the contemporary urban vernacular and parodies this way of speaking and the stereotypes associated with it. In order to understand how the mass media in general and *It's still veiling* with the sketch *Gangster talk on the phone* in particular draw on and contribute to the typification of the contemporary urban vernacular, I will now offer examples of a couple of the most influential (in regard to dissemination and public debate) media representations of the contemporary urban vernacular. This serves as a prelude for a more detailed analysis of the sketch, and this analysis will serve as a background for understanding how the sketch's typification of the contemporary urban vernacular is perceived by the pupils in my study.

An early example of a media production parodying the language use of minority youth is the online computer game *The Mujaffa Game* ("Mujaffaspillet"). It was launched in the year 2000 on Denmark's Radio's website and was originally called *The Perker Game* ("Perkerspillet"), but due to complaints the people behind the game changed the name. The protagonist of the game is the character Mujaffa, who reflects stereotypic assumptions about a particular minority persona. Mujaffa is a young male immigrant, wearing Adidas sweatpants, a white tank top, a gold watch, two gold necklaces and a red baseball cap worn backwards. The object of the game is to drive around Copenhagen in a BMW, collecting gold necklaces, saluting your friends with the phrase *wallah my cousin* ("wallah min fætter") and picking up blond girls. Quist and Jørgensen (2007) show both how the word *Mujaffa* has become a cover-term for this stereotype and how the expression *wallah my cousin* has gone through Androutsopoulos' (2001) life-circle from the streets to the screens and back again. Quist and Jørgensen (2007) argue that this is an example of crossing (Rampton 1995, 2006), where an expression (*wallah my cousin*) is picked up by speakers with no first-hand knowledge of the speech of minority youth. Thus *The Mujaffa Game* is an example of a media production that plays on a stereotypic minority youth identity while using linguistic resources associated with the contemporary urban vernacular. It can be argued that by displaying an existing (negative) stereotype, the game helps to destabilize that stereotype. However, although the game presents this existing stereotype with humoristic distance, it also partly helps to reinforce and spread the knowledge of this stereotype.

There have also been several examples of media productions parodying the contemporary urban vernacular on Danish national TV. One example is a seasonal Christmas show from 2007 targeted at adults. In Denmark there is a tradition of showing one episode of so-called Christmas calendar shows every day from the 1st to the 24th of December as a countdown to Christmas Eve. Thus they are TV-series in 24 episodes, and they are primarily targeted at children. In 1974 a Christmas calendar show called *Jullerup Færgeby* (which translates as something like *Christmasville Ferrytown*) was shown, and this show was mimicked in 2007 by the adult Christmas calendar show *Yallahrup Færgeby*. Both shows are in 24 episodes and the characters are hand puppets, but the story is moved from an old-fashioned harbour town with a lighthouse to an urban ghetto-like environment. In the original the protagonists were children with names such as Anton and Knud (very traditional and old-fashioned Danish names) whereas the protagonists in the parody are Ali and Hassan, two minority boys who use resources associated with the contemporary urban vernacular and idolize the American gangster rapper Tupac. Like *The Mujaffa Game*, *Yallahrup Færgeby* is an example of a parody of both a certain stereotypic minority identity and of the contemporary urban vernacular. Similarly, like the expression *wallah my cousin* in *The Mujaffa Game*, the expression *proper sick (gangster)* in *Yallahrup Færgeby* has gone from the streets to the screens and back again. However, where the parody in *The Mujaffa Game* was based solely on minority youth and their speech style, the parody in *Yallahrup Færgeby* equally targets other societal stereotypes through the other characters in the show. These include the majority Danish pupils, the teachers, the school librarian etc. Nonetheless, though the typifications in *Yallahrup Færgeby* are more complex and more sophisticated than in *The Mujaffa Game*, the show arguably still helps to reinforce the different stereotypes portrayed in the show. In particular the prejudices about minority boys can potentially be fortified and offered further distribution through the show.

These two examples have shown that parodying the contemporary urban vernacular is not a new phenomenon, and I have argued that the parodies can potentially facilitate the dissemination of the different stereotypes. I will now move on to a more detailed analysis of the sketch show *It's still veiling* and the sketch *Gangster talk on the phone* and see what exactly the sketch is making fun of, in order to understand what the pupils in my study are reacting to.

5 It's still veiling

It's still veiling premiered in January 2013 on the national TV-channel DR2. DR2 was launched in 1996 by the public media corporation DR (Denmark's Radio) and was focused on "culture and society, lifestyle, food, and movies" (DR 2013c). It was targeted at adults and only featured programs from late afternoon and into the evening. It was known for featuring themed specials twice a week, documentaries, and satirical TV-shows. The above-mentioned *Yallahrup Færgeby* was also aired on DR2 and can still be viewed on the channel's website. Even though the pupils in my study are not the target audience for *It's still veiling*, they still all know the show and most of them have watched it. However, the fact that the show isn't targeted at them may shine through in their reactions to the show.

The title of *It's still veiling* plays on a Danish comedy from 1962 ("Det slører stadig" vs. "Det støver stadig", *It's still veiling* vs. *It's still dusting*), featuring some of Denmark's most famous actors of that time. According to the show's official website: "It's still veiling is a satire show with 4 ethnic girls, who give everything from burqas to pork roast a loving treatment. Meet among others Latifah visiting the police, Muslim sex-counseling and Paradise Hotel in Saudi Arabia" (DR 2013a, my translation). This quote underlines one major production difference between this show and the media texts mentioned in the previous section, namely that the people behind the show explicitly present themselves as minority Danes, which means that they can be perceived as having status as insiders when making fun of minority Danes.

The show's Facebook page recaps the lyrics to the show's theme song: "What's going on behind the lace curtains, a whole other world, I don't know what it's like. Look at yourself, get your facts straight, I know about more than falafels and taxis" (DR 2013b, my translation). Both of these quotes clearly outline the theme of the show. Lace curtains and pork roast index stereotypic traditional Danishness whereas falafels, taxis and burqas index stereotypic minority culture, or at least majority Danes' prejudices about minority culture. From these quotes we can see that the people behind the show present it as a satirical show, made by minority Danes and confronting prejudices about stereotypical minority culture exemplified by burqas and falafels. Furthermore the contrast between majority and minority Danes seems to be central to the show (falafels vs. pork roast).

Nožić (2013) carries out critical discourse analyses of two of the sketches of *It's still veiling* and includes perception analysis based on data collected by playing the two sketches for viewers with both majority and minority background and recording their reactions. Her analyses indicate that sketches that are intended to make fun of majority Danes' prejudices about minority Danes can be perceived by some (minority) viewers as making fun of the minority people in the sketch. This corresponds with the point Hill (2008) has made about what she calls *Mock Spanish*. Hill presents examples of jocular use of Spanish by non-Spanish speaking Americans such as saying "cerveza" instead of beer, and she argues that even though the language users may claim that their use of Spanish is respectful and meant to celebrate the Spanish language, the different uses of Spanish center on negative stereotypes about Spanish speakers, such as the stereotype of Spanish speakers as "lazy procrastinators" (2008: 120) or the stereotype of the "drunken Mexican" (2008: 42). Thus Hill argues that even a seemingly benign joke can reinforce the negative stereotype upon which it is based. Based on Nožić's findings I argue that the same phenomena are taking place with regard to "It's still veiling". As the sketches in the show all center on stereotypic assumptions about minority (and in some cases also majority) Danes, knowledge of the negative stereotypes about minority Danes is necessary in order for the sketches to be funny. Although the different sketches may aim to challenge the stereotypes, on which they are based, they can still help to disseminate the knowledge of these stereotypes among a wider public. With this in mind I will now turn to the sketch "Gangster talk on the phone".

6 Gangster talk on the phone

The gangster talk sketch opened the second program in the series. The scene shows two girls sitting on the grass in a park. One of the girls has blond hair and light skin while the other has dark hair and dark skin. The girls wear similar clothes and both have long hair. The dark-haired girl is wearing big, black, horn-rimmed glasses. The blonde girl is holding a notebook, while the dark-haired girl is holding a textbook and a pen. The sketch opens with the blonde girl asking the dark-haired girl to explain an assignment and the dark-haired girl points in the blonde girl's notebook and says that she would write it differently while the blonde girl nods in agreement. The dark-haired girl then continues with a monologue about the wonders of nuclear physics while using academic vocabulary such as *atomic level* ("atomarts niveau"), *concern yourself with the properties of the substance* ("beskæftiger sig med stoffets egenskaber"), and *left its mark on the world of philosophy* ("sat sit aftryk i filosofiens verden").

This is interrupted by the dark-haired girl's phone ringing, which she answers simply by saying *hello* ("hallo") followed by a pause. The dark-haired girl then begins a conversation over the phone and as she does so there is a clear shift in register. While on the phone the dark-haired girl uses a range of linguistic resources associated with the contemporary urban vernacular: lexical (*eow*, *wallah*, *koran*, *kalp*), phonetic (affricated and palatalized t-pronunciation, fronted s-pronunciation, and voiceless pronunciation of initial uvular r), and prosodic (distinct tonal pattern). Furthermore, there is a distinct shift in indexical fields (Eckert 2008) from the conversation in the park to the conversation on the phone. In the conversation in the park the dark-haired girl constructs a school-oriented persona demonstrating academic skill both regarding the topic of the conversation and the linguistic resources she employs. This persona is recognized and reinforced by the blonde girl, who asks the dark-haired girl for help with schoolwork and accepts the dark-haired girl as an authority on the subject. This is in sharp contrast with the conversation on the phone, where the dark-haired girl talks about a girl who owes her money. She describes a conflict with this other girl, wherein the dark-haired girl asked the girl to pay her the money, but the girl ran off before the dark-haired girl could catch her. The dark-haired girl then goes on to ask her interlocutor to help her catch this girl before ending the conversation by saying that she will call later because right now she is in the middle of something. While on the phone the dark-haired girl constructs a physically threatening persona using expressions such as *how the fuck should I know* ("hvor fuck skulle jeg vide det fra"), *tie her to my dad's satellite dish* ("bind hende op på min fars parabol"), and *cram her into a dumpster wallah* ("prop hende ned i en skraldespand wallah"), and this persona is highlighted by the shift in register.

Overall the sketch portrays the dark-haired girl as both a linguistically and an academically skilled person, who displays her mastery of two different sets of linguistic resources in two different settings. The sketch thus highlights that a person can speak the contemporary urban vernacular and accordingly align with the stereotypic values that this register indexes (such as toughness, street culture, and lack of academic skill), while at the same time displaying academic skill and school-orientation in a different setting. This persona differs from the one presented by the blonde girl, who only speaks to ask a question or agree with what the dark-haired girl has said. The blonde girl is seen to be surprised at the dark-haired girl's change in persona on the phone, and she appears to be confused when the dark-haired girl hangs up and immediately switches back to speaking about nuclear physics.

The fact that the contemporary urban vernacular is portrayed as a style that the speaker can shift in and out of is a notable change from the earlier media parodies of this way of speaking. The protagonists of both *The Mujaffa Game* and *Yallahrup Færgeby* are depicted as speaking the contemporary urban vernacular at all times. That these media texts portray the contemporary urban vernacular as amusing either in itself (as in *The Mujaffa Game* and *Yallahrup Færgeby*) or in contrast with an academic standard as in *Gangster talk on the phone*, is in line with the public discourse of this way of speaking as "poor" and "ugly" language, a sign of lacking intelligence and education (a discourse that can be found e.g. in countless online debates on minority youth and language).

I argue that the gangster talk sketch works on several different levels. On one level it makes fun of the two extremes, both in language and persona, especially in the way that the blonde girl reacts to them. On another level it makes fun of the blonde girl for being less proficient, both in regard to schoolwork and also in regard to the dark-haired girl's style shifts. However, the main aim of the sketch seems to be to make fun of the prejudices that the viewers may have both of minority versus majority students and of the two different ways of speaking. The stereotypes of both the prototypical good student and the prototypical gangster are challenged, as they coexist in the same character, who swiftly switches back and forth between the two. Still the stereotypic connection between register and conduct is not questioned as the contemporary urban vernacular is connected to physical threats and toughness and the academic speech style is connected to schoolwork.

7 Class session

During the class session the pupils seemed generally to be amused by the sketch. Many of them showed that they knew both the sketch show and the sketch beforehand (for instance by singing along to the jingle or by commenting on what would happen next). They all laughed at the sketch, especially when the dark-haired girl was on the phone and made threats at the girl, who owed her money. We showed them the sketch several times, once as an introduction to the session, then again after they had seen the questions and once more before discussing the sketch with the entire class. Nonetheless, they kept asking to see it again. During the class discussion the most eager participants were boys, and in particular a group of boys with ethnic minority background. During this session these boys all self-identified as speaking the way the girl did on the phone (i.e. the contemporary urban vernacular), which corresponded well both with what I had observed at the school and heard on the different recordings. Since these boys dominated the class discussion, their points of view were the ones picked up by JSM and written on the blackboard. For this reason I have chosen to focus on some of their comments when selecting what excerpts to analyse in this paper.

As can be seen in Figure 1, the group (in the front to the left) consisted of six boys in total, but only four were active during the conversations I have included (Naveed, Aurelio, Kamal, and Waqas). None of these four boys were in general especially active during lessons and seldom put up their hands to answer the teachers' questions, which meant that this class session differed very much from the other lessons, I had observed over a span of three years. In general Iman, one of the girls with minority background, was the only girl who participated in the class discussion (see also Lundqvist's chapter, this volume). The other girls can be heard on the group recordings, but hardly ever participated in the class discussion, which is also the reason why Iman is the only girl participating in the interactional excerpts I treat here. Iman was portrayed by the teachers as a very active and capable student, and according to my observations she was one of the most active pupils in the class.

Figure 1

8 Ethnicity and authenticity

The different stereotypes connected to the use of the contemporary urban vernacular in mass media parodies, serve as a background for understanding the analyses in the following section, which looks at some examples of the pupils' reactions to the sketch. Through three examples I will show, firstly, how the pupils link the contemporary urban vernacular to ethnic categorizations, secondly, how ethnic categorizations become relevant for perceptions of authenticity, and thirdly, how the speaker's authenticity (i.e. the dark-haired girl's) and the pupils' senses of identification (with the contemporary urban vernacular) can influence the reception of the sketch and render the sketch potentially insulting.

An aspect that was significant to the pupils' reactions was the role of ethnicity and authenticity. Both concepts were brought up repeatedly by the pupils in the discussion of the sketch, and it was clear that both influenced how the pupils perceived the sketch and the two different ways of speaking.

The first example I discuss is from the group discussion, where two of the boys are discussing how to describe the ways of speaking that are performed in the sketch, when Kamal (who was working with Waqas and Nusaibah, a girl who was silent during this sequence) brings up ethnicity. All three pupils had an ethnic minority background and Kamal and Waqas both belonged to the group of boys who often constructed tough streetwise identities (although Kamal did this more frequently than Waqas). During this session they clearly self-identified as speakers of the contemporary urban vernacular.

Excerpt 1

	Original	Translation
Kamal:	jamen jeg ved ikke hvordan	well I don't know how
	jeg skal forklare det jeg	to explain it I
	vil rigtigt vil jeg jeg	really want I I don't want
	gider ikke blive racistisk	to be racist
	men ellers vil jeg sige på	but otherwise I'll say one
	den ene måde snakker hun	way she speaks
	som en dansker på den anden	like a Dane the other
	måde snakker hun som en	way she speaks like a
	perker	perker
Waqas:	præcis det er også det jeg	excactly that's also what
	tænker fordi	I'm thinking because
Kamal:	men hvordan skal jeg sige	but how should I say you
	man kan ikke bare sige hun	can't just say she's speak-
	taler som en dansker	ing like a Dane
Waqas:	ja men som en ja men som en	yes but like a yes but like
	racist over for de andre	a racist toward the other
	danskere	Danes
Kamal:	ja det er det	yes that's it

As they are trying to describe the two different registers Kamal offers the distinction of ethnicity as a possibility: one way of speaking is that of a Dane and the other is that of a "perker". However, he shows reluctance to apply the ethnicity category as an explanatory factor and equals this kind of explanation to racism. Waqas defends Kamal's use of the term "speaks like a Dane" by refining it; saying that she speaks like a Dane who is racist towards other Danes, thereby distinguishing between two types of Danes, of which one group is racist towards the other. Thereby Waqas succeeds in keeping the distinction based on ethnicity, but it is no longer Kamal who is being racist. Rather the way the girl is speaking when she speaks "like a Dane", or the stereotypic speaker associated with this way of speaking, is racist toward the other Danes, i.e. the ones who do not speak that way.

Thus we see that in their attempt to describe the two different registers, Waqas offers the explanation that they end up agreeing on; namely a distinction between two kinds of speakers: Those who speak "like a Dane" and the ones who do not, and those who do are racist toward the "other Danes".

It is interesting to see firstly how categories related to ethnicity are ascribed merely on the basis of language use, and secondly how closely linked the discourse of ethnicity is to racism for both boys. That it is in fact language use that is the base for the ascription of ethnicity-related categories is evident since it is the same girl who uses two different registers associated with different ethnic categories. For Kamal typification based on ethnicity seems to be so tightly linked to racism that he hesitates to even bring it up. Being a racist is clearly a very undesirable trait in the views of the boys. Nonetheless, Waqas does not hesitate to associate speaking the conservative standard with being racist. This does not seem to be in conflict with the fact that it is the same girl who uses both registers in the sketch. However, the ethnicity of the girl who speaks on the phone seems to be relevant for the pupils' understanding of the sketch, and as the following example shows there seems to be some disagreement about how to understand the sketch.

In the next excerpt JSM was listing on the blackboard the different labels that the pupils had offered for the two different ways of speaking. When he later asked the pupils to explain the different labels, Aurelio, another boy, who self-identifies as speaking the contemporary urban vernacular, explained why he used the term "wannabe language".

Excerpt 2

	Original	**Translation**
01 JSM:	okay og du siger et wan-	okay and you say a wannabe
02	nabesprog	language
03 Mohamed:	[wannabe] ((griner))	[wannabe] ((laughing))
04 Aurelio:	[fordi] hun er en hun er	[because] she's a she's
05	en dansker og hun snakker	a Dane and she's speak-
06	perkersprog det er	ing perker language that's
08	wannabe jo	wannabe right
09 Delia:	hun er ikke dansker	she's not a Dane
10 Kamal:	[du ved godt hvad wannabe	[you do know what wannabe
11	betyder]?	means]?
13 JSM:	[hun er en dansker og	[she's a Dane and speaks
14	snakker perkersprog]	perker language]

	%com:		((In the background Narges, Delia, and Iman all say that she isn't a Dane))
15	Aurelio:	ja ((svar til Kamal))	yes ((answering Kamal))
16	Kamal:	hvad betyder det?	what does it mean?
17	Aurelio:	Xxx	xxx ((unintelligible))
18	Kamal:	[ja hvordan kan det der så	[yes so how can that be
19		være efterligning]	fake]
20	Naveed:	[det er jo bare en plas-	[it's just a plastic perker
21		ticperker jo]	you know]
22	Uni:	plasticperker ((griner))	plastic perker ((laughing))
23	Iman:	nej hun er ej [til Naveed]	no she isn't [to Naveed]
24	Kamal:	hun gør bare [hvad en	she's just doing [what a
25		perker]	perker]
26	Aurelio:	[hun hun hun] er jo en	[she she she] is a Dane and
27		dansker og snakker perk-	speaks perker language you
28		ersprog	know
29	Christian:	[hun var ikke dansker	[she wasn't a Dane Aurelio]
30		Aurelio]	
31	Kamal:	[hun gør det for	[she's doing it for fun]
32		sjov] det er en skue-	it's an
33		spiller	actress

When JSM asks the class how the girl speaks on the phone there are a lot of different answers from the class and one of them comes from Aurelio, who says she is speaking *wannabe language* ("wannabesprog"). A little later JSM picks up on this and Aurelio voices the understanding that the girl's use of the contemporary urban vernacular is inauthentic since she is a "Dane" who speaks "perker language", which makes her a "wannabe". This sets off a discussion in the class regarding the girl's ethnicity and several of the other pupils remark that she is not a Dane. Kamal privately questions Aurelio's understanding of the term "wannabe" and asks how it can be "fake"; thereby showing that he disagrees with Aurelio's understanding of the girl as a Dane. Christian backs this view up further by saying loudly across the class that the girl is not a Dane. Kamal then employs a different strategy. Where the other arguments against Aurelio have centered on the girl's ethnicity (categorizing her as a non-Dane), Kamal argues that she is an actress and "doing it for fun".

Naveed also takes part in this discussion by saying that the girl is a *plastic perker* ("plasticperker"), which according to the pupils is a term used about people who act and speak like *perkers*, but who are not really *perkers*. Thus it seems that Naveed (as the only one) agrees with Aurelio that the girl isn't a *perker*, but he doesn't help Aurelio convince the others that it is *wannabe*.

After this JSM moves to the other side of the class and asks whether the girl is a Dane, to which a lot of the pupils simultaneously answer no. JSM calls on Mohamed who explains that she was a Dane in the beginning but became a "perker" later on. JSM then calls on Nada who says that you can tell by looking at the girl that she is not a Dane. The notion that being a "perker" has something to do with appearance is also introduced by Narges earlier on. While the class is talking about the contemporary urban vernacular ("slang language"), Christian (who elsewhere very explicitly disassociates himself from this way of speaking) performs a stylization of the contemporary urban vernacular, which seems to annoy Narges, since she calls him a "fucking little dwarf" ("din fucking lille gnom"), asks if he is "acting up" ("kommer du og spiller op") and says "you really don't look like a perker" ("hvor ligner du ikke en perker").

In this discussion the pupils use the word "wannabe", which is a commonly used expression among younger people about people acting out personas they are not granted the right to. Aurelio, however, uses it not about the girl herself but rather about the concept of being one thing and speaking like another, namely being a "Dane" and speaking like a "perker". During this debate none of the others support Aurelio's claim that it is "wannabe", and there are two different arguments against him. The main one centers on ethnicity: the girl is in fact **not** a "Dane" and hence her speaking "perker language" cannot be "wannabe". In this argument "Dane" is opposed to "perker" and being a "perker" equals having the right to speak "perker language". The other argument comes from Kamal, who points out that it is fictional. The girl is an actress and doing it for fun, and to Kamal this means that it cannot be "wannabe". This argument is the only one not focusing on ethnicity, but rather on the sketch as a performance. This does not mean, that for Kamal the contemporary urban vernacular is not associated with ethnicity, but rather that her ethnicity is not relevant in this situation since she is an actress and therefore by definition not an authentic speaker.

It is clear from this example that there are diverging interpretations of the sketch. While most of the pupils perceive the girl, who speaks on the phone, as a "perker", Aurelio and Naveed think that she is a Dane, and clearly, being a "perker" influences whether or not one is understood as having the right to use the contemporary urban vernacular. Besides dealing with ethnicity this discussion also involves legitimacy and sense of ownership. I will examine the latter concepts more closely in the following paragraph.

9 "They're dissing us" – rights and ownership

The previous examples have shown that in the pupils' discussion of the two registers ethnicity played an important role. On one hand categories related to ethnicity ("Dane" and "perker") were ascribed on the basis of language use, while on the other hand membership of an ethnic category seemed to determine whether or not a speaker was perceived as authentic when using the two different registers. This perceived personal relation between speaker and language has also been noted by Møller and Jørgensen (2012) when studying the processes of enregisterment among the school leavers. As Jørgensen (2010) points out speakers may both "own" and "command" language, although the two are not necessarily interdependent. This phenomenon is also documented by Harris (2006), who observes that young people in London can claim a language as their own while denying having expertise in the use of the language. This sense that some language belongs to "us" and not to "them" (cf. Gumperz', 1982: 65 notion of "we-code" and "they-code") is expressed in the following excerpt:

Excerpt 3

		Original	Translation
01	Naveed:	hallo de disser os	hey they're dissing us man
02		mand	
	%com:	(...)	(...) ((here several of the pupils shout Ibo, which is the name of another comedy character who uses resources associated with the contemporary urban vernacular))
03	JSM:	var det sjovt?	was it funny?
04	Naveed:	nej det var ikke sjovt	no it wasn't funny
05	JSM:	hvorfor [hvorfor øh]	why [why uhm]
06	Naveed:	[koran hvad er] det disser	[koran what is] it dissing
07		os for?	us for?
08	JSM:	hvad?	what?
09	Naveed:	skal jeg rejse mig op eller	do I need to stand up or
10		sådan noget?	something like that?
11	JSM:	ha	Ha

		(...)	(...)
			((after Naveed's remark the teacher comes up to him and asks him to raise his hand before speaking. When JSM tries to bring the discussion back on track Iman raises her hand.))
12	Iman:	vi me ja altså altså vi	we thi yes well well we
13		mener ikke at hun øh (.)	don't think that she uh (.)
14		hvad er det hvad hedder	what is it what's it called
15		det nu hun disser ikke	she's not dissing the girl
16		hende ved siden af hende	next to her you know but uh
17		vel men øh nogle der tror	some who think she's dissing
18		hun disser os fordi det er	us because it's some there
19		nogle der er nogle måske	are some maybe speak you
20		snakker du ved ligesom	know like her and it may be
21		hende og det kan være hun	she has you know uh what's
22		har du ved øh hvad hedder	it called insulted us
23		det nu fornærmet os	
24	JSM:	mm	mm
25	Iman:	lad os sige det sådan	let's put it like that
26	JSM:	hvem hvem er os?	who who is us?
		(...)	(...)
27	JSM:	nå os os det er dem der	oh us us that's those who
28		snakker ligesom hende	speak like her
29	Iman:	der er ikke så mange der	there aren't that many who
30		snakker ligesom hende	speak like her
31	JSM:	nej	no
32	Iman:	nej men hun v de gør grin	they're making fun of how
33		med hvordan man sna taler	you ta speak and it makes
34		og det gør xxx	xxx ((unintelligible))

As soon as the video clip of the sketch has stopped playing Naveed comments loudly across the class "hey they're dissing us man". This remark isn't directed at anyone in particular but seems to be offered as a joke to the amusement of the entire class, which can also be seen by the fact that many of the pupils, as well as JSM, laugh. Following this, many of the pupils call out the name Ibo, which is the name of another 'perker'-character from an online sketch show. Then JSM asks whether the sketch was funny to which Naveed answers "no" and accuses "them" of dissing "us". Several of the semiotic resources Naveed employs can be associated with the contemporary urban vernacular, such as his intonation and the use of the word "koran" as an interjection. This goes hand in hand with the construction of a tough, masculine persona through his confrontational questions to JSM. His final question ("do I need to stand up or something like that?") is accompanied by a threatening gesture where he raises his open hand to the level of his face with the back of his hand facing JSM.

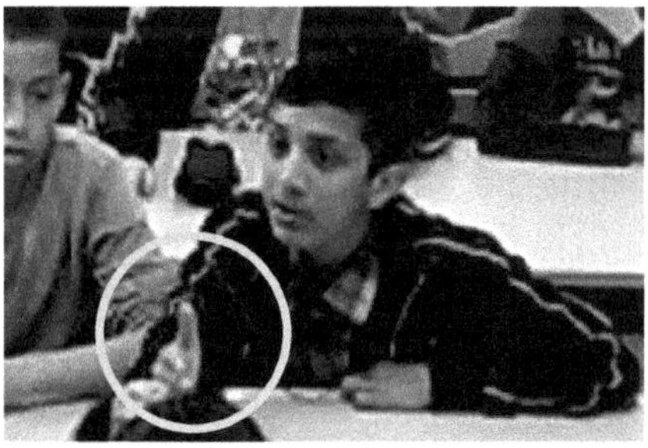

JSM laughs in response, showing that he interprets Naveed's remark in a jocular frame, and asks Naveed to explain, but Naveed is cut off by the teacher, who reprimands him for not having raised his hand. When making the gesture Naveed continues the joke from his previous comment by constructing a gangster persona and acting offended by the sketch – or by the researchers who played the sketch for him. That his remarks are intended as amusement can be seen by the fact that both he and his classmates are laughing and that his page buddy, Kamal, jokingly reaches over and covers Naveed's mouth with his hand.

The discussion then shifts to what it means to "diss", but a little while later Iman raises her hand and offers clarification for Naveed's statement. Her argument is, that since some in the class speak the contemporary urban vernacular, they may be offended and feel that the sketch is making fun of them and the way they speak. Iman uses the generative pronoun "man" (*you* or *one*) whereby she avoids specifying who speaks like that, as "man" can either include or exclude the speaker as well as the hearer. This follows a discussion of who "us" is, and "us" is defined as the people who speak the contemporary urban vernacular. Iman, however, on several occasions both during this session, during interviews, and in everyday interaction very explicitly disassociated herself from that way of speaking and the people who speak like that. Therefore, it makes sense for her to be vague about who is insulted by the sketch, since she does not usually presents herself as a part of that group, and since being part of that group, in her view, carries negative implications.

In this excerpt Naveed responds to the sketch by expressing offence while displaying tough masculinity and using resources associated with the contemporary urban vernacular. In doing so he introduces the concepts "us" and "they" whereby he constructs two groups, one to which he belongs, and one to which the creators of the sketch belong; and Iman picks up on this division.

This positioning corresponds well to my knowledge of the involved students from both ethnographic observations and audio and video recordings. Iman on several occasions disassociated herself from semiotic practices that could be connected with the contemporary urban vernacular and even on occasion reprimanded some of her classmates when they employed some of the resources associated with this way of speaking. Naveed on the other hand often used resources associated with this register and belonged to a group of friends who were often constructed (both by themselves and by others) as speaking "ugly". Later on in the discussion they were also mentioned by their classmates as examples of people who speak like the girl does in the sketch (i.e. the contemporary urban vernacular).

This example shows that not only is authenticity linked to perceptions of ethnicity, but in the case of this media production it also seems to affect its reception among the people represented by it (cf. Jaffe 2011). In Excerpt 2 we saw the discussion of whether or not the girl was a "perker" and hence an authentic speaker of the contemporary urban vernacular, and here we see that the pupils, who identify with the contemporary urban vernacular and its indexicalities, can potentially view this media representation of "their" way of speaking as insulting and its use of this register as inauthentic.

10 Conclusion

In this chapter I have discussed how the contemporary urban vernacular in Copenhagen has been presented in different mass media products, and how a group of pupils, for whom this way of speaking is a vital part of their everyday interaction, responds to one of these representations. The different media products parodying the contemporary urban vernacular have in common that they play on some of the same stereotypes regarding speakers of this register, although the later representations are more nuanced. The latest one, "It's still veiling", differs from the others in that the people behind it (and starring in it) have minority background themselves. Even so, by playing on the negative stereotypes surrounding this way of speaking all of these media representations of the contemporary urban vernacular can possibly reinforce these stereotypes and contribute to their distribution among Danish audiences. Thus, like Hill (2008) has observed with respect to the use of Mock Spanish, even well-intended media parodies of the contemporary urban vernacular can be potentially harmful in spreading negative stereotypes about the speakers of this register.

The sketch "Gangster talk on the phone", like the other examples of mass media productions featuring the contemporary urban vernacular, is an example where a part of the enregisterment of this way of speaking is taking place in mass media, since this register has gone "from the streets to the screens" (Androutsopoulos 2001). Though the pupils in this study are not the intended audience of the sketch, the majority of them knew both the show and the sketch beforehand, and their reactions to the sketch also show that at least some of them feel that they are represented by the sketch, since the girl in the sketch speaks like they do.

The pupils' reactions to the sketch make evident different properties of both the contemporary urban vernacular and of the sketch. Firstly, we can see that the contemporary urban vernacular is closely associated with aspects of ethnicity, and that a person can be subject to categorization as "Dane" or "perker" based on the use of this register (Excerpt 1). Secondly, we can see that regarding the contemporary urban vernacular signs of ethnic categorization can potentially influence perceptions of authenticity (Excerpt 2), since a discussion of whether or not the girl is an authentic speaker with the right to use that register becomes a discussion of whether she is to be considered a "perker" or a "Dane". Finally, the sketch can potentially be perceived as insulting to speakers of the contemporary urban vernacular (Excerpt 3) if the girl is viewed as inauthentic and hence "making fun of" and "dissing" the people who speak like that.

This clearly shows that the reception of a media text by the people potentially represented by it can differ greatly from what was intended by the people behind the production. Thus the pupils' reactions to the sketch justify Hill's (2008) argument: even though the sketch is intended to make fun of prejudices towards speakers of the contemporary urban vernacular and not the speakers themselves, it still plays on the existing stereotypes and can therefore be perceived as insulting.

Andreas Stæhr

Normativity as a social resource in social media practices

1 Introduction

Digital communication technologies and social media have become important resources in people's everyday communication (Baron 2008; Barton and Lee 2013). Therefore there is reason to believe that the increased use of new technologies has resulted in an increase of written texts (Kress 2005). The sociolinguistic image of the Internet as a space for linguistically exciting interaction contrasts with a more conservative image of computer mediated communication (CMC) as a threat towards the standard language. This view of CMC is voiced in unison by authors, politicians, so-called experts, 'authorities' and linguists (see Stæhr forthc. a). The claims about the disappearance of the orthographic standard are regarded as a morally reprehensible (Blommaert and Velghe 2012: 10) and as an expression of a "moral panic" (Cameron 1995) concerning declining standards, as described by Thurlow (2006) in his study of the public debate on language and digital communication technologies in English-language news articles.

In this chapter I describe how adolescent Facebook users from Copenhagen orient towards different norms of language use through self-corrections and other-corrections. The study of writing and orthographies has largely been neglected from a social point of view and studies of language and social meaning have traditionally involved analysis of spoken language (Sebba 2012: 1). In this chapter I suggest that the correction of language use give information about social relations among language users. I study the link between *linguistic form* and *social relations* by showing how young people use form corrections to more than just informing about and pointing to norms of language use. The correction practices of the adolescent Facebook users I study include various types of linguistic orientation. When we speak about norms in relation to writing we do not always (or only) refer to standard orthography. Other levels of normativity (such as peer generated norms, norms of writing online etc.) are also valid (Agha 2007). Because normativity is a co-constructed interactional accomplishment (Agha 2007), and because no language use is inherently correct or incorrect (Jørgensen 2010), typos, spelling mistakes and deviations can only be categorized as such in relation to the particular interactional and situational context. This means that what appears as a spelling mistake from a standard orthographic point of view is not necessarily perceived as such; other norms may be more situationally relevant. The adolescents I study sometimes correct all spelling mistakes, typos and orthographic variations in their own or others' utterances, but at other occasions they only single out some of the deviations. Often they correct themselves and each other on the basis of different norms of language use dependent on the interactional context. Sometimes several different norms are applied simultaneously within one sequence of written interaction. This indicates that corrections of language use are about more than mere orientation towards linguistic correctness.

In this chapter I wish to nuance the uniform description of social media as orthographically unregulated spaces. I also wish to discuss the conception that young people's use of social media is to blame for their alleged lack of spelling proficiency. I do this by studying how a group of adolescents orients towards different norms and norm centres in their Facebook interactions and what metalinguistic strategies they use in their correction practices. By carrying out sequential analyses of Facebook interactions I will show how interlocutors accept or contest each other's behaviour and how norms of writing are treated as situationally relevant. To study this we need to look into the activities' particular unfolding, the social meanings of the corrections (both their metapragmatic and micro social aspects), and the implications of them. I examine this from the perspective of the participants. After an introduction to my understanding of writing, spelling and normativities in social media I provide a description of my empirical methods. In the subsequent sections I analyse the use of self- and other-corrections.

2 Writing and spelling in social media

Today writing is a frequent means of everyday communication in many parts of the world (Baron 2008) and written language is crucial in vernacular activities of everyday life (Barton and Lee 2013: 16). Young people in particular are known as keen and skilled users of digital communication technologies, but such new communication forms are not limited to any specific age group (Barton and Lee 2013: 10). Barton and Lee (2013: 16) further argue that new technologies provide people with new and distinct writing spaces. It is particularly new that texts can no longer be thought of as relatively fixed and stable, but instead they are becoming more fluid (Barton and Lee 2013: 16), and increasingly interactive and multimodal. For example established notions such as "audience", "author" and "authorship" are also becoming more complex (Barton and Lee 2013: 16). Social media have also introduced a more complex relation between the notions of speech and writing and many more hybrid forms are identified on the web (Barton and Lee 2013;

Tannen 2013; Stæhr 2014). The relation between what I refer to as *new forms of writing* and *vernacular writing* is that the new forms of writing are often (but by no means always) vernacular rather than standard (see also Androutsopoulos 2011). Coupland and Kristiansen (2011: 20) even suggest that people's use of social media provide them with opportunities for the creativity and vernacularisation of writing in ways similar to developments in spoken language.

Individual variation within written genres is not a new phenomenon, nor is the scholarly study of it. Individual variation (not least in spelling) has been documented in letters and other private documents since the 17th century, that is, long before the onset of digital communication technologies (Pedersen 2009: 53). Nevertheless, today social network sites represent a striking contrast to newspapers, books and other print media produced for publication by mainstream publishers exactly because there is such wide-spread individual variation (Sebba 2012: 5). This indicates that different types of writing are regulated differently (Sebba 2012: 5) and more particularly that the orthographic standard plays different roles. According to Sebba, types of writing can be placed on a continuum in terms of the extent to which they are subjected to regulation. Some types of writing such as newspapers and books are highly regulated, while other types such as graffiti and texts on social network sites are not, or: at least not from the point of view of standard orthography. Sebba (2012: 5) characterises the new forms of written discourse (e.g. text messages and texts on social network sites) as belonging to the "unregulated orthographic space" where standard spelling is frequently disregarded. If we accept Sebba's premises, including his (standard orthographic) vantage point, Sebba certainly has a point. Yet, if we in describe the different kinds of writing that the young people produce in social media environments as "unregulated", there is a danger of oversimplification because that social media writing, as I will show below, is characterised by various, sometimes competing, forms of regulation. I will argue that in order to achieve a more nuanced understanding of (the complex regulation of) social media practices, it will be necessary to attend to the various linguistic resources writers have access to, and to the fact that social media has only enhanced this access. In this way networked writing breaks with the sociolinguistic assumption that spelling is an invariant linguistic practice (Androutsopoulos 2011; Shortis 2009; Sebba 2009). Sebba (2009: 36) further points to the fact that even if there is a standard orthography for a 'language', there is also variation. Such variation can be legitimate and widely accepted or not. Along these lines Androutsopoulos (2011: 151) argues that the grapheme structure of written online discourse is important as a level of linguistic variation. However, as Androutsopoulos (2011: 156) reminds us, vernacular spelling conventions do not replace standard orthography. Rather the orthographic standard is supplemented by other conventions. These may differ from the orthographic standard in many ways. For instance they may be recognised by fewer people, that is, have a smaller range.

In sum, the Internet has not had a revolutionary impact on spelling in the sense that it has changed the possibilities of spelling. The production of new forms and new conventions of spelling also happened long before the onset of digital communication technologies (Shortis 2009: 240). Even so, the Internet has introduced: "a looser, more permeable sense of what counts as spelling. Spelling is becoming a deployment of choices from a range of options" (Shortis 2009: 240). Hence, writing in social media is not a 'free for all', but depends on different levels of normativity. In this way social media interaction does not just follow a standard spelling norm but other norms as well, and the norms applied or oriented to may inform about the ways the participants relate to each other. Thus, we are looking at "orthography as social action" (Sebba 2012; Jaffe et al. 2012) and at normativity as consisting of various levels.

3 Normativities

According to Agha (2007: 126) linguistic normativity can be divided into three levels. The first level is *norms of behaviour*. This is described as a statistical norm or frequency distribution in some type of behaviour (Agha 2007: 126). The second level is *a normalised model of behaviour*. This contains reflexive models of social behaviour recognised as 'normal' or typical by (smaller or larger) groups of people, and what I will later refer to as *peer generated norms* fits this description. Finally, the third level of normativity is *the normative standard*, which is "a normative model, linked to standards whose breach results in sanctions" (Agha 2007: 126). I will refer to this level as *the Standard* or *standard orthography* in my analysis. Agha (2007: 147) argues that the ideals linked to the Standard tend to "naturalize perceptions of the register as a baseline against which other registers appear as deviant, defective varieties of the language". In this way standard registers in well-developed standard-language communities are hegemonic (Silverstein 2003: 219). Norms are often hierarchically organised because the Standard functions ideologically as "the "neutral" top-and-centre of all variability that is thus organized around-and-below it" (Silverstein 2003: 219). In that sense standardisation often influences what people consider as "normal" behaviour and "valid" norms. In fact, as Shortis (2009: 239) argues, standard orthography has been ubiquitous in the age of print. Standard language further commonly becomes emblematic of speakers level of education, academic skills and status in society (Agha 2007: 169) and standard language registers are given legitimacy and prestige over non-standard alternatives (Garrett 2010: 34). Denmark is a highly standardised speech community (Kristiansen 2009: 167), with a history of linguistic uniformity of spoken language, and a strong prevalent standard ideology (Pedersen 2009: 52). This has also been the case regarding the written language. The institutionalised norm of writing has been administered by The Danish Language Board, an institution under the Ministry of Culture, since 1955. Due to the ideological position of standard orthography in well-established standard language communities such as the Danish, it can be socially stigmatising (Goffman 1963) or just have negative social effects not to adhere to the orthographic standard. However, this does not entail that deviations from other norms may not have social consequences as I show in my analysis.

It is important to recognise, however, that social normativity is a "polycentric" (Blommaert 2010) phenomenon. This means that people, on every occasion, may orient to, or feel accountable towards, various social and linguistic norms which are tied to different norm centres. Such norm centres consists of one or more evaluative authorities. For instance, young students may orient towards school and teachers, peer groups and different kinds of popular and sub cultures such as music, films, skateboarding, sports etc. Also, different normative centres are taken to be relevant in different situations and genres. Thus, what counts as good or bad language varies from situation to situation because different settings, such as for example social network sites and school, are differently ordered spaces with different normative centres. In addition, people have different normative preferences, and the same individual may draw on different centres for different social purposes. Yet, in fact, almost every situation people engage in is polycentrically organised because more than one possible norm centre can often be distinguished (Blommaert 2010: 40). Even within a single social network site we find that young people orient towards different norm centres as I will show in my analysis. In this way, young people's linguistic repertoires are polycentrically organised (see also Karrebæk et al. forthc.).

So, settings differ with regard to which norms are relevant. We motivate, and show to our interlocutors, what norms are relevant through the use of metasigns that point towards different norm centres, and through our linguistic behaviour in general. Furthermore, we judge from the responses we receive to what extent others agree on our normative interpretation. In that respect, the metapragmatic activity of correction is about establishing footing (Goffman 1981) and interpersonal alignment. This methodological approach to the study of correction, i.e. as an interactional and social process, illuminates people's own perceptions of what count as valid norms in a given situation.

4 Self- and other-corrections on Facebook

It is a common practice among the adolescents I study to correct each others' language use on Facebook. In the literature concerning the phenomenon of *correction* (or *repair*) a distinction is commonly drawn between self-corrections and other-corrections (Schegloff, Jefferson, and Sacks 1977). I maintain this distinction in this chapter. Schegloff, Jefferson, and Sacks (1977: 362) find that self- and other-correction are related organisationally and that self-correction is preferred over other-correction. Most studies of repair have focused on spoken interaction while there is only little research on repair mechanisms in online written interaction (Meredith and Stokoe 2013: 2). For example Schönfedt and Golato (2003) study repair in multi-party web chats and show how participants often adjust their repair practices in accordance with the particular conditions of the web chat. Collister (2011) studies repair in chat interaction in the online game 'Word of Warcraft'. More specifically she studies what she calls '*-repair' which her participants use to correct misspellings. The functions of '*- repair' will be explained in more detail below. More recently Meredith and Stokoe (2013) have examined self-repair in one-to-one quasi-synchronic Facebook chat. They show that self-initiated self-repair is frequently occurring in this online space and that repair occurs in similar and contrasting ways to repair in spoken conversation. Furthermore, the preference for self-correction also holds in online interaction (Meredith and Stokoe 2013: 22).

Self- and other-correction are turn-taking formats with a range of social functions. Yet, each function depends on the situational and interactional context. The term *correction* often refers to the process of a perceived "error" being replaced with something perceived as "correct" (Schegloff, Jefferson, and Sacks 1977: 363). In line with Schegloff, Jefferson, and Sacks (1977) I view self-corrections as a type of self-initiated repair of a stretch of discourse. I view the correction of others' spelling as dis-alignment. This can be dis-alignment with the original producer whose choice of linguistic form has been corrected, with somebody else, with a register of practice, situated context, etc. When carrying out self- and other-corrections the adolescents orient towards different norms of language use, and the normative preferences are often connected with the interactional and situational context of the metalinguistic activity. The potential orientation towards different norms is a fundamental element in Facebook interaction because the conversations take place in a semi-public space (Ellison and boyd 2013) where different people with different normative preferences constantly engage with each other and are confronted with each other's writings and normative orientations. The corrections typically concern either what are treated as spelling mistakes or uncertainties about correct spelling. Yet, remember that, in my account, spelling mistakes are not only viewed from a standard orthographic point of view (Agha's third level of normativity).

I observe different interactional strategies of self- and other-corrections among the adolescents, which I will illustrate with the following examples. One strategy of self-correction is to explicitly display one's uncertainty about the orthographical conventions. The adolescents typically mark such uncertainty by writing *(staves)* ('to be spelled') in brackets after a word. Another metalinguistic strategy is self-correction of a misspelled word by adding an asterisk followed by the correct spelling. Collister (2011: 921) refer to this as '*-repair' and argues that this innovative form only exist in writing as there is no pronounceable version of an * (other than saying the word asterisk). Furthermore, she finds that this form of repair can be deployed both for self- and other-repair. Among the adolescents uncertainty about spelling and corrections can be signalled through explicit statements such as 'I don't know how to spell this word', 'oops I wrote it with an "e"', 'I know it is [wrong] it is because I am writing on my phone', 'I know I misspelled it so don't correct it', etc. Such metalinguistic comments on correctness serve different social functions in the local interactions among the participants in my study. Common to all self-corrections are that they are conducted to highlight the writers' mastery of language norms. Corrections of others' language are also practiced in various ways. Sometimes the adolescents merely mark the correction with an asterisk (as described for self-corrections), and sometimes corrections are articulated more explicitly, such as: 'it is spelled this way', 'you spelled it wrongly', 'learn how to spell', 'can't you spell', etc. Such statements differ in terms of what meta-message is communicated. For instance, comments such as 'can't you spell' are potentially more face-threatening than utterances such as 'it is spelled this way'. Most of the corrections are often followed by (explicit) metapragmatic comments on the linguistic form in focus of the correction. These evaluations often label or categorise the correction, or explain its motivation, and thereby they constitute a key to understanding its social function.

There are many corrections in my data, yet the young people certainly do not correct everything which could be corrected. They may comment on a couple of deviations, misspellings and typos in an utterance but ignore others. Sometimes they do not correct anything at all. Furthermore, it differs whether they orient to standard orthography or to other norms when making corrections. They may even orient to different levels of normativity at the same time. Before I turn to my analysis of self- and other-corrections I describe my data collection.

5 Data

In this chapter I use data collected among the 7th – 9th graders in the focus school. After this part of the collaborative study ended (2011) I continued to meet with some of the adolescents and I kept following all of them on Facebook. In 2010 most of the young people in our study had a Facebook profile and they regularly engaged with each other through this social network site. I gained access to these interactions in the following way. I created a Facebook profile on behalf of the project and advertised our new profile when I talked to the adolescents during fieldwork. Soon we began to receive friend requests on Facebook. We never took initiative to befriend them and we have explicit consent from them that we can use the data, provided that all names are anonymised (for a detailed account of the data collection see Stæhr 2010, 2014). The adolescents in focus of this paper all lived in the same area of Copenhagen, but in terms of cultural and linguistic backgrounds they varied extensively. To the extent this is of any importance for my analysis I will account for it during the analyses. The Danish text in the excerpts contains orthographically non-conventional forms. Some of them become the focus of the participants' attention, whereas some are not commented on. I attempt to represent these variations from Danish standard orthography in the English translations if they are important for my analysis. I have divided my analysis into two parts. In section 6 I investigate the social functions of self-corrections in Facebook interaction while in section 7 I focus on corrections of others' language use.

6 Self-corrections on Facebook

The first excerpt shows an example of self-correction. It exemplifies how the strategy of writing *(staves)* ('to be spelled') after a word form is used and responded to. The participants are Negasi and her friend Alima. Negasi is born in Denmark, and her parents come from Eritrea. Alima does not attend any of the classes I followed, but from my online ethnographic fieldwork I know her to be a close friend of Negasi. This is also reflected in the fact that Negasi has added Alima as her sister in the family relation section on her Facebook page (despite them not being sisters in a traditional understanding of this concept). The excerpt is from Negasi's Facebook wall where she has posted a YouTube clip called "The Duck Song". To accompany the video Negasi has the following status update:

Excerpt 1: "Negro humor*" (October 2010)

Original:

Translation:	**Negasi:**	YOU NEED TO SEE THIS ONE! :'D haha I died the first time I saw it!
	Alima:	love it!
	Negasi:	Hahhah negrohumour? (to be spelled)
	Alima:	negro humour* Yeeeeees!
	Negasi:	hihihih :D

Negasi initiates her status update by strongly recommending the video she has uploaded. Note her use of capitals and the exclamation mark, by means of which she urges people to watch the video. Subsequently she describes her personal experience with the video clip, as she writes that she 'died' the first time she saw it. This is slang for laughing a lot ('dying with laughter'). Judging from Alima's response she shares Negasi's enthusiasm. In the following comment Negasi categorises the content of the video as *neger humor* 'negro humour' followed by a question mark and the metalinguistic comment *(staves)* ('to be spelled'). This comment signals insecurity about whether she has spelled the word correctly. She separates the noun into two words which is a deviation from the standard rules for compounds in Danish (I have adjusted the English translation to English orthographic standards to represent the misspelling). Although certainly worth closer sociolinguistic scrutiny, the meaning of 'negro humour' is not the main issue of my analysis; rather as Alima writes *Jaaaaaa!* 'Yeeeeees!' it seems to be the case that the girls share an understanding of it. It is striking that Negasi orients towards the standard orthographic spelling of the word 'negro humour' and also that Alima responds to this metalinguistic comment as if it is an invitation to correct the word. Thus, she replies by writing *negerhumor* 'negro humour', i.e., in the correct way, followed by an asterisk in the subsequent comment. The asterisk indicates that the utterance should be understood as a correction. In this instance Alima's correction appears as a friendly gesture. This is a common way for the adolescents to react to self-corrections. In the next excerpts I show how self-correction can also have other social functions.

Excerpt 2 and 3 illustrate the interactional strategy of self-correction involving the use of an asterisk as a metapragmatic comment on an incident of misspelling. Excerpt 2 is a part of a longer thread consisting of 85 comments from the young participants' shared Facebook page. They used the page to arrange after-school activities such as trips to the cinema, parties etc. The thread is initiated by a comment written by one of the boys called Bashaar. He writes that he cannot attend their next event because he is ill. Shortly after Jamil writes that he cannot attend either for the same reason. Some of the others suggest that Jamil is lying. This triggers an argument between Jamil and the others that results in accusations and name-calling. This is the context of the exchange below. As a response to Bashaar and Jamil's excuses Fatima writes:

Excerpt 2: "I have already corrected it!! :D" (October 2011)

Original:

Fatima Eeeijj I SKAAAAL KOMMER :-(
2. oktober kl. 21:33 · Synes godt om
Fatima Kommee*
2. oktober kl. 21:33 · Synes godt om
Safa Haha, self glemmer jeg ikke ;) og nej Jamil , jeg tjekkede ikke facebook selvom den har redet mig et par gange ;)
2. oktober kl. 21:33 · Synes godt om · 1 person
Jamil komme*
2. oktober kl. 21:34 · Synes godt om · 1 person
Fatima JEEEG HAAAR RETTET !! :D
2. oktober kl. 21:34 · Synes godt om

Translation:	**Fatima:**	Nooo YOU HAVE TO COMING :-(
	Fatima:	Comee*
	Safa:	Haha, ofc I will not forget ;) and no Jamil I did not check facebook even though it saved me a couple of times ;)
	Fathi:	Come*
	Fatima:	I HAVE ALREADY CORRECTED IT !! :D

In Fatima's first comment she urges the boys to attend the class activity. However, in doing so she writes *kommer* 'coming' which is in the present form rather than the expected standard infinitive form *komme* 'come'. Fatima immediately notices this within less than a minute. Yet, she makes a typing error as she writes *kommee* ('comee') instead of *komme* ('come'). This does not pass unnoticed. Jamil who is already in the business of provoking the others seizes the opportunity to correct Fatima and writes **komme* ('*come'). Fatima responds within the same minute and states that she has already corrected the typing error. She uses capitals and exclamation marks to emphasise the message of her comment but she also mitigates what could be seen as an aggressive tone by adding a laughing smiley. It appears as if she does not notice the typo in her self-correction until later in the excerpt (in a part not showed here) where she writes *og hvaaa så Komme** ('so what come*') diminishing the importance of the typo. Yet, we can still conclude from her comment that the act of self-correction is an important practice, and her use of the '*-repair' certainly demonstrates linguistic skills and an awareness of correctness in her Facebook writing. In addition, Fatima's response to Jamil's correction suggests that once you have made a self-correction you are 'protected' against comments on your lack of spelling proficiencies and the like within the same sequence of interaction. Along these lines such self-corrections are a way of doing *face-work* (Goffman 1955), in this case as an interactional strategy to protect oneself from being categorised as illiterate, stupid, non-academic and other character traits associated with not mastering the Standard. In this way it appears as if Jamil's correction of a seemingly trivial typo is a way to call attention to Fatima's (alleged) poor spelling skills, and, standard orthography is used as a resource associated with (academic) status and success – an association, also often seen within the more general public discourse of language and correctness.

Standard norms of orthography and grammar were in focus in the two previous excerpts as linguistic strategies of managing peer-group relations. However, self-correction also orients to other norms than the Standard and the institutionalised formal correctness. In the next excerpt the level of peer-group normativity becomes prominent as we shall see how self-corrections are carried out in relation to peer norms. Also, explicit statements on misspellings are employed as an interactional strategy of correcting language use. In this excerpt Fatima writes a status update on her wall about a visit to the dentist. According to her, it is written in a way associated with a particular way of being Danish, which I will elaborate on later:

Excerpt 3: "Are you on bad terms with the dictionary ;D" (March 2010)

Original:

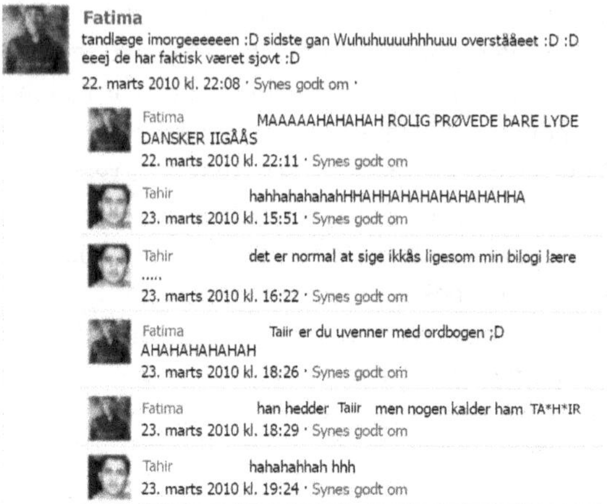

Fatima
tandlæge imorgeeeeeen :D sidste gan Wuhuhuuuuhhhuuu overstååeet :D :D
eeej de har faktisk været sjovt :D
22. marts 2010 kl. 22:08 · Synes godt om ·

Fatima MAAAAAHAHAHAH ROLIG PRØVEDE bARE LYDE DANSKER IIGÅÅS
22. marts 2010 kl. 22:11 · Synes godt om

Tahir hahhahahahahHHAHHAHAHAHAHAHAHAHHA
23. marts 2010 kl. 15:51 · Synes godt om

Tahir det er normal at sige ikkås ligesom min bilogi lære
.....
23. marts 2010 kl. 16:22 · Synes godt om

Fatima Taiir er du uvenner med ordbogen ;D
AHAHAHAHAHAH
23. marts 2010 kl. 18:26 · Synes godt om

Fatima han hedder Taiir men nogen kalder ham TA*H*IR
23. marts 2010 kl. 18:29 · Synes godt om

Tahir hahahahhah hhh
23. marts 2010 kl. 19:24 · Synes godt om

Translation:

Fatima: Dentist tomorrow :D last time Wuhuhuuuuhhhuuu over and done with :D :D
Well okay they [read 'it'] has actually been fun :D

Fatima: MAAAAAHAHAHAH EASY NOW I JUST TRIED TO SOUND DANE **RIGHT**

Tahir: hahhahahahahHHAHHAHAHAHAHAHAHAHHA

Tahir: it is normal to say **all right** just as my biology teacher
...

Fatima: Taiir are you on bad terms with the dictionary ;D

Fatima: his name is Taiir but some call him TA*H*IR

Tahir: hahahahhah hhh

Fatima's status update describes her last visit to the dentist but it turns out that the propositional content is not the only information worthy of interest. A few minutes later, she adds a metapragmatic comment which directs the attention to the linguistic style of the update as she writes: *rolig prøvede bare at lyde dansker iigåås* 'easy now I just tried to sound Dane right'. By doing so she associates her way of writing with a specific understanding of Danish-ness. It is a very general characterisation and we cannot know what specific features or models of behaviour she associates with sounding Danish or for that matter, what it means to her to be Danish. However, her metalinguistic comment suggests that the adolescents are not only aware of their spelling skills, but also of how spelling is associated with social and cultural models. Consequently Fatima is able to exploit her insight into spelling as a way to demonstrate her perception of how to "sound Danish". Such awareness illustrates the reflexivity in social media interaction (see also Stæhr 2015). That is, young people's productions on social media (both with respect to outcome and process) force them to look at themselves, sometimes from a new perspective, which may result in subsequent modification of self-representation (Weber and Mitchell 2008: 41). To underline the message of her metapragmatic comment on her linguistic or behavioural appearance Fatima ends her comment with the word *IIGÅÅS*. This is an alternative spelling of standard *ikke også* ('right') and it appears to be marked in several ways. Firstly, judging from Tahir's reaction, it is not perceived as part of Fatima's routine behaviour. To begin with, Tahir shows that he finds her utterance funny by laughing. Half an hour later he comments on it as he repeats the word *IGÅÅS*. This he associates with their biology teacher (with majority background) and the style of writing allegedly represents her normal way of speaking. The fact that he highlights the word *IGÅÅS* and associates it with a majority speaker of Danish indicates that he sees it as a central element of Fatima's performance of sounding Danish. Also, even though Tahir's spelling of the word *ikkås* differs from Fatima's it still highlights the same pronunciation features. They both write "å" instead of "o" and they both contract the word which reflects casual speech. Danish is considered as a deep orthography (Seymor, Aro, and Erskine 2003) due to its inconsistent relations between phonemes and graphemes but regardless of this pronunciation features may be represented in writing, and they certainly are among the adolescents on Facebook. Secondly, Fatima's use of multiple vowels and capital letters flags her utterance in relation to her previous utterance. In this way the stylisation functions as a metamessage (Tannen 2013) commenting on the construction of a persona from which she distances herself and highlighting a performed and insincere (note the laughter) way of being Danish which is recognised by Tahir.

In general Tahir's comments are interesting as his spelling deviates from the orthographic standard. For example, *normal* 'normal' is spelled *normalt* and *biologi lære* 'biology teacher' is spelled *biologilærer* 'biology teacher' in the standard orthography. Furthermore, *ikkås* 'right' should be *ikke også* ('right'). Yet, it would be misleading to characterise this as a spelling mistake in the present context as it illustrates a representation of a specific (understanding of a) pronunciation of the word. The alternative spellings are indeed noticed by Fatima who asks Tahir if he is on bad terms with the dictionary. This should be understood within a frame of teasing, judging from her use of emoticons and her somehow iconic representation of laughter. But it is important to recognize that although Fatima orients towards the dictionary (a common practice among the adolescents), this should not be seen as an invitation to stick to standard orthography. Fatima's own status update also contains typos and deviations from the orthographic standard, and the fact that she only orients to Tahir's misspellings (and not her own) shows that here there is more in play than an interest in correctness and orthography. I suggest that her corrections and references to the Standard (dictionary) serve to (re)produce academic reputations among peers. Just after drawing attention to Tahir's relation with the dictionary she motivates her spelling of his name by writing: 'His name is Taiir but some call him TA*H*IR'. The asterisks mark the letter "H" as in focus of the correction. Thereby Fatima shows awareness of the relation between pronunciation and the standard spelling of his name. Keeping in mind the way asterisks were used in excerpt 1 and 2 we may assume that her use is a way to pre-empt others' potential corrections. Approximately an hour after Fatima's correction and self-correction Tahir replies with laughter. It does not seem to bother him to be depicted in this way, i.e. as academically less competent, and I also know from my ethnographic fieldwork that he is often positioned as non-academic both by peers and teachers. Fatima thereby confirms more widely circulating perceptions of Tahir's lack of academic ambitions.

The next excerpt illustrates a similar use of self-corrections, but in addition it highlights that the interactional context plays a crucial role in relation to what norms are applicable and to who has the right to write in certain ways in different situations. This excerpt involves a correction from 'learner Danish' to standard orthography. It comes from a status update from Jamil's Facebook profile. To understand the following interaction it is necessary to know that Jamil has minority background while the other boy appearing in the excerpt, Rasmus, has majority background. In the status update Jamil explains that he is going to have a very long day. He writes:

Excerpt 4: "long time no seen, what you do" (October 2011)

Original:

Translation:	**Jamil:**	Long day tomorrow, get off at 17,05!
		[...]
	Rasmus:	I start 8:00 and get off at 17:30, and that's the way it is every Monday
	Jamil:	Yes, but then you are earlier off the rest of the days
	Rasmus:	Not that early
	Jamil:	Don't lie nigga
	Rasmus:	Well I don't snowman
	Jamil:	long time no seen, what you do
	Rasmus:	I look at the soccer in the telly, and listen to the music from the youtube
	Rasmus:	*I watch soccer at the telly and listen to music on youtube :D
	Jamil:	the postman always rings twice [written in Japanese]

Rasmus, one of Jamil's classmates, is one of the first persons to comment. He writes that he is going to have an even longer day and he hints at long workdays being perfectly normal for him. In this way he tries both to outdo Jamil and to trivialise the content of Jamil's update. This also changes the activity into a (mock) competition which is continued in the subsequent comments. One more change happens, and this time it concerns the moral character of the participants. This happens when Jamil writes: *don't lie nigga* whereby he implies that Rasmus is not sticking to the truth. Jamil performs this change of footing through a shift into what is similar to a Black English vernacular style of writing. Rasmus reacts by writing: *Det gør jeg da heller ikke snemand* 'Well I don't snowman'. These two utterances introduce an element of colour and ethnicity to the conversation and it appears as if the two boys switch colours and ethnic affiliation.

The exchange of roles or identities is further underlined linguistically by Jamil who addresses Rasmus in a stylised learner variety of Danish associated with newly arrived immigrants. This is equivalent to what Rampton (2001: 271) describes as 'foreigner talk' (see also Jaspers 2011a). He writes: *lang tid siden, hvad **du lave*** 'long time no seen, what you do'. According to the grammatical standard a correct sentence would be: *hvad **laver du*** 'what are you doing' and the non-inversion of subject and finite verb is indexical of this style of speaking. Rasmus replies by adopting the same style of writing as he writes: *Jeg ser den fodbold i den fjernsyn og høre den music på den youtube* 'I look at the soccer in the telly, and listen to the music from the youtube'. In this case the excessive use of the definite article makes his utterance characteristic of what could be described as 'learner Danish'. Rasmus would not normally be seen as a ratified user of this style by the others (see Stæhr forthc.) but he accommodates to Jamil's style of writing and becomes a ratified user in this local interaction between the two boys. Strikingly, he corrects the sentence into standard Danish marked by an asterisk shortly after. In this way he "translates" the utterance into a style of writing that is more recognisably as his. The fact that he adds a smiley in the end indicates that either the translation or the previous utterance should not be taken entirely seriously. His translation draws on the *form* of self-corrections as he uses the asterisk to frame the act and thereby the utterance can be seen as face-repair.

We cannot say for sure what motivates Rasmus to rewrite the utterance, but it may have to do with the fact that their conversation takes place on Jamil's wall (and not in a private chat) and therefore can be viewed by all of their Facebook friends. We know of at least two other participants because Lamis and Massima (two girls from their class) *synes godt om* 'like' some of the comments. So, even if Rasmus feels comfortable writing in the learner style of Danish in the presence of Jamil (note also that Jamil initiated the activity) he might not feel comfortable or entitled to use this in public. For that reason Rasmus' face-work can be viewed as a way to manage his public identity and an interactional strategy which protects him from being sanctioned and receiving comments on his language use. Consequently his motivation for correcting himself should not only be found in the local interaction, but can also be seen as a reflection of a shift into a public persona. Elsewhere I have observed how Rasmus is sanctioned when crossing (Rampton 2005) into styles or registers not perceived as belonging to him (see Stæhr forthc. a for a detailed description). Thus, his act of face-repair through self-correction is a way of managing how he positions himself in relation to others and other language styles. It is harder to explain the meaning of Jamil's subsequent comment. Jamil posts a link written in Japanese script saying: 'the post man always rings twice' (citing the title of a novel by James M. Cain). This link leads to a Facebook page (with content from Wikipedia) written in Turkish about the movie "Tutko" which is the Turkish title of the Italian movie "Ossessione" ('Obsession'), which is also based on Cain's novel 'The post man always rings twice'. The use of Japanese script could be a comment on the fact that Rasmus changed his spelling and wrote like a foreigner as Jamil does a similar thing. Yet, without losing sight of the actual content, he also seems to propose that Rasmus watches the film. And more generally, Jamil's post could be an example of his frequent use of absurd (black) humour which is often hard to follow, judging from the reactions of his peers. Yet, it fits the general frame of play in the excerpt where the two boys play with linguistic resources and social categories. In sum, the example demonstrates how the adolescents use the self-correction format to do other things than correcting typos and orthography. Another central aspect of this excerpt is that it illustrates how the adolescents' linguistic repertoires are polycentrically organised, because they orient towards both Black English vernacular, learner Danish and standard orthography in their Facebook interaction.

In this section I have described different interactional strategies of self-correction and how the adolescent Facebook users draw on these forms of correction when performing other social acts (such as face-work and protecting one's personae). Self-corrections have in common that they are used to draw attention to the writer's spelling proficiencies or language usage in general. In this way different kinds of metalinguistic commentary (the '*-repair' and '(to be spelled)') highlight misspellings and point out the possibility that a word is not spelled correctly. Self-corrections function as face-work and aims at protecting the person against others' evaluations of one's spelling and the possibility of being constructed as a bad speller and thereby non-academic, stupid etc. My analysis so far indicates that the act of self-correction (excerpt 1, 2 and 3) and correction of other's language use (excerpt 2 and 3) show more than the orientation towards standard orthography, peer generated norms and correctness. Furthermore, correction practices are used by the adolescents for teasing (sometimes with spelling skills), for conjuring up foreign speakers, and for politeness reasons (by insisting on writing correctly and helping out with spelling). Moreover, self-corrections involve awareness of rights of language use as we saw in excerpt 3 and 4. In these cases I illustrated how the adolescents adapt to the local genre and to the nature of the medium of Facebook as a private and a public space at the same time. Thus, excerpt 3 and 4 showed that self-corrections do not only involve corrections on a lexical level but also reflection about the use of different ways of writing that are indexical of specific values and speakers. In the next section I will look further into how the adolescents negotiate social relationship in their Facebook interactions through the use of different other-correction practices. In the first part I focus on corrections involving standard orthography. Afterwards I look at corrections involving peer group generated norms and co-occurrence of different norms.

7 Correcting others' language use

The first example of other-correction (excerpt 5) illustrates how orientation to standard orthography is used as a resource in negotiation of local peer status and heterosexual relations among the adolescents. Fatima posts an update on her wall where she accuses one of her friends called Saleem of abusing her. Saleem does not attend one of the two classes I followed, but he lives in the same street as Fatima and they correspond frequently on Facebook, often in a flirtatious way involving teasing and jocular verbal beating. Fatima initiates the update by writing:

Excerpt 5: "I don't know WHO is that bad at spelling hahaha ;)" (February 2010)

Original:

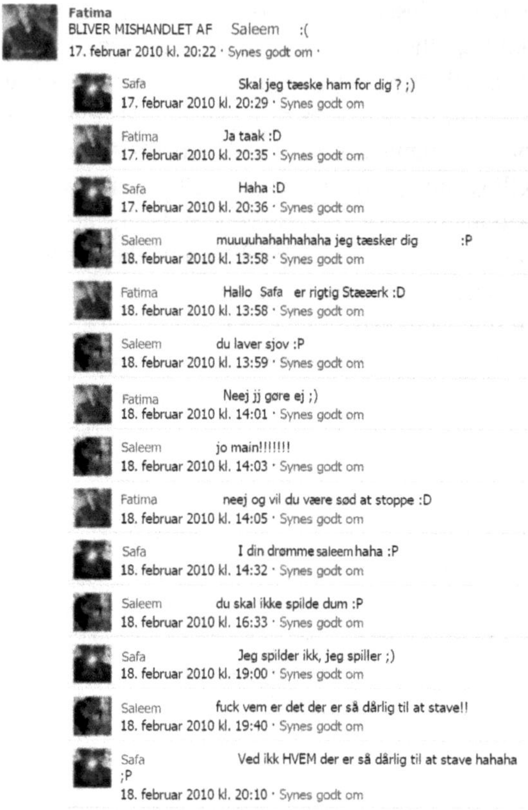
Fatima
BLIVER MISHANDLET AF Saleem :(
17. februar 2010 kl. 20:22 · Synes godt om ·

Safa Skal jeg tæske ham for dig ? ;)
17. februar 2010 kl. 20:29 · Synes godt om

Fatima Ja taak :D
17. februar 2010 kl. 20:35 · Synes godt om

Safa Haha :D
17. februar 2010 kl. 20:36 · Synes godt om

Saleem muuuuhahahhahaha jeg tæsker dig :P
18. februar 2010 kl. 13:58 · Synes godt om

Fatima Hallo Safa er rigtig Stææérk :D
18. februar 2010 kl. 13:58 · Synes godt om

Saleem du laver sjov :P
18. februar 2010 kl. 13:59 · Synes godt om

Fatima Neej jj gøre ej ;)
18. februar 2010 kl. 14:01 · Synes godt om

Saleem jo main!!!!!!!
18. februar 2010 kl. 14:03 · Synes godt om

Fatima neej og vil du være sød at stoppe :D
18. februar 2010 kl. 14:05 · Synes godt om

Safa I din drømme saleem haha :P
18. februar 2010 kl. 14:32 · Synes godt om

Saleem du skal ikke spilde dum :P
18. februar 2010 kl. 16:33 · Synes godt om

Safa Jeg spilder ikk, jeg spiller ;)
18. februar 2010 kl. 19:00 · Synes godt om

Saleem fuck vem er det der er så dårlig til at stave!!
18. februar 2010 kl. 19:40 · Synes godt om

Safa Ved ikk HVEM der er så dårlig til at stave hahaha ;P
18. februar 2010 kl. 20:10 · Synes godt om

Translation:

Fatima: I AM BEING ABUSED BY Saleem :(
Safa: Do you want me to beat him up? ;)
Fatima: Yes pleease :D
Safa: Haha :D
Saleem: Muuuuhahahhahaha I beat you up Safa :p
Fatima: Hey Safa is really strong :D
Saleem: You are joking :P
Fatima: Noo I don't ;)
Saleem: You are, man!!!!!!!
Fatima: Noo and would you please stop :D
Safa: in **your** dreams Saleem haha :P
Saleem: don't **blay** stupid :P
Safa: I don't **blay**, I play ;)
Saleem: fuck **ho** is that bad at spelling!!
Safa: I don't know **WHO** is that bad at spelling hahaha ;)

Fatima's use of capitals seems to be a way to draw others' attention to her post. It is possible that both Saleem and Fatima are present while Fatima writes the update because Saleem does not comment until the next day. In addition, Fatima writes in the present tense which may indicate Saleem's presence during the writing. Fatima's update can be characterised as flirtatious because her description of her experience with Saleem is reminiscent of the often physical and flirtatious teasing among teenagers. Her 'cry for help' is heard a few minutes later where her classmate Safa offers her assistance to beat up Saleem. Fatima accepts the offer after a few minutes. The first part of their correspondence happens on the 17th of February in the evening, and the conversation continues the following day when Saleem responds to Safa's offer. With an iconic written representation of an evil voice ('muuuuhahahhahaha') he threatens to beat up Safa instead. In the next few comments Fatima and Saleem argue about whether Saleem is stronger than Safa. Note that the conversation takes place within a play frame signalled by the adolescents' use of emoticons and the iconic representations of laughter. Half an hour later Safa re-enters the conversation by writing: 'in your dreams Saleem haha'. Saleem reacts to this confrontational (but still playful) comment by writing: *du skal ikke* ***spilde*** *dum* 'don't **blay** stupid' and while doing so he makes a common spelling mistake as he writes *spilde* ('spill') instead of *spille* ('play'). Safa does not hesitate to take advantage of this as she draws attention to Jamil's spelling mistake in her reply: *Jeg* ***spilder*** *ikke, jeg spiller ;)* 'I don't **blay**, I play'. The winking smiley could indicate joy over Saleem making this mistake. In the next comment Saleem tries to deliver a snappy comeback, by writing: *fuck* ***vem*** *er det der er så dålig til at stave!!* 'fuck ho is that bad at spelling!!'. We cannot know whether he speaks about Safa's spelling proficiencies in general or about the typo in her previous comment where she writes: *I* ***din*** *drømme* (equivalent to 'in your dream') instead of *I* ***dine*** *drømme* 'in your dreams'. In any case he is not very successful as he makes one more spelling mistake or typo by writing *vem* (the equivalent mistake would be 'ho' in english) instead of *hvem* 'who'. Again Safa takes advantage of the situation and rephrases Saleem's comment into a question. Furthermore, she highlights the correct spelling of *hvem* 'who' by writing this word in capitals. This silences Saleem. Thus, proficiency in spelling becomes a social resource as Safa (whom I know to be very school ambitious) uses it to position Saleem as a bad speller twice, and she (successfully) overrules his attempts to put her down. In this way the interaction illustrates how spelling can be a resource used for teasing and for navigating the risks and rewards of flirting in the same way as (alleged) physical strength was treated as a resource earlier in the excerpt. Judging from the fact that Saleem leaves the conversation, it appears as if academic skills and knowledge of standard orthography succeeded in beating physical strength on this occasion. I have observed several similar incidents where academic skills such as spelling are used as a status resource. In this way spelling proficiencies becomes a resource for constructing identities associated with academic success.

The next excerpt focuses on how norms of language use can be put up for negotiation. It further deals with the orientation to peer norms and to the mixing of different levels of normativity. I have divided the excerpt into two sections as it exemplifies two different aspects of correction of language use. The status update is written by Bashaar who writes:

Excerpt 6a: "fuck it, people know what I mean anyway >:)" (August 2010)

Original:

Bashaar
7. august 2010

Shuf hendes Gøt !

Ceyda HAHA göt**
7. august 2010 kl. 21:54 · Synes godt om

Bashaar Ved det, men jeg kan ikke finde ud af at lave det
7. august 2010 kl. 21:54 · Synes godt om

Ceyda ok først denne her ¨ også o prøv
7. august 2010 kl. 21:55 · Synes godt om

Bashaar ¨o
7. august 2010 kl. 21:55 · Synes godt om

Ceyda du skal ikke lave mellem rumm !!ö ¨=o
7. august 2010 kl. 21:56 · Synes godt om

Bashaar ¨O
7. august 2010 kl. 21:56 · Synes godt om

Ceyda HAHA Nej ö ¨o du skal trykke på ¨ogso lave et o!
7. august 2010 kl. 21:57 · Synes godt om

Bashaar ^Kan ikke, finde ud af det..
Fuck oogså det, fol ved godt hvad jeg mener >:)
7. august 2010 kl. 21:58 · Synes godt om

Ceyda Okay Det lyder også som det samme
7. august 2010 kl. 21:59 · Synes godt om

Bashaar Jaa...
7. august 2010 kl. 21:59 · Synes godt om

[...]

Translation:

Bashaar: Shuf ['look at' in Arabic] her gøt ['ass' in Turkish, however spelled with Danish 'ø' instead of 'ö']
Ceyda: HAHA göt
Bashaar: I know, but I don't know how to make it
Ceyda: Okay first this one ¨ and then o try
Bashaar: ¨o
Ceyda: You are not supposed to press space !!ö =o

Bashaar: O¨
Ceyda: HAHA no ö ¨o you have to push ¨and then make an o!
Bashaar: ^Can't do it..
fuck it, people know what I mean anyway >:)
Ceyda: Okay it sounds the same anyway
Bashaar: Yes..

In Bashaar's status update he encourages the reader to *Shuf hendes Gøt* 'look at her ass' without explaining whose *gøt* he is writing about. This remains a mystery, as it never gets attention in the following interaction. Ceyda corrects his spelling of *gøt* 'ass' in accordance to the Turkish standard orthographic spelling of it as *göt*. I do not know Ceyda, but judging from her name and her comments it appears as if she is a proficient writer in Turkish. During the first seven comments Ceyda instructs Bashaar in how to make the sign "ö" on the keyboard. Yet, despite her persistence, she does not succeed. After many attempts Bashaar gives up and writes: '^can't do it..fuck it, people know what I mean anyway'. By doing so he shifts from a focus on *word form* to the *meaning* of the word and questions the relevance of and reason for formal correctness as important for the communicative aim of their conversation. It turns out that Ceyda agrees as she writes 'Okay it sounds the same anyway'. Thereby, a breach of standard orthography is locally accepted motivated by pronunciation (they sound similar). In the second part of the excerpt Bashaar's language use once again gets sanctioned. Negasi, whom we have already met, initiates the correction by writing:

Excerpt 6b: "What a language huh?" (August 2010)
Original:

Negasi ?
7. august 2010 kl. 22:09 · Synes godt om

Bashaar ??
7. august 2010 kl. 22:09 · Synes godt om

Negasi Sikke et sprog var ?
7. august 2010 kl. 22:10 · Synes godt om

Bashaar Hhaha!...
Det er det, eneste sted min Mor ikke, kan se den måde jeg udtrykker mig Negativt, på . .. Det er derfor Negasi
7. august 2010 kl. 22:12 · Synes godt om

Ceyda HHAHA
7. august 2010 kl. 22:27 · Synes godt om

Negasi hahahhah det samme her !
7. august 2010 kl. 22:36 · Synes godt om

[...]

Translation:	**Negasi:**	?
	Bashaar:	??
	Negasi:	What a language huh?
	Bashaar:	Haha!.. It is the only place where my mother can't see the way I express my self negatively. .. that's why Negasi
	Ceyda:	HHAHA
	Negasi:	hahahhahh same here!

Negasi's correction consists of a comment containing a question mark. Judging from Bashaar's reaction he does not understand what she hints at with this question mark. Negasi further elaborates by more explicitly directing his attention towards the nature of his language use. Bashaar now understands Negasi's comment as disapproving of his language use. This is evident from how he reacts in the following post where he more or less apologises for his writing. He does so by saying that Facebook is the only space where his mother cannot sanction what he says. Negasi laughingly agrees in the comment below and thus Bashaar has succeeded in producing an adequate explanation that ratifies his language use.

Excerpts 6 a+b teach us that sanctions of language use not only concern corrections addressing deviations from the standard orthography. Corrections are also conducted to sanction pragmatically unacceptable language use as shown in excerpt 6b. In this way correction practices are both carried out on the level of *form* (the correction of *gøt*) and on the level of *meaning* (the negotiation of what is appropriate and language use). Furthermore, the excerpt shows that when the young people orient to standard norms it may be the Standard in other languages than Danish; besides Turkish orthography I have observed orientation to English orthography. And finally, the excerpt illustrates that even breaches of standard orthography can be brought up for negotiation, and accepted, if the argumentation works.

8 Conclusion

In this chapter I have shown examples of self- and other-initiated corrections on Facebook. The adolescent Facebook users oriented towards different norms of language use and used different metalinguistic strategies in doing so. Different types of corrections involved different kinds of social positioning. I illustrated how a Facebook user wrote *(staves)* ('to be spelled') in brackets after a word which caused another user to help out with the spelling. In this case the metalinguistic act called for cooperation regarding the spelling. I also demonstrated how standard orthography was used as a social resource on a par with other social resources (e.g. physical appearance), and in these cases metalinguistic acts of correction functioned as interactional strategies for teasing the others about lack of spelling skills and highlighting particular students' lack of academic ambitions. Furthermore, we have seen how self-corrections involved awareness of rights of language use. Instances of other-corrections often entail negotiation of linguistic competences and it is not uncommon to see how they evolve into competitions of who is the most competent speller. Self-corrections regularly function as hedges against other-corrections and my data suggests that it is not regarded as a sign of so-called netiquette to correct other people once they have corrected themselves. Metalinguistic strategies of self- and other-correction indicate that mastery of the standard orthography is a resource associated with status and academic competences. Correction practices, therefore, reveal how linguistic competences are used as a social resource when the adolescents are flirting, teasing each other, helping each other out with spelling words correctly, constructing themselves as competent spellers, showing awareness of rights of language use, etc.

The adolescent Facebook users in my study are reflexive language users and their reflexive linguistic behaviour does not confirm the uniform allegations that young people's spelling proficiencies worsen as a result of their everyday use of social media. In fact, when the adolescents orient towards standard orthography by carrying out either self- or other-corrections this in itself indicates the continuing relevance of standardisation for these adolescents. Yet, my analyses show that the adolescents orient towards peer-group norms as well as standard norms, and they furthermore demonstrate to be capable of navigating in relation to the different centres of normativity. Thus, the adolescents correct some spellings while others are only questioned when it makes sense according to the interactional context. The interactional context, and the semi-public character of Facebook interaction, also influences the adolescents' self- and other-corrections. I argued that the "presence" of others could influence the choice of linguistic style in the local interaction. Thereby correction practices can contribute to our knowledge about how Facebook users navigate in relation to the affordances and limitations of social media.

It is not a new insight that language users correct each other linguistically. Yet, my study contributes to an understanding of how such practices are brought into play in social media interaction in contemporary society. This is timely considering the large number of critical comments about young people, social media and orthographic competences. Correction practices on Facebook are important parts of adolescents' everyday languaging because such practices reveal the complex relation between linguistic form and social relations. The correction practices described in this paper further reflect the poly-centric organisation of linguistic repertoires among adolescent Facebook users and the values associated with different centres of normativity. For example, while corrections of standard orthography involve values such as stupid, non-academic etc., orientations towards peer norms involve aspects of appropriateness, rights of language use etc. Furthermore, correction practices not only involve orientation towards linguistic correctness or regulation of linguistic behaviour, but also local status and power relations. On the basis of this we can conclude that social media (such as Facebook) are not unregulated orthographic spaces and that regulations of linguistic behaviour have social functions ranging beyond the matters of correctness.

Astrid Ag

Rights and wrongs – authority in family interactions

1 Introduction

Recent language socialization studies of family relations agree to discard static understandings of family relations and instead look at the practices that constitute them (Goodwin 2006a). In order to understand practices and routines of families it is important to study interactions between family members, because as Kendall (2007: 3) notes: "Families are created in part through talk: the daily management of a household, the intimate conversations that forge and maintain relationships, the site for the negotiation of values and believes". A particular kind of practice which plays an immense part in constructing and negotiating such family relations is members' indexing of morally correct behaviour towards each other: "[t]he flow of social interactions involving children is imbued with implicit and explicit messages about right and wrong, better and worse, rules, norms, obligations (...) and other dimensions of how to lead a moral life" (Ochs and Kremer-Sadlik 2007: 5). Such messages about right and wrong behaviour not only function as a way to comment on and regulate others' behaviour per se, they also function as social resources in constructing and negotiating relations and authority in the family. When parents e.g. correct their children's language or their table manners, they position themselves as authorities. The children can comply and thereby co-construct the parents' authority, or they can ignore the parents' statements and thereby negotiate and challenge the authority construction of the parents. Similarly, a sibling's display of authority towards another sibling might not be successful if she or he does not see the other as a legitimate authority, and if she or he does not accept the position of subordinate. It follows from this that construction and negotiation of authority is highly intertwined with construction and negotiation of interpersonal relations. Therefore, a study of authority relations in families automatically becomes a study of family relations.

This chapter includes data from five families. I look at instances of family members' explicit messages about right and wrong behaviour in interactions. These are part of socialization practices, and the analyses of them enable me to investigate two central aspects of family interactions, namely 1) how authority is constructed and negotiated and 2) how family members construct and negotiate interpersonal relationships.

The five families have ethnic, linguistic, and religious minority backgrounds. The children are all born and raised in Denmark, whereas their parents are born in Pakistan, Jordan, and Lebanon, and have moved to Denmark for various reasons and at different points in their lives. The minority category is highly focused upon in the media. I do not pay particular attention to the category of minority in my analysis of authority and interpersonal relations, but this chapter contributes to the public debate on ethnic, linguistic, and religious minority families in Denmark exactly by not taking for granted the significance of their backgrounds. The interactions shown in this chapter tell another story about what takes place in minority families than what is usually highlighted in the Danish public and political debate. In Danish media, stories about ethnic, linguistic, and religious minority families are often negatively framed (Jacobsen et al 2013: 17; Hussain, Yilmaz and O'Connor 1997: 259). When doing a search on "etniske familier" [ethnic families] on Google four of the first 12 hits read as follows: "Co-operation with ethnic families doesn't work", "Problems in ethnic families are difficult to solve", "The family maintains ethnic minority women in violent relationships", and "The invisible violence in ethnic minority families" (translated from Danish). Such stories not only frame ethnic minority families negatively, they also construct ethnic minority families as different from ethnic majority families. However, the interactions of the five families presented in this chapter show that there is not anything invidious about these families. On the contrary, the way authority relations and interpersonal relations are constructed, challenged, and negotiated by the families will presumably be something most families in Denmark are familiar with.

2 Language socialization

Socialization into appropriate behaviour is part of families' everyday life. Gaining knowledge about the everyday life is exactly at the heart of both Linguistic Ethnography (see chapter 1) and Language Socialization: "One of the most significant contributions of language socialization research is the insight it has yielded into everyday life – the mundane activities and interactions in which ordinary individuals participate, constituting the warp and woof of human sociality" (Garrett and Baquedano-López 2002: 343).

Language socialization (e.g. Kulick and Schieffelin 2004; Ochs and Schieffelin 2012) is the study of socialization through the use of language and to the use of language (Schieffelin and Ochs 1986b: 163). My study is not a language socialization study per se. According to Kulick and Schieffelin (2004: 350), a language socialization study is ethnographic and longitudinal, and it should demonstrate acquisition (or lack of acquisition) of particular linguistic and cultural practices over time and across contexts. The recordings I have from the families are, in most cases, collected within the same period of time. As a consequence, it is not possible to demonstrate changes of linguistic or cultural practices over time. Therefore, the part of my project which focuses on the family context does not meet the criteria set up by Kulick and Schieffelin (2004: 350). Accordingly, this should rather be regarded as "a study of language and social interaction" (Kulick and Schieffelin (2004: 350). In this sense, my study is exactly that, namely a study of language and social interaction, but I adopt a language socialization perspective on my data.

Early research on language socialization primarily looked at socialization practices between novices and more experienced persons, often between children and parents (e.g. Schieffelin and Ochs 1986). Later, both peer groups and siblings have been studied (see review of studies on peer socializations in Goodwin and Kyratzis 2012). This study is special in that it looks at socialization practices not only in parent-child interactions and not only in siblings interaction, but between all of the interacting family members. The reason for this is that every family member can produce messages about right and wrong behaviour, and authority is an interactionally achieved practice which involves all interacting parties, and which is co-constructed through the responsive behaviour. I will return to this.

3 Authority

In the words of Pace and Hemmings (2007: 6) authority is "...a *social relationship* in which some people are granted the legitimacy to lead and others to follow" (italics in original). Who is being granted the right to a position as authority differs from context to context and from one participant constellation to another. *Traditional* authority refers to authority granted to those in ruling positions. This is typically seen in parent-child and teacher-student relations; here children and students are expected to do what they are told by the parents and teachers simply because of the institutional positions held by parents and teachers (Pace and Hemmings 2007: 6). *Professional* (Pace and Hemmings 2007: 7) or *knowledge* (Wilson and Stapleton 2010: 50) authority is based on a person's expertise within a given field. With that expertise follows the authority to evaluate others' utterances on the given topic. *Moral* authority refers to when someone is indexing appropriate behaviour towards others. Durkheim (1956: 29) for instance describes how the "work of education" is to make "...the egoistic and asocial being that has just been born (...) capable of leading a moral and social life". *Religious* authority or "authority in (and trough) God" (Wilson and Stapleton 2010: 58) can be granted persons who speak on behalf of a God (e.g. the Pope) or it can be used when someone refers to God or religious scripts as a guideline for norms of behaviour. Finally, *interactional-structural* authority occurs when someone controls the interactional floor and thereby decides who speaks when and about what (Sinclair and Coulthard 1975; Wilson and Stapleton 2010: 55; Karrebæk 2012b: 33)

These different types of authority relations should not be understood as an exhaustive list. But they are the ones relevant to my analyses of family interaction (see Karrebæk 2012b for analyses of authority relations in school among the participants in our collaborative study). Also, the different authority relations are not supposed to be taken as bounded categories. Religious authority can overlap with legal authority, when religion and state are coterminous, or with moral authority, when God is seen as the highest moral authority (Wilson and Stapleton 2010: 58). And a teacher in a classroom will often perform both institutional authority and knowledge authority.

There are two important facets of authority to bear in mind when studying authority relations. Firstly, as mentioned authority is co-constructed. One can be an institutional authority, e.g. a teacher, but if the students do not comply with what the teacher wants the students to do, the teacher is not authoritative from a performance perspective (Wilson and Stapleton 2010: 49). The same is the case with parents, and perhaps older siblings. They might inhabit a potential status as authoritative given their respective roles in the family, but it is not certain that their children (or younger siblings) view them as such. Therefore it is important to understand authority as being interactionally constructed and negotiated. In the following I show how authority in family interactions is not necessarily the outcome of pre-established roles, but is constructed, negotiated, and challenged interactionally.

Secondly, authority relations are not limited to the given persons interacting. We also orient to what Blommaert (2010: 39) refers to as *centres of authority* outside the interaction:

> "...authority emanates from real or perceived 'centres', to which people orient when they produce an indexical trajectory in semiosis. That is, whenever we communicate, in addition to our real and immediate addressees we orient towards what Bakhtin (1986) called a 'super-addressee': complexes of norms and perceived appropriateness criteria, in effect the larger social and cultural body of authority into which we insert our immediate practices vis-à-vis our immediate addressees".

These centres can be individuals like teachers, or the coolest guy in class, they can be collectives such as peer groups, or they can be abstract entities or ideals such as the church or democracy (Blommaert 2010: 39). The centres can also be, as examples will show, God, a day-care teacher, a mother, or an imagined health book. Talking about something being *outside* of an interaction of course raises the question about how to determine what is *inside* and what is *outside* of an interaction. In this case, however, I simply refer to centres of authority outside of an interaction when the interacting parties construct an authority by orienting to someone or something which does not participate actively in the conversation. As we shall see, the notion of centres of authority is highly relevant when analyzing authority relations in family interactions.

4 Method, data, and participants

The collaborative project builds on data from a range of different everyday settings (see chapter 1 for a general description on data and method). The data examined in this chapter are from the young participants' homes. After having carried out ethnographic fieldwork among the 7th–9th graders at school for some time, I began to focus on some of the participants' homes. I intended to observe in their homes as well, but I did not succeed in gaining access. Even though I got to know the young participants quite well, and they were used to having me around at school (see Ag 2010), they were hesitant about having me in their private home. A possibility is that they associated me too much with their life at school and did not feel comfortable with mixing that with their family life. Also, they were not too eager when I asked them to talk to their parents about participating in an interview. They kept telling me that they had forgotten to ask or that their parents were busy, and it would be better if I asked them later. It turned out to be easier to participate in a parent-teacher conference, where many of the parents were present, and ask the parents myself if I could interview them. Before the parent-teacher conference I asked the participants if they were okay with me asking their parents, and they all were.

Apart from when I visited the young participants' houses to interview their parents, I did not conduct ethnographic observations in their homes. I did, however, get the young participants to bring small audio recorders home and make recordings while they were interacting with their families. These recordings give me an insight into their family life which I would not have had otherwise. In total I collected 26 recordings from 11 families. This chapter is based on recordings made in five families. Eight parents and 18 children appear in those recordings, and seven parents and 11 children participate in the interactions discussed in this chapter. Also, I interviewed the parents, and I use some of the interviews to shed light on different issues talked about in the recordings.

The activities taking place in my recordings differ. This does not come as a surprise because when the young participants asked what to record at home, I told them that they could record while they were having dinner, when they were watching TV, doing homework, or simply just talking to each other. My data were meant to cover a broader range of family activities than what is typically seen in studies on family discourse which is often based upon dinnertime interactions (e.g. Ochs et al. 1992; Ochs and Taylor 1996; Paugh 2005; Paugh and Izquierdo 2009; Perregaard 2010). One recording is made while the family members are all gathered around the dining table having dinner. This recording is initiated by the mother whom I interviewed the day before. I told her – as I told the young participants – to record whatever she wanted for instance while the family was eating or while she was talking with her children about their homework. She chose to record while they were eating, and the recording begins and ends during dinner. The other recordings, which were initiated by the young participants, are not as strictly tied to one activity. Several different activities take place during the recordings. In these recordings it is sometimes difficult to understand what is being said and by whom if, for instance, some of the participants are in another room than the recorder, or if a speaker is speaking loudly about a football match on television. The transcriptions of these recordings are affected by that.

It applies to all of the transcriptions that I only note or comment on particular linguistic features, e.g. emphasis, if they are relevant to the analyses (for transcription key see appendix). The recordings include linguistic resources associated with Arabic, Urdu, Punjabi, Danish and English. As to the recordings with Arabic, Urdu and Punjabi I have been working with two translators who have transcribed and translated the recordings and afterwards gone through the transcriptions with me. I present the transcriptions using Latin script only. I do not use different fonts for resources associated with e.g. Danish and Urdu in the transcriptions, as I do not wish to reproduce the interactions as consisting of "different languages" (see also Blackledge and Creese 2010: 76). Instead, I only use one font as a way to illustrate that the speakers are *languaging*, i.e. using whatever linguistic resources at their disposal to achieve their communicative aims (Jørgensen 2010; see also introduction to this volume).

As mentioned I look at interactions from five families. Table 1 provides an overview of the families. I mention the age of the children as they occur in the chapter. All participants are anonymised.

Table 1

Families	Size of family	The parents' country of origin	Appear in the following examples
Family one	Mother, father, five sons, one daughter	Pakistan	1, 5
Family two	Mother, father, two sons, one daughter	Lebanon (mother) Jordan (father)	2a, 2b
Family three	Mother, father (who does not live with them), three daughters	Pakistan	3, 6
Family four	Mother, father, two daughters, one son	Pakistan	4
Family five	Mother, father (who is a away from the family while the recordings were made), two daughters, two sons	Pakistan	I am not including a transcription, I only refer to it (after example 1)

5 Parents' display of authority towards their children

I have listened to the 26 recordings from the 11 families in order to identify sequences where family members give explicit messages about right and wrong behaviour. I found various kinds of display and negotiation of authority in the interactions, and I will illustrate this with six examples from the five families. In the six examples we see a movement from parents displaying authority towards their children over children challenging their parents' authority to siblings displaying and negotiating authority between each other.

Excerpt 1 is an example of a father displaying *moral authority* towards his son while also including another centre of authority, namely God. The example is from a recording made by 17-year old Shahid. In the beginning of the recording Shahid and his siblings are watching a football match on TV while Shahid is doing his homework. An hour and a half into the recording Shahid's father comes home and watches the football match as well. After five minutes with no talk, except from the TV speakers, Shahid's father asks him a question (line 02). It is not possible to hear what the father says, but Shahid answers that he has not betted (money on the match I assume). The father then tells him, and his other children who are overhearers of the conversation, that he does not approve of betting.

Excerpt 1: "dear God (if only) my children right will be spared from this thing"
Recording from family one. Participants: Shahid (Sha); Father (Fat).

		Original	**Translation**
01	Sha:	xxx	xxx
02	Fat:	aap ne kaisey xxx	how did you xxx
03	Sha:	mein ne mein ne kheli nahi	I have I have not betted
04		hai mein nahin khelta lekin	I don't bet but I xxx made
05		mein ne xxx ko jataya tha	win Chelsea
06		Chelsea ko	
07		((xxx er muligvis et navn))	((xxx might be a name))
08	Fat:	mein ne kasam se nahin khela	I swear I didn't bet right
09		na ((sagt i samme tone som	((said in same tone of voice
10		Shahid))	as Shahid))
11	Sha:	jee	yes
12	Fat:	xxx lekin patta kya hota hai	xxx but do you know what
13			happens
14	Sha:	jee	yes
15	Fat:	bandey ka mein abhi na	a persons' a moment ago
16		bathroom mein gaya hoon na	when I was in the bathroom I
17		mein ne kaha ya Allah mere	said dear God (if only) my
18		bechein na is cheez se	my children right will be
19		pache rahe	spared from this thing
20	Sha:	mm jee	mm yes
21	Fat:	jab mere bachein bilkul un ka	when my children can decide
22		apna ikhtyar ho hoon	for themselves right
23	Sha:	jee	yes
24	Fat:	jab bande ki apni marzi ho	when you start to decide for
25		jati hai ?kyounke mama? Ab	yourself ?because mom? now I
26		mein aap ko ko waisey hi	just want to tell you in a
27		kahoon ga akhlaqi taur pe	moral/friendly way
28	Sha:	jee	yes
29	Fat:	lekin mein kar kuch nahin	but I'll not be able to do
30		sakoon ga theek hai	anything okay
31	Sha:	jee	yes
32	Fat:	aaj aap chotey hain aaj mein	today you are young today I
33		puri kosish karta hoon ke yeh	try hard to make sure it
34		na ho na	doesn't happen right
35	Sha:	mm	mm
36	Fat:	to sirf is liye yeh soch	so only because of that (.)

ke ke yeh bohot hi	from that point of view (.)
	that it's really

Ochs and Kremer-Sadlik (2007: 5) note that "[a] universal function of the family is to raise children to think and feel in ways that resonate with notions of morality that relate to social situations…". In example 1 Shahid's father is doing exactly that. He tells Shahid that he should not bet on football matches. He does not construct his authority as *traditional authority* where his son would be expected to do what he is told simply because of the institutional position held by the father (Pace and Hemmings 2007: 6). He does not use arguments such as "you are not allowed to do so because I say so", and he does not use directives, a speech act which is usually linked with authority, control, and dominance (e.g. Bhatia 2000: 157; Goodwin 1990: 127). Instead he displays *moral authority* by stating that soon Shahid and his sibling are old enough to decide for themselves (line 21–24), and then he will not be able to do anything (line 29–30). Rather than simply stating that they are not allowed to bet he seems to frame his point about avoiding betting as a piece of good advice. He does so with the meta-comment in 25–27 "now I just want to tell you in in a moral/friendly way". The word *akhlaqi* can be interpreted as "in a moral way" or "in a friendly way". Both interpretations point to the father as framing his point as good advice given by a father to his older child.

It is interesting that there is one more relevant participant evoked in this conversation, namely God. The father introduces God as an addressee when he paraphrases his own conversation with God. In that conversation, which has just happened, he prayed for his kids to avoid betting (line 15–19). In an interview the father explains how listening to Na'at (religious poetry) or to prayers in the mosque makes his heart so soft that he will be calm and forgiving even if someone would come by and behave in an ugly manner towards him. With that in mind, his inclusion of God in their conversation might be because the father has faith in that God will help his children avoid betting. His inclusion of God can be seen as a strategic attempt to strengthen his argument "…through an alignment with the highest moral authority of God" (Wilson and Stapleton 2010: 59). But it can also be that the father chooses not to appear as the authority – as the analysis above also points towards – but instead as an animator (Goffman 1981: 144). The father does not display *moral authority* with reference to his institutional role as a parent, but seems to construct a role as a messenger of morality from God. In excerpt 5 we see a similar situation in which a girl animates her mother when correcting her brother.

Finally, with regard to the interactional structure of the interaction, the example bears resemblance to a conversation between a father and his 14 year old daughter over the phone (family five). In this telephone conversation the father initiates a longer statement on norms of behaviour which last for almost two and a half minute. He displays *moral authority* by explicitly instructing his daughter on how she should behave by saying that she e.g. should walk directly home from school, look out for her siblings, read the Koran every morning, implement Islam in her every day practices, and be affectionate to her siblings. In both example 1 and the telephone conversation the interactional structure is characterized by monologues delivered by the fathers and minimal responses delivered by the (teenage) children. The two cases, however, differ with regard to the fathers' way of displaying moral authority. Where Shahid's father in example 1 does not appear as an authority, but includes God as a centre of authority, Massima's father displays *traditional authority.* In the telephone conversation he almost exclusively uses directives, which as mentioned is usually linked with authority, control, and dominance (e.g. Bhatia 2000: 157, Goodwin 1990: 127). Massima's father's use of directives, and the fact that Massima does not challenge or negotiate them, illustrate Massima and her father's co-construction of his authority. At the same time there are other equally important and relevant dimensions in the telephone conversation. Tannen (2007: 46–47) argues that family discourse is often studied exclusively with a focus on power and hierarchy and at the expense of intimacy and connection. Both the dimension of solidarity and power are indeed explicitly present in the telephone conversation, because Massima's father also praises her for being a smart, good and caring daughter while giving her these instructions on how to behave.

In this section I will turn to an example with an interactional structure which differs significantly from the monologue structure of example 1 and the telephone conversation. Excerpt 2 illustrates another instance of parents socializing a child into becoming a moral child, but this time it is done by both parents simultaneously. A father, a mother, Israh (14) (see Møller (this volume) for analyses of other interactions with Israh) and Khatib (3) are having dinner while talking about an incident where Khatib hit another child in the day-care:

Excerpt 2a: "Haven't I told you not to hit anyone"
Recording from family two. Participants: Father (Fat); Khatib (Kha); Mother (Mot); Israh (Isr)

Original	**Translation**
01 Fat: līah ḍarabtū līah ḍarabtū	why did you hit him why did
02	you hit him
03 Kha: hūa kharmashnī hīk hīk hīk	he scrathed me like this like
04	this like this

Mot:	↑kharmashak	↑scrathced you
Fat:	inta līsh bitiḍarabū mish	why did you hit him haven't I
	qiltillak mā tiḍrabshi ḥadā	told you not to hit anyone
	hā	haven't I
Kha:	hīk hīk	like this like this
Fat:	iḥkī	then tell me
Kha:	hīk hīk	like this like this
Fat:	anā bas'alak līsh ḍarabtū	I'm asking you why did you hit
		him
Mot:	līsh mā qiltū lil pīdāgo līsh	why didn't you tell the
	mā qiltū lil pīdāgo mamnū'	daycare teacher why didn't
	tiḍrab	you tell the daycare teacher
		you're not allowed to hit
Kha:	hīk hīk hīk kharmashnī hīk	like this like this like this
	hīk hīk	that's how he scratced me like
		this like this like this
Mot:	līsh mā qiltū lil pīdāgo	why didn't you tell the
		daycare teacher
Kha:	hūa	he
Mot:	hm inta lāzim tiqullah	huh you have to tell the
	lil pīdāgo	daycare teacher
Fat:	mish anā illī qiltillak mā	haven't I told you not to hit
	tiḍrab ḥadā yā walā hā iḥkī	anyone boy now tell me why did
	līsh ḍarabtū marra thanī	you hit him you are not
	mamnū' fāhim wa la lā'	allowed another time
	mamnū' baqullak marra thanī	do you understand
	fahim	
Kha:	hīk hīk	like this like this

The excerpt is only a smaller part of their conversation about the incident, but it illustrates the nature of the entire conversation. The interactional structure differs from the two previous ones by being more dialogical, firstly because of the questions-answers structure, and secondly because of the co-parenting (Gordon 2009: 83) by the mother and the father. The mother and the father display *interactional-structural authority* in that they control the interactional floor. During their conversation about the incident, the father asks Khatib nine times about what happened and why he hit the other child. The father invites Khatib to give his side of the story. He does not, however, seem to pay much attention to the answer. Instead he tells Khatib eight times that he is not allowed to behave like that.

The parents provide Khatib with the opportunity to defend his actions as they tell him to explain what happened. Yet they construct an alliance against him and thereby give him very little leeway. Both of them participate in the correction of their son's behaviour; they tell him to explain why he hit the other child, and they repeat each other when setting up rules for him: "you are not allowed (to hit)" (line 17, 28–29) (see Gordon 2009: 85). The parents, however, differ in their performance of authority. The mother draws on another centre of authority, namely the day-care teacher, and wants to know why Khatib did not tell the day-care teacher that the other child had scratched him (line 14–16, 21–22). She wants him to orient to the *institutional authority* of the day-care teacher (line 24–25) instead of taking matters into his own hands. The father, on the other hand, does not take into account that the incident occurred in a situation where there was another *institutional authority* present. His account of why Khatib should not behave like that is: "haven't I told you not to hit anyone". Thereby the father orients to himself and emphasizes himself as a *moral authority*.

The corrections of Khatib's behaviour construct the mother and the father as a parenting team (Gordon 2009: 83). They act similarly towards their teenage daughter Israh. Just prior to the conversation about the incident with Khatib, the mother encourages Israh three times to eat her fish. Israh responds by saying that she will eat it in a moment, that she needs to finish what she is eating, and finally, while laughing, that she loves fish. This is neither rejection of nor compliance with the directive, but rather a way to postpone dealing with the mother's request. At the end of the conversation about Khatib, the parents' resume their focus on Israh (line 04):

Excerpt 2b: "eat fish"
Recording from family two. Participants: Father (Fat); Khatib (Kha); Mother (Mot); Israh (Isr)

Original	**Translation**
01 Fat: marra thaniya mamnū' fahim hā	you can't do it again do you
02	understand huh
03 Kha: im xxx	mm xxx
04 Fat: yallah kulī al-samak kulī kulī	come on eat fish eat
05 Isr: akaltū	I have eaten it
06 Mot: kulī kulī haydā	eat eat this

The father continues along the same lines as the mother in telling Israh to eat her fish. Israh to some degree challenges her father's authority – as she did with her mother – by not simply complying with his directive, and instead argues that she has already eaten the fish. The mother does not seem to accept the answer or maybe she wants her to eat another piece. She repeats the father's directive while instructing Israh to eat. Paugh and Izquierdo (2009) find similar examples of food negotiations in their study of dinnertime interactions. Such food negotiations illustrate the "...tensions between parental authority and individual agency..." (Paugh and Izquierdo 2009: 199) of the children. Furthermore, both of the examples from the family dinner illustrate that messages about how to behave and how not to behave do not only work as socializing tools, they can also constitute parents as a team in their dialogical display of authority.

6 Children's negotiation and challenge of their parents' authority construction

Several parents state in the interviews that they disapprove of 'bad' linguistic behaviour, and they exemplify this with swearing. The mother of Shahid (family one, see excerpt 1) says in an interview that they are considering moving out of the neighbourhood. She and her husband do not like it for several reasons and one of them being the negative influence the other kids have on her children's language. She gives the example that the children have started swearing at home.

Excerpt 3 illustrates the use of a swearword and how it is reacted upon. The four-year old girl Kiran is sitting next to her 13-year old sister Dimah who is ill. The mother and the oldest sister Yasmin are in the kitchen. Dimah is talking with the mother about homework and school. At the same time Kiran is talking to herself:

Excerpt 3: "Mommy your daughter is swearing"
Recording from family three. Participants: Kiran (Kir); Dimah (Dim); Yasmin (Yas); Mother (Mot)

Original			**Translation**
01	Kir:	er du allerede tre år: (1.2)	are you three yea:rs already
02		hvor mege:t(1.1) tre: (2.0)	(1.2) that's a lo:t (1.1)
03		så bli:ver du (1.6) er du	three: (2.0) then you wi:ll be
04		allerede m f: se:ks (1.2)	(1.6) are you already m f:
05		se:ks ((klapper)) no no ma ma	si:x (1.2) si:x ((clapps))
06		((synger)) (1.2) er du	no no ma ma((sings)) (1.2) are
07		allerede seks år å:rh det er	you six yea:rs already wo:w
08		rigtig mange er det sådan her	that's a lot is it like this
09		xxx ?what? xxx er det bare	xxx ?what? xxx is it just like

	sådan her (1.0) hva:d	this (1.0) hu:h
Dim:	… lærere de spørger som om de	…the teachers they ask as if
	ikke selv kender svaret	they don't know the answer
	((taler i baggrunden))	themselves ((talks in the
		background))
Kir:	fuck hvor mange år er du	fuck how old are you
Dim:	åååh	oooh
Yas:	xxx	xxx
Dim:	mama din datter bander	mama your daughter is swearing
	(1.2)	(1.2)
Kir:	↑n:	↑n:
Mot:	Kiraaan	Kiraaan
Kir:	((griner))	((laughs))
Dim:	og så sidder hun med den her	and then she is sitting with
	helt oppe ((griner))	this thing up here ((laughs))
Mot:	hvorfor hvorfor g hvorfor	why why d why do you say
	siger du sådan noget	such things
Kir:	((uforståelig lyd))	((unintelligible sound))
	(1.0)	(1.0)
Mot:	hva:d	wha:t
Dim:	hun har lært det af Fiddah	she has been taught by Fiddah
Mot:	xxx	xxx
	(1.2)	(1.2)
Kir:	nej Malik	no Malik
Dim:	nå [Malik]	oh [Malik]
Mot:	[man] skal ikke sige	[do] not say something
	sådan noget lige meget hvem	like that no matter whom
	man har lært det af	you've been taught by
Dim:	det er Malik	it's Malik
Kir:	Malik har lært det[xxx mi:g]	Malik has taught [xxx me:]
Dim:	[((skriger))]	[((screams))]
Mot:	xxx	xxx
Dim:	mama hun har lige tyret sin	mama she has just tossed her
	albue ind i øjet på mig Kiran	elbow into my eye Kiran
	vil du gerne flytte dig hvis	please move if you are going
	du skal være sådan	to be like that
	(1.5)	(1.5)
Mot:	Kiraaan	Kiraaan
	(1.0)	(1.0)

Kir:	MALIK HAR LÆRT MIG DET	MALIK HAS TAUGHT ME SO
Mot:	OG DERFOR SKAL DU IKKE SIGE DET VEL (1.1) bare fordi du har lært det af en eller anden	AND THAT'S NOT A REASON FOR SAYING IT YOU KNOW (1.1) just because someone has taught you so

Billig (1999: 94) argues that "...the demands of politeness create the temptation of rudeness" and that "...each time adults tell a child how to speak politely, they are indicating how to speak rudely" (see also Kulick and Schieffelin 2004: 356–359). The way Kiran suddenly uses the word "fuck" after having talked to herself in a funny way for quite some time without any reactions, probably indicates that she is very well aware of the fact that she is using a "forbidden phrase" (Billig 1999: 94). Also, she may try to get attention from the others. If this is the case, she succeeds. Her sister Dimah reacts right away by saying "oooh", probably meaning either "did you just say that" or "you are in trouble now". Subsequently Dimah calls for her mother's attention: "mommy your daughter is swearing". One time prior to this extract and one time after the extract, Dimah in similar ways calls for their mother. It is probably motivated by her finding Kiran's behaviour annoying. She might do so to draw in another centre of authority, i.e. their mother, and make their mother stop Kiran's behaviour. In those two cases the mother, who is cooking while talking to Yasmin in the kitchen, does not react. But she reacts when Dimah tells her that Kiran is swearing. Apparently swearing is a more serious breach of norms than being annoying towards a sister. In an interview with the mother about her attitudes toward her children's language, she says that she is tolerant with regard to different ways of speaking, but that she does not want to listen to swearwords. This is certainly illustrated in the excerpt. The mother asks Kiran why she says "such things". Kiran does not respond immediately, and Dimah mentions a girl who she believes has taught Kiran the word. Kiran corrects her sister and mentions another person (Malik) who has taught her the word. The mother tells her that she should not say something like that no matter whom she has been taught by. Kiran does not just simply accept the correction, but challenges the mother's authority. She raises her voice and defends herself by mentioning the friend who has taught her the word, maybe in an attempt to legitimize her usage of the word and not take responsibility for it. However, the mother does not accept her explanation and repeats: "and that's not a reason for saying it you know just because someone has taught you so".

Interestingly this mother has pointed out to us that most of the time it is actually her children who comment on and correct her language and not vice versa. They correct her Danish if she makes errors according to a normative standard understanding of Danish, such as non-standard grammatical gender. She says that the children get annoyed, and that they ask her if she cannot hear it is wrong. The mother tells that Dimah is very talented when it comes to language, and that she is the one to criticize her the most, by saying "it hurts in the ears hearing you speak Danish". Also, if she uses words like "nice" (the English word "nice" is used in Danish in the same way as in English – especially used by young people) and "lækkert" ("delicious") they, again according to the mother, tell her that "it is a little too Danish", "don't speak Danish as a Dane you are Pakistani", and "you are way too integrated" (see Ag and Jørgensen 2013; Madsen 2013a; Møller and Jørgensen 2011a for further readings on the participants' detailed descriptions of language norms). The mother's portrait of her children's attitude towards her language shows two things. Firstly, the mother accounts for her children's corrections while laughing heartily. This suggests that the children's criticism of their mother's language is not a serious threat to her social status and authority. More likely it is to be understood as a common jocular ritual among the family members and thereby parts of the routines and practices that constitute them as family (see also Gordon 2009: 27–28). Secondly, the interactions in the family illustrate how different persons can assume and be granted authority in different situations. Whereas the mother displays *moral authority* in example 5 by correcting Kiran's behavior, the children, according to the mother's description, display *knowledge authority* with regard to Danish. Their "expertise" in Danish apparently gives them authority to evaluate the mother's Danish whether it concerns grammatical errors, her use of slang words, or her way of speaking Danish (as a Dane).

The next analysis focuses on negotiations of frames, social relations, and authority by a mother and her two daughters (family four). The excerpt is from a recording made by 15-year old Nasha who is at home with her six years younger sister Yalda and their mother. The mother is rehearsing religious narratives and prayers with Yalda. In an interview the mother describes how she has read the Koran with her three children every evening for 20 minutes as she does not think that going to the mosque once a week is sufficient.

Earlier in the recording Yalda and her mother have discussed the activity. Yalda does not want to say the prayers from the beginning, but the mother corrects her for constantly forgetting how the prayers begin. Prior to this excerpt the mother asks when and where the Prophet got his first calling, and they talk about that. The mother continues by asking the following question:

Excerpt 4: "not like that you don't interrupt"
Recording from family four. Participants: Mother (Mot); Yalda (Yal); Nasha (Nas)

	Original	Translation
Mot:	shabash aur hamare nabi ko jo	good and will you tell our
	woh baat kahani pataein gi ke	Prophet's that talk story that
	jab pyaare nabi ko paas kaun	when who came to our beloved
		Prophet
Yal:	så skal du ikke afbryde mig	so do not interrupt me
Mot:	nej okay det skal jeg nok	no okay I will not
	lade være	
Yal:	okay og jeg må hvis jeg	okay and I can if I make
	har fejl så kan du fortælle	a mistake you can say so
	det til sidst	afterwards
Nas:	up up [in the] sky ((synger))	up up [in the] sky ((sings))
Mot:	[okay]	[okay]
Yal:	ik okay pehle	right okay first
Mot:	danish bolna nahin	don't speak Danish
Yal:	mama woh dua kar rahe they na	mom they were saying prayer
	phir farishta aa gaya tha phir	right when the angel came then
	unhon ne kaha tha kya kehte	he said what did he say what
	they kya kaha tha unhon ne	did he say
Mot:	iqra ((Arabic)))	read ((Arabic))
Yal:	iqra [phir]	read [then]
	[((ler))]	[((laughs))]
Mot:	aisey [nahin] kehna	don't [say it that] way
Yal:	[((ler))]	[((laughs))]
Yal:	iqra [phir]	read [then]
Mot:	[nahin] iqra [bhi nahin]	[no] not read [either]
Yal:	[xxx] se du	[xxx] see
	afbrød mig	you interrupted me
Mot:	okay	okay
Yal:	((griner triumferende)) phir	((laughs triumphantly)) then
	nabi ne kaha tha mein nahin	the Prophet said I can't
	parh sakta phir ((tøver))	read then((hesitates))
Nas:	((ler))	((laughs))
Yal:	((ler))	((laughs))
Mot:	araam se slap nu af	take it easy calm down
Yal:	phir unhon ne phir kaha tha	then they said read then
	iqra phir nabi ne hamare	the Prophet said our beloved

	pyare nabi kaha mein nahin parh sakta mein parha likha nahin hoon	Prophet I can't read I'm not well educated
Mot:	mm	mm
Yal:	phir seene se zor se lagaya aur kaha iqra [phir]	then he hugged firmly and said read [then]
Nas:	[bismi] rab bikal lazee khalaq ((arabisk))	[in the name of] your lord who created ((Arabic))
	(1.3)	(1.3)
Mot:	is tarah na afbryder nahin karna hota	not like that you don't interrupt
Nas:	men det var forkert det hun sagde	but what she said was wrong
Mot:	nahin aisey nahin keh aisey hi	don't say not like that just like
Yal:	phir unhon ne jaldi se keh liya aur phir øh ja	then he said rapidly and then ehm yes
	(1.0)	(1.0)
Nas:	DRIVHUSHUSGASSERNE TILLADER solens kortbølgestråling at passere jordens xxx((læser nok op fra en bog))	THE GREEN HOUSE GASSES ALLOW the short-wave radiation of the sun to pass the earth's xxx ((probably reads out loud from a book))
	((Yalda og moren fortsætter))	((Yalda and the mother continue))

During the recording the girls do not question or challenge the fact that the mother wants them to rehearse religious narratives and prayers, neither that she wants them to answer questions about e.g. the name of the flag of the Muslim community they belong to. Thereby they co-construct the mother's authority in religious socialization as well as the relevance of this type of socialization. While the girls do not challenge whether or not they should undertake the activity in itself, they do however in several ways challenge the framing and the interactional structure of the activity.

There is a discrepancy between the mother's and the two daughters' understanding of how seriously the activity should be taken. Sometimes (not shown in the extract) the mother is making fun and talks with her daughters about all sorts of things, but at other times, and illustrated in the extract, she frames the activity almost as a lecture. In fact, earlier in the conversation the mother labels the activity a teaching activity when she says to Nasha “move over a bit Nasha, let me teach her a bit”. Furthermore, the way the mother asks Yalda questions regarding the prayers or narratives, for instance in line 01–04, is reminiscent of the way a teacher asks a student a question. Yet, the girls do not orient to the serious, educational framing of the situation constructed by the mother, all the time. The sisters laugh twice in the extract. The first episode happens when Yalda has forgotten what the Prophet says and asks her mother (line 17–18). The mother gives her the answer, namely “iqra”, which in Arabic means ‘*read*’. Yalda then pronounces the word highly emphasized to Nasha’s amusement. The mother on the other hand does not approve of her pronunciation of the word, maybe because she finds it disrespectful. In continuation of Nasha’s laughter, Yalda laughs as well, and thereby she aligns with her sister and against their mother. A moment later, Yalda again seems to have forgotten the word “iqra”. She hesitates, and her hesitation is enough to make the two girls laugh once again, presumably because Yalda seconds after having learned the word has already forgotten it again. The mother tries to re-establish the educational frame for the interaction by asking them to calm down and be quiet and asks Yalda to continue.

In line 55–57, Nasha very explicitly and loudly tries to reframe the situation. Apparently she reads out from a schoolbook. She reads out very loudly the moment Yalda ends her utterance. No one reacts though, and Yalda and the mother continue with the rehearsal. It is difficult to point to Nasha’s reasons for doing this. Maybe she feels that Yalda has got enough attention from their mother. Maybe she finds the activity boring. Or maybe she wishes to display positive orientation to school to the recorder and thereby to the researchers. Anyhow, we see how the girls’ orientation to the activity does not align with the mother’s framing of it.

The girls also challenge the interactional structure of the activity. In line 05 Yalda challenges the mother’s *interactional-structural authority* in that she does not comply with her mother’s request for saying the narrative. She sets up conditions for how the mother should behave in order for Yalda to say the narrative. Thereby she assumes an authoritative role with regard to the arrangement of the activity. The mother “agrees with the terms”, but nonetheless interrupts Yalda twice (line 22 and 25) during Yalda’s rehearsal of the narrative. After the second correction, Yalda complains about her mother’s interruption. When the mother says “okay”, Yalda laughs triumphantly as if to signal that she was right about the fact that her mother would interrupt her. We see how it is not only the mother who is correcting the children, but also the other way around. In line 43–44 Nasha is the one to correct. While Yalda is rehearsing the narrative, Nasha interrupts. She completes the prayer in Arabic which Yalda is trying to complete. The mother, however, tells her that “you don’t interrupt”, and thereby teaches her rules of turn-taking as well as politeness. Apparently, the mother does not disagree with the content of Nasha's correction, but she disagrees with the way Nasha corrects her sister.

Overall, we see how the two sisters during the interaction co-construct, resist and reframe their participation (Garrett and Baquedano-Lopez 2002: 346), and how they construct and negotiate authority and social relations in the family. Also, we see the function that the religious rehearsal has as a socializing tool for not only religious skills and values, but also for norms of interactional behaviour.

7 Display and negotiation of authority between siblings

So far we have seen corrections of behaviour as well as constructions and negotiations of authority between parents and children. In the two final examples I focus on authority constructions and negotiations between siblings. The analysis that follows examines regulation and evaluation primarily carried out by another child. The example is from a recording between a group of brothers and a sister and their mother (family one). The siblings are sitting eating at a table, and the mother is in the kitchen. The two children in focus of this analysis are Elias and Hayat. Elias and Hayat are younger siblings to Shahid (see example 1). Elias who is seven years old is being corrected by his sister Hayat who is three years older:

Excerpt 5: "Elias come back"
Recording from family one. Participants: Hayat (Hay); Mother (Mot); Elias (Eli)

Original	**Translation**
Hay: mama	mommy
Mot: ja	yes
Hay: han har ikke spist færdig han er gået	he didn't finish his food he left
Eli: jamen jeg kommer nu	but I'm coming now
(9.0)	(9.0)
Mot: vil du have mælk	would you like some milk
Hay: nej jeg vil have te	no I want tea
Mot: nej ikke mere te	no not tea
((Elias hvisker, og et yngre barn laver pjattelyde))	((Elias is whispering, and a younger sibling makes silly noises))

Hay:	spis nu spis nu rigtig	eat eat properly Elias
	Elias se alle dine brødre	look all your brothers are
	spiser rigtig	eating properly
	((flere stemmer siger noget	((multiple voices are speaking
	samtidigt))	simultaneously))
	((17 sekunder senere))	((17 seconds later))
	((musik, måske fra et spil))	((music, maybe from a game))
Hay:	luk nu: du larmer rigtig	shut the: you're making a
	meget [xxx]	lot of noise [xxx]
Eli:	[xxx] ((fjollelyde)	[xxx] ((silly
		noises))
Eli:	er du min lillesøster eller	are you my little sister or
	hvad	what
	(2.0)	(2.0)
Hay:	mor han larmer rigtig	mom he's making a lot of
	meget	noise
Mot:	Elias lad være	Elias don't
	(1.5)	(1.5)
Eli:	undskyld	sorry
	((stilhed i 13 sekunder))	((silence for 13 seconds))
	((to børn hvisker))	((two kids are whispering
Hay:	mor Elias larmer rigtig meget	mom Elias is making a lot of
	moar	noise mommy
Eli:	xxx	xxx
	((30 sekunder senere))	((30 seconds later))
Hay:	mor Elias er gået	mom Elias left
Mot:	Elias kom tilbage Elias	Elias come back (.) Elias
	(2.8)	(2.8)
Hay:	Elias kom tilbage hun kalder	Elias come back she is calling
	på dig en gang ikke tre gange	you once not three times (1.0)
	(1.0) kom tilbage (2.0)godt	come back (2.0) good (1.2) I'm
	(1.2) jeg er din mor jeg	your mother I'll tell you what
	bestemmer over dig	to do
	(4.0)	(4.0)
Eli:	xxx (pjattelyde))	xxx ((silly noises))
Hay:	xxx	xxx
Eli:	mm mm mm	mm mm mm
Hay:	godt Elias du skal spise selv	good Elias you have to do it
	godt	yourself good
Eli:	xxx	xxx

Hayat is highly engaged in Elias' behaviour. She alternates between commenting on his behaviour to their mother (line 03–04, 27–28, 34–35, 38) and correcting him herself (line 13–15, 20–21, 41–45). When Hayat in line 03–04 tells their mother that Elias has left, he mitigates his behaviour by saying that he is on his way back. This is the only time Elias aligns with Hayat's comments. In the rest of the extract he reacts to her comments by being obstructive. In line 24–25 he asks her in a somewhat provocative tone if she is his little sister, even though she is three years older than him. He also reacts by making silly noises while she is talking to him (line 22 and 47). Judging from his reactions he does not accept Hayat's self positioning as a *moral authority*. The opposite is the case when the mother corrects his behaviour. He says sorry and starts to whisper instead. It is the first and only time he reacts to the corrections by apologizing. He complies with his mother's directive and does not challenge her authority.

Hayat is very persuasive in her construction of a parent-like identity. Not only is she parenting her brother by indexing inappropriate behaviour through directives, she also praises him when she evaluates his behaviour as appropriate (line 50–51). Thereby she displays both power and solidarity which as Tannen (2007: 28) points out are characteristic for family interaction. Her use of expressions typically associated with adults functions as a resource to negotiate social order (Goodwin and Kyratzis 2012: 366). However, it is not entirely clear how seriously her utterances should be understood. Some of her comments appear serious (e.g. line 20–21) while some of them seem to be keyed (Goffman 1974: 45) as less serious, for instance in line 41–45 when she presumably parodies the voice of her mother – or maybe of mothers in general. I do not know Hayat from my ethnographic fieldwork in school. As a consequence, it is difficult for me to know with certainty if and when she is parodying, as I am not familiar with her normal voice. Nevertheless, we see again how another centre of authority, this time the mother, is invoked in the construction and negotiation of authority and social relations. Hayat constructs her role as the one holding the positions of authority, power, and control while simultaneously calls out for the mother and draws on the mother's *traditional authority*.

The final example is from the same recording as example 3 (family three). The oldest sister Yasmin, who is 15 years old, is our project participant, and she has been asked to make recordings at home. In this recording, it is her four-year old sister Kiran who is carrying the audio recorder. The three sisters are talking to each other while their mother is in the kitchen. 13-year old Dimah, who has a fever, lies in a bed or a couch. Her younger sister Kiran wants to put a pack of cold butter on her forehead:

Excerpt 6: "be quiet she is sick"
Recording from family three. Participants: Kiran (Kir); Dimah (Dim); Yasmin (Yas)

	Original	**Translation**
Kir:	der står hvis man er syg så	it says that if you're ill you
	skal man bare lige have sådan	just need some butter in your
	noget smør i hovedet (1.0) på	face (1.0) on your forehead
	panden	
Dim:	Yasmin	Yasmin
Kir:	det står der	it says so
	(1.2)	(1.2)
Dim:	kan man godt øh	can you ehm
	(2.0)	(2.0)
Yas:	hvad	what
Dim:	xxx kan man godt få xxx	xxx can you get xxx
Yas:	hvorfor	why
Dim:	lad mig dog få noget	come on let me have some
	privatliv	privacy
Yas:	nå men du må sige alt	but you can say anything
Dim:	?vi? sidder da og [snakker	?we? are sitting and [talking
	?pænt? til hinanden]	?nicely? to each other]
Kir:	[jeg skal	[I just
	li:ge xxx]	need to: xxx]
Dim:	det er der da ingen der skal	no one should listen to that
	høre	
Yas:	jamen du skal ikke tale pænt	but don't speak nicely speak
	snak normalt ((griner))	normally ((laughing))
Dim:	nej men det er der da ikke	no but no one should hear that
	nogen der skal høre at jeg	I'm xxx today
	xxx i dag	
Yas:	nej xxx det skal være helt	no xxx it has to be perfectly
	normalt	normal
	(1.2)	(1.2)
Kir:	YASMIN [TI] STILLE HUN ER SYG	YASMIN [BE] QUIET SHE IS ILL
Dim:	[ja ja]	[okay]
Dim:	[((griner))]]	[((laughs))]]
Yas:	[xxx ((mumler))]	[xxx ((mumbling))]
	((moren og Yasmin snakker i	((the mother and Yasmin are
	baggrunden))	talking in the background))
Dim:	((hoster))	((coughs))

Goodwin (2006a: 516) writes that "[n]egotiations involving acts of control are central to the organization of family life...". We see how all of the sisters display acts of control towards each other. Yasmin tries to convince Dimah that it is okay that their conversation is being recorded, by saying that she can say anything, and that she should just speak normally (line 15, 22–23). Dimah on the other hand is reluctant to the recording and disaligns with Yasmin's arguments (line 13–14, 16–17, 20–21, 24–26). Kiran tries to stop their arguing by telling Yasmin in a loud voice that she should be quiet because Dimah is ill (line 30). Kiran, who is only four years old, constructs – like children often do – an adult-like identity (see e.g. Goodwin 1990: 126–135). During the recording she assumes a role as a caretaker towards her sick sister by comforting her, being next to her, and – in a not so typical adult-like way – trying to make Dimah feel better by cooling her forehead with butter (line 01–04). In the extract she tries to legitimize her somewhat alternative treatment with reference to a center of authority, namely some kind of imagined health book "it says that if you're ill you just need some butter in your face (1.0) on your forehead". Her sisters, however, do not pay any attention to her.

The way she interferes in her two older sisters' discussion by in a loud voice telling Yasmin to be quiet because Dimah is sick can mean several things. Firstly, it could be a part of Kiran's construction of a caretaker. Dimah is ill, and therefore Kiran argues that it should be peaceful around her. Secondly, it could be a way to show alignment with Dimah, now that she – by doing the recording despite Dimah's reluctance – has indirectly been aligned with Yasmin (earlier in the recording Yasmin and Dimah have discussed whether to record or not). Thirdly, the directive to Yasmin about being quiet could also be a way to construct and negotiate her own position within the sibling-group, because as Goodwin (1990: 127) argues "...directives constitute the principal means through which children realize positions of dominance and submission between characters...". However, whether or not Kiran realizes a position of dominance between the three sisters is not entirely clear. On the one hand, Yasmin actually stops arguing with Dimah and starts talking to their mother. On the other hand, Dimah reacts to the directive by laughing. Her laughter could be a way to signal to Yasmin that Kiran is on Dimah's side, but it could also – given the slightly surprised tone in her laughter – indicate that she does not accept Kiran's attempt at being authoritative as legitimate. This might tell us, that authority is not always simply interactionally achieved. The age make-up of the group might affect the outcome of the interaction, in that Kiran's transportable identity (Zimmerman 1998: 90–91) as a little girl and as the youngest sister might affect how serious Dimah treats Kiran's directive as well as to what degree she treats Kiran's display of authority as legitimate.

8 Conclusion

In this chapter I have examined messages about right and wrong behaviour in family interactions for what they can tell us about authority relations and interpersonal relations. Firstly, I argue that in a study of authority relations and social relations in family interactions it is necessary to look at all the interacting parties. One reason for that is that I see authority as dialogical and co-constructed. Another reason is that I find that indexing appropriate and inappropriate behaviour is not a practice only undertaken by parents. I find that children too index appropriate and inappropriate behaviour both towards their parents and towards their siblings.

Secondly, in this chapter I have demonstrated just how diverse authority relations can be. Authority relations take different forms depending on various contextual factors, e.g. the participant constellation, the age of the participants, and the subject of the conversation. Due to the dialogical and co-constructed nature of authority it is not certain that e.g. a person granted institutional authority in one situation can be sure to be accepted as such by the interlocutors. Thereby, authority is not simply something one possesses once and for all, rather it is something that is being constructed, challenged, and negotiated interactionally. Furthermore, authority relations are as we have seen not limited to the participants interacting. The family members also orient to what Blommaert (2010: 39) refers to as centres of authority outside of the interaction. It has shown to be highly relevant to include the notion of centres of authority in a study of authority relations in families. In several of the examples presented in the chapter the family members orient to centres of authority outside of the interaction. These centres of authority can be as diverse as a God, a day-care teacher, a mother, and an imagined health book. The chapter thereby provides empirical examples of how the theoretical notion of centres of authority is worked out in practice in family interaction. Finally, I argue that family members' display of authority in correcting each other is not only about socializing someone into appropriate behaviour. It is also a resource used to construct, re-establish, challenge, and negotiate social situations, positions, and relations within the family.

Ulla Lundqvist

Becoming a "smart student": The emergence and unexpected implications of one child's social identification

1 Introduction

Critical studies within linguistic anthropology of education show that teachers and students co-construct identities and learning (Bucholtz et al. 2012; Wortham 2008; Rymes and Pash 2001). Some of these studies find that teachers and students jointly orient themselves moment by moment to local actions, and that they compare these local actions to metapragmatic models of identities. Across moments in time teachers may ascribe comparable, or even similar, school-relevant identities to particular students, for example "disruptive" or "unpromising" or, conversely, "smart" and "promising". These processes of social identification may constrain or support learning in the classroom (Wortham 2006, 2004). Although such social regularities are pedagogically problematic, they are common in Western societies. Both models of disruptive and smart students are widely circulated and culturally predominant in Western school settings. We know much about the unfortunate situations of students who are labelled and identified as "clueless", "dumb", "silent", "learning disabled" or "learning deficient" (Heyd-Metzuyanim 2013; Ogbuagu 2013; Hirst 2007; Varenne and McDermott 1998; Mehan 1996). But we know less about the situations of students who are identified as "smart", "intelligent", "good" or "gifted".

The existing anthropological literature on "successful students" mainly describes how the cultural production of "intelligence" or "smartness" in schools involves labelling of students along with institutional and societal expectations of students' class, racial or gender identities (Hatt 2007, Korp 2011). These explanations generally describe typical patterns of identity construction, and they generally describe participants as homogeneous groups who follow predictable trajectories of success. But trajectories of identification are heterogeneous, contingent and likely to deviate from typical patterns. The present article takes a first step to fill this gap in the existing literature on successful students by taking a closer analytic look at one child's atypical trajectory of identification.

As we will see, the social identification of my focal child increasingly points towards a metapragmatic model of the smart student. But, noticeably, his trajectory of identification becomes socially and pedagogically consequential in unexpected ways. I suggest that teachers' positive identification of certain children may constrain these children's learning chances. I argue and provide evidence that when a teacher, as a rule, identifies a student as "smart" and assigns him or her a favoured position and special rights within the classroom, that student is likely to become socially vulnerable and his or her learning chances may subsequently be reduced. In addition, in this situation the overall learning environment becomes less responsive to other students' initiatives and efforts.

This chapter covers one child's trajectory of social identification in an Arabic heritage classroom in Copenhagen, Denmark. The focal child, Mohsen, shifts between being a student among other students – although he is a smart and favoured student – and a different and qualitatively more privileged position in which he has rights to symbolic and material resources. Other students in the classroom do not have these rights. We will see that the regular identification of Mohsen as a smart student is so strong that the teacher draws on it even when Mohsen's actions are not in accordance with the local smart student model. My analyses build on recordings from three Arabic classes, in particular from two classes taking place within a month. I focus on these specific classes because they constitute a trajectory during which the identification of Mohsen increasingly points towards a metapragmatic model of the smart student. Thereby, the identification of Mohsen as a smart student solidifies. The solidification of Mohsen's identification becomes socially consequential when other students in the class contest his favoured position and special rights.

I do not claim that background characteristics and personal properties, such as intelligence, family background, academic and linguistic experience etc., are without significance for Mohsen's social identification. Rather, I turn attention to classroom *processes* of social identification in order to understand how such processes are carried out, and how participants make characteristics and properties of these processes significant and salient. In so doing I draw on theories of participation (Goffman 1986, 1981, [1974]) and social identification (Wortham 2006). Although the case study involves an Arabic heritage classroom in Denmark, comparable processes and problems are likely to be widespread in other Western school settings.

2 Data and setting

During an eleven months long ethnographic fieldwork I followed a group of fifth to sixth form students (eleven to twelve years old) in their mandatory classes and in Arabic heritage classes in a school in central Copenhagen. I followed Mohsen for a year in his home near the school. I conducted participant observation, interviews and other semi-structured activities. Data consists of audio and video recordings and transcripts of these, photographs, field notes and various other literacy artefacts. All participants are anonymized.

As mentioned, this chapter concentrates on the Arabic classes. Children officially identified as speakers of the Arabic mother tongue were offered free Arabic heritage classes until the sixth form. Fourteen third to fifth form students (nine to twelve years old) followed the Arabic classes, but during the spring term approximately half of them left. The students had different national backgrounds (Iraqi, Moroccan and Lebanese), competences in different varieties of Arabic and to different degrees. Some children did not have an active command of Arabic at all, while others used it in everyday communication with their parents.

Mohsen was twelve years old (2013) and from a family with a Lebanese background. He was born in Denmark as the second of four children. In everyday communication Mohsen's parents mostly practised Lebanese dialect with their children. In addition, Mohsen's mother had taught him and his siblings some basic Modern Standard Arabic. The family visited Lebanon every second or third year. During these visits Mohsen mainly practiced Lebanese dialect with family and friends. According to Mohsen's parents and the Arabic teacher, Aslan, Mohsen had a good command of Arabic.

Aslan had a Kurdish Iraqi background. During school and teacher training in Iraq he practised Sorani, Iraqi dialect and Modern Standard Arabic. Aslan also taught Danish as a second language, and he knew most of the students from the compulsory classes. The class had an assistant teacher: Noor. She had a Lebanese background. Noor was the mother of one of the students in the class, Duha. Noor had no formal education, and both Aslan and Noor talked about her as a "trainee". Usually, Aslan and Noor divided the class into two groups and taught one each. Class activities included grammar exercises and different types of assignments. Moreover, Aslan often engaged the children in quizzes, involving other languages than Arabic, typically Danish, Swedish, German and English. Aslan explained that this was a pedagogical strategy, which he used to make the children draw on all available linguistic resources in their acquisition of Arabic.

I participated, made recordings and observations during ten lessons and two fieldtrips in the spring term 2013. The term was severely affected by a month-long national lockout where the children hardly attended any classes (including the mandatory classes). In addition, the teachers cancelled a few classes. Consequently, my data covers almost all of the term's Arabic lessons. All fifth form students stopped after the spring term as this was the last year in which they were entitled to free Arabic classes.

3 Social identification

I consider social identification to be interpersonal processes through which individuals identify and are identified as instantiations of socially recognised "metacultural" or "metapragmatic" models of identities (Agha 2007a; Wortham 2006: 32–40; Urban 2001). Metapragmatic models of identities are models of socially recognisable types of people, for instance "disruptive" or "smart students", and/or of characteristic actions that relate to such types. People orient towards metapragmatic models, but they are not necessarily conscious of doing so. A quick search on the Internet results in various instructions on how to become a "good", "smart" or "successful" student along with caricatures of such stereotypes. Good studentship is widely associated with modesty and friendliness, and with individuals who complete assignments on time, participate eagerly in class, answer correctly and demonstrate moderate behaviour. Some scholars describe how notions like "giftedness", "intelligence" and "genius" emerge as culturally produced ideas, which influence social practice and understandings of success in school (Borland 2011; Sternberg 2007; McDermott 2006). In accordance with Agha, Wortham and Urban, I consider such notions to be heterogeneous models that may emerge from various and unpredictable practices and ideas of different sociohistorical origins.

Moreover, social identification emerges and may solidify both in patterns and over time:

> Social identification happens across a trajectory of events as signs of identity and metapragmatic models are consistently applied to and inhabited by an individual. Widely circulating categories and models are essential to social identification, but only as they are contextualized within local settings and particular events. In settings like a classroom, local versions of more widely circulating models often develop and participants in these settings draw on those models as they identify themselves and each other. (Wortham 2006: 49).

In a classroom setting, the act of delivering a correct answer to the teacher's question may be regarded as a distinctive sign of the well-behaved and compliant student. It may also be part of the local model of the smart student and, thereby, along with other behavioural signs, contribute to the identification of a student as smart over time and across events. Some students may strive to be identified as smart students; other students may not (seem to) aspire to it at all, for many different reasons. Teachers tend to see the actions of some children as signs of the smart student, whereas other students are rarely identified as such, although their actions could lead to such identification. Thus, social identification occurs in moments, it is not pre-established, and yet it draws on already existing understandings, models and resources. Importantly, local interactional processes are constantly influenced by the unpredictability of the moment, and thereby social identification is never entirely stable, unambiguous and predictable.

4 Frame, keying and participation framework

As tools for the analysis of social identification in the class interaction, this section introduces three of Goffman's central analytical notions: frame, keying and participation framework. Goffman (1986: 10–11) refers to frame as the 'principles of organization which govern events' including the participants' subjective involvement in them. For example, frames can be transformed by being *keyed* with different meanings (Goffman 1986: 45). When re-keying happens participants in a given activity acknowledge that a systematic alternation reconstitutes what goes on. All activities can also be described from a different, but complementary perspective, namely as enacted participation frameworks (Goffman 1986: 3). A participation framework is a structural description of the social organisation of situated encounters, including the relations between activities, participants and participants' utterances and other actions. The notion may refer to an activity in its entirety or to smaller subactivities or sequences, such as an interactional exchange.

Activities framed as teaching typically generate the expectation that they include a teacher, some students and, in the case of literacy-oriented classes, literacy artefacts, such as pencils, papers and books – and in the case I will analyse, a digital whiteboard. Frames also generate expectations about the specific enactment of the participation framework and of interactional formats. For instance, the IRE format is common in classrooms (Cazden 1988: 29; Mehan 1979). IRE consists of teacher initiation, student response and teacher evaluation, and as I show, the format was practised in the Arabic classes. In teaching activities we also expect participants to have institutionalised and unequal power relations. We expect the teacher to demonstrate what is regularly interpreted as superior status, for instance by giving instructions, asking questions and evaluating contributions, and by referring to these types of actions as his or her responsibility and obligation. The students demonstrate deference by following the teacher's instructions, answering the questions and accepting the evaluations. Yet, participants may act differently than expected from their institutional roles. As we will see, students may fail to give the correct answer, and they may re-key an activity framed as teaching into a joke. Moreover, teachers may transfer the responsibility for instructing the class to students.

5 Incipient social identification of a smart student

This section gives two examples (from May second) of what I saw during my fieldwork as a recurrent positioning of Mohsen. I argue that we here witness incipient identification of Mohsen as a smart student. This identification becomes even clearer and is solidified a couple of weeks later, as evident from the examples analysed in section six. In examples one and two there is still ambiguity and uncertainty in the interpretation of behaviour as signs of identity. The involved students are Duha, Mohsen and Sakira. Aslan, the teacher, introduces a reading exercise.

My transcripts place the English translation directly below the original example. The Arabic original is in dashed underline, the Danish original is in *italics*, and the Swedish original is in **bold**.

Excerpt 1: (May second, audio recording)
Participants: Aslan (ALN), Duha (DUH), Mohsen (MOH), Sakira (AKI)

01 ALN: okay (.) e:h u Sal=el bint ethaniya shu isemha Duha elli
okay (.) e:h and Sal=the other girl what's her name Duha? that
02 teh ki ma'Aminah
talks to Aminah?
03 (1.8)
04 MOH: °Salma°
°Salma°
05 DUH: ahm s: °l°
ahm s: °l°
06 (2.7)
07 MOH: [°*kom nu ha*°]
[°come on ha°]
08 DUH: [Sarah]
[Sarah]
09 ALN: huh Sarah
huh Sarah?
10 DUH: ay
yes
11 ALN: ente shu raáyak Mohsen
what is your opinion Mohsen?
12 MOH: Salma
Salma

```
13 ALN:  e:h Duha inte muqtun'a bi raí Mohsen (.) sahih (.)
         e:h Duha are you convinced by Mohsens opinion (.)
14       elle Mohsen biúlu
         is it right? (.) what Mohsen says?
15 DUH:  e:hm (.) ay
         e:hm (.) yes
16 ALN:  okay (.) Sakira enti mettefá ma'ahum
         okay (.) Sakira do you agree with them?
17 AKI:  mm
         mm
```

In lines one and two Aslan asks Duha about the name of a girl in the text they are reading. Duha hesitates. Mohsen, whispering, gives Duha the correct answer, "°Salma°". Duha begins to answer, but she hesitates, stutters and then she stops. With a token of laughter Mohsen encourages her to continue, probably because he is uncomfortable, but still wants to support her, "°come on ha°". Simultaneously, Duha responds, "Sarah", which is not the correct answer (the correct answer is Salma). Thereby, the two children construct Duha as a student who cannot answer for herself; Mohsen provides her with the answer, and yet she fails. In contrast, Mohsen demonstrates being a helpful and knowledgeable student.

Aslan says to Duha, "huh Sarah?" This sounds like an attempt to initiate a correction sequence in which Duha is given the chance to provide an alternative to her first answer, but she does not do that. She merely confirms her response. Aslan neither gives her a second chance nor a more specific indication of what she is expected to do. Instead he addresses Mohsen, "what is your opinion Mohsen?". By doing this Aslan puts Mohsen in a privileged position vis-à-vis the other students. Neither Duha nor Sakira, who is also present, are selected as addressees in this interactional exchange. Notice also that Aslan asks for Mohsen's opinion. Aslan does not clarify of what Mohsen should have an opinion; however, the most likely interpretation is that he elicits Mohsen's evaluation of Duha's answer, i.e. whether he agrees with Duha or not. Again, this puts Mohsen in a privileged, although maybe also slightly awkward position, where he may have opinions (rather than just knowledge) that are worth listening to, and even opinions on the other students' contributions. Mohsen does not refer explicitly to Duha's answer, but circumvents the expectations of Aslan's question by providing his own answer, which is correct (1.12).

Although the required information is now publically available, Aslan asks Duha if she is "convinced" by Mohsen's contribution. Duha could have refused to answer, but by giving a successful or correct reply to Aslan's invitation she will most likely position herself as inferior and explicit acknowledge Mohsen's superiority. Thus, the relative hierarchy between the two students is established, confirmed and underlined, both through their publically available and different understandings of the text, and through the teacher's positioning of them. And it is validated once more when Sakira, on Aslan's invitation, demonstrates agreement too.

Mohsen is not only a knowledgeable student. He also receives rights that none of the other students have. This is illustrated in excerpt two, which is drawn from the same recording, half a minute after the first excerpt. Aslan asks the children how you say "good morning" in different languages.

Excerpt 2: (May second, audio recording)
Participants: Aslan (ALN), Duha (DUH), Mohsen (MOH), Sakira (AKI)

```
01  ALN:  <godmorgen> hvad betyder det på engelsk?
          <good morning> what does it mean in english?
02  MOH:  good morning
          good morning
03  UNI:  ah ha
          ah ha
04  ALN:  på tysk?
          in German?
05  MOH:  eischoschei ha ha [jeg ved det ikke ha]
          eischoschei ha ha [I don't know     ha]
06  ALN:                    [ha ha              ]
                            [ha ha              ]
07        All participants laugh
08  ALN:  ☺okay okay☺
          ☺okay okay☺
```

Aslan initiates a teaching routine when he asks the students what the English equivalent to the Danish word "*godmorgen*" is. Mohsen replies with the correct answer ("good morning"). Thereby, he positions himself in accordance with expectations both on a structural level (on the level of the participation framework) and on the level of content (providing the requested information). Aslan asks another question, "in German?", and Mohsen replies, "eischoschei". This sounds German, but it is not a recognised German word, and much less the correct answer. Mohsen's response shows that he accepts being part of the same participation framework and frame; he answers the question and acts in accordance with expectations to a compliant student involved in teaching activities. Yet, he does not provide the requested information, probably because he does not know it; at least that is how he accounts for his "German" contribution (2.5). Aslan's question seems to have put Mohsen in a difficult situation. Mohsen is willing and eager to answer the question, and he wants to give the correct answer, but he is unable to do both. As a solution he fulfils the structural requirements (by answering), but he contributes with clearly wrong, though socially harmless information, which, at the same time, demonstrates his phonological German skills. He also demonstrates that he is aware that his answer is wrong, and that it should be treated as a benign joke rather than as a threat to the teacher's authority; this is indicated by his discrete token of laughter and his mitigating "I don't know" immediately after the "German" turn.

Aslan accepts Mohsen's re-keying by laughing. In fact, everyone laughs, and Aslan once again ratifies Mohsen's contribution, this time with a positive evaluation in the form of a smiling voice, "☺ okay okay ☺". Unlike what is usually the case when the other students fail to answer a question, Aslan does not repeat his question when Mohsen fails to answer. Thus, no other student is given the chance to answer the question. Aslan acts as though the requested information is not missing, and he continues with the class.

These two examples show incipient identification of Mohsen as a smart student. In both examples the teacher treats Mohsen differently than the other students. Aslan asks Mohsen to evaluate another student's incorrect answer, whereas Mohsen's incorrect answer is treated as acceptable. The other students are asked to validate Mohsen's correct answers. Of course, Aslan's explicit questions to Mohsen could be interpreted otherwise; he might consider Mohsen a student who needs encouragement to speak (compare Wortham 2006: 31). However, from the mandatory classes Aslan is familiar with Mohsen's reputation as a good student. Teachers in the mandatory classes refer to Mohsen as one of the "best" students in class. This is also noticed by Knoop-Henriksen (2013). Moreover, Mohsen is a regular participant in classroom interaction in Arabic classes. Therefore, this seems to be an unlikely interpretation.

Mohsen demonstrates being compliant, eager to answer, friendly and funny. He also demonstrates being sufficiently knowledgeable to answer correctly and to give competent wrong answers. In addition, he demonstrates being aware that the answer is wrong, thereby not running the risk that anyone should believe otherwise. My argument is that this co-construction of Mohsen by all present participants – as knowledgeable and special – is part of a process throughout which he is increasingly identified as smart. The model of the smart student involves all of this: knowing the answer, being compliant, friendly and fun etc., and it leads to special rights. We shall see that demonstrated in full force in the following section.

6 The solidification of social identification

This section demonstrates (through five examples from May seventeenth and June thirteenth) how Mohsen's identification solidifies and increasingly points towards a local metapragmatic model of the smart student. On May seventeenth five students attended class. The class worked with Arabic flags and countries, which the students located on Internet sites. All teaching activities included and focused on the digital whiteboard.

In the beginning of class Aslan asked Mohsen to get the keyboard from the cabinet. Although Dina, Duha and Iman were all situated closer to the digital whiteboard than Mohsen, Aslan selected Mohsen for the task. Aslan told Mohsen to log on to the computer; subsequently, Mohsen started navigating the digital whiteboard, and he continued doing so throughout class. In excerpts three, four and five Aslan teaches a group consisting of Dina, Duha, Iman and Mohsen. Noor concentrates on the last student. The following situation happened six minutes after Aslan assigned Mohsen control over the digital whiteboard.

Excerpt 3: (May seventeenth, video recording)
Participants: Aslan (ALN), Dina (DIA), Duha (DUH), Iman (INA), Mohsen (MOH)

```
01 ALN:  eh (.) ya' ya'ni matʰalan teshtrun aiskrim aw
         well for example you can buy ice cream or you
02       [teshretun shaghlat]
         [can buy things    ]
03 INA:  [°yes°             ]
         [°yes°             ]
         { raises head  }
04 MOH:  ice cream Iman [det er     ]
         ice cream Iman [that's     ]
05 INA:                 [ice cream] jeg ved godt det er is ha ha
                        [ice cream] I know it's ice cream ha ha
                        {turns towards Mohsen}
                                  {smiles, lifts hand, Iman > Aslan}
06 ALN:  ja  (.) ushu tssamena bil biswidi
         yes (.) and what would you call it in in Swedish?
07 INA:  øhm
         ehm
08 ALN:  min min menkum ye'raf
         who who of you know it?
```

```
09  INA:   [slik (.) på sve øh svensk     ] det betyder (.) øh godis
           [candy (.) in Swe eh Swedish ] it means (.) eh godis
           {lifts hand, moves forefinger back and forth}
           ((godis = Swedish for candy))
10  ALN:   [nej Iman                      ]
           [no  Iman                      ]
```

Mohsen says, “ice cream Iman [that’s]”. Although officially addressing Iman, Mohsen speaks loudly and thereby constructs the other participants, including the teacher, as overhearers. Mohsen initiates an activity that focuses on linguistic form. He uses a part of Aslan’s turn (ice cream) as a starting point for this and thereby demonstrates that he has important information related to what Aslan just said. Moreover, Mohsen positions himself as having the symbolic right to determine what information is important and what is not and to provide the other students with this information. Iman interrupts Mohsen to say that she already knows, “[ice cream] I know it’s ice cream ha ha”. This seems to respond to Mohsen’s contribution as an invitation to a knowledge competition between Mohsen and Iman, a regular practice between these two students. Iman smiles, raises her hand and gazes towards Aslan (3.5) inviting him to respond.

Aslan accepts the invitation to join the students and frames the activity as teaching adding the classic IRE format, “yes (.) and what would you call it in in Swedish?” Iman responds minimally, “ehm.”, probably because she does not know. Aslan repeats his question, this time addressing all the students, but Iman demonstrates that she does want to answer the question by replying, “[candy (.) in Swe Swedish] means (.) eh **godis**”. This is not the information Aslan asked for (*glas* “ice cream” in Swedish); it is related information and it falls in the relevant turn in the IRE format. In many ways Iman’s contribution resembles Mohsen’s fake German in excerpt two, one significant difference being that Mohsen, unlike Iman, demonstrated awareness of the erroneous character of his answer. Whether this is the reason why Aslan treats the two children’s contributions differently we cannot know, but it is evident that Aslan does not accept Iman’s information in the same way as he did Mohsen’s. Aslan interrupts Iman before she is able to reply: “[no Iman]”. Not only are Mohsen’s contributions treated differently than Iman’s, Mohsen also benefits from symbolic and material resources which Iman and the other students do not have. Excerpt four is from the same lesson and it occurs a few seconds after excerpt three.

Excerpt 4: (May seventeenth, video recording)
Participants: Aslan (ALN), Dina (DIA), Duha (DUH), Iman (INA), Mohsen (MOH)

01 MOH: *jeg ved det godt*
I know it
{Mohsen > Aslan}
02 ALN: [o o shu ismu] bil swidi: (.) el e:h el el
[and and what is it called] in Swedi:sh? (.) the e:h the the
03 aiskrim
ice cream?
{Mohsen enters a search engine on the Internet}
04 MOH: [*jeg ved det godt*] *(.) >jeg ved det Asla=Asla=Asla<*
[I know it] (.) >I know it Asla=Asla=Asla<
{Mohsen > screen}
{enters Google Translate}
05 ALN: *NEJ MOHSEN DU SKAL IKKE GOOGLE*
NO MOHSEN YOU SHOULD NOT GOOGLE
06 {Aslan turns towards screen}
07 DIA: ha ha
ha ha
{Dina, Duha and Iman turn towards screen}
08 MOH: ☺*jo*☺
☺yes☺
09 ALN: *NEJ MOHSEN*
NO MOHSEN
10 All participants > screen
11 Dina and Iman laugh
12 Aslan turns smiling towards Mohsen
13 MOH: *<jamen ø:h>*
<but e:h>
{moves cursor back and forth between different language options in Google Translate}
14 Aslan coughs
15 INA: *PÅ SVENSK*
IN SWEDISH
16 {Mohsen chooses "Swedish", writes something and clicks on "translate"}
17 MOH: [*glas?*]
[glass?]
18 INA: [**glas**]

[ice cream]
((glass = Swedish for ice cream and Danish for glass))
19 ALN: *glas ja* [ha ha]
glass yes [ha ha]
{turns away from screen}
20 MOH: [☺*er det glas? (.) glas?*☺]
[☺is it glass? (.) glass?☺]
{Mohsen > screen} {turns upper body forwards and backwards and smiles to Aslan}
21 ALN: *ja det er glas*
yes it's glas
{smiles to Mohsen}

In line one Mohsen claims that he has the requested information (*glas*, Swedish for ice cream). Aslan ignores Mohsen and repeats his question addressing all the students. Simultaneously, Mohsen conducts an online Google search. He excitedly repeats his claim, “[I know it] >I know it Asla=Asla=Asla<”. Mohsen speaks quickly, repeats Aslan’s name three times and enters Google Translate. It is not likely that Mohsen actually knows the Swedish word for ice cream. If that was the case, he could have given the answer immediately. Furthermore, Mohsen seems surprised when he realises that the Swedish word for ice cream is *glas*, which in Danish means glass (4.17–20).

In lines five to six Aslan responds ambiguously to Mohsen’s claim. Verbally he participates as the thoughtful teacher attempting to limit Mohsen’s right to material resources, “NO MOHSEN YOU SHOULD NOT GOOGLE”. On the other hand, Aslan turns to watch Mohsen’s Internet search. Dina responds by laughing, and she, Duha and Iman turn towards the screen (4.7). Now Mohsen has the attention of all the participants. He speaks in a smiling voice, “ ☺ yes ☺ ”. This is probably to show that he is aware that he is transgressing classroom norms, but that his Internet search only constitutes a minor transgression. Once more Aslan makes an ambiguous contribution, “NO MOHSEN”. This time all the participants immediately turn towards the screen. Dina and Iman laugh, and finally Aslan accepts Mohsen’s search, as he turns smiling towards him. The others respond to Mohsen’s performance as a funny move. In the following moments Mohsen seems uncertain of how to continue the search; he speaks slowly and hesitantly he moves the cursor back and forth between different language options in Google Translate. Iman takes over the instruction and supports Mohsen with the relevant cue, “IN SWEDISH”. Doing so, she demonstrates being friendly, supportive and knowledgeable. In lines seventeen and eighteen Mohsen and Iman simultaneously reaffirm that the requested information has been provided, and Aslan reaffirms this. Noticeably, Mohsen is struck by surprise: "[☺is it glass? (.) glass?☺]".

Next, Aslan assigns different Arabic countries to the students, and Mohsen locates the flags of these countries on the Internet. Aslan assigns Tunisia to Duha. Twelve minutes later we see how Mohsen's right to both material and symbolic resources consequently makes the teacher struggle between two juxtaposed participation frameworks.

Excerpt 5: (May seventeenth, video recording)
Participants: Aslan (ALN), Dina (DIA), Duha (DUH), Iman (INA), Mohsen (MOH)

01 {All participants look at screen. Mohsen holds keyboard.
Mohsen scrolls down through pages with flags}
02 MOH: Tunis *jeg ved godt hvordan den ser ud*
Tunis I know what it looks like
{scrolls down a website with pictures}
03 ALN: *ja det ved jeg også men m vi skal finde det til Duha ja* (1)
yes I know too but b we have to find it for Duha yes (1)
04 *det er* lah Tyrki [je had^{h}a]
this is not Turkey [this is]
{Mohsen holds
cursor on Turkish flag, half of it opens}
05 MOH: [*de:t Tyrkiet*]
[i:t's Tyrkey]
06 ALN: *ja* (.) byeshbah had^{h}a (.) el'alam abyad^{h} fi eh (.)
yes (.) it looks like this one (.) a white flag in e:h: (.)
07 elard^{h}iya bed^{h}a eh
white background
{Mohsen removes cursor from Turkish flag, starts scrolling
up again}
…((side event has been cut out))
08 ALN: [*ø:h:*]
[e:h:]
09 MOH: [*kan vi f*]*inde det her?*
[can we f]ind it here?
10 {Mohsen clicks on a photo}
11 ALN: Mohsen mumkin tekteb 'al al eh display
Mohsen can you please write on the eh display?
{Aslan points towards the screen}

12 {Mohsen closes a frame, half opens another frame, closes a frame and scrolls up and down again, looks at keyboard. A new Google links list appears. Mohsen moves cursor in Google list}
13 INA: *Tunesien*
Tunisia
14 INA: °*flag (2.7) skriv fla:g*°
°flags (2.7) write fla:g°
{Pictures with maps of Tunisia, camels etc. appear. Mohsen scrolls up to top of page}
{Mohsen turns towards keyboard and starts writing}
15 MOH: °*slap af Iman*°
°relax Iman°
16 {Pictures of Tunisian flag appear. Mohsen scrolls to top of page}
17 ALN: okay Duha shufti
okay Duha did you see?
18 DUH: ay:
yes:
19 ALN: okay
okay

Mohsen claims, "Tunis I know what it looks like". Simultaneously, he tries to locate something on the Internet. In the beginning it is not clear what it is. Tunis may refer to the capital, the flag or a map of the country Tunisia. But Mohsen initiates a search on the Internet, and all the participants concentrate on his actions. Aslan responds, "yes I know too but b we have to find it for Duha". This utterance is ambiguous. On the one hand, Aslan acts the institutional role as teacher, telling Mohsen that if it was a question of gathering this information he would have done so. Singling out Duha as the reason for this teaching activity may serve as a correction of Mohsen; Aslan may be telling him that this activity should include all of the students, not only Mohsen. If this is the case, Aslan's use of the first person plural pronoun "we" refers to all of the participants. On the other hand, Aslan's use of "we" may include only Mohsen and Aslan and thus establish the two of them in a unit of epistemic authority. An epistemic authority is, in Raviv et al.'s (2003) understanding, a reliable source of knowledge that defines the scope and enables the other participants to learn and access the information required in the situation. In this line of interpretation, Aslan not only emphasises Mohsen's role as a knowledgeable student expected to deliver the required information (Tunis), but also ascribes him a favoured position beyond his position as student.

I argue that Aslan struggles between the participation framework establishing himself and Mohsen as epistemic authorities, and another participation framework aimed at teaching all of the students. Moreover, the participation of Duha and Iman, respectively, in the situation supports the interpretation that Mohsen participates in and is ascribed a favoured position. Consider this argument while looking at the continued interaction. In line four Aslan comments on Mohsen's finding, "yes this is not Turkey [this is]". Simultaneously, Mohsen reaffirms his finding, "[it':s Turkey]". Noticeably, next Aslan switches to Arabic and explains colour similarities between the Tunisian and Turkish flags, "yes. (.) it looks like this one (.) a white flag in u:h: (.) white background". Thus, he performs his role as Arabic teacher and addresses all of the students in order to frame the activity as teaching.

In lines nine to eleven Aslan and Mohsen again work on two different participation frameworks. In line eight Aslan hesitates, and Mohsen suggests a strategy, "[can we f]ind it here?". Moreover, he clicks on a picture and continues to search for the requested information on the digital whiteboard. Mohsen tries to solve the task, but he has difficulties. Mohsen displays one way of navigating, but Aslan guides him in a different direction, "Mohsen can you please write on the eh display?" Aslan continues to speak in Arabic, trying to steer and frame the activity as Arabic teaching of all the participants. All of the students will be able to see what Mohsen writes in the search line. Moreover, Aslan points to the screen of the digital whiteboard.

In line fifteen Iman challenges the epistemic authority of Aslan and Mohsen by giving an instruction, "Tunisia". Thus, she demonstrates being knowledgeable and having relevant information. Mohsen scrolls down, and Iman repeats and elaborates her suggestion in a lowered voice, "°flags (2.7.) write fla:g°". Mohsen turns towards the keyboard and starts writing (5.14). Next, he locates pictures of the Tunisian flag (5.16). Aslan summons Duha, "okay Duha did you see", and Duha reaffirms. This is the first time Aslan addresses Duha during the activity. This is noticeable, because Duha was singled out as the reason for the activity. However, she is not invited to participate actively.

These three examples demonstrate that Mohsen increasingly is identified as a smart student. We have seen that the teacher treats Mohsen noticeably differently than the other students. Aslan accepts Mohsen's fake German. Although Iman demonstrates being knowledgeable in a comparable way, Aslan rejects her wrong answer (godis). Aslan selects Mohsen to control the digital whiteboard. Aslan grants Mohsen the symbolic right to select what information is relevant, thereby providing the other students with the information, transgressing classroom norms and forming part of an epistemic authority including Mohsen and Aslan.

Mohsen demonstrates that he is eager to answer, friendly and funny. However, he does not demonstrate being knowledgeable, able to answer correctly or sufficiently skilful to navigate the digital whiteboard. Mohsen's special rights are not only a privilege; at this point they also become a burden, because the teacher transfers teaching responsibilities onto him (instructing the other students and controlling the digital whiteboard). Thus, we have seen examples of how Mohsen's social identification solidifies. His favoured position in the classroom fosters other students' contestation, and in the following we will see conflicts unfold with increasing force.

At least five conflicts occur in the lesson on May seventeenth. Conflicts emerge when other students attempt to gain the right to the material resources of the digital whiteboard and are denied this right. For example, Duha tries to take the keyboard from Mohsen fourteen minutes after the Tunesian flag episode. Aslan tells Duha that she cannot have it. Less than a minute later, Iman attempts to take over the navigation of the digital whiteboard, and both Mohsen and Aslan reject her attempt. Later, Duha makes another attempt to gain control of the keyboard while Mohsen is locating Arabic countries on the screen. Mohsen struggles with the task, and Aslan shows him where on the map he can find what he is looking for. Duha takes Mohsen's chair (by the keyboard) and is about to take control of the digital whiteboard when both Mohsen and Aslan tell her to "let go". When Duha does not react immediately, Aslan disciplines her: "NO IT'S NOT FUNNY".

In the beginning of the lesson on June thirteenth Mohsen asks Aslan if he wants him to navigate the digital whiteboard. Aslan confirms this, and Mohsen controls the digital whiteboard throughout the lesson. Eight minutes after the episode Aslan is about to initiate a teaching activity. Iman goes over to the screen, but Aslan asks her twice to sit down. Iman however continues to stand by the screen for three and a half minutes, and when Aslan comes over she addresses him.

Excerpt 6: (June thirteenth, video recording)
Participants: Aslan (ALN), Duha (DUH), Iman (INA), Mohsen (MOH), Zara (ZAR), unidentified speaker (UNI)

```
01          Iman and Aslan stand by screen. Mohsen controls digital
            whiteboard.
02          Aslan and Mohsen > screen
03  INA:    Aslan (.) Aslan
            Aslan (.) Aslan
04  ALN:    [ja    ]
            [yes   ]
```

05 ZAR: [*ASLAN*] *(.)* [*ASLAN*]
[ASLAN] (.) [ASLAN]
06 INA: *hvorfor gør vi ikke* [*ligesom vi*] *plejer?* (.)
why don't we do [like we] usually do?(.)
07 [*så vi skiftes?*]
[so we take turns?]
08 ALN: [*Mohsen højreklik*]
[Mohsen right click]
09 MOH: *ja men det er også højreklik*
but it's right click
10 ALN: [*højreklik (.) sæt ind*]
[right click (.) paste]
11 ZAR: [xxx *ve:nstre:*]
[xxx le:ft:]
12 (.) Aslan and Mohsen > screen
13 INA: *Aslan (1.1) du ved Aslan* [xxx]
Aslan (1.1) you know Aslan [xxx]
14 ALN: [*ja det (.) to sekunder*]
[yes it (.) two seconds]
{Turns towards Iman, raises both arms in an abrupt gesture}
15 *Iman DU PISKER MIG*
Iman YOU ARE WHIPPING ME
16 INA: =☺*undskyld:*☺
=☺sorry:☺
{Aslan and Iman > screen}
17 MOH: ☺*du pisker ham*☺
☺you are whipping him☺
{Mohsen picks up a piece of paper from the floor}
18 All children laugh
19 MOH: *se lige*
look
{Mohsen > screen}
20 INA: °*jeg har ingen pisk så kan jeg ikke få den*°
°I don't have a whip then I cannot get it°
{goes around the table, smiles and sits down}
21 UNI: ha ha
ha ha
22 ALN: *jeg snakker med Mohsen så siger du hele tiden*
I talk to Mohsen and then all the time you say

```
23          >Aslan Aslan [Aslan]<
            >Aslan Aslan [Aslan]<
24   DUH:                [årh: ]ha ha
                         [arh: ]ha ha
25          Duha and Iman turn towards each other
```

Aslan and Mohsen concentrate on the screen. They engage in a cut-and-paste activity by the keyboard (6.8–10). In line three Iman addresses Aslan for the first time, "Aslan (.) Aslan". Aslan gives Iman permission to speak, "[yes]", and simultaneously Zara loudly calls Aslan. Iman suggests that the students control the digital whiteboard in turns, "why don't we do [like we] usually do? (.) [so we take turns?]". In addition, Aslan's guidance of Mohsen overlaps with Iman's turn, "[Mohsen right click]". I argue that in this moment two juxtaposed participation frameworks conflict. Aslan struggles between a participation framework aimed at preparing the teaching activity and a conflicting participation framework in which Iman challenges Mohsen's right to the digital whiteboard. In line eleven Zara contributes with an instruction, "[xxx le:ft:]". Neither Aslan nor Mohsen reacts. Iman resubmits her proposal, "Aslan (1.1) you know Aslan". Aslan's response to Iman supports my claim that he struggles between two participation frameworks, "[yes it (.) two seconds] Iman YOU ARE WHIPPING ME". Although Aslan interrupts Iman, he initially acts the role of the thoughtful teacher, confirming her turn and asking her be patient, "[yes it (.) two seconds]". Then, he seems overwhelmed and has an emotional outburst. Aslan raises his voice, turns towards Iman, clearly annoyed, and raises both arms in an abrupt gesture. Thus, he treats Iman's proposal as disruptive.

Iman takes advantage of Aslan's loss of control and rekeys his outburst into a parody, "= ☺ sorry: ☺ ". On the one hand, Iman apologises and demonstrates respect for the teacher. On the other hand, her latched pronunciation and smiling voice suggest that her apology may be insincere. Mohsen is not late to join the parody with a double voiced contribution, " ☺ you are whipping him ☺ ". Bakthin (1984: 193–199) refers to the presence of different speaking positions within one utterance as double voicing. A double voiced utterance aligns with two, real or imagined, speakers or speaker positions. On the one hand, Mohsen's utterance reuses and aligns with Aslan's outburst. On the other hand, his smiling voice may be a parodic refraction of the teacher's voice. All of the children laugh, and Iman constructs the other participants as overhearers, "°I don't have a whip then I cannot get it°", as she walks around the table, smiles and sits down. Her smile and actions add to the impression that she is constructing a parody.

Moreover, Aslan's response suggests that he is affected by the children's parody, "I talk to Mohsen and then all the time you say >Aslan Aslan [Aslan]<".

Aslan teasingly reuses Iman's proposal, speaks quickly and repeats his own name three times. Again, he positions Iman as "disruptive". The implication is that Iman interrupts the two serious interlocutors, Aslan and Mohsen. Less than a minute later, the conflict escalates into a more explicit contestation of classroom order, including Mohsen's special rights.

Excerpt 7: (June thirteenth, video recording)
Participants: Aslan (ALN), Duha (DUH), Iman (INA), Mohsen (MOH), Zara (ZAR)

```
01  ZAR:  nej du behøves ikke at gøre sådan der
          no you don't have to do like that
          {Mohsen opens scroll bar in the word processing programme.
          All participants look at screen}
02        Duha turns towards Zara and winks
03  MOH:  så prøver jeg igen
          then I try again
04  ALN:  ja så prøv lidt igen
          yes then try a little again
05  INA:  °det er der den skal være°
          °that is where it is supposed to be°
                              {Mohsen inserts part of webpage in text}
06        Mohsen removes inserted part again
          (1.1)
07  ZAR:  nej det er ikke så:dan
          no it is not like tha:t
08  MOH:  jeg får spat (.) [gider du ikke blande dig udenom]
          I get annoyed (.)[will you just stay out of it   ]
                           {Mohsen turns towards Zara}
09  ALN:                   [Mohsen prøv lige langsomt      ]
                           [Mohsen just try slowly         ]
10  ALN:  lad mig [lige låne låne låne      ] musen
          let me  [just borrow borrow borrow] the mouse
                                            {Points towards screen}
                       {Takes mouse out of Mohsen's hand}
11  DUH:          [HALLO: HØJREKLIK         ]
                  [HALLO: RIGHT CLICK       ]
                  {Looks at Zara and turns torso towards Mohsen}
12  MOH:  hvad tror du jeg GØ:R
          what do you think I am DO:ING
```

{Mohsen turns towards Duha. Aslan puts mouse on the teacher's desk}
13 DUH: *skrid med dig*
you buzz off
{Mohsen > Duha, Duha > Mohsen}
14 MOH: *skrid selv Duha*
buzz off your self Duha
{Mohsen looks down and on screen, holds up piece of paper to his chin}

In line one Zara positions Mohsen as "unable" to solve the task (cut and paste) in a satisfactory manner, "no you don't have to do like that". Duha turns towards Zara and winks at her, probably because Duha supports Zara's contestation of Mohsen's favoured position. Mohsen makes another attempt to insert the clip, Aslan confirms, and Iman quietly positions Mohsen as able to perform the task, "°that is where it is supposed to be°". However, Mohsen has difficulties navigating the digital whiteboard; he inserts a part of a webpage in the text and removes it again (7, 5–6). Zara once again points to Mohsen's difficulties, "no it is not like tha:t". Mohsen abruptly turns towards Zara and exclaims, "I get annoyed (.) [will you just stay out of it]". Mohsen is affected and under pressure – he is responsible for controlling the digital whiteboard. If this was not the case, he could have asked for help or not responded to Zara.

Aslan supports Mohsen, "[Mohsen just try slowly]", and during the second part of his turn Aslan changes strategies and politely takes over from Mohsen, "let me [just borrow borrow borrow] the mouse". In this situation Mohsen is not allowed to stand out as the smart student. Why the teacher relieves Mohsen of the pressure, we cannot know. But noticeably, none of the other students are allowed to solve the task. Duha seizes the moment to retaliate. Mockingly she says out loud, "HALLO: CLICK RIGHT", elongating the vowels as she instructs Mohsen. The implication is that she is speaking to a dumb person. Mohsen returns the gesture, "what do you think I am DOI:NG", and turns sneering towards Duha. The conflict escalates further when Duha tells Mohsen to "buzz off", and he returns her insult.

We have seen how Mohsen faces uncomfortable moments of disqualification when he is unable to navigate the digital whiteboard, and how other students increasingly contest his favoured position, including his rights to material and symbolic resources. Moreover, how Aslan consequently rejects the other students' contestation of Mohsen's favoured position. Iman proposes a more equal distribution of the digital whiteboard, and her behaviour could have been interpreted in accordance with the local smart student model; she demonstrates being compliant and friendly. Nevertheless, Aslan treats her proposal as disruptive. In addition, in an interview in June 2013 Aslan spontaneously identifies Mohsen as a "very smart student", who "has found the path to language acquisition". This adds to the understanding that Mohsen indeed is identified as a smart student.

7 Conclusion

Mohsen's social identification increasingly points towards a metapragmatic model of the smart student. This local smart student model involves knowing the correct answer, being friendly, compliant and funny etc. Aslan grants Mohsen, and nobody else, the right to the material resources of the digital whiteboard. My material contains at least a dozen examples from May seventeenth and June thirteenth where Aslan asks Mohsen, if he has left his seat, to return to the keyboard. Mohsen's identification increasingly leads to rights to symbolic and material resources, and Aslan ascribes Mohsen epistemic authority. Thereby, Mohsen is granted the right to perform the role as expert and give instructions. This can be considered a symbolic resource that merely adds to the established hierarchy.

Mohsen is probably assigned the right to the digital whiteboard because he has a good command of Arabic, is knowledgeable and likely to act in accordance with the local smart student model and thus help the teaching activities along. Moreover, Mohsen already has a favoured position in class (the incipient identification). However, the skewed distribution of material resources certainly adds to the hierarchy in the classroom, as it enables Mohsen to deliver the required information on more than one occasion, and thus it reinforces his symbolic rights. Sometimes Mohsen's social identification overrules the locally most straightforward and reasonable interpretation of signs and actions. In several examples Mohsen is positioned as a smart student even when his actions can hardly be said to be in accordance with this local model. Noticeably, the locally constructed hierarchy is further validated when other students contest Mohsen's privileged position – and when the teacher rejects their contestation.

In this chapter I have covered one child's social identification in an Arabic heritage classroom in Copenhagen. Although social identification in other settings, including mandatory classrooms, will not be identical to this case study, comparable processes of identification, involving models of good studentship, intelligence and smartness, are likely to be widespread in Western school settings.

Social identification involving models of smart, intelligent or good students may have highly unfortunate pedagogical implications. Teachers are at risk of transferring the responsibility of the teaching to smart and favoured students; we saw how Aslan transferred responsibility to Mohsen. Favoured students are at risk of being given teaching responsibilities they are not qualified or supposed to hold; we saw how Mohsen faced uncomfortable moments of disqualification when he was unable to navigate the digital whiteboard. In addition, if learning is understood in terms of delivering the requested information in a given situation, students like Mohsen may learn less when they are given the information in advance or allowed to give wrong answers without being offered appropriate support to find the right answer. Moreover, favoured students may become socially vulnerable when they interact and engage with peers; we saw how Zara and Duha positioned Mohsen as unable. It is difficult to participate simultaneously as a friend and a smart and favoured student.

Moreover, the learning chances of students assigned inferior positions in the classroom are likely to be reduced. When the teacher favours certain students and assigns them special rights, the learning environment becomes less responsive to the initiatives and efforts of other students; we saw how Aslan singled out Duha as the reason for the activity involving the Turkish and Tunisian flags. Yet, Duha remained passive throughout the event. Had she been actively included in the activity, this would have increased her learning chances. The skewed distributions of material resources also reduces the learning chances of students like Iman, Duha, Zara and Dina, who are denied access to the digital whiteboard or other literacy resources. In the long term students who are assigned inferior positions in the classroom are likely be educationally discouraged.

Lamies Nassri

"Well, because we are the One Direction girls" – Popular culture, friendship, and social status in a peer group

1 Introduction

> Michelle and Rana are gossiping about how Hasna, the new girl who will start in their class tomorrow, might talk about the other girls in Arabic with Rana. Rana comments that she hopes the new girl isn't harsh and assures Michelle that if Hasna says anything bad about One Direction, Rana will be the first to defend them [i.e. One Direction] (Field diary, 13.08.2013, LN)

Research on gender has traditionally described girls as talkative, empathetic and willing to socialize with other girls, and boys as assertive, dominant and goal oriented (Leaper and Smith 2004: 993–994; Leaper 1994; Maccoby 1998; Maltz and Borker 1982). However, this view of girls is undergoing a change. On the basis of extensive research on preadolescent girls in different elementary schools across the United States, M. Goodwin has noted that girls are not always empathetic and affirmative (Goodwin 2006b). The girls she observed spent a great deal of time talking about and assessing the behaviour of others, and she described their peer socialization as ripe with conflicts (Goodwin 2006b: 17–18). Coates (1999) and Eckert (2011) showed how girls, through media and consumer culture, were socialized into a gendered heterosexual semiotic practice in which they (co) constructed in- and out-groups. As children grow into preadolescence, they distance themselves from childhood through a peer social structure, which includes the orientation toward heterosexual desire (Eckert 2011: 89). At this early stage, heterosexuality is more about social value than about enacting it. This becomes clear as young girls (and boys) focus more on the desire of distant (and inaccessible) individuals, such as celebrities, rather than their more approachable (and accessible) peers (Eckert 2011: 89). Nevertheless, such heterosexual orientation is highly meaningful and significant as the children negotiate and gain social status – even dominance – possibly allowing them to become part of the "popular crowd" (Eckert 2011: 86). Girls present and perform different relations through gender; for a girl to be understood and recognized as a girl, she needs to move within a heteronormative order, where homosociality and heterosexuality are the main elements and borders. Thereby, bonds of friendship and sexual desire are understood in terms of social systems of norms, assessment, limits and regulations – what Ambjörnsson calls the heteronormative market of desire (Ambjörnsson 2003: 106, my own translation). *Homosocial* here describes “a social bond between persons of the same sex” (Sedgwick 1985: 1).

This chapter discusses how Rana, a 9-year-old girl, enacts friendship, and how a popular culture phenomenon, the boy-band One Direction, is managed strategically to do this. Thus, I analyse how Rana creates different relations to other girls and in particular how she, along with her (occasional) best friend Michelle, maintains hierarchy in the girls’ homosocial unity through the use of One Direction. For example, the excerpt from my field diary above describes how Rana, who is well-recognized by her peers as a One Direction fan, constructed an imagined scenario, in which a new girl was represented as a potential villain, threatening the treasured object of One Direction by talking bad about them, even before she had met the girl. Rana represented herself as the loyal One Direction fan who would defend her friendship with Michelle through protecting their favourite band.

Much research on minorities has focused on issues such as on how minorities act, speak and socialize in different situations. I look beyond the understanding of certain people as ‘minorities’ who inherently contrast with a majority. I do this by comparing and analyzing data from two institutionally divided settings – Rana’s Arabic class and her ordinary class – to show and compare how she performs fan identity. Rana does not separate her fan identity depending on the different settings, nor does she or others orient much towards ethnicity anywhere. However, there are certainly differences in how she negotiates and uses One Direction to build friendship and hierarchy. While in her ordinary class, Rana is competing with a number of girls to be part of the in-crowd, in the Arabic complementary class-room she only engages with one other girl, at least in the situations in which One Direction is introduced. In fact, rather than ethnicity, an important keyword seems to be socio-economic difference.

Thereby this chapter constitutes a case study on a specific girl, in a specific primary school, during a specific time. Yet it also casts light on the general understandings of the construction of friendship among girls and on preadolescents’ linguistic use of popular culture resources. I concur with Goodwin (2006b) that girls’ peer group socialization is not necessarily harmonious; rather, it includes hierarchy and a pursuit of social status even at the expense of others.

2 Data and method

I carried out 12 months of ethnographic fieldwork at the focus school. Here I followed a cohort of second graders in their ordinary classes and in their after school complementary Arabic classes. My fieldwork observations include Arabic classes, ordinary classes, after-school activities, field trips and breaks, and my data consist of field diaries, audio- and video-recordings, self-recordings, group conversations, and interviews with parents and teachers.

Rana's ordinary class consisted of 23 pupils, while 12 had a Danish majority background, 11 had a minority background. These pupils' parents came from a variety of different countries, including Thailand, Pakistan, Somalia, Eritrea, Lebanon, Palestine, Iraq and Morocco. Until third grade, Rana was one of two girls with minority background and the only Muslim girl in her class, and she oriented towards her majority Danish female classmates while at school. In the group of boys, 8 had minority backgrounds – with 6 of the boys being Muslim. The parents' socio-economic backgrounds also differed. While some parents were well-educated, others only had a ninth grade or high-school degree; some parents were disability pensioners or on social welfare, others worked in high status positions.

Rana's ordinary class differed from the two other second grade classes. In terms of social dynamics it had a core group of strong girls led by Michelle. These girls were much more concerned with their (expensive and fashionable) clothes, music and food than in the others. A classmate identified Michelle, Rana and Mathilde as best friends. However, the girls' 'best friend' relation was often changing and negotiable, and I observed how Rana and Mathilde were treated as outsiders on different occasions. Mathilde differed from Rana and Michelle, as she was considered to be neither popular nor particularly diligent. As the leader, Michelle had the power to assess what was socially 'cool'. Their main teacher, Simon, commented on this in two separate interviews conducted by a fellow researcher (in 2012 and 2014, when the girls were in first and third grade). In both interviews, Simon described Michelle as the class' queen bee – the girl who had it all: social skills, looks, fashion, intelligence and wealth. She stood out based on her expensive clothes and costly vacations. Simon noted that Rana paid much attention to Michelle's outfits and was eager to please Michelle. All of this corroborates my observations. Simon described Rana as a "superstar," sweet, smart, diligent and quiet. She was independent; she read the weekly curriculum by herself and wrote to her teacher if she had any remarks or questions. Simon further described Rana as a girl who knew all she needed to know, was fashionable and progressive, especially in regards to One Direction. According to Simon,

Rana and Michelle began the fad of One Direction at their school. In fact, Rana was the first in the class to wear a One Direction T-shirt.

Rana was the only girl from her class who attended Arabic classes. These took place in direct continuation of the ordinary classes, twice a week, each session lasting one hour and ten minutes. Rana's Arabic class consisted of first and third graders. There were 15 pupils with different Arab backgrounds: Iraqi, etc. While there were 3 girls and 8 boys from second grade, and 3 boys and 1 girl from first grade.

During the Arabic lessons, Rana spend most time with Aisha, another second grader who attended the same after-school centre as Rana. The Arabic teacher described Aisha as a sweet, quiet and intelligent child. The two girls sat together during Arabic classes and a frequent conversational theme between them concerned Aisha's (occasional) second hand clothes and the fact that Aisha's family was not particularly well-off. Rana and Aisha lived next to each other; in fact, they told me that they played together when at home and in the after-school centre, and that they hoped that their same age baby brothers would become best friends. Importantly, Michelle went to a different after-school centre, so Rana had to find different friends during these afternoon hours. Aisha told us that she, Rana, and a third girl from their after-school centre – were best friends. However, this was not what we heard from Rana, and I never observed Rana and Aisha play in the schoolyard during the regular school day.

3 Identity, symbolic capital and stance taking

The following analyses of friendship, social relations and hierarchies are based on Rana's identity work. Individuals construct identities through complex uses of the semiotic resources available in their (identity) repertoires which are conditioned by their access to different identity building resources (Blommaert 2005: 207). I include different semiotic resources deployed by Rana to construct her identity as a One Direction fan. In addition, I consider identity as an on-going process, rather than a condition – that is, as an "identification." The particular identity work carried out therefore depends on situational needs and opportunities (Brubaker and Cooper 2000; Blommaert 2005). As Blommart (2005) writes, in order for an "identity to be established..." (205). This means that Rana and Michelle cannot successfully identify themselves as "the One Direction girls" unless others recognize them as such.

Bucholtz and Hall (2004) offer us a good basis for treating the creation and maintenance of group relations. They explain that social groupings are not based on pre-existing intra-group similarity and homogeneity. Rather, similarity is created through the down-toning of difference, while simultaneously accenting difference to other (perceived) groups. In essence, we are us because we are not them (Ibid: 370–371). The construction of difference introduces an intra-group hierarchy, too, as those who have the power to construct difference also have the power to determine who is included and who is not (Ibid: 372–373).

I use Bourdieu's notion of symbolic capital to describe how Rana constructs hierarchy and social relations in class. Bourdieu (1991: 72) describes symbolic capital as the legitimization and recognition of resources a person or group acquires through other individuals or institutions. In other words, symbolic capital is the accumulated prestige of an individual in a specific social context (ibid: 14). The legitimization that follows symbolic capital transforms 'resources' to 'power'; when legitimized, it has to power – and value to be realizable (Skeggs 2010: 347).

I look at how the girls display taste of and stance in relation to popular music as a way to create hierarchy and social status, as stance-taking equals positioning and aligning or dis-aligning with others (Du Bois 2007: 163; Bucholtz 2007: 378–379). Taste is a manifestation of symbolic capital (Skeggs 2010: 347). In other words, it is important to be aware of the different values ascribed to various types of knowledge.

4 Popular culture and music

According to Storey (2001: 1), popular culture is defined in opposition to something else. Storey (2001: 6–14) sketches six different understandings: 1) something widely liked (highlighting the popular and qualitative measurement in popular culture); 2) the 'left over' culture (compared to 'high' culture); 3) mass culture (commercialized and produced for the masses); 4) culture produced by 'the people' for 'the people' (bottom-up as opposed to top-down); 5) as hegemony; and 6) from a post-modern viewpoint (not being able to draw a line between high and popular culture). I am concerned with the use of popular music as a resource and adopt Frith's (1996) perspective. Frith (1996: 108–109) argues that popular music should be looked at from how it produces, affects and creates an experience in a recipient. We can only take in this experience through a subjective *and* collective identity. Through music, we experience ourselves – music becomes an experience of our "self-in-process" (Frith 1996: 109).

Music, like identity, is both performance and story. It describes the social in the individual and the individual in the social, the mind in the body and the body in the mind; identity, like music, is a matter of both ethics and aesthetics (Frith 1996: 109).

This perspective on popular music provides not just a sense of self, but also a sense of others, of how to be part of something bigger: "(...) the type of popular culture we consume might give us our identity and separate us from other groups" (Fedorak 2009: 4).

In addition to the music, fan merchandise played an important role in Rana and Michelle's construction of themselves as One Direction fans. For example, Rana had a few One Direction pens while Michelle had 25 posters from her recent trip to Italy, a shirt and a bracelet. We even have records of Rana commenting, to Michelle, that she is willing to use all her allowance and her 'Eid money' (that is, money she got during the Muslim holiday, Eid) to buy One Direction paraphernalia from a recently opened One Direction pop up shop (more on this below).

In the following sections, I will show how One Direction fan practices are used as a resource for Rana (and Michelle) to construct symbolic capital, create identity and negotiate social relations in the classroom.

4.1 One Direction and Directioners

One Direction is an Irish-British band consisting of five young men: Liam Payne, Niall Horan, Zayn Malik, Louis Tomlinson and Harry Styles, all 19–21 years old (2014). The five boys were put together as a boy band by one of the guest judges in the UK television show, *The X-factor*, in 2010. Although they only came third place, they quickly gained a lot of popularity among young girls and in particular female tweens (aged 8 to 12 years old). By 2013, One Direction had sold over 19 million singles and 10 million albums and won a number of music awards. According to the British tabloid newspaper The Mirror, their single "One Way or Another (Teenage Kicks)" was a number 1 hit in 63 countries, including the UK, USA, Argentina, Singapore, Egypt and New Zealand (Wood 2013). In addition to being a band, One Direction has become a brand with a vast amount of fan merchandise, including clothing, posters, pencils, inline scooters, singing toothbrushes and Build-a-Bear® (an interactive make-your-own stuffed animal) with built-in One Direction songs. In 2013, the One Direction brand marketed a perfume, published a book ("Where We Are") and made a movie ("This Is Us"). Fans of One Direction go by the name of "Directioners" and they are spread all over the Globe. They use social media to share emotions based on news related to the band and some describe being a Directioner as similar to being part of a cult as it involves loyalty to One Direction as well as loyalty towards other Directioners (Styles 2013).

5 Being a Directioner at the school

Rana did not approve of anyone else in school besides Michelle identifying as a Directioner, and the two girls decided what constituted a real fan. They excluded the others with the justification that they did not know enough about One Direction. Rana also demonstrated insight into the general rules one (supposedly) needed to follow in order to be a Directioner. On wikiHow (a user-generated platform for how-to guides), 30 people co-authored an eight-step guide for how to be the "perfect Directioner". The steps included: supporting One Direction through buying merchandise, albums, and writing to them; respecting all the members of One Direction, as well as other Directioners, equally; and not getting easily offended by non-Directioners, etc. Rana bought the One Direction albums, memorized many of their lyrics, and knew each member's full name and blood type. Though previously Rana exclusively idolized Zayn Malik, she started claiming to have the same degree of affection for all members because choosing one "would be like having to choose between her parents – she liked them to the same degree" (Field diary, 17.12.2013, LN).

Of course, Rana (and Michelle) did not have to adhere to the rules they put up, but they did not accept any other way of being a One Direction fan either. Rana told me that a younger girl from her after-school centre who self-identified as fan of One Direction, was not a real fan as she did not know everything about the boys and did not have enough One Direction songs on her iPad:

> She tells me that she [Rana] is a really big fan, so is Michelle, and Mathilde is a little bit, but she doesn't know that much about them. I ask if some of the children from the after-school centre are One Direction fans and she answers no. I ask her: what about the younger girl from your after-school centre? Well yes, but she doesn't know as much as herself, she explains. (Field diary, 17.12.2013, LN)

Similarly, the following fieldnote excerpt shows how Michelle did not allow the girl Hasna to identify as a One Direction fan. Hasna has just moved to the school and it is her first day in her new class:

> While Rana is away from her seat, Michelle picks up one of Rana's One Direction pens and flaunts the pen in Hasna's direction while she says, "LOOK how ELEGANT he is!" Hasna grabs the pen and says jokingly: "He is MINE." Michelle quickly grabs the pen from Hasna and demonstratively, and within just the right distance, shows her the rest of her pens. Michelle accuses Hasna of not even knowing their names. (Field diary, 14.08.2013, LN)

The example shows 1) how Michelle, through One Direction and One Direction fan merchandise, orients towards a standardized heterosexual femininity; 2) how she uses One Direction as a resource to maintain or break bonds in a peer homosocial setting; and 3) how symbolic capital in the form of knowledge is constructed as an important part of being a One Direction fan. This latter point is further underlined, when Michelle accuses Hasna of not knowing the One Direction members' names, thereby excluding her as a One Direction fan.

One Direction was also significant to Rana when Michelle was not around. It was made relevant in all types of situations in which I followed her: in class, recess, the after-school centre and the Arabic complementary class. While Rana was fighting for social status during ordinary class, she was including Aisha much more readily in her fan-ship during the Arabic class, even though Aisha did not in fact identify as a One Direction fan. This was not without its conflicts, though, as I will show in the following.

6 The mother tongue class

6.1 Heterosexual desire

During my fieldwork, I noticed that Rana oriented towards a heterosexual norm through fan culture and practice, in which she would imagine certain scenarios with the members of One Direction. The following two extracts are from the mother tongue class with Rana and Aisha. The two girls are sitting in the hallway with their Arabic books. Rana has just started singing along to a Justin Bieber song that is playing in the background. Aisha says that Rana is a fan of Justin Bieber. Rana is quick to correct Aisha, telling her she is actually a fan of One Direction. They change the subject for a couple of minutes but then return to it again, when Aisha shares this following piece of information:

Excerpt 1a: 'I would have cried if Liam waved at me'
Recording from outside the Arabic class, May 2013.
Participants: Aisha (AIS); Rana (RNA).

		Original	Translation
01	AIS:	ha ha du er klart over min	ha ha you do realize my my
02		min lærers børn de har været	teachers' children saw One
03		inde at se One Direction	Direction
04	RNA:	ja ja det VED jeg godt	yes yes I already KNOW that

AIS:	og Liam han vinkede til dem	and Liam waved to them ((Rana
	((Rana gisper)) Liam (3.4)	gasps)) Liam (3.4) it's true
	det er rigtigt de var inde	they went to a One Direction
	at se One Direction koncert	concert and then Liam and
	og så var det Liam så var det	then Liam he waved [to] NAME
	at han vinkede [til] NAVN	
RNA:	[nej]	[no]
	nej	no
AIS:	og NAVN	and NAME
RNA:	ne:::j	no:::
AIS:	hvad er der galt	what's wrong
RNA:	nej nej nej aj nu begynder	no no no uh I am going to cry
	jeg at græde	now
AIS:	hvorfor hvad er der galt	why what's the matter
RNA:	jeg vil også gerne møde dem	I also want to meet them (.)
	(.) ved du hvad jeg ville (.)	do you know what I would do
	jeg ville have grædt hvis	(.) I would have cried if
	[Liam vinkede til mig] (4.8)	[Liam waved at me] (4.8)
AIS:	[først] det er rig- Liam	[first] It's tru- Liam waved
	vinkede til NAVN og NAVN	to NAME and NAME
RNA:	ja ja det ved jeg godt du	yes yes I know that you just
	har lige sagt det	told me
AIS:	er det ikke FEDT	isn't it AWESOME
RNA:	du er ikke fan af One	you're not fan of One
	Direction så du kan ikke sige	Direction so you can't say
	at det er fedt (1.3)	that it's awesome (1.3)
AIS:	øh det ved du ikke	uhm you don't know that
		((Rana starts to sing along
		one of the songs playing
		in the background (Justin
		Bieber: Beauty and a Beat))

Aisha presents two pieces of information about One Direction. First, that her teacher's children went to a One Direction concert. Second, that one of the members (Liam) waved to them (line 5). As Aisha tells Rana this, she assigns value to the fact that it is *her* teacher's children who saw Liam waving at them (line 1–5). She inherits a bit of glamour from her closer relation to these fortunate beings. Contrary to what Aisha first told her, and what apparently was old information, Rana clearly finds this second piece of information new and interesting, as she gasps in response (line 5–6). Rana positions herself as a fan through gasping (line 5–6), telling Aisha that she feels like crying (line 16–17), sharing her desires (line 19) and explaining her reactions if Liam waved to her (line 19–22). Rana thus positions herself as a Directioner through an imagined scenario, which includes crying if you see your idols wave at you. Through her construction of this scenario, Rana creates a moment of intimacy and alignment with Aisha in her turn, "I also want to meet them (.) do you know what I would do (.) I would have cried if Liam waved at me" (line 20–22). She not only positions herself as a One Direction fan, but through her fanship, she also displays an orientation to a heterosexual norm. Possibly, as a way to build a homosocial bond with Aisha. However, Aisha does not pick up on Rana's fan practice nor on her orientation to a heterosexual norm, for example by agreeing with Rana or by co-constructing Rana's imagined scenario. Thereby the excerpt illustrates a mismatch between Aisha and Rana, and the asymmetry in the girls' reactions escalates throughout the sequence (line 15, 18). Aisha, who initiates the sequence and at first succeeds in raising her status with Rana, ends up dis-aligning with Rana, as she reveals that she does not have the social capital to discern what counts as valid reactions. As such, Aisha does not react as she is 'supposed to,' according to normative fan practice behaviour or to a heterosexual norm. Interestingly Rana, in the beginning, actually picks up on Aisha's initiative and appears to build common ground with her; that is, Rana emphasizes their similarities by downplaying the differences (line 5–24). She does this despite the later introduced information that Aisha does not count as a One Direction fan (line 28–29). Aisha does not succeed in re-aligning with Rana, and maybe this is why Rana changes her strategy (lines 23–35). In any case, Rana starts emphasizing the differences between them by asserting that Aisha does not have the authority to state that the event was awesome (lines 27–30). Aisha does not succeed in turning the knowledge into capital. More precisely, she *succeeds* in bringing up a relevant topic, but she *does not succeed* in arguing for having sufficient legitimacy within the practice related to the topic.

A couple of minutes later Aisha returns to the subject:

Excerpt 1b: 'I would really like to kiss Zayn Malik'
Recording from outside the Arabic class, May 2013.
Participants: Aisha (AIS); Rana (RNA).

	Original	**Translation**
AIS:	hvem synes du er mest (.)	who do you think is the most
	mest dummest i One Direction	(.) is the most stupidest in
	allermest dum	One Direction the most stupid
RNA:	Aisha	Aisha
AIS:	Hvem	who

RNA:	dig (1.0)	you (1.0)
AIS:	mig	me
RNA:	hallo jeg har SÅ meget lyst	hey I would REALLY like to
	til at kysse Zayn Malik (0.9)	kiss Zayn Malik (0.9)
AIS:	virkelig (.) hvem	really (.) who
RNA:	Zayn Malik (1.1)	Zayn Malik (1.1)
AIS:	hi hi	hi hi
RNA:	hvad	what
AIS:	har du lyst til at kysse ham	do you want to kiss him
RNA:	ja det har jeg faktisk	as a matter of fact I would
	(2.0)	(2.0)
AIS:	hvorfor (1.1)	why (1.1)
RNA:	FORDI det er Zayn Malik (.)	BECAUSE it's Zayn Malik
	°og han er så lækker°	(.)°and he is so hot°
AIS:	hvem er Zayn Mali- nå det er	who's Zayn Mali- oh is it
	ham der med det sorte hår og	him with the black hair and
	sådan lidt farve (1.3)	a little bit of colour (1.3)
	hvorfor har du lyst til at	why do you want to
	kysse ham	kiss him
RNA:	fordi han er for lækker	because he is way too hot
	(0.7) og han er god til at	(0.7) and he is good at
	synge (1.7)	singing (1.7)
AIS:	[ved NAVN det godt] (0.7)	[does NAME know] (0.7)
RNA:	[ja jeg kan sige at han er	[yes I can say that he is
	lækker] hvad	hot] what
AIS:	ved NAVN det godt	does NAME know
RNA:	hun hun har hun har lyst til	she she wants to kiss with
	at kysse med Louis (1.8)	Louis (1.8)
AIS:	Louis (0.8)	Louis (0.8)
RNA:	mmhhmm Louis (3.9)	mmhhmm Louis (3.9)
AIS:	ham med det brune hår ikke	the one with brown hair right
	(1.2)	(1.2)
RNA:	faktisk har han sådan lidt	actually he has kind of
	jov lidt	yeah a little
AIS:	han har sådan lidt langt hår	he kind of has long hair
	lidt	
RNA:	nej det er Harry (0.6)	no that's Harry (0.6)
AIS:	så Louis det er ham med	so Louis he is the one with
	selerne	the suspenders
RNA:	ja (7.9)	yes (7.9)

In line 36–38, Aisha asks Rana who she thinks is the most stupid member of One Direction, presupposing that one (or more) of the members of One Direction is stupid. This shows that Aisha is unfamiliar with the fan practice of respecting all members equally, that is, none of them can be regarded as stupid (see section 4.1.). Rana replies "Aisha" (line 39), implying that no one from One Direction is stupid and that Aisha is stupid for asking that question. Rana expresses her stance not only towards One Direction, but towards Aisha as well, choosing to align with One Direction rather than with her peer. However, even though Rana dis-aligns with Aisha in her fan construction, she continues to align with her in dis-playing an orientation to a heterosexual norm. This is evident as Rana soon changes the subject and states: "Hey I would REALLY like to kiss Zayn Malik" (line 43–44). Once again, Rana depicts an imagined scenario that draws on heterosexual desire as a sign of fanship. She does this by telling Aisha that she would like to kiss one of the members of One Direction because he is part of the band, hot and can sing (line 43–44, 49–51, 53–54 and 60–61). Aisha's inquiries could be seen as moral questions as she perplexedly asks Rana "really?" (line 45), to which Rana affirms, "as a matter of fact" (line 50) to restate her desire. Aisha and Rana's replies might indicate that Aisha does not see it fit for Rana to display heterosexual desire. Immediately, Aisha asks Rana if a mutual friend of theirs, who is a year older, knows of Rana's desires. Rana confirms this and adds that their friend shares them, as she wants to kiss another member of One Direction, Louis (line 63–68). Thereby Rana uses her (older) friend's desires to back up and warrant her own desires. One Direction is a way for Rana to enter the heterosexual market, marking herself as a leading figure in the transition from childhood to adulthood.

In line 69–70, Aisha questions Rana's answer, to which Rana expresses agreement in a rather superior manner. There is an almost four second long pause, which could imply that Rana has "won" the argument. Aisha then changes the structure of her questions from being about the desiring subject (Rana/the friend) to the desired object (Zayn/Louis). She also claims to have knowledge about a band member – Louis (line 71–80). Rana is about to dispute Aisha's claim that Louis has brown hair, but ends up agreeing: "Yeah a little." In line 75–76, Aisha then calibrates Rana's statement (line 73–74) that begins with that Louis "Actually has kind of (...)." Thus, Aisha attempts to finish the sentence by reusing Rana's former words: "He kind of has long hair." Even though Aisha, through format tying (Goodwin and Goodwin 1987: 215–227), aligns with Rana, Rana does not reciprocate. Rana's answers are brief (line 77, 80) and she does not attempt to build mutual ground for connection.

The excerpt shows how Rana is positioned as the expert; Aisha is doing all the asking, while Rana is answering (line 45–46, 49–51, 52–54 and 55–62). The excerpt shows how Rana is displaying heterosexual desire by using One Direction as a resource. She positions herself as a fan and displays knowledge of fan practice while she conveys an insight to adult heterosexual behaviour, which is affirmed when the older girl is brought into the picture. Even though Rana shares her desires with Aisha, she does so as the expert, rather than a peer at Aisha's level. Hence, while Aisha recognizes and aligns with Rana, Rana dis-aligns from Aisha.

Together, excerpts 1a and 1b show a fluid and situational friendship, and the importance of symbolic capital and hierarchy. While Rana builds common grounds and aligns with Aisha in excerpt 1a, through the discursive construction of heterosexual desire and by drawing on One Direction as an identity resource, the very same elements are used to create difference from Aisha in excerpt 1b. Here Rana dis-aligns with Aisha and excludes her from her heterosexual construction. In excerpt 1a, Rana involves Aisha by asking questions such as, "Do you know what I would do?" (line 20). In excerpt 1b, Rana is assertive and she demonstrates that their social hierarchy has shifted from being somewhat balanced to Rana being on top.

As the rest of the chapter will show, not many peers were allowed to be involved in Rana's (or Michelle's) desires toward One Direction. One Direction was used between Rana and Michelle to create friendship in the girls' homosocial unity, and they had the exclusive social right to assess and talk about One Direction. Aisha might have been an exception, as she was not involved in the power struggle in the mainstream class. Therefore she did not pose a threat against the friendship. Also, Rana used Aisha to test the boundaries of the heteronormative market of desire. She thereby treated the social space created with Aisha as a safe zone. Hence, it seems to be important that Rana actually attempted to involve Aisha.

7 The ordinary class

7.1 Quid pro quid – negotiating global fan practice locally

In the following section, I will show how Rana and Michelle locally negotiate friendship, hierarchy and social status through fan practice. The following excerpts are from Rana's first day in the third grade. The pupils have been allowed to choose where (and with whom) to sit. Rana is sitting next to Michelle and Mathilde and Freja are opposite them, at the same table. Because it is their first day after summer vacations, they are doing an exercise at the table where they are supposed to discuss their summer vacation. However, Rana and Michelle are not too focused on this; One Direction seems to be more important. To understand the following excerpt, it is important to know that a nearby mall had just opened a month-long pop-up shop entitled “One Direction World” – which was dedicated to One Direction themed merchandise. This was supposed to exist from August 10th to August 25th 2013. Prior to the excerpt, Michelle has told all the girls at the table that she bought 25 One Direction posters and a One Direction bracelet during her vacation in Italy. Mathilde sighs and whimpers that she wants to go to Italy as well. Rana, who had previously remained silent, then contributed to the conversation and said:

Excerpt 2a: ‘You know what’
Recording from the ordinary class, August 2013.
Participants: Rana (RNA); Michelle (MIH); Mathilde (MLD).

		Original	**Translation**
01	RNA:	ved du Michelle den	you know Michelle the twenty-
02		enogtyvende den enogtyvende	first the twenty-first I
03		fortæller jeg dig hvorfor	will tell you why I went to
04		jeg var i field's	field's
05	MIH:	ved du hvad jeg kan ALLE	you know what I know ALL
06		deres navne og deres mellem-	their names and their middle
07		navne i One Direction	names in One Direction
08	RNA:	hvad	what
09	MIH:	jeg kan ALLE deres navne	I know ALL their names AND
10		OG deres mellemnavne i One	their middle names in One
11		Direction	Direction
12	MLD:	har I hørt det der nye	have you heard that new
13	MIH:	fulde navne jeg kan med	full names I know with their
14		deres [mellemnavne]	[middle names]
15	MLD:	[tre timer]	[three hours]
16	RNA:	(.) nej (.) nej okay jeg	(.) no (.) no okay I will
17		lærer dig efternavnene og du	teach you the last names and
18		skal lære mig det her	you will teach me this
19	MIH:	okay okay det skal jeg nok	okay okay I will

It is noteworthy to observe that Rana does not tell Michelle about the One Direction shop on the 12th of August, which is the date of the recording and the day Rana has planned to go to the mall. Instead, Rana announces that she will only reveal the reason for going there on August 21st, the day she believes the shop will close (line 1–4). It is quite likely that Rana is jealous of Michelle's new One Direction acquisitions from Italy, a country she cannot easily visit, and therefore she tries to get a head start with the One Direction shop. At least, Rana explicitly excludes Michelle from something that is surely of interest to her. Also, while Michelle's acquisitions are real objects and represent a material value, Rana's information is only of symbolic value. Michelle responds to Rana's (rather mystifying) comment by saying, "you know what I know ALL their names and their middle names in One Direction" (line 5–7). As Michelle format-ties to Rana's previous utterance, "You know" (line 1), Michelle indirectly also responds to Rana's face-threatening act (Brown and Levinson 1987), by ignoring the fact that she is kept intentionally in the dark, but also by defending a line as a One Direction fan. At the same time she challenges Rana by constructing a competition-like frame (Goffman 1981). Michelle saves her own face by presenting herself as an expert in the "competition", potentially making Rana loose face. Michelle could have chosen not to include "you know," and instead merely stated that she knew all the names of the members of One Direction, but through format-tying, Michelle embeds Rana as her opposition; in essence, it becomes a "you" versus "I" argument.

Rana responds "(.) no (.) no"; the short pauses could indicate that this is to be taken as disbelief rather than negation. In any case Rana chooses to mend the social damage by reciprocating Michelle, and she does so by asking her to teach Rana the boys' middle names while Rana proposes to teach Michelle their last names. Michelle claims (line 13–14) to know the boys' full name but regardless of that she agrees with the proposed arrangement and as such both girls' faces are saved. This excerpt thereby shows that the girls' fan practices are not about gaining knowledge about One Direction (as Michelle claims she has the knowledge already), but about taking a stance, using knowledge to that, and thereby co-constructing friendship. The excerpt also shows that there is much at stake. Hierarchy is important, and exclusion is a risk for Rana, as it is for the other girls. At some point, Mathilde tries to join the conversation, by asking Rana and Michelle (line 12) what is probably a question about One Direction, but Rana and Michelle do not respond. Instead they continue to address each other exclusively (line 13–19). I will elaborate on this observation below.

In the following excerpt 2b, which fell a couple of minutes after excerpt 2a, Rana decides that she will not wait until the 21st to tell Michelle why she is going to the shopping mall later that day:

Excerpt 2b: 'Michelle can you keep a secret'
Recording from the ordinary class, August 2013.
Participants: Rana (RNA); Michelle (MIH); Mathilde (MLD)

		Original	**Translation**
20	RNA:	aj jeg skal jeg skal i	uh so I'm going I'm going to
21		field's i dag jo	field's today
22	MIH:	det er godt det er godt det	that's good that's good
23		er godt	that's good
24	RNA:	aj Michelle kan du holde på	uh Michelle can you keep
25		en hemmelighed det holder til	a secret it's until the
26		den enogtyvende	twenty-first
27	MIH:	nå jo hvad	oh yeah what
28	RNA:	det holdte det holder fra den	it's until it's until the
29		tiende til den enogtyvende	tenth to the twenty-first
30	MIH:	hvad	what
31	RNA:	i field's i field's er	in field's in field's there's
32		der en butik KUN med One	a shop ONLY with One Direc-
33		Direction det hele er KUN	tion everything is SOLELY
34		med One Direction ((Rana	with One Direction ((Rana
35		hvisker hemmeligheden til	is whispering the secret to
36		Michelle)) det hele og du må	Michelle)) everything and you
37		ikke fortælle det til nogen	cannot tell anybody ((Rana
38		((Rana snakker nu i en normal	now speaks in a normal tone
39		stemmeleje))	of voice))
40	MIH:	nej nej nej ((som i, at det	no no no ((as in I won't))
41		vil hun ikke gøre))	
42	MLD:	hvad	what
43	RNA:	(1.2) ikke noget	(1.2) nothing

Before revealing the big secret, Rana makes Michelle promise that she will not tell it to anyone else – at least not until the twenty-first (line 24–26, 28–29). As Michelle agrees, Rana moves closer and whispers the news about the One Direction shop (line 31–35). Then she again stresses that Michelle should keep this a secret: "...and you cannot tell anybody" (line 36–39). Michelle reassures Rana that she will keep her promise. As they shift from whispering to a normal voice, the other present girls are (again) positioned as overhearers (Goffman 1981). Mathilde asks what they are talking about, and after a short pause, Rana replies "nothing" (line 43). Both Rana and Michelle are relevant as a next-speaker and present an answer to Mathilde. None of them do that at first and the resulting pause seems to be a strategy to demonstrate ignorance and create exclusion. Rana's response (line 43) excludes Mathilde from the co-constructed unit and the intimacy with Michelle, and it positions Mathilde as an eavesdropper (Goffman 1981).

In this excerpt, Rana selects Michelle as the sole addressee for a 'secret' piece of information (line 24-29); she makes it clear that Michelle is not allowed to tell anyone else (line 36–39), and she verbally and physically excludes the other girls at the table, in particular Mathilde (line 42–43). Rana thereby creates a moment of intimacy and alignment with Michelle, creating and displaying a closer bond between the two girls (line 31–41). The girls thereby reciprocate with each other and build on their friendship and homosocial bond by very apparently constructing an exclusivity of information sharing and being part of their friendship.

Immediately after this excerpt, recess begins. During recess, Rana and Michelle accidentally meet two groups of pupils who both inform them about the One Direction pop-up shop. The first incident includes two older boys, while the second incident includes Ella from their class. Clearly, schoolmates regularly identify Rana and Michelle as One Direction fans.

With the cat out of the bag, Rana no longer hesitates sharing her plans for today with the rest of the children. This leads to the following incident:

Excerpt 2c: 'Well, because we are the One Direction girls'
Recording from the ordinary class, August 2013.
Participants: Rana (RNA); Michelle (MIH); Mathilde (MLD)

		Original	**Translation**
44	RNA:	(.) aj jeg skal i One Direc-	(.) uh I am going to the One
45		tion butikken i dag ikk'	Direction shop today right
46		og så skal jeg i Bog & Ide	and then I'm going to Bog &
47		((en bogbutik))	Ide ((a book store))
48	MIH:	hva skulle du lære det der	so did you want to learn you
49			know what
50	RNA:	hvad for noget ja (.) tak	what yes (.) thanks HEY
51		HEY PIGER vi skal li:ge sige	GIRLS we just have to tell a
52		en hemmelighed	secret
53	MLD:	nå: One Directi::on	o:h One Directi::on
54	MIH:	HURRA i skabet men xxx	CONGRATULATIONS you hit the
55			mark but xxx
56	RNA:	aj Mathilde gå lige	uh Mathilde you have to go
57		det er en hemmelig[he::d]	it's a sec[re::t]
58	MLD:	[det er ik]ke sjo:vt	[it's not] funny
59	RNA:	[det er en HEMMELIGHE:D]	[it's a SECRET]

60	MLD:	[xxx] hallo det er KUN jer	[xxx] hey it's ONLY you who
61		der må vide hvad de	are allowed to know what their
62		[hedder]	[names are]
63	RNA:	[JA:::]FORDI ALTSÅ VI ER ONE	[YE:::S] WELL BECAUSE WE ARE
64		DIRECTION PIGERNE:	THE ONE DIRECTION GI:RLS
65	MLD:	ja: og det må vi andre ikke	ye:ah and the rest of us are
66		være eller hvad	not allowed to be one as well
67			or what
68	RNA:	nå men du kan finde en anden	well you can find another
69		gruppe (.) måske	group (.) maybe

After Rana has shared that she is going to the One Direction shop (line 44–45), Michelle asks if she wants to learn "you-know-what" (line 48–49), hinting at their agreement in excerpt (2a). Rana gets the hint and loudly announces to those around them: "HEY GIRLS we just have to tell a secret" (line 50–52). Even though Rana says it aloud, the "we" only includes Rana and Michelle, as Rana then insists that Mathilde has to leave because "it's a secret" (line 56–57).

During this sequence, there is an explicit negotiation about who the One Direction girls are and who are allowed to be part of that group – in this case only Rana and Michelle (line 56–70). It is also clear that the informational content of the secret is not the most important part of the group dynamics. Rana explicitly and very loudly says: "HEY GIRLS we just have to tell a secret" (line 50–52), but the secret primarily functions as a way to ascertain their group identity as separate from the others; at least, Mathilde knows what the secret is about as she states, "Oh One Directi::on" (line 53). Michelle sarcastically congratulates Mathilde for knowing this, thus confirming Mathilde's assumption (line 54–55). In line 56–63, Rana asks a clearly unamused Mathilde to leave, insisting on the legitimacy of her request by repeating, "It's a SECRET" (line 59). Mathilde expresses insight into the secret (i.e. the boys' names [line 60–62]), and neither Rana nor Michelle tries to conceal the secret (line 63). It is not the secret itself that is important; rather, it is the sharing and being part of the secret. It is the project of sharing secrets exclusively from others. The names of the boys in One Direction are used to make friendship and construct hierarchy and relations in the girls' homosocial peer setting. In line 63–64, Rana argues that they are allowed to exclude her because "WE ARE THE ONE DIRECTION GI:RLS". Rana once again uses an exclusive "We" intended only for her and Michelle. As Mathilde questions this exclusive "We" in line 65–67, Rana tells Mathilde to find another group, adding a "maybe" (line 69) after a short pause, as though suggesting that she actually cannot do that.

By excluding others (Mathilde), Rana and Michelle create a "we/us" structure. But the excerpt also depicts how not everyone holds the same potential to construct particular identities. Identity is a dialogical process and not everyone has equal access to the same identity resources. We see that knowledge about what is considered valuable knowledge (i.e., One Direction's names) is not always sufficient to be included; it was not enough for Mathilde to become part of Rana and Michelle's fan practice or friendship group. Rana and Michelle effectively employ their knowledge of One Direction as symbolic capital, successfully constructing their friendship and maintaining social status in their school. But they also decide when this symbolic capital is relevant and sufficient for obtaining group membership. Thereby One Direction is merely one of their tools to co-construct friendship.

Later, when they return to the classroom, Mathilde shows to feel offended because of the exclusion:

Excerpt 2d: 'You could just as well search the Internet'
Recording from the ordinary class, August 2013.
Participants: Rana (RNA); Michelle (MIH); Mathilde (MLD); Unknown (UKE)

	Original	**Translation**
RNA:	vi sagde en hemmelighed	we told a secret
MLD:	det er ikke derfor Rana	that's not it Rana
RNA:	det har du selv sagt	you said it yourself
MLD:	jeg har ikke sagt det til	I didn't say that to anyone
	nogen	
RNA:	du sagde xxx (4.4)	you said xxx (4.4)
MLD:	det er kun jer to der skal	it is only you who are
	vide det driller du så med	allowed to know will you
	nej jeg kan bare ikke sange	then tease me with no I
	(.)	don't know all the songs (.)
RNA:	har vi nogensinde sagt det	did we ever say that
MLD:	JA det har I (7.1)	YES you have (7.1)
UKE:	Mathilde Mathilde: i næste	Mathilde Mathilde: in the
	frikvarter vil I to så gerne	next recess do you two want
	lege (5.7)	to play (5.7)
MIH:	du kan også bare søge på	you could just as well search
	internettet	the Internet

Mathilde points out to Rana that she is not mad at Rana and Michelle for sharing a secret. Rather, she is annoyed because they claim to be the only ones who are allowed to know the One Direction members' names. Secret-sharing creates an us-versus-them situation, as it presupposes that someone is not part of the secret.

In this case, even though Mathilde knows what the content of the secret is, Rana and Michelle still holds on to this function of the secret, i.e. the social exclusion attached to not being part of the secret-sharing. They thereby implicitly suggest that they are the only ones allowed to talk about One Direction and to identify as One Direction fans.

In line 77–80, Mathilde adds that even if she were to join them in their One Direction activities, she would be teased for not knowing the songs. Rana denies ever having excluded her, but Mathilde asserts that this is indeed the case (line 81–82). Allegedly she has previously been teased about not having enough One Direction resources, nor capital, to be recognized as a group member. The excerpt indicates that Rana and Michelle have social status, which is probably both due to the fact that they form a unit, and to the fact that they share an interest in the contemporary t(w)een phenomenon One Direction. After a longer pause (5.7 seconds), Michelle suggests to Mathilde that she "Could just as well search the Internet" (line 86–87). Referring Mathilde to the Internet is a direct way of stating that what is at stake is not knowledge about the members, but rather the social act of secret-sharing.

As described in section 4.1, some Directioners perceive One Direction fan culture as a sort of cult, involving loyalty to One Direction and to other Directioners. However, the opposite seems to happen in Rana and Michelle's situation. One Direction is used as a resource to exclude others, even though they demonstrate interest in One Direction. Because of their symbolic capital, Rana and Michelle can define who is allowed to identify as a One Direction fan, thereby joining their group. Hence, they re-interpret a fan practice to create a group, and generate social capital and value locally.

Rana occasionally aligned with Aisha, despite the fact that Aisha did not usually identify as a One Direction fan (compare section 6.1). In contrast, when Mathilde expressed knowledge about One Direction in effort to be part of the group, she was quickly turned away.

Something similar occurred in Rana's after-school centre. I was standing with Rana and a younger girl, who self-identified as a One Direction fan:

> I ask Rana if her older sister is a One Direction fan as well, "no not really," she answers, "no, but I am trying to teach her". Rana tells me that she knows everything about them, among other things their blood type. A younger girl and Rana start talking about something concerning One Direction, I don't quite get the essence of it. Rana closes their discussion by telling the younger girl that she knows the answer (which has to do with One Direction) but doesn't want to tell her. Rana turns to me and tells me that she knows her own blood type as well. When I ask her what blood type Zayn is, she comes closer and whispers me the answer, the same happens when I ask her about Nials blood type (field diary, 16.12.2013, LN)

This excerpt demonstrates how Rana selects whom she wants to share One Direction information with. She is teaching her older sister – who is not a fan; she is also happy to inform me about Zayn and Nial's blood types – although I am not a fan either. But the younger girl – who in fact is very interested in One Direction – is not as lucky. Similarly to Mathilde she is excluded and Rana does not want to share One Direction information with her. There may be different reasons for this. I may get special treatment because she is flattered by the attention of a grown-up. And her sister and I are both outside of the peer group hierarchy and social order, we are in no way competing with her, and therefore not threatening to her One Direction fan status.

8 Conclusion

In this chapter, I have illustrated how Rana constructs an identity as a One Direction fan. I have shown how she uses three semiotic resources in her local negotiations: heterosexual desire, knowledge, and the fan merchandise to gain symbolic capital and social status in different social settings. I have shown, how Rana successfully demonstrates the power of a band such as One Direction not just for entertainment, but for identity construction. By constructing herself as a One Direction fan, Rana is able to create relationships with those who will be an asset to her, while claiming social status in the school environment. I have discussed how she displays heterosexual desire and knowledge to distinguish herself from other girls, during her transition from childhood to adulthood in the girls' homosocial peer unit.

By looking into how Rana creates fan identity in Arabic classes and in ordinary classes, I have argued that the institutional settings affect Rana's strategic identity construction. One relevant aspect concerns the number of (potential) participants and competitors. Rana aligns with Aisha in Arabic classes and involves her in her fan practises. Rana also uses this setting as an opportunity to flirt with the heterosexual market and the heterosexual norm. Arabic class only involves one other girl, it is safe for Rana to test her boundaries here, rather than in the ordinary class, where she is involved with a group of girls. When Aisha tells Rana that her attraction to One Direction is odd, Rana claims that her older friend has the same yearnings. By using her older friend, she positions herself as just as mature and justifiable as her elder peer. In her ordinary class Rana is hesitant to include others, reserving her fan practices only for Michelle. Although Rana's peer relations are situational and fluid in all cases, they are certainly more complex in the ordinary class, and she has to prove her symbolic capital and social status to a lot of others (excerpt 2a–2d). I have shown how Rana's relation with Michelle, her (occasional) best friend, is just as locally constructed as her relationship with other peers, and how one recurrent method of creating close social bonds and friendship is to exclude others. Michelle and Rana become an "us" because they create a "them".

In addition, I have argued that One Direction is not the protagonist of Rana and Michelle's fan practice; rather, the band, brand, and associated merchandise, is exploited to create intimacy by excluding others through secret-sharing, stance taking and demonstrations of heterosexual desire. It is also used by the two girls in mutual challenges.

Rana has the symbolic capital to successfully identify as a One Direction fan in different contexts and settings (Arabic class, ordinary class, after after-school centre), and she succeeds to maintain a social status as desirable in all settings. She also seems to align with and include people whom she can gain social status from or who do not threaten her social status in class – such as the popular girl Michelle, Aisha, her sister and me. In her ordinary class, Michelle is the 'queen bee', and without Michelle Rana's position is much less safe. The stakes are higher in the ordinary class than in Arabic class and after-school care, as more children compete for social status, making the situation more complex.

Lian Malai Madsen

'The Diva in the room' – Rap music, education and discourses on integration

1 Introduction

The integration of ethnic minorities into majority society is a recurrent theme in public debates related to diversity in contemporary Western Europe (e.g. Blommaert and Verschueren 1998; Rennison 2009; Jaspers 2005; Extra, Spotti, and Avermaet 2009, Hogan-Brun et al. 2009). In the Danish context a significant aspect of the integration debate is an assumed connection between participation in organised leisure activities and successful involvement in society in general. That participation in leisure communities leads to social inclusion is a well established idea within the field of sports at various levels from policymaking to local participation in club activities (e.g. Anderson 2003, 2005; Boeskov and Ilkjær 2005; Agergaard 2008; Agergaard and Bonde 2013; Madsen 2012, 2013c, 2015), and such assumptions are internationally widespread (e.g. Dagkas and Armour 2011; Segaert et al. 2012). However, in Denmark there is a particularly long and strong tradition of voluntarily organised leisure activities. With a population of just above 5.5 million people, Denmark today has more than 16,000 sports clubs, and eight out of ten Danes have, for a period in their lives, engaged in organised sports (Ibsen and Ottesen 1996). In addition to this there are various other forms of associations and organised activities, such as scouting, music and political communities, and it is a salient feature of the Danish public discourse to emphasise the importance of club membership involving contact with adults. In fact the lack of participation in such structured adult-led leisure activities is considered a symptom of problematic societal integration (Andersen 2010: 32). One aspect of this idea is illustrated by the category "foreningsløse børn" (club-less children) which figures in social problem statistics (e.g. Anderson 2005: 168).

This chapter addresses the idea of 'integration through leisure activities' by focusing on a group of boys who spend most of their time out of school practicing rap music. There are certain differences between music cultural activities and membership of a sports club, one being that rap music-making is not usually practiced within the frame of a club with a traditional democratic organisation. However, there are also several similarities. Sports are often not supported and practised merely for sports' sake, but increasingly also with welfare-ideological and societal purposes (Munk and Lind 2004), and in many cases, so are rap and hip hop[1]. Hip hop has become an internationally rather well-described vehicle for educational projects (e.g. Alim 2011; Hill 2009; Pennycook 2007), and critical hip hop (language) pedagogies often invest in transferring semiotic competencies from hip hop culture into more formal, official contexts of school and training (cf. Alim 2011; Hill 2009; Ibrahim 1999; Alim, Ibrahim, and Pennycook 2009). These frameworks usually emphasise creative, limitless and counter-hegemonic linguistic practices as a significant part of the educational potentials of hip hop culture and consider political engagement through hip hop music a means of constructive identity building and engagement of youth in society.

In the case I discuss, the leisure activity of rap music-making is clearly understood as beneficial for the general social development of the young Copenhageners in question. The boys' rap mentors cooperate with council supported projects and schools, and feature in youth political integration initiatives (DUF 2010). Additionally, the adolescents themselves express the understanding that rap activities have "saved" them from bad behaviour and instead made them value educational progress (Stæhr 2010; Madsen 2011; Stæhr and Madsen 2015: Madsen and Karrebæk 2015). In the following therefore I look into how these young rappers participate in rap activities, how rap is related to educational activities and ideologies and, in particular, how linguistic practices are part of the bringing about of different cultural orientations. I also discuss to what extent adolescents' engagement with rap in this context involves social processes that correspond to those articulated in different ways as 'integrating'.

I begin by considering integration as a political and theoretical concept in connection with recent initiatives directed at voluntary clubs and associations in order to establish the theoretical, methodological and empirical framework for discussing the idea of integration in relation to rap. Next, I account for my approach and describe the data, participants and the local rap community they engage in. Finally, I turn to specific examples of adolescents' rap practices, their musical productions and linguistic conduct to discuss how these data inform understandings of socio-cultural adaptation and participation. I argue that what seems like practices of cultural incorporation (e.g. Faist 2009; Foner and Bertossi 2011) as they play out in local rap activities do not entirely reflect processes of

1 International hip-hop scholars and critics usually treat rap music as a distinctive element within the wider frame of hip hop culture. Hill (2009: 33) describes how the youth he studies deploy the distinction between 'rap' and 'hip hop' as a distinction between 'real' (hip hop) and 'fake' (rap) representations of this popular culture. Yet, the participants in our study as well as their rap mentors exclusively use the term rap to refer to their cultural practices. Therefore I use the term rap when I am concerned with the participants and the local rap environment, but when I relate to the international research I use the wider circulating term hip hop (see also Stæhr and Madsen 2015).

mutual adaptation. Rather the linguistic norms of the local rap community seem to rest strongly on hegemonic educational ideologies. In conclusion, I argue that it is essential to attend to 'the Diva in the room', that is to participants' stakes and skills in relation to the practiced activities whenever organised leisure activities are viewed as potential sites for societal cohesion and social development.

2 What is integration?

The notion of integration has been prominent in the Danish public and political debate since the mid 1990s (Olwig and Pærregaard 2007: 18). Yet in the general debate as well as in much research, it is rather unclear what the concept of integration refers to precisely (Ejrnæs 2002). As Ejrnæs notes integration as term, as it is most often used, covers two different meanings, namely one-sided adaptation (assimilation) or mutual adaptation (pluralistic integration) (Ejrnæs 2002: 8). The idea of integration is closely linked to common understandings of cultural diversity that articulate different perspectives, values and norms and circulate through various communicative channels, that is different *discourses* on diversity (e.g. Fairclough 1992; Blommaert 2005). Rennison (2009) identifies no less than eight different discourses on diversity related to the integration debate in Denmark. She identifies a rights- and anti-discrimination-discourse, a discourse on "broadness" and acceptance, an empowerment-discourse, and a multiculturalism-discourse (mainly characteristic of human rights organisations, particular political organisations, and cultural research). She also identifies a market-discourse, an innovation-discourse, and a competence-discourse (characteristic of the field of business and of a neoliberal ideology). These types of discourses all in different ways emphasise the potential benefits of diversity for society and businesses and rest on an understanding of mutual adaptation. Within this understanding, integration is also viewed as an economic issue for society (or individual businesses). Thus, successful integration according to these discourses equals contribution to society by minority members through participation in education and the labour market.

Yet, the most dominating discourse in Danish media and current policy making maintains an ethnocentric perspective (Yilmaz 1999: 180–81; Rennison 2009: 120–158). According to Rennison (2009: 121), this ethnocentric discourse is closely related to a collective "moral panic" which results in resistance to strangers' cultural practices, and emphasises values related to culture. Culture itself is understood as inherited, static, and tied to birthplace and nation, and cultural differences are seen within the stereotypical frames of "us" and "them", with the "us" imagined as a coherent cultural and national community (Rennison 2009: 128–131; Anderson 1991; Yilmaz 1999). Nationalist ideology is central to this discourse and the view of integration is assimilationist. Ethnic minorities are regarded as either "un-adapted strangers", or as "disciplined strangers" if they are well integrated (Rennison 2009: 153), and the goal for integration is to reach monocultural coherence through assimilation of cultural minorities into the majority culture. This ethnocentric discourse on integration is certainly not an exclusively Danish phenomenon, it is characteristic of public debate and policy making in a range of Western European countries (e.g. Blommaert and Verschueren 1998; Yilmaz 1999; Jaspers 2005; Extra et. al 2009). Since integration projects are firmly situated in this discursive climate, dominating political discourses on integration are central to the case I investigate here.

Because of this discursive climate, however, social and anthropological research has raised concerns about the use of integration as an analytic research term. As Olwig (2010: 180) describes it:

> integration is not just an analytic term measuring levels of social incorporation according to pre-defined parameters of achievement within, for example, employment, housing and education. It has become an emic term denoting the ability to conform to social norms and cultural values defined in dominant discourse as basic to proper citizenship (see also Olwig and Pærregaard 2011).

To avoid confusion with the emic understandings of integration, terms like social incorporation has been used (Faist 2009; Foner and Bertossi 2011). Yet, in order to address, understand, or challenge the societal framing of particular social processes as integration, some research have maintained the term as theoretical and analytic notion by relating the political notion to the sociological concept of *social integration* (Olwig and Pærregaard 2011; Agergaard and Bonde 2013). As a theoretical notion in classical sociology, social integration describes the general social processes that occur when individuals take part in social communities and refers to the degree of connectivity between different parts of a society (Durkheim 2006, org.1897). In more recent sociological and anthropological studies of leisure communities in Denmark, social integration is understood to concern negotiation, change and maintenance of social communities among all participants involved (e.g. Olwig and Pærregaard 2007, 2011; Agergaard and Bonde 2013), and this research often set out from Giddens' definition of integration (see contributions in Olwig and Pærregaard 2007; Agergaard and Bonde 2013).

According to Giddens (1984: 28) "'Integration' may be understood as involving reciprocity of practices (of autonomy and dependence) between actors or collectivities.", and he further distinguishes *system integration* from *social integration*:

> Social integration then means systemness on the level of face-to-face interaction. System integration refers to connections with those who are physically absent in time or space. The mechanisms of system integration certainly presuppose those of social integration, but such mechanisms are also distinct in some key respects from those involved in relations of copresence (Giddens 1984: 28).

Hence Giddens' definition of integration describes processes of social transformation that involve reciprocity rather than incorporation. System integration refers to processes of reciprocity across time and space, whereas social integration entails co-presence and refers to reciprocity processes in face-to-face encounters. In this way the two-part distinction reflects a macro and a micro perspective. Clearly political integration discourse and sports-political projects work at the level of system integration providing the structural and discursive conditions for potential spaces of reciprocity (although political rhetoric often emphasises assimilation rather than reciprocity) and assumes that this will lead to social integration. Policy and institutional organisations set the frames for bringing different individuals and groups together, in this case to do sports. Yet, as Giddens points out this is only part of the story. Social integration as mutuality of practices does not just happen at the level of institutions, but a significant part of these social processes consists of face-to-face encounters. In Madsen (2012, 2013c, 2015) I have pointed out that local norms, identity affiliations and symbolic values are significant to social integration processes in Giddens' sense in the context of a martial arts club. I argue that in Giddens' definition of social integration there is basis for tuning in a lot closer than what is usually done in the sociology and anthropology of sports to investigate practices of reciprocity. To answer the question of how one can talk about practices of reciprocity, connectivity or cultural incorporation through organised leisure activities it is therefore crucial to look further into details of how aspects of autonomy and dependence, norms, affiliations and values play out in face-to-face interactions.

To attend to the details of such interactions I need particular methodological tools capable of capturing practice on the ground and its wider implications across a range of context levels. Linguistic Ethnography (Rampton et al. 2004; Blommaert 2007) is a fruitful approach for this, as it is sensitive to how individuals participate in communities and how social categories and structures are being produced and reproduced in everyday life (see introduction, this volume). Furthermore, consideration of the local, socio-cultural meanings given to particular semiotic resources and its relation to wider cultural models can be accounted for through the notion of *indexicality* (Ochs 1992; Silverstein 2003). Indexicality refers to the associations between forms and (typical) usage, contexts of use and stereotypes of users that are (re-)created in communicative encounters through linguistic and other signs. Indexical associations are metapragmatic because they characterise signs' links to pragmatically usable systems of signs or cultural models (Agha 2003, 2007a). Hence, the approach in this contribution can be characterised as a discourse analysis from a linguistic ethnographic perspective (Blommaert 2005). I combine ethnographic accounts, analysis of indexicality and linguistic micro-analysis of situated interactions, with a focus on speech as sequential actions and on interpersonal relationships.

The discourses on cultural differences, integration, and leisure sports include understandings of what culture is and means for social life in contemporary diverse (but previously less diverse) societies, what it involves to participate in society, and how organised social activities play a part in successful socialisation. These assumptions inevitably relate to understandings of what identity is and how identity relates to culture (Madsen 2015). Current approaches to identity within sociolinguistics are influenced by poststructuralist thinking and emphasise that identity is the product rather than the source of linguistic and other semiotic practices; that identities may be linguistically indexed through labels, implicatures, stances, styles or features; and that identity work does not merely involve strategically controlled acts, but through semiotic displays social category associations may 'leak' from our behaviour in less controlled ways (Coupland 2007: 111; Bucholtz and Hall 2005: 585). In addition, a central part of identity work is the ascription and reception of social category belonging by others (Blommaert 2005: 206; Bucholtz and Hall 2005: 585; Agha 2007a: 234). For the purpose of this work I need, specifically, to relate situated identifications to wider processes of discursive formation and a suitable framework for grasping this relationship is the concept of *positioning* (Davies and Harré 1990). This concept describes how participants locate themselves in relation to others by jointly producing, aligning or dis-aligning with story lines with links to particular discourses or *moral orders* (Davies and Harré 1990). In this sense I approach identity work as stories the participants tell about social belonging through their linguistic and other semiotic practices in situated activities.

I engage with wider discourses on integration in organised leisure activities, but because I engage with these ideas I also aim to discuss whether processes that can be considered socio-culturally incorporating occur on the ground. Thereby, I relate to both integration as discourse and to the processes of reciprocity in the situated positionings and alignments, that is social integration in Giddens' theoretical sense.

Before turning to the empirical case and its local ethnographic context, I shall elaborate on the political assumptions about integration and organised leisure activities, by looking closer at two publications about voluntary integration efforts from the period where our fieldwork among the adolescents took place (both from 2010). The first is a purpose description of a governmental funding scheme supporting integration work in sports- and voluntary associations. The second is a special issue of a publication from the Danish Youth Council (an umbrella organisation for voluntary youth organisations in Denmark aimed at strengthening democracy) with a focus on the integration of "New-Danes in the association life" (DUF 2010, New-Danes is the commonly used euphemism in Danish public discourse for immigrants or children of immigrants, see also Møller, this volume). This publication includes an article about one of the rap mentors of the boys from our study.

3 Integration and organised leisure activities

In 2010 the incumbent government at the time had established a distinct Ministry of Integration (this was abandoned by the government in seat from 2011–2015, but has been reinstated in 2015). This ministry initiated several funding schemes aimed at improving integration through participation in leisure clubs (Agergaard 2013). One of these was the fund for "The voluntary integration work and participation in sports- and association life" (my translation). The description of the overall purpose of the scheme stated that:

> The associations offer a value- and interest-community across the borders of social, political and ethnic divisions. People come together because they share the same interests and people are accepted within the values of the community" (p. 1, my translation).

Thus, on this political level the discursive construction of integration builds on the idea that being together and sharing an interest will lead to acceptance in a community. The description of the criteria of success for the projects seeking funding makes clear that success is measured by an increase in the number of members, by involved parents, and by voluntary leaders "with an ethnic background different from Danish". In the description of the purpose it is further claimed that:

> Participation in the voluntary association life and the local sports and association life gives people with an ethnic background different from Danish a good opportunity to learn about Danish society in general, including democratic rules, Danish values and norms (p. 1, my translation).

This articulation of integration corresponds closely to the common ethnocentric understanding of integration in political and media discourse. Similar values are emphasised in the introduction to the special issue of the Danish Youth Council's magazine:

> New-Danish youth learn Danish, democracy and societal engagement, when they participate in scouting, pupils' council or youth politics (DUF 2010: 1, my translation).

But through quotes incorporated into the introduction from a politician from the Danish People's Party (Dansk Folkeparti, a right wing party with a strong nationalist profile, see also Møller this volume), democracy is presented as a particular Danish value that can be acquired through participation in voluntary associations:

> In the associations one learns to cooperate and to respect others and not to be selfish. It is extremely important that young immigrants get to know the democratic Danish traditions and understand the value of these (DUF 2010: 1, quoting Peter Skaarup, my translation).

The publication from the Danish Youth Council contains articles exemplifying the voluntary integration work, such as one about an ethnic minority troop of scouts in an urban area, a Turkish homework café and school chess. In addition it presents a range of members of a new political initiative: the "New-Danish Youth Council". This council consists of young adults with minority background and with interest in and experience with integration. The purpose of the council is to give advice to the Minister of Integration. So these political texts articulate the assumptions that: 1) Meeting to share an interest will lead to inclusion in a community; and 2) Ethnic minorities will learn about democratic and Danish values and norms by being involved in organised leisure activities, and in that way they will become integrated.

A different perspective on the socially incorporating potential of leisure activities is represented by the practitioners of hip hop. The vice convener of the "New-Danish Youth Council" is, in fact, a rapper, Ali Sufi, who is also one of the mentors of the participants in our research. From a music market point of view, at the time of the fieldwork he was a relatively underground artist predominantly publishing his music through digital media. He is presented in the article as an "intellectual rap-star" with migration background and parental links to the Iranian resistance movement (PMOI – People's Mojahedin Organization) and an academic degree in public policy studies. Sufi's perspective, as it is displayed through quotes in the article, emphasises an approach to integration with a focus on the dangers of societal discrimination of, particularly, minority boys. According to him the hostility towards minority boys can result in their turning to "alternative environments such as immigrant gangs and fundamentalist organisations" (DUF 2010: 7, my translation), and he aims at reaching out to these boys through rap music by, for instance, engaging in voluntary teaching in writing lyrics and performing rap. Sufi's approach to integration certainly represents a different perspective from the dominating ethnocentric conception of integration. He articulates a view of minority boys as victims of more structural inequalities that place the boys at the bottom of the societal hierarchy, and he strives for improving their cultural and social resources (DUF 2010: 7). In line with Sufi's approach is the organisation *Ghetto Gourmet* with a so called rap academy aiming to take "wisdom, inspiration, strength, courage, crafts and skills [...] back from the ivory tower and out to the streets" (translated quote from webpage, see Madsen and Karrebæk 2015: 254), and similar potentials are emphasised by the international hip hop pedagogical studies (Alim 2011; Hill 2009; Pennycook 2007). This work pays particular attention to the critical language awareness involved in creating rap lyrics. Hip hop is considered a cultural form with great potential for expressing political ideas, identity affiliations and for engaging with societal issues, and a crucial part of these expressions is of course linguistic. Furthermore, hip hop as cultural genre is viewed as a vehicle for expanding traditional views of language by allowing for creative linguistic practices, such as mixing, innovative slang etc. (Alim 2011).

But it is worth considering further to what extent and exactly how 'sharing an interest' may lead to inclusion in a community and development of mutual values and skills? The common understandings of integration through voluntary association work at the political level as well as among activists seem to presuppose that participants are accepted in a club or leisure community simply because they share an interest and attend regular meetings; but how members are included in or sometimes excluded from local communities is rarely taken into consideration. Similarly, the ways participants orient to the activities themselves and the relationship between skills, social status and conditions for participating in a given leisure community are not often addressed by socio-political projects or by research reporting on such projects (Madsen 2012, 2013c, 2015). It can, for instance, be vital to be good at the activities to be accepted by the other members, and what it takes to be considered good may vary among different members. There is a need for more nuanced considerations of what it entails to participate in organised leisure activities, and a problem with integration projects is a tendency to overlook the significance of the peer-community among the children and youth. The building of shared values and norms does not only happen through a transfer from adult role models to younger pupils. The building of social relations between peers is likely to be the most important part of the everyday engagement in leisure activities. To approach these issues form a participant perspective it is in place to introduce the young rappers and turn to the details of their participation in rap activities in different contexts.

4 Data and participants

In this chapter I focus on three boys from the group of participants in their final years of school (see introduction). We followed these boys from grade 7 to the end of grade 9 (in 2009–2011, when they were 13–15 years old). Mahmoud has a Moroccan, Bashaar an Iraqi and Isaam a mixed Palestinian-Lebanese background. During our field work they were heavily engaged in a rap-band, here called the *Mini G's*. They signalled affiliation with rap culture through the way they dressed, the music they listened to and their own music compositions and lyrics, a topic they often discussed during school breaks and in the youth club. Their rap activities were highly visible in the classroom when we began our research. For instance, they wore T-shirts with their group name, and articles from local newspapers about their performances were hung on the classroom wall. During our fieldwork they also participated in various local and national hip hop and rap events (see also Madsen 2011; Stæhr 2010; Madsen and Karrebæk 2015; Stæhr and Madsen 2015). In this chapter I primarily discuss excerpts from audio-recordings in youth club settings where the boys are engaged in producing or talking about rap music. I also include a few excerpts from a field diary and I refer to quotes from rap lyrics from YouTube videos (documented in more detail in Stæhr and Madsen 2015). Three of the data examples are from the same recording in the studio in a suburban youth club. I have marked them 'studio 1', 'studio 2' and 'studio 3' to indicate their chronological relationship (I discuss 3 before 1 and 2). For transcription key see appendix.

5 The local rap community

As an artful cultural form hip hop and rap are musical and lyrical means of expression. The production and performance involve literacy, musical, rhythmical, and kinaesthetic skills, but in many ways the approach to rap in the context of our study exceeded the merely artful interests. The *Mini G's* practiced their rap music predominantly in connection with activities in and around two youth clubs. One was the local club in the neighbourhood close to the school at Amager where we conducted our research (I refer to this as 'the local youth club'). The other was a youth club in a suburb to Copenhagen (I refer to this as 'the suburban youth club').

Through the local youth club the boys came into contact with a rap mentor who taught and produced rap music with local adolescents on a voluntary basis. The boys refer to him as their "manager" (see excerpt 1). He was a leading figure in the organisation *Ghetto Gourmet*, with the rap academy as one of its activities. This organisation also offered workshops to Copenhagen schools, and the boys' two school classes participated with their Danish teachers in one of these as an alternative way of learning about poetry (in the 8th grade, October 2009, see Madsen and Karrebæk 2015). Through the involvement in Ghetto Gourmet the boys participated in a concert where they met another rapper, Ali Sufi (mentioned above). The Mini G's approached him and asked if he would cooperate with them on a production, and he agreed. Sufi was involved in teaching rap at the suburban youth club, and because Bashaar had a family contact who worked at the club, they also began to attend the club regularly and work with him there. Sufi initiated another rap association that Issam and Bashaar were members of, the KGB (meaning: "*Kaster Guld Barrer*", "Throws Gold Bars"). This organisation was presented (in an introduction video on YouTube) as a "musical commune", and it was organised in a similar way to traditional leisure associations with convenor, treasurer etc. Both communities overlapped in participants and activities and they provided the main framework of activities for the boys' rap interests. Through these they participated in local concerts and national rap competitions as well as in the regular meetings in the youth clubs. Also it was characteristic of both rap associations that they drew heavily on the infrastructures provided by social media (YouTube and Facebook in particular), and other initiatives by Sufi were a dedicated digital rap channel, *RapMoves TV*, and a digital production company, *Sorte Får* (Black Sheep).

Educational aspects are clearly central to the activities in the rap communities. The mentors provide advice and guidance in relation to rap-related skills such as composing, producing and performing, but both at the levels of ideology and practice there are also links to more official schooling. Sufi's own rap texts, for instance, appeal to knowledge as a significant capital, and Isaam in a retrospective interview describes Sufi as strongly involved in the boys' educational progress (helping with homework and urging them to get an education). In addition, the activity of teaching poetry through the medium of rap in schools illustrates a very direct engagement with formal education. In the next section I discuss data examples suggesting that a connection between education and rap was also relevant to these young participants' own perceptions and practices.

6 Rap and school-related activities

Our research among the adolescents documents how Bashaar, Mahmoud and Isaam displayed enthusiasm and ambition in relation to school work (Stæhr 2010:

chapter 6; Madsen 2011). During breaks at school they often worked on school assignments and in the youth club after school they frequently did homework together. In class they usually participated actively, although they sometimes focused more on entertaining classmates and challenging teacher authority than on the teacher led activities (Madsen 2014). At some occasions rap music-making was part of their homework, as we shall see below, because their teachers made efforts to incorporate the hip hop interest into school activities (Madsen 2011; Madsen and Karrebæk 2015). The young rappers themselves, in fact, expressed the understanding that their rap music involvement had an impact on their attitude to school. In this interview they explain to the interviewer how rap has made them take school more seriously:

Excerpt 1: Rap saved us
Group-interview with Andreas, May 2009. Participants: Mahmoud (Mah); Bashaar (Bas); Isaam (Isa); and researcher, Andreas (And),
My translation. Focal parts emphasised in **bold.**

	Original	**Translation**
And:	hvad er der sket	what's happened
Bas:	vi er blevet mere modne	**we've become more mature**
Isa:	ja og vi er begyndt at tage	yes we've begun to **take**
	det seriøst rappen	**it seriously the rap ((music))**
	før var vi bare sådan nogle	before we were just some
	knægte ballademagere men nu	kids trouble makers but **now**
	gider vi ikke spille smart	**we don't want to play smart**
	og være aggressiv	**and be aggressive**
Bas:	og før kan jeg huske i	and before I remember in the
	fjerde klasse at øh vi hele	fourth grade that eh we
	tiden pjækkede fra timerne	skipped classes all the time
	vi løb væk fra ((navns))	we ran away from ((name's))
	timer og sådan noget	classes and stuff
Isa:	vi var rigtig nogle bøller	we were like real brats
	men nu (.) efter rappen (.)	but now (.) after the rap(.)
	rappen reddede os kan man	**rap saved us you can**
	sige	**say**

18	Bas:	har reddet os også selve	have saved us also
19		skolen har vi taget mere	**school itself we've taken more**
20		seriøst	**seriously**
21	Isa:	mm så	mm so
22	And:	er det rigtigt	really
23	Bas:	ja	yes
24	Mah:	[før jeg lavede ikke]	[before I didn't do]
25	Bas:	[for eksempel jeg jeg]	[for example I I]
26	Mah:	så meget lektier før	much homework before
27	Isa:	vi kan takke vores manager	**we can thank our manager**
28		((navn)) [for det her]	((name)) [**for this**]
29	Bas:	[prøv at hør her]	[listen]
30		jeg er gået fra nul til ti	**I've gone from zero to ten**
31		og tolv (1.3) bare fra	**and twelve** (1.3) just from fourth
32		fjerde og her og nu	grade and here and and now

The researcher talks to the boys about a noticeable difference between rap productions they have posted on YouTube in 2008 and one in 2009 – the earlier ones with focus on "dissing" "wannabes", gangsters and violence, and the latter about explicitly rejecting gangster rap, and focussing on being brave enough to be yourself (I attend to more details of the content and style in the following section). They explain the different types of songs as part of a trajectory towards a more mature approach to rap. The most significant point to take from the interview here is that the development towards maturity and seriousness in relation to rap music is presented as closely related to improvement of school performance (line 19–20 and 30–31). The boys construct a story line as having been "saved by rap" and even express thanks to their manager, an act that is indexical of the 'thank you speech' genre within the field of music and arts. So they are not only positioning as good students, but also as rap artists. In this positioning they draw on an understanding of leisure activities and mentor-relationships as important for their educational development, and in this way they appear to re-construct the well-established discourse within voluntary association and community work described above (see also Stæhr 2010: chapter 6; Madsen and Karrebæk 2015; Stæhr and Madsen 2015).

In excerpt 2, however, a different understanding of the relationship between rap music and school is expressed by a friend in the local youth club. The excerpt illustrates part of their rap-related activities in club. Mahmoud and Bashaar are writing a climate rap, which is also homework for school, but the activity takes place in a leisure context in which they often worked on their music. This makes the setting for the activity somewhat hybrid and the linguistic practices they employ during this sequence relate to similar hybrid relationships between peer and school cultural resources. The boys jointly create the lyrics for the song, and Mahmoud writes them down. Before this sequence the writing has led Bashaar to make fun of and correct Mahmoud's spelling of the word "temperature" (see Madsen 2011; Stæhr 2010: chapter 6). So the school-oriented frame and a norm of correctness have indeed been made relevant. A third participant joins the conversation at the beginning of excerpt 2, Madiha, a girl, who is also a regular to the youth club.

Excerpt 2: Do your homework
Recording from the youth club, October 2009. Participants:
Bashaar (Bas); Mahmoud (Mah) and Madiha (Mad). Rap marked in *Italics*.

	Original	**Translation**
Mah:	[*den stiger*] ((rapper))	[*it rises*] ((rapping))
Mad:	[Koran xxx kom nu] lav	[Koran xxx come on] do your
	jeres lektier få jer en	homework get yourself an edu-
	uddannelse (.)	cation (.) ↓rap Koran do you
	↓rap Koran tror I I får	think you'll get
	penge [for det]	money [for it]
Bas:	[HVOR MEGET] HVAD	[HOW MUCH] WHAT
	HVAD TROR DU JEG FIK I	WHAT DO YOU THINK I GOT IN
	FRANSK I DAG (.) TI	FRENCH TODAY (.) TEN
	HISTORIE FIK JEG TOLV	HISTORY I GOT TWELVE
	MATEMATIK FIK JEG TI	MATH I GOT TEN
	LAD VÆRE MED AT SNAKKE	DON'T TALK
	WALLAH	WALLAH
	(2.0)	(2.0)
Mad:	?ej hvor skulle jeg vide det	?well how would
	fra?	I know?
Mah:	[*temperaturen* (.)	[*the temperature* (.)
	den stiger] ((rapper))	*it's rising*] ((rapping))
	[øh JA I FORHOLD TIL ANDRE]	[eh YES COMPARED TO OTHERS]
Mad:	HVAD FIK DU MOUD	WHAT DID YOU GET MOUD
	Mahmoud fik sgu også ti	Mahmoud also got bloody ten
Bas:	TI I FYSIK OG	TEN IN PHYSICS AND
Mah:	KE↑MI (0.3) TOLV I	CHEMIS↑TRY (0.3) TWELVE IN
	BIOLO↑GI	BIOLO↑GY

((wallah, Arabic origin = I swear))

Madiha interrupts Mahmoud's rap with the suggestion that the boys do homework instead of rap music in order to get an education (lines 1–6). Thereby she seems to articulate an assumption that rap does not lead to income (as education does) or she, perhaps, implies that the boys' rap music is not at a level that will lead to economic success. So Madiha constructs a contradiction between the youth cultural practices such as rap music and general measures of societal success, at least in relation to Mahmoud and Bashaar. However, to do so, she employs non-standard linguistic features characteristic of the vernacular speech style frequently used among the youth in our study (the contemporary urban vernacular (Rampton 2011) described in several contributions in this volume e.g. Hyttel-Sørensen; Karrebæk; Agha, see also Madsen 2013a). The linguistic features include a particular prosodic pattern and the slang expression *Koran* used as intensifier (line 2 and 5), and they index peer culture and streetwise values rather than educational skills (e.g. Madsen 2013a). Bashaar does not argue against the expressed assumption, nor does he claim that they are in fact engaged in doing homework. Instead he defensively and loudly asks Madiha a rhetorical question about his marks and continues by listing a range of the high marks he has recently received in school as an answer (line 7–13). This seems to function as a demonstration of his academic capabilities, and a way of positioning himself as school-skilled (in line with his earlier spelling corrections). Still, similar to Madiha, he deploys linguistic features associated with the vernacular speech style. These are both prosodic and lexical (e.g. the expression *wallah*, line 13). Finally, Mahmoud, too, lists high marks in several subjects using the same intonation (lines 22–24). Excerpt 2 thereby illustrates how the boys defend their school competence as a reaction to the idea that rap-culture and school success are incompatible. The example shows that the close relation between school competence and rap activities expressed by the boys is not uncontested – in this case it has to be defended. But like above the boys manage a simultaneous positioning as both good students and rap artists, and this example is typical of how these boys in many ways successfully blend dominating educational norms and positive school orientation on the one hand with peer and popular cultural norms and semiotic activities such as a linguistic vernacular forms and rap on the other (Madsen 2011; Madsen and Karrebæk 2015). In this way it illustrates a sense of mutual adaptation of different cultural models at the level of face-to-face interaction.

The next excerpt, however, shows how rap activities can also be constructed as an obstacle for school work. The excerpt is from the recordings in the studio in the suburban youth club with Ali Sufi. Throughout the recording in the studio Bashaar expresses annoyance with spending time listening to the other group members re-recording their parts of the song (I will attend to details of this positioning below). Several of the sequences from this recording are characterised by the conversational flow being broken up by relatively marked pauses. This is likely to be related to Bashaar's complaints that lead to disagreements as we shall see. Excerpt 3 illustrates one such sequence. Just before this part there has been a long stretch of silence (7.2 seconds) and Bashaar has suggested to their mentor: "from now on can't you just say like those who are recording have to come". The mentor has replied that he will not know in advance who has to record again. In addition, another group member, Salim, has just argued that he suggested they spend the time writing lyrics while the others record:

Excerpt 3: Could have been at home doing homework (Studio 3)
Self-recording by Bashaar in suburban youth club, March 2011. Participants Bashaar (Bas); Isaam (Isa); another rap group member, Salim (Sal), rap mentor, Sufi (Suf).

	Original	Translation
	(1.2)	(1.2)
Sal:	> jeg ↑sagde til dig lad os	> I said to you let's
	skrive <	write <
Bas:	[> hvor↑dan skal vi skrive	[> ↑how shall we write
	i↑mens <]	↑while <]
Sal:	[og så sagde du jeg føler]	[and then you said I feel]
	mig bedre tilpas i studiet	more comfortable in the
	jeg sagde vi kunne	studio I said we could
	(.) gå [ud og skrive]	(.) go [out and write]
Bas:	[der var ikke] nogen	[there wasn't] any
	bærbar > han sagde der var	laptop > he said there wasn't
	ikke nogen bærbar <	any laptop <
	(1.9)	(1.9)
Men:	°to sekunder°	°two seconds°
Sal:	ja men alligevel	yes but anyway
Bas:	hvordan alligevel (0.5)	how anyway (0.5)
	skulle vi lave beatbox	should we do beatbox
	eller ↑hvad	or ↑what
	(0.2)	(0.2)
Sal:	tsk lad være med det der	tsk ((tuts)) don't do that
	Bashaar	Bashaar
Bas:	okay jeg siger det bare yani	okay I'm just saying it
	jeg kunne have været hjemme	yani I could have been at
	nu og lavet lektier	home now doing homework

((yani, Arabic, equivalent to 'like'))

After some silence, Salim repeats the previous argument that he has already suggested they use the waiting time to write. The possibility for doing this is questioned by Bashaar (line 4–5), and in overlap with Bashaar's "how shall we write while", Salim further accounts for his efforts to make use of the time. In his explanation for why the writing did not work out, he positions Bashaar as the obstacle by pointing out that Bashaar had said he felt more comfortable in the studio (line 6–9). Referring to this objection attributes to Bashaar a personal emotional and perhaps irrational orientation. Bashaar contests this positioning by underlining the lack of a laptop as the reason for not being able to write. The argumentative character of this exchange is underlined by the utterances being spoken faster than surrounding utterances and in several parts simultaneously (line 4–5 and 9–10). After another relatively long pause, Salim with his "yes but anyway" (line 15) partly signals agreement, but also hints at the lack of a laptop not being a sufficient reason for rejecting the suggestion. Yet, he does not further account for why, in spite of Bashaar's following repair. Instead Salim reacts to Bashaar as unreasonable with an annoyed tut and a request that Bashaar stops his complaints. Bashaar responds to this by pointing out that he could have spent the time doing homework. Thereby he constructs the rap activities as a disturbance to school work. This act has to be seen in the light of its situated purpose of Bashaar arguing that he is wasting his time being in the recording studio. Instead of attempting to directly counter Salim's positioning of him as *unreasonable* and irrational, the strategy seems to be to suggest how he could have made *more reasonable* use of the time. Such a strategy must build on the presupposition that the other interlocutors share a view of homework as being important. In addition, referring to a preference for doing homework – usually considered a sensible and rational activity (and valued by their rap mentor) – could be said to contrast with the unreasonable and irrational positioning. So while the rap-activities here are situationally constructed as an obstacle to school-related activities, this construction still rests on an emphasis of school and homework as significant.

The excerpts discussed in this section show that education is of great concern to the young rappers and that in their everyday interactions (and the understanding they present in the interview) there is a close relationship between being good at rap and being school ambitious. Furthermore, we see how they boys combine youth cultural and educational indexes in their interaction around rap. Still, the data examples illustrate an awareness of a possible understanding of an opposition between formal education and rap culture. This is articulated by Madiha and exploited by Bashaar in his account for considering certain parts of their rap activities a waste of time. But how do these observations of educational aspects and different cultural and linguistic indexes relate to the boys actual rap productions?

7 Rap productions – content and linguistic practice

An important part of the boys' participation in rap activities was the writing, performing and recording of rap music and lyrics. The boys' rap productions were recorded in the youth clubs with their rap mentors and often shared afterwards through social media sites like YouTube and Facebook (Stæhr and Madsen 2015). Therefore it is worth looking into the boys' rap productions, and here I shall focus on the form and content of the lyrics. During our fieldwork we collected eight rap productions in the form of videos that had at some point been publicly shared by the participants on YouTube (with their permissions). Table 1 provides an overview of the rap songs with information about the year they were shared, the main content and general observations regarding the linguistic style of the lyrics.

We saw in excerpt 1 how the interviewer's interest in the change between the two rap songs from 2008 and the production with Ghetto Gourmet from 2009 *Just a rapper* led to the participants linking rap to education. They suggest that *Just a rapper* represents the kind of rappers that take education seriously. What is striking about the change of rap style in these productions is that it illustrates a shift from what the participants themselves describe as "gangster rappers" to "serious rappers", and this seems to involve a change in linguistic style as well, occurring after the boys' involvement with Ghetto Gourmet and later KGB with Sufi. In the early songs the adolescents express affiliation with the local street gang, violence in the neighbourhood and opposition to the police. In *Wannabe*, "wannabe G's" (G for gangster) are presented as worthless compared to the song protagonists. In addition the lyrics contain explicit meta-linguistic commentary, as the text addresses local hybrid speech practices and demonstrate what is referred to as "our language":

> **Ew** you're losers – you copy – You call yourself a **G** – **do you wannabe?** – You have no value do I'm not 'Danish People's Party'- So try to listen – we are in front 'cause it's here in Amar' we speak our language – **acra para vur abow**?
>
> (*Ew* 'hey'; *acra* 'police'; *para* 'money'; *vur* 'fist fight'; *abow,* an exclamation, quote from "Wannabe" 2008, my translation, features not traditionally associated with Danish in bold)

The linguistic style of the song is equivalent to the everyday peer style of the adolescents and illustrates the poly-lingual character of their languaging (Jørgensen 2008; Jørgensen et. al. 2011) by including features that can be associated with Danish, English, Kurdish and Arabic (see also Madsen and Karrebæk 2015; Stæhr and Madsen 2015). The rap text also involves a political dimension through the

Table 1: Overview of rap productions (see also Stæhr and Madsen 2015)

Title and year (My translation)	**Main topics of content**	**Linguistic style of lyrics**	**Group name and Affiliation**
'Where we come from' YouTube video, 2008	The local street gang Affiliation with violence and crime in the local neighbourhood Identifying as 'Pakis' – contrasted to nationalist right wing politics Opposition to police	Predominantly monolingual Danish with a few slang and swear words, English expressions and features of minority languages	Mini G's
'Wannabe' YouTube video, 2008	The local street gang Worthless wannabes – contrasted to real 'G's' Multicultural youth – Contrasted to nationalist right wing politics	More hybrid linguistic style with incorporation of English and vocabulary from minority languages – explicit meta-linguistic comments and demonstration of mixing	Mini G's
'Just a rapper' YouTube video, 2009	Meta-rap Competent rappers 'Anti-gangster'	Predominantly monolingual (standard) Danish with vocabulary indexing up-scale culture	Mini G's/ Ghetto Gourmet (Ali Sufi)
'Obama' YouTube video, 2009	Addressing US president about problems ranging from crime in local neighbourhood to poverty in Palestine, Guantanamo, and climate problems	Predominantly monolingual (standard) Danish with a few English and slang expressions	Mini G's / Ghetto Gourmet
'It's how we do it' YouTube video, 2009	Meta-rap about qualities of community of Ghetto Gourmet and their music	Predominantly monolingual (standard) Danish with a few English and slang expressions	Mini G's/ Ghetto Gourmet
'The problem solver' YouTube video, 2009	Love rap with 'anti-gangster' aspects: *'you're not my bitch you're my life saver'*	Predominantly monolingual (standard) Danish with a few English and slang expressions	KGB/ RapMoves (Ali Sufi)
'New side' YouTube video, 2010	Meta-rap about qualities of community of KGB and their music	Predominantly monolingual (standard) Danish with a few English and slang expressions	KGB/ RapMoves (Ali Sufi)
'Move steps' YouTube video of live performance from release concert of Ghetto Gourmet, 2011	Meta-rap about being competent city rapper seeking to improve	Predominantly monolingual (standard) Danish with a few English and slang expressions	Mini G's/ Ghetto Gourmet

positioning as “not Danish People’s Party” – the above-mentioned right wing nationalist party, and links the hybrid speech style to not affiliating with this nationalist party.

In what the adolescents call their more “serious” rap, the linguistic style of the lyrics is predominantly monolingual standard Danish and it includes a range of expressions associated with more upscale cultural norms, notably in the chorus (marked in bold): “Well you know who we are – On the stage and we dare – **Poetry** and **harmony –** Gangster rap **spare me**” (Quote *Just a rapper* 2009, my translation). *Just a rapper* was created during the boys’ participation in Ghetto Gourmet’s rap academy. The content of this song is primarily a meta-rap message, emphasising distance to gangster rap and celebrating the art of competent rap. The boys’ musical productions after 2009 (created during the involvement with the local rap mentors), continue to be concerned with positioning as competent rappers, but some also focus on societal problems and political issues. For instance, the *Obama* song addresses political problems on a local as well as a global scale: “Hey Obama – you will hear from me – there’s also crime here at Amager”, and it includes the explicit statement “I’m a political rapper, but I’m not a diva” (Quote *Obama* 2009, my translation).

So do these musical and lyrical productions in any way relate to processes that can be considered educational or socially incorporating? With respect to the content, there is certainly a shift from the early occupation with gang, gangster and violence culture, to the later productions that show societal and political engagement and reflections (mostly the Obama song). This development would certainly be approved of by political integration initiatives. Yet, there is also a central concern with rap for rap’s sake. Improving rap skills, claiming and demonstrating competence in the art of rap is in fact the main focus of most of their rap productions. Both in content and style there is less emphasis on ethnic minority identity aspects and the cultural diversity of the young rappers everyday life in the later songs. From identifying as a ‘perker’ (a term used about and among Danes of minority decent with varying connotations, see Hyttel-Sørensen; Nørreby; Møller, this volume) and employing a local linguistically hybrid vernacular speech style, the productions made within the Ghetto Gourmet and KGB communities can be characterised as being more standard and monolingual. It is important to add that the boys’ pronunciation of the lyrics in their performance is not always standard Danish, but it is more standardised in the rap performances than in their everyday speech. At the level of vocabulary their linguistic style in the later rap songs is indeed more standard, and at times with clear academic and up-scale cultural connotations. In the meta-linguistic reflections we have collected from the participants they specifically describe such vocabulary as a prime characteristic of the speech style they refer to as ‘integrated’ – a speech style associated with teachers and adults, respect, academic skills and up-scale culture (e.g. Madsen 2013a; Møller and Jørgensen 2013). In this linguistic sense the young rappers seem to become more 'integrated' through their rap trajectories. The fact that the participants refer to academic standard speech as 'integrated' shows an awareness of integration discourses, but also a re-construction of the concept perhaps involving a certain ironic reference to the societal adaptation it involves in the stereotypical meaning. Before concluding this section, I will consider an excerpt from an interaction during a table football match in the youth club, which illustrates how the notion of integration was explicitly addressed in relation to rap music-making and similarly re-constructed and playfully brought about as a potential topic for a rap song:

Excerpt 4: It's about integration

Self-recording in the local youth club by Bashaar, June 2009. Participants: Bashaar(Bas); Mahmoud (Mah); Israh (Isr); Selma (Sel). Singing in *italics*.

		Original	Translation
01	Bas:	eow har I hørt vores nye	eow have you heard our new
02		omkvæd mig og Mahmoud	chorus me and Mahmoud
03		(det har han ikke) vi skal	(he hasn't) we are
04		lave en sang i Mini G's den	making a new song in Mini
05		handler om integration	G's it's about integration
06		(vi siger sådan der)	(we go like)
07	Isr:	hvis det er jer der har	if it's you who
08		lavet den	made it
09		[så er den dårlig]	[then it's bad]
10	Sel:	[lad være med at]	[don't play]
11		spille integreret	integrated
12	Bas:	(vi siger sådan der) *endnu*	(we go like) *another*
13		*en fremmed* (.) *hun er bare*	*stranger* (.) *she's just*
14		*en fremmed* (.) *hun er en*	*a stranger* (.) *she's*
15		*dansker på Nørrebro*	*a Dane in Nørrebro*
16		((synger))	((sings))
17		(.) gi'r det ikke mening?	(.)doesn't that make sense?
18	Mah:	næ:	no:

((eow, Kurdish origin, equivalent to 'hey'))

Bashaar calls for the others' attention to listen to the chorus of a new song and adds that the song is about integration (an imaginary song it turns out – the group did not actually make a song about integration). He employs the expression "eow" and the intonation associated with the urban youth speech. This speech style is commonly used by all the boys in particular in casual peer contexts. The concept of integration as a process of adaptation involving minority and majority relations is clearly relevant to the suggested lyrics of the rap song performed by Bashaar. The chorus refers to a "dansker" ('Dane') in "Nørrebro" (an area of Copenhagen known for its highly ethnically diverse population) as a "fremmed" (stranger), and thereby he turns the stereotypical societal discourse upside down. A different meaning of integrated is at play in Selma's teasing comment before this. In the expression "play integrated", integrated is employed as a derogative term and in this combination it invokes elements of fakeness. This is also a regular usage of the notion of integrated among the participants in our study to point out peers' uncool, fake or too (adult/majority/school-related) adapted behaviour (Madsen 2013a). The explicit engagement with the notion of integration as a topic of a song occurs in a playful pretend rap and is reacted to with teasing rejection. Thereby it is not treated sincerely as a suitable theme; rather Selma's reaction suggests it relates to some element of inauthenticity and involves negative connotations.

In sum, based on the development of the young rappers as it is reflected in their rap texts, we see that their involvement with the grassroots rap-political workshops and the mentors results in:

- A disaffiliation with gangster-rap and its associated values
- A certain political engagement (with problems of inequality and crime) expressed in their lyrics (but with limitations to what counts as a suitable topic)
- Identity positioning as part of particularly competent urban rap communities and a central concern with meta-rap
- Less use of non-standard and mixed youth vernacular linguistic practices and more use of a standard, academic style (corresponding to their own descriptions of 'integrated' speech)

The self-presentations expressed by the young rappers in their texts certainly emphasise affiliation with the interest communities of the rap organisations and a development of seemingly shared values within a particular moral order e.g. involving the qualities of good rap and distance to generally negatively evaluated counter cultures (of gang and crime activities). What is surprising, compared to the international sociolinguistic literature on hip hop, is that linguistic indexes of local youth culture (and the hybridity it involves) are hardly ever used in their rap music after they become involved in these communities. Judging by their artistic expressions one could be tempted to say they are linguistically mainstreamed rather than emancipated. But is this a result of an explicit normativity of the mentors? Or is it a sign of hegemonic linguistic and educational ideologies?

Excerpt 5 from Stæhr's notes from a field trip to the suburban youth club suggests that Sufi distances himself somehow from the everyday speech practices of the participants:

Excerpt 5: That stuff about paki language
[...] *after a while he [Sufi] asks what I do. I explain briefly about language. He interrupts and says "that stuff about 'perker' language ethnolect" and "have you heard the language they speak at Amager". I don't get chance to answer, because Bashaar says 'yes he knows all the words, we can't hide anything from him anymore' and laughs* (Field diary, Stæhr, 23rd of March 2011, my translation).

The field diary describes how the mentor labels the linguistic practices of the participants as "'perker' language ethnolect". The reaction of Bashaar treats the researcher's access to the speech style as requiring explanation, and the local construction of the style involves associations with ethnicity, a particular urban area and unintelligibility. This suggests that the boys' vernacular speech practices are ascribed a relatively peripheral, or at least peculiar status.

In 2014 Isaam became a rap teacher himself, and in a retrospective interview I asked him about whether they were taught about choice of linguistic style in their rap music by their mentors and how he approached language in his own teaching. He explained that he would advise his own rap pupils to only occasionally use what he refers to as "perkerdansk" ('perker' Danish) and otherwise stick to "ethnic Danish" (in the meaning 'the Danish spoken by ethnic majority Danes'). The reason for this was a concern with the recipients of the music, as he continued to explain:

Original	**Translation**
"Ja man skal prøve at få fat på folk til at lytte din musik (.) så du så (.) så du kan også sige for eksempel (.) ah det er sgu det er sgu sådan nogle perkerunger der laver sådan noget musik det gider vi ikke lytte til (.) men nej hvis du kan få fat på selve de etniske danskere og synes det er fedt så har du succes"	"yes you should try to get to people to listen [to] your music (.) so you so (.) so you can also say for example (.) ah but it's it's some bloody 'perker' kids making that kind of music we don't want to listen to that (.) but if you can get to the ethnic Danes themselves and [they] think it's cool then you have success"

(Isaam, retrospective interview, February 2014)

According to Issam the considerations about linguistic style were related to ambitions of success as rappers which involved reaching a wider audience and not being rejected as a "'perker' kid". Isaam further explained that in particular their teachers in Ghetto Gourmet often corrected their grammar and sought to teach them linguistic correctness. When I asked why, his answer was:

Original	**Translation**
"man skal heller ikke lyde som en dum (.) altså en ufaglært person du ved (.) for så så bliver selve din tekst eller dit budskab useriøst (.) og det er vigtigt at få sit budskab ud på den rigtige måde"	"one shouldn't sound like a stupid (.) like an uneducated person you know (.) because then then your text or your message becomes unserious (.) and it's important to get your message out in the right way"

(Isaam, retrospective interview, February 2014)

So in addition to aiming at a wider outreach and at artistic success there seems to be a concern with coming across as intelligent in order to be taken seriously. Isaam told me that he was trying to create a new rap association independent of the youth clubs with its own facilities, and that his main aim with this was to create an environment for the local youth with interest in rap to become skilled and successful as rappers. So whereas it can be alluring to explain the dominance of linguistic standard practices in the rap productions as linked to the ideologies of education, Isaam's accounts point to rap cultural ambitions as an important part of the explanation. In the final section before I conclude, I will look closer at this individualistic orientation to art as it plays out in specific interactional episodes and at times conflicts with the ideologies of solidarity and community often considered a key affordance of association life.

8 Solidarity in the recording studio and the Diva in the room

Although the *Obama* song discussed above included the statement of being a political rapper and not a "diva", excerpt 6 from Stæhr's field diary in the suburban youth club reports how Bashaar describes all the young rappers as divas:

Excerpt 6: Divas
We sit down in some armchair like chairs. First Salim has to re-do his strophe. There's a lot of dissing going on and Bashaar thinks it's a waste of time. Bashaar tells me how they're all Divas and can be jealous if someone gets a better spot in the song than someone else (Field diary, Stæhr, 23rd of March 2011, my translation)

According to Bashaar "Divas" are concerned with their own position in the rap productions, and he describes jealousy as a part of their participation in the rap activities. This description illustrates a dimension of identifying as an individual rap artist with particular personal stakes in the activities. Such an approach to rap appears to conflict with the solidarity and democratic values central to the ideals of a commune like the KGB.

By attending to one final excerpt from the interaction in the recording studio, I will discuss the conflict between these two aspects of the boys' participation in the rap community in more detail. Due to the length of the sequence, I will treat it in two separate parts (marked a and b). As described in section 5 (introducing excerpt 3 from the same recording), and as noted in the field diary quoted above, Bashaar is complaining about wasting time listening to the others' re-takes. Just before this example Isaam has had several attempts at re-recording (but has still not successfully completed his part), and Bashaar has repeatedly expressed annoyance. At the start of this sequence, the researcher (Andreas) has just left to go home, and Isaam has also temporarily left the room. Bashaar is wearing the recording equipment:

Excerpt 7a: Re-recording (Studio 1)
Self-recording by Bashaar in suburban youth club, March 2011. Participants Bashaar (Bas); Isaam (Isa); another member og rap commune (KGB), Salim (Sal); rap mentor, Sufi (Suf).

		Original	Translation
01	Bas:	det er det jeg siger wallah	that's what I say wallah we
02		vi spilder al tiden på at at	waste all the time by by re-
03		genindspille	recording
04	Suf:	hvad ↑mener du det er sgu da	what do you ↑mean it's not a
05		ikke spild af tid	bloody waste of time
06	Bas:	det er det da	sure it is
07	Suf:	der er da brug for det fordi	well there's the need for it
08		det lyder federe jo	because it sounds cooler
09	Sal:	det lyder bedre	it sounds better
10	Suf:	[ja]	[yes]

Bas	[så] ↑tag det på ↑første	[then]↑do it in the ↑first
	↑take wallah ↓mand	↑take wallah ↓man
Suf:	hvad mener du hvad hvis han	what do you mean what if he
	vil gerne have det ?første	would like to have ?first
	gang?(.) sagde han han lagde	time? (.) he said he took it
	det ned han (syntes)det var	down he (thought) it was good
	godt så ville han lave det om	then he wanted to redo it
Bas:	men sådan ER DET	but that's HOW IT
Suf:	?DU KAN LIGE SÅ GODT? GØRE	?YOU MIGHT AS WELL? DO IT
	DET [EN ANDEN GANG]	[A SECOND TIME]
Bas:	[MEN SÅDAN ER] DET HVER GANG	[BUT THAT'S HOW] IT IS EVERY
	JO IKKE	TIME RIGHT
Suf:	OG [HVAD SÅ:]	AND [SO WHA:T]
Sal:	[VI ?krydser?] JO IKKE PÅ	[WE don't] ?cross? ON
	DIG fordi du ikke vil gøre	YOU because you don't want
	det en anden [gang]	to do it a second [time]
Suf:	[er] er	[are] are
	folk professionelle ↑her er	people professionals ↑here
	det ikke xxx første gang	isn't it xxx first time
	eller hvad (.)	or what (.)
	[HVIS DU VILLE GØRE DET	[IF YOU WANTED TO DO IT YOU
	VILLE DU OGSÅ VÆRE GLAD]	WOULD ALSO BE HAPPY]
Isa:	[hvad hvad er der sket hvad	[what what's happened what's
	er der sket her]	happened here]
Suf:	for du havde en mulighed for	that you had a possibility
	at lægge det om igen	to re-take it again

((wallah, Arabic origin = I swear))

Until this point in the interaction, Bashaar has expressed irritation, but here he explicitly voices a complaint about wasting time. Sufi initially responds with what seems like a rhetorical repair as he immediately continues to contest Bashaar's claim. Thereby he articulates an oppositional stance and the argument about whether or not it is a waste of time to do re-recordings continues throughout the interactional sequences in both excerpt 7a and 7b. Bashaar's complaint is not only resisted by Sufi. Salim and Isaam also occasionally support Sufi's resistance to the attitude displayed by Bashaar, but the main participants in the dispute are Bashaar and Sufi. Bashaar reacts to Sufi's contestation by plainly reaffirming his own claim without further accounts, but Sufi continues by accounting for the value of re-recordings with reference to a better ("cooler") result, and this is supported by Salim. Bashaar does not reject the value of a good result, but with an annoyed response in the imperative form: "then do it in the first take wallah man" (line 12) he hints at the possibility of a good result in the first take. In saying this he positions those who need to do re-takes as less competent. In his initial complaint, Bashaar does not mention specific participants as the cause of his annoyance, and he employs an inclusive 'we' in his utterance: "we waste all the time" (line 1–2). Yet, Sufi in his response resists the idea that re-recording signals a lack of competence and refers to a personal pronoun '*he*', as if he has understood Bashaar's complaint as directed at someone in specific. Sufi argues that 'he' could have thought it was good the first time, but still want to redo it (line 13–17). Both Salim and Isaam have re-recorded at this point, but since Isaam is not present and has had his attempts immediately before Bashaar's complaint, it is likely that Sufi understands the annoyance as directed at Isaam.

From line 19 on the participants become heavily invested in the dispute and their exchange is characterised by loud volume and overlapping contributions. Bashaar maintains that repeated re-recordings are a nuisance, but he is challenged by both Sufi and Salim now turn to arguments that appeal to solidarity. Salim points out that the others are not criticising Bashaar because he does *not* want to re-record (line 24–26), and Sufi points out that people are not professionals in this context (line 28–29) and that Bashaar would appreciate the possibility too *if* he wanted to re-record (line 31–32). Both of these arguments, in fact, potentially criticise Bashaar for not wanting to spend time on re-takes and thereby not striving to do better. By complaining about wasting time on the others' repeated attempts Bashaar also constructs the activity of re-recording as irrelevant to himself. Through this he positions himself as more competent than those who need more than one try. But this story line that links rap competence to being able to make a good recording in the first take is challenged by Sufi and Salim. The story line they jointly construct emphasise making an effort and showing solidarity as important qualities, and through this they counter position Bashaar as someone who lacks these skills. During the heated dispute Isaam suddenly joins the conversation asking what has happened. This suggests that he has just entered the room. At first he receives no response to his question, and he repeats it:

Excerpt 7b: Waste of time (Studio 2)
Self-recording by Bashaar in suburban youth club, March 2011. Participants Bashaar (Bas); Isaam (Isa); another rap group member, Salim (Sal); rap mentor, Sufi (Suf).

		Original	**Translation**
01	Isa:	hvad er der sket	what's happened
02		(0.3) ((Bashaar sukker))	(0.3) ((Bashaar sighs))
03	Isa:	hvad diskuterer I	what are you discussing
04	Suf:	fordi han: bruger tid på at	because he: spends time on
05		en skal genindspille det er	someone re-recording well
06		da nor↑ma:lt hvis du ikke	it's nor↑ma:l if you don't
07		synes xxx det er jo ↑meget	think xxx it's a lot
08		federe ↑DU ER OGSÅ PÅ	cooler ↑YOU'RE ALSO ON THE
09		↑SANGEN så du skal være glad	↑SONG so you should be happy
10		for at han gør lægger noget	that he's doing a take of
11		der er bedre jo	something better
12	Bas:	?men? så fjern mig fra	?but? then remove me from
13		sangen ↓wallah øh	the song ↓wallah eh
14		(0.2)	(0.2)
15	Suf:	hvorfor har du (.)hver gang	Why have you (.) every time
16		han øh tror du det er det	he eh do you think that's
17		(.)det (det) handler om	what it(.) it's about
18	Bas:	↑ne:j men	↑no: but
19		[det er ↑bare yani]	[it's ↑just yani]
20	Suf:	[det xxx betegner] som det	[it xxx signifies] like it
21		bliver også bedre for dig	also becomes better for you
22		hvis ↑han laver noget der er	if ↑he does something that's
23		fedt	cool
24	Bas:	det er ikke ?bedre end? mig	It isn't ?better than? me it
25		det afhænger ikke af mig jeg	doesn't depend on me I have
26		har mit vers [så lad dem	my strophe [then let them
27		spille deres vers]	play their strophe]
28	Suf:	[nej du er	[no you're like
29		sådan rigtig xxx er du ikke]	really xxx aren't you]
30	Bas:	jeg har ↑mit så lad dem	I have ↑mine then let them
31		passe ↑sit yani	look after ↑theirs yani
32	Isa:	(nej men) hvis sangen er	(no but) if the song is
33		slatten så er det jo	sloppy then it's like

34	Suf:	sådan er det jo ikke i en	that's not how it is in a
35		gruppe hvis hvis der er e:n	group if if there's o:ne who
36		der laver noget der er fedt	does something cool then it
37		så smitter det af på alle	reflects on everyone (0.2)
38		sammen (0.2) og omvendt	and the other way round
39		((dørklokke høres i	((doorbell sound in the back-
40		baggrunden, ringer 2 gange))	ground, rings twice))
41		(4.5)	(4.5)
42	Bas:	°jeg synes bare det er spild	°I just think it's a waste of
43		af tid°	time°

((wallah= I swear; yani, Arabic origin, equivalent to 'like'))

When Isaam enters and asks what has happened a potentially uncomfortable moment occurs. Since Bashaar has uttered his objection after Isaam's failed recordings, and has hinted that this suggests a lack of competence he has positioned Isaam as incompetent in his absence. Bashaar's initial response to Isaam is a noticeably bothered sigh, and this makes Isaam understand that he is the actual cause of Bashaar's annoyance. When Isaam asks again what they are discussing, Sufi explains. This time he uses the indefinite pronoun "en" referring to 'someone re-recording' (line 5) rather than a personal pronoun. He continues to defend re-recording, reject it as a sign of incompetence, appeal to values of solidarity and loudly emphasises that Bashaar features on the same song and benefits from others improving their performance. With the raise in volume from line 8, Sufi's utterance comes across as a reprimand of Bashaar and in this part of the utterance he shifts to using personal pronouns: "You're also on the song', 'you should be happy', 'he's doing a take of something better". So here the avoidance of making it a personal issue seems abandoned. By employing this authoritative voice Sufi puts Bashaar in the position of a disobedient novice. Bashaar's reaction to this is a request to be removed from the song, and this plain refusal to cooperate functions as an expression of offence that enhances the sense of dispute. Sufi questions Bashaar's reaction and repeats the argument that he benefits from the others' efforts, but Bashaar rejects their interdependence and maintains an emphasis on separate individual performances (line 24–27 & 30–31). Sufi continues to argue against this approach and explicitly addresses suitable group behavior in a final corrective utterance. After a long stretch of silence, Bashaar silently persists that it is a waste of time, as if, at least as an afterburn (Goffman 1971), to get the final word in the dispute. Throughout the interactional sequence Bashaar deploys linguistic features of the Copenhagen youth vernacular (characteristic intonation and Arabic expressions), and Sufi's language use is predominantly standard, but involves some pronunciation features associated with the regional variety of Århus (where he has lived). However, none of these linguistic practices appears as marked in this interactional context. They were regularly used among the participants in leisure settings as we have seen in the other excerpts. Bashaar's use of the peer-related speech style, however, can be taken as an indication of Sufi having a different teacher status from the formal school teachers (with whom the participants reported to speak more 'integratedly', Madsen 2013a).

In excerpt 7a and 7b we see conflicting story lines emerge. Bashaar articulates an orientation to individual artist identity (or a "Diva" identity to use Bashaar's own term) that builds on a moral order of autonomy and values personal ambitions and rap skills. This clashes with the orientation articulated by Sufi to a group-member identity, building on a moral order of dependence and values of solidarity, joint efforts and investment in the common best result. The simultaneous presence of artistic and more society-building ambitions are also evident in Isaam's consideration in the 2014 interview. Here he describes developing rap talents as a primary motivation for building up a new rap association, and, as we saw in section 7, the ambitions for becoming successful artists play a significant part for the language practices of the rappers. At the same time Isaam explained that the location he was aiming for, for a new studio was an important consideration, as he hoped to connect youth from different areas of Amager to help resolve conflicts between different local neighborhoods. Although these are just a few examples from a case study there are good reasons to believe it illustrates a tension between different values and investments which is of more general relevance to discussions of social integration through participation in leisure activities and interest communities. I shall elaborate on this in the conclusion below.

9 Conclusion

In this chapter I have shown that educational achievements and skills of relevance to formal education are certainly central to the local rap community in focus of this case study. I have also shown that the participants in the rap activities attribute their educational ambitions to their involvement in this leisure activity. In this sense it seems that the participation in rap associations and the contact with rap mentors entail values corresponding to those assumed by political approaches to integration. In 2014, five years after we began our fieldwork, only Isaam is still actively involved in the rap music communities. Bashaar still has a keen interest in rap music, but does not participate in any organised rap activities. Mahmoud stopped his involvement with rap at the end of grade school, and he is no longer in regular contact with the others. Bashaar is in the beginning (a second attempt) and Isaam at the end of high school (or A-level) qualifications (Danish 'Gymnasium'). Hence, based on their educational trajectories so far Bashaar and, in particular, Isaam promise to be examples of what – within the dominant discourse of integration (as assimilation) – could be considered somewhat successfully integrated members of Danish society. They have been involved in interest communities and in addition gained support for educational ambitions through their rap activities.

However, I have demonstrated that this conception of integration does not capture what happens among participants in leisure associations. We have seen how personal artistic ambitions were central to the boys' engagement with their leisure interest. The interpersonal relationships among the participants in the rap music-making also implied hierarchical positioning based on rap skills. As was evident in the examples from the recording studio this rap-cultural orientation could conflict with ideologies of solidarity and community-belonging. In Giddens' (1984) definition social integration is the reciprocity of practices of autonomy and dependence. But the data I have discussed illustrate how the 'Diva' norms of autonomy in practice were hard to reconcile with the norms of group-membership and dependence. I have reported on parallel observations of the influence of interpersonal status hierarchies linked to competence in the context of a martial arts club (Madsen 2012, 2013c, 2015). In the martial arts club being good at competition fighting was significant to a central involvement in the club community, and this study of the young rappers confirms the importance of taking competence and competition into consideration. Dimensions of investment in the activities and interests as such on the one hand and investment in the interest community on the other are both relevant to participation in leisure associations and clubs. It is by no means impossible for participants in leisure activities to combine both orientations, but my case study points to problems with assuming that participants necessarily come to share values because they share an interest.

Finally, I have shown that Copenhagen adolescents employed indexical signs stereotypically associated with different cultural models (e.g. formal school marks and linguistic vernacular style) in peer interactions around rap and that these interactional practices can be seen as moments of social (micro) integration (Giddens 1984). However, the vernacular and hybrid linguistic practices were strongly reduced in public musical displays and productions. Taking Isaam's explanation into account this seems to relate partly to the influence of hegemonic language ideologies of standard and correctness. But the dominance of standard-linguistic practices in the rap productions was also related to adaptation to the

Danish majority population to achieve success as musicians. This standard adaptation indeed contrasts with global hip hop that is closely associated with African American Vernacular English to the extent that white or Asian hip hoppers adopt AAVE as part of their hip hop affiliation or performance (Cutler 1999). The case of this rap environment in Copenhagen is certainly different from the sociolinguistic studies of hip hop (Androutsopoulos and Scholz 2003; Pennycook 2007) and the work within the critical hip hop pedagogies (Hill 2009; Alim, Ibrahim, and Pennycook 2009) documenting hybrid and counter-hegemonic linguistic and literacy practices (see elaborate account in Stæhr and Madsen 2015). Linguistically this local rap community is not counter-hegemonic, and rather than bringing linguistic indexes of minority status and youth culture to the front stage, these young rappers assimilate to linguistic majority terms in search of success, intelligence, and a little Diva-ness.

Thomas Rørbeck Nørreby

Ethnic identifications in late modern Copenhagen

1 Introduction

```
Vidste du at over halvdelen af verdens befolkning ser op til Jamil
Perkersen Nielsen Rasmussen ;);););):)):)
```

<u>Eng trans:</u> *Did you know that over half of the world's population looks up to Jamil Perkersen Nielsen Rasmussen ;);););):)):)*

(Jamil's facebook profile, 12.09.11)

This Facebook update was produced by a young man named Jamil in the summer of 2011. At the time of the update Jamil is 17 years old and he lives in Copenhagen with his family who has a background as immigrants and has family ties in Palestine and Lebanon. Jamil's real surname is neither Rasmussen, Nielsen nor Perkersen. In a both subtle and creative way his status update brings about aspects of the societal conditions for a young man with minority background living in late modern Denmark. Nielsen and Rasmussen are very common Danish surnames and together they are shared by over 5 % of the Danish population (according to www.dst.dk). Perkersen is a construction building on the lexical item "perker", which roughly speaking is a Danish derogatory term for people with non-Western backgrounds, and the addition of the Danish surname suffix "-sen". Perkersen is thus not a "genuine" surname but (probably) created by Jamil for the occasion. By identifying himself as Jamil Perkersen Nielsen Rasmussen, Jamil presents himself as "a Dane" on the one side (Nielsen, Rasmussen), and an immigrant on the other (Perker(sen)), and thereby he illustrates the socio-cultural complexity of late modern Denmark by suggesting to inhabit a sort of Danish *and* non-Western joint ethnicity.

This example of complex identity formation emphasizes what many scholars have argued (and continue to argue); namely that the change many Western societies are going through both in terms of demographic composition and in terms of communication possibilities, should change the way we view, describe and understand social life in late modernity (e.g. Vertovec 2006, 2007; Baron 2008; Blommaert & Rampton 2011). One of the main arguments is that we need to replace the orderly model of multiculturalism as it does not suffice in dealing with a reality which is characterized by complexity, hybridity, mobility and change – a reality in which "belonging, loyalty and attachment are not parts of a zero-sum game based on a single nation-state and society" (Vertovec 2007: 5). The multiculturalism model that Vertovec argues is now an insufficient perspective on contemporary Western Europe's urban contexts, has for a long time dominated UK's political discourses and administration (Burton et. al. 2008, Vertovec 2010a). In Denmark, however, the multiculturalism discourse has only played a minor role e.g. in human rights arguments (Rennison 2009, also see Madsen this volume). Instead the far most dominant discourse projects an *ethnocentric* view on the nation of Denmark in which individuals that are not considered to be "real" Danes are treated as one more or less homogenous group. Within this discourse, categorisations such as "second generation immigrant", "person with another ethnic background" and "bilingual" are frequently used as means for drawing up this binary image of the population of Denmark – as divided into the Danes and the non-Danes. The following are examples of the use of some of these identity categories from three different news sources:

> Tosprogede halter efter etniske danskere i folkeskolen
> *Bilinguals lag behind ethnic Danes in the public schools*
>
> (Information 22.04.13)

> Det er mislykkedes folkeskolen at løfte tosprogede til et niveau, der er i nærheden af de danske elever
> *The public schools have failed to raise the bilinguals to a level that is close to the Danish students*
>
> (Politiken 01.04.11)

> 2. generations indvandrere lever meget mere som danskere end deres forældre gjorde, viser forskning
> *Research shows that 2nd generation immigrants' way of living resembles the Danes' way of living to a much higher extent than in the case of their parents*
>
> (www.dr.dk 13.09.13)

Whereas the category "second generation immigrant" occurs in many different contexts and incorporates a rather obvious element of ethnic relations pointing to people who have parents that were born outside the national borders of Denmark, the category "bilingual" is mostly seen in political discourses on education. It is used for dividing the school children of Denmark into two groups and thereby to imply the existence of various important socio-cultural differences between the groups. In this way, as an identity category "bilinguals" is actually given explanatory power and it is used to explain why some pupils perform poorly at school. Furthermore the division is so firmly embedded within debates about school and education in Denmark that it is usually (if not always) done without adding any sort of explanation as to what it is exactly that separates "the bilinguals" from "the (ethnic) Danish pupils". So, to judge from the categories alone, one can only say for sure that the bilinguals apparently are *not* ethnic Danes, which then indicates that the division is based on ethnic relations. A diachronic look at the use of the term bilinguals in public discourse in Denmark would reveal that this indication is not farfetched (see e.g. Karrebæk 2006). Since it was first introduced in an announcement from the Ministry of Education in 1996, bilingual as a term has gone through what could be characterized as a process of iconization (Irvine and Gal 2000). It has gone from being used to describe (all) schoolchildren in Denmark with other mother tongues than Danish to becoming more or less a symbol of ethnicity and (re)producing a binary discourse where having a non-Western background is both contrasted with having a "Danish" background and associated with being low in resources from a socio-cultural, socio-economic and linguistic perspective. Therefore the division of the schoolchildren in Denmark into at least those two groups could be seen as an example of a covert way of exercising discrimination. This is parallel to developments in other late modern, democratic societies where explicit racist discourses are no longer accepted in the public sphere (Blackledge 2005). Today the term bilingual shares the same indexical values and operates in the same paradigm as "second generation immigrant" and "person with another ethnic background". It has simply become a new word for non-Western ethnic minority in a binary image of Denmark's contemporary demography.

The ideological and political implications that could motivate such a division are reminiscent of the discourses of integration prevalent in many Western European countries (see Madsen this volume) and I claim in this chapter that this popular and firmly embedded way of grasping late modern demographic diversity (in Copenhagen) is both insufficient and inadequate. In fact it seems to provide us with far more questions than answers. For instance how do you position yourself in this image of reality if you were born in Denmark but by parents with non-Western backgrounds? What are the consequences for those pinpointed as bilinguals? And what about the possibility of one individual being both Danish and non-Danish? The aim of this chapter is to provide answers to these questions. Based on three years of fieldwork I investigate what role ethnicity plays in the social everyday of Jamil (the young man with the Facebook update) through interactional discourse analyses. My aim is to show how ethnicity is constructed and constituted through social action, to align with the growing awareness that newer approaches are needed to replace the insufficient model of multiculturalism (Blackledge and Creese 2010; Blommaert and Rampton 2011, Arnaut 2012) and thereby support my main argument; namely that in late modernity and despite of what is seen in most public discourse, it is perfectly possible for an individual to be both a Dane and a non-Dane[1].

2 Copenhagen in late modernity

Late modern society is characterized by human mobility. In globalization (Giddens 1991; Baumann 1998) people are presented with possibilities for moving and communicating over long distances with greater speed and they have become less tied to specific geographical places than what used to be the case even just 30 years ago. As a result of human mobility the demographic composition of our society is becoming more complex. The late modern city is inhabited by individuals with different cultural, political, religious, social and linguistic backgrounds and this is of great significance to our social everyday life. I refer to our society as late modern in accordance with the understanding of the concept presented by Giddens (1991) and Beck (1992) arguing that the societal changes we have witnessed for decades should not be seen as a resolution of the modern society but rather a development of the modern society.

Vertovec (2006, 2007a) coined the term *superdiversity* to describe the socio-cultural and socio-economic complexity globalization has brought about. We see superdiversity reflected in the city of Copenhagen when young people use a wide range of the resources at their disposal to challenge, investigate and rearrange traditional connections between language, country of origin and ethnicity (Møller forthcoming). Jamil's status update, as presented in the introduction, could be seen as an example of just that. Superdiversity complicates the understanding of people as organized in so-called ethnic groups and makes it inexpedient to assume that individuals who share national backgrounds also share values and norms and act in similar ways. However, despite the societal changes there are still strong tendencies in educational, public and academic discourse to treat ethnicity as a stable, natural and intrinsically meaningful phenomenon; to take the existence of bounded groups associated with one ethnicity as a given (Brubaker 2004); and to treat ethnicity as a key explanatory category. This prevalent understanding of ethnicity and ethnic groups fails to grasp that among the members of these (imagined) communities (Anderson 1991) we find a number of differences in terms of migration processes, social positions, religious beliefs, linguistic, cultural and educational capital, and all of these factors influence the social profiles of each individual member. This leaves the overall category of ethnicity with

1 This chapter is based on the work previously presented in: Nørreby (2012)

poor (if any) explanatory power in itself. In this regard it is important to view the concept of superdiversity in light of the national romanticist ideologies of homogeneity that have characterized the western modern society for decades and to some extent still do (as illustrated in the introduction). Therefore I refer to our society as *late* modern.

Jamil lives in an area of Copenhagen with a relatively high number of families who immigrated to Denmark from the 1970's and onward (around 30 % according to the statistical information available at www.dst.dk). It used to be a traditional working class area, but it is now very socially, culturally and ethnically diverse. The general diversity of the area is reflected overall at the school in which Jamil in 2010–2011 attends 9th grade; in the school's two 9th grade classes, respectively 75 and 82 % pupils have family backgrounds outside of Denmark, and Arabic, Urdu, Danish, Punjabi, Croatian, Icelandic and Russian (to name a few) are among the pupils' self-reported mother tongues (Møller and Jørgensen 2013). If we weigh in the technological developments of communication possibilities (e.g. the internet) the societal conditions in Copenhagen can be characterized as being superdiverse, entailing a lack of predictability with regard to the relations between language, religion, family background and country of origin, etc. In superdiversity new layers are added to difference in the sense that when we talk about "a 17 year old Copenhagen boy" today we are not able to predict or know, much if anything, about him purely on the basis of this information. We are not able to predict what "languages" he speaks or is acquainted with, where his family comes from, which cultural and religious values he affiliates with (if any), what his interests are, etc. In today's societal settings these relations are empirical questions that call for ethnographic research on a micro-level rather than preliminary research conditions. According to Blommaert and Rampton (2011) these recent developments have changed the task for sociolinguistic research:

> [...] research instead has to address the ways in which people take on different linguistic forms as they align and disaffiliate with different groups at different moments and stages. It has to investigate how they (try to) opt in and opt out, how they perform or play with linguistic signs of group belonging, and how they develop particular trajectories of group identification throughout their lives. (Blommaert and Rampton 2011: 5)

3 Identity practices

I align with these notions presented by Blommaert and Rampton (2011) of how to investigate late modern social reality and I base my study on the assumption that macro-level sociolinguistic developments cannot be understood without engagement with micro-level language use in interaction (Agha 2005b; Rampton 2006). The effects of globalization processes are seen on both a macro- and a micro-level so in order for us to be able to address and investigate the ways in which people use the resources at their disposal to grasp, organize and change the contemporary world we need methodological tools and dynamic concepts that can sufficiently encapsulate connections between language on a micro-level and social structure on a macro-level. Linguistic ethnography (Rampton et al. 2004; Creese 2008) is well suited as a method for this (see introduction, this volume). Blommaert's (2005) theoretical work on discourse and identity is characterized by the same dynamics. Blommaert argues that identity is something we constantly construct, negotiate and ascribe to each other through interaction and he proposes that we see identity as "[...] *particular forms of semiotic potential, organised in a repertoire*." (Blommaert 2005: 207, italics in the original). Blommaert uses the term *repertoire* to illustrate how we, as social beings, are able to draw on different identity features in given situations of communication, and that it is possible for us to take on/claim different identities when we engage in semiotic activities. However, identities should not be seen as being individually produced or as results of something that was already there. Agha (2007a) argues that identities are not only constructed by the individual, they are also ascribed to the individual by others: "[...] when one's self-conception (or rather, a given time bound version of it) becomes fixed or definite for a while, it is only relevant to social life insofar as it is perceivable by others." (Agha 2007a: 233–234). In order for an identity to become valid, and to be ascribed, some kind of recognition or approval by others is required. Identities should thus be understood as inter-subjectively produced; hence something that are brought about in interaction. This means that some identity markers and identity ascriptions are (made) more relevant and valid in some situations than in others, for cultural, social or contextual reasons (Blommaert 2005: 206). Locally valid identity features or markers are not just transferable to new contexts as their indexical meanings (may) vary from one context to another. Furthermore, people are not free to construct any identity they want or could imagine, as there are restrictions to their legitimate access to semiotic potential.

I treat identity as a social categorization resource. This means that the analytical focus is *practice*, that is, contextualized social, semiotic and linguistic acts. I do not intend to describe identities as situated achievements of one or another social role; rather I seek to gain my insights through the study (of processes) of identification (Brubaker & Cooper 2000, Madsen 2015). Dealing with identities as expressions of action instead of as inherent qualities allows us to gain new understandings of concepts such as ethnicity, ethnic group(s), and nationality. If we accept the premise that e.g ethnicity and nationality are constructed through semiotic activity then an investigation of the concepts must necessarily involve an investigation of semiotic activity.

4 Ethnicity

In my approach to the concept of ethnicity I draw on the work of Brubaker (2004) who describes ethnicity as a social psychological phenomenon that is used by individuals to perceive, interpret and represent the social world. Ethnicity is a social construct i.e. a perspective on the world which basically means that it is something we should seek to explain and not something we can use to explain thing *with* (Brubaker 2004: 9). By approaching ethnicities as socio-cultural (and political) *interpretations located in practice* I am able to study how ethnicity is constructed, negotiated and ascribed through social action in a specific situated time and space. This allows me to break with the macro-discursive understanding of ethnicity as "something you have" and to look at *ethnicization* instead, that is, ethnicity as a political, social, cultural and psychological process (Brubaker 2004: 11). This approach can be used to point out an interesting perspective with regard to the ethnocentric discourse in Denmark that was outlined in the introduction to this chapter. On the one hand, the discourse ethnicisizes in a way that ethnic minority (being non-Danish) is made relevant for all sorts of things (like when it is used to explain academic achievements in school) while at the same time it abolishes ethnic groupings and differences between different minorities to a high degree. As already mentioned I find that the discourse represents a rather problematic and inadequate view on the contemporary Danish society. Nevertheless it is interesting to see how all this comes into play in the social everyday life of Jamil.

Before moving on to the analyses, though, I wish to make a final claim of analytical importance; namely that cultural interpretations that involve ethnicity always build on a (perceived) connection/a sense of belonging based on historical conditions, i.e ancestry or so-called "roots". In this perspective my definition of ethnicity is inspired by Edwards who characterizes ethnic identity as:

> [...] allegiance to a group – large or small, socially dominant or subordinate – with which one has ancestral links. There is no necessity for a continuation, over generations, of the same socialization or cultural patterns, but some sense of a group boundary must persist. This can be sustained by shared objective characteristics (language, religion, etc.), or by more subjective contributions to a sense of 'groupness', or by some combination of both. (Edwards 1995: 128)

Ethnicities are collective social identifications that are connected to historical backgrounds in one way or another. However, the connection can be based purely on a *perceived* sense of an ancestral background. Whether the connection is perceived or "real" is not important; it is however essential that the social identification is anchored in a sense of belonging. Another important point about ethnicization as a social practice is that "[...] categories such as [...] ethnicity, nation [...] identity [...] language or power must be understood as contingent, shifting and produced in the particular, rather than having some prior ontological status." (Pennycook 2007: 39). Thus, when Jamil for instance performs Lebanese or Palestinian ethnic identifications in Denmark he at the same time adds new meaning to these ethnic categories.

In the case of Jamil's ethnicity practices there exists a constant dialectic relation between the (in lack of better words) "global" and the "local" which I argue is not only characteristic of the concept of ethnicity in late modernity but more generally of the superdiverse environments that shape Jamil's everyday life. Ethnicities are constructed through the use of semiotic resources in processes of identification and they do not just 'tag along' when individuals move through country- and continent territories; the travel of resources from one context to another has consequences for the associated indexical meanings and values. Ethnicities can be transnational and transcultural, and like other transnational and transcultural products ethnicities that from a national perspective "come from the outside" are reshaped and added new meaning when they are (re)constituted and (re)produced in "new" contexts (Connel and Gibson 2003: 191). When Jamil for instance uses his ancestral background as Palestinian as an identity marker, it is insufficient to characterize these practices as merely expressions of a Diaspora link. Jamil was born and raised in Denmark so when he self-identifies as a Palestinian in Denmark, he at the same time re-contextualizes the ethnic identity category "Palestinian". Furthermore Jamil is part of – and in contact with – many different social and cultural trails in the superdiverse environments he experiences during a typical everyday, and ethnic identifications such as Dane, Palestinian and Lebanese are never unambiguous. As I intend to show they are multifaceted, dynamic and complex identifications and they are used in different ways and for different purposes.

5 "Local" affiliations and alignments

During my ethnographic fieldwork I followed Jamil closely both in- and outside the school in the attempt to cover his everyday communicative encounters comprehensively. This allowed me to collect a large set of data. The data include: self-recordings where Jamil is wearing an mp3-recorder on his shirt or jacket while in school or while spending time with friends in his neighborhood; one-to-one interviews in which Jamil and I talk about his social everyday life; and finally various Facebook activities that I was able to gain access to through a Facebook friendship between Jamil and our research group (see Stæhr this volume). I have divided my analyses into two sections; the first focuses on situations in which Jamil performs different identifications related to Danishness while the second deals with situations in which Jamil performs different non-Danish identifications using his ancestral background as Lebanese and Palestinian as identity markers.

The first example is taken from the wall of Jamil's Facebook profile. It relates to a practice that was common for the pupils in Jamil's class during the last year of school. It involved sending various questions regarding different topics to friends on Facebook. One then answered by either picking one of the proposed answers or by adding a new possible answer. When a new possible answer was added it was then included below the question when forwarded to another Facebook user. Sometimes the pupils composed the questions themselves, and sometimes the questions were composed by other Facebook users. This practice was usually carried out in a jocular and non-serious manner which was typically reflected in the possible answers.

In this first example Jamil is presented with a question which brings associations to Billig's (1995) *banal nationalism*. With the feet firmly planted in "the nation of Denmark" a random Facebook user poses a question and lines up three different possible answers: You can either choose to be a Dane, a foreigner or a mix of the two.

Jamil besvarede spørgsmålet Er du Dansker, udlænding eller et mix?:P med Dansker.

Eng trans: Jamil answered the question "Are you a Dane, a foreigner or a mix?" with A Dane

(Jamil's facebook profile, 12.09.11)

As we can see Jamil has chosen to answer the question by explicitly categorizing himself as a Dane. Through his answer he presents himself for everyone (or at least those who are members of Facebook) as closely affiliated with Denmark. In this particular case I do not know who started the survey and made up the specific categories; neither do I know if Jamil knows this. It is also impossible to say anything about who Jamil is directing his response at. His choice of "A Dane" is nevertheless interesting as it constitutes an example of Jamil using semiotic resources at his disposal (in this case a question that is sent around on Facebook) to perform an ethnic identification; in this specific situated time and space as a Dane.

The next example is an excerpt from one of two interviews that I conducted with Jamil during my fieldwork. Both interviews were conducted at the university, and both times only Jamil and I were present. The theme of the interviews was his social everyday life. This chapter will present excerpts from both interviews in which Jamil tells many stories. Obviously I am in no position to know if all he tells is true, if it is made up, or a combination. Luckily neither of this is of analytical importance since I am purely interested in Jamil's perspective on the world, i.e. in Jamil's constructions of a lived reality. So whether or not things went on exactly like Jamil says they did, does not change my analyses.

In the following Jamil tells me that he is going to Lebanon in the summer to visit his family. Then he starts going through some of his previous experiences from Lebanon.

Gas-like air

Jamil:	øh deres luft derhenne den	*eh their air over there it*
	er sådan øh forurenet du	*is like eh polluted you*
	trækker ikke sådan	*don't breathe in like*
	normal luft som her i	*normal air like here in*
	Danmark du trækker ben-	*Denmark you breathe*
	zinluft agtig ((griner))	*gas air like ((laughs))*
	[Thomas: ((griner))] lige	*[Thomas: ((laughs))] right*
	da sådan lige da de åbnede	*when they like opened the*
	flyet så kan jeg bare mærke	*plane then I can just just*
	xxx damen ved siden af mig	*feel xxx the lady next to me*
	hun siger på arabisk sådan	*she says in Arabic like*
	jeg oversætter lige på	*I am just translating into*
	dansk orh hvor jeg elsker	*Danish oh how I love eh the*
	dog øh Libanons øh duft jeg	*scent eh of Lebanon I*
	sagde til hende sådan der	*said to her like this*
	øh er du mærkelig sådan på	*eh are you strange in*
	arabisk øh kalder du det	*Arabic eh do you call that*
	der for ren luft sådan der	*clean air like that*
	hun sagde sådan ren luft	*she said like clean air*
	kalder du det der for ren	*do you call that clean*

21		luft den er mere foru-	*air it is more polluted*
22		renet end øh jeg [skider	*than eh when I [take a*
23		på toilettet ((griner))]	*dump at the loo ((laughs))]*
24	Thomas:	[((griner))]	*[((laughs))]*
25	Jamil:	jeg kunne slet ikke holde	*I really couldn't bare it*
26		det ud	

In his story Jamil tells about the difference between the air in Denmark and the air in Lebanon. “You don’t breathe in normal air like here in Denmark” (lines 2–4) he says, referring to the air in Lebanon which he also calls “polluted” (lines 2 & 21). By asking the woman on the plane if she is strange (line 16), Jamil expresses very clearly that he does not understand how she can actually like the Lebanese air. Jamil furthermore says that the woman refers to the Lebanese air as being clean (line 19) which he also has a hard time understanding. This is evident when he refers to the air in Lebanon as “gas-like” (line 6) and with his statement that the air in Lebanon is more polluted than when he takes a dump (lines 21–23). I interpret his toilet remark as an overstatement with a humoristic effect which is illustrated by our shared laughter. Nevertheless it is still a critical evaluation of the woman’s view on the Lebanese air.

Throughout the entire excerpt Jamil positions himself as an outsider in relation to Lebanon. He says “over there” (line 1) and he talks about “their air” (line 1). With these remarks he expresses a disassociation with Lebanon whereas when he talks about Denmark he expresses the opposite, that is, closeness, e.g., in utterances such as “here in Denmark” (line 4). In the utterance “their air” Jamil depicts a community of Lebanese people that does not include himself, thereby creating an opposition between “me” and “them”. He expresses an attitude towards some societal phenomena in Lebanon by comparing them to conditions in Denmark and positions himself as someone who regards Denmark as the normal state of affairs.

It is very likely that the story Jamil tells in this excerpt is influenced by my presence as the interviewer and the fact that Jamil regards me as “a Dane” (he has categorized me as a Dane on several occasions throughout the years). In any case, the “Danishness” that Jamil draws on in this excerpt is inter-subjectively produced in the situation by him positioning himself in relation to me as a white Danish interviewer and researcher.

The section’s last excerpt is from a self-recording in a suburb to Copenhagen. In the excerpt I am having lunch with Jamil and seven other participants. I am at one end of the table while Jamil, who is wearing a recorder, is at the other end. A boy from Jamil’s class has just told about the food habits of the English, and this leads to Isaam telling us about food habits in Lebanon. Isaam’s parents came to

Denmark from Palestine and Lebanon before he was born, just like Jamil's, so Isaam also has family in Lebanon that he visits.

Dogs and hyenas

01	Isaam:	i Libanon ik der spiser de	*in Lebanon right they eat*
02		chips i stedet for pommes	*crisps instead of French*
03		frites	*fries*
04	Thomas:	mmh	*mmh*
05	Isaam:	de er hunde så tager de	*they are dogs then they take*
06		xxx ((latter og larm))	*xxx ((laughter and noice))*
		(5.0)	*(5.0)*
07	Jamil:	de er hyæner dernede	*they are hyenas down there*

Because of all the noise and the fact that they all speak at once I cannot tell what Isaam is saying after "they take" (line 5) but I know from my field notes that he gives an explanation of why he describes the Lebanese people as dogs. After the explanation there is a short break, and subsequently Jamil calls the Lebanese people hyenas. Both Isaam and Jamil perform their ascriptions of the Lebanese people on the basis of what they perceive to be Lebanese food habits. In line 1–3 we see how Isaam says that the Lebanese eat crisps "instead of" French fries and he uses this comparison between the Lebanese food habits and his own as the reason for the ascriptions. My view is that when he says the "instead of" he refers to the fact that the Lebanese eat crisps where he "ordinarily" would eat French fries. I view Jamil's utterance in line 7 where he calls the Lebanese people "hyenas" as a sign of him sharing Isaam's view on the Lebanese's food habits as being different and odd. Therefore the excerpt could be interpreted as an example of the two boys constructing Denmark as home and "the norm" by focusing on what they experience as alien or deviant in their stories about their Diasporas. This particular practice has been observed in other studies on ethnicity (e.g. Harris 2006, Stæhr 2010) with conclusions similar to mine. Both Isaam and Jamil refer to the Lebanese people as "they" and thereby make a distinction between themselves and the Lebanese people. They both articulate a dissociation to these people (and their food habits) and in line 7 Jamil enhances this impression as he uses the expression "down there". This illustrates an alienation, a dissociation and a distance to Lebanon and to the Lebanese people.

In the three excerpts of this section Jamil performs different identifications that are all in one way or another anchored in Danish relationships. He does so by employing different semiotic resources: Through a questionnaire on Facebook he includes himself in the collective social identity category of Danes. He uses the air in Denmark as a resource for disassociating himself with Lebanon and the societal conditions “over there” while at the same time constructing Denmark as “home” or as “the norm”. Finally Jamil, and Isaam deploy food for making fun of the Lebanese people and their habits while at the same time performing a dis-identification with Lebanon. Jamil simply exploits the semiotic resources made available to him by the surroundings to perform different identifications in order to present and position himself in what he finds to be situationally satisfactory and appropriate ways. The next section will focus on situations in which Jamil performs ethnic identifications by drawing on positive alignments and affiliations with Diasporas in Palestine and Lebanon.

6 “Diasporic” affiliations and alignments

The first example of this section, the text box below, is taken from Jamil’s Facebook profile. Here he has participated in a survey where one picks one’s five favorite countries.

Pick your 5: My Favourite 5 Countries !

Jamil picked:

1: Palestine

2: palestine

3: palestine

4: palestine

5: Palestine 4 us

(Jamil’s facebook profile, 21.08.10)

English in the original

I know that this question box was sent to Jamil by Isaam who has a similar family background to Jamil, as already mentioned. Isaam has chosen Palestine five times and it is likely that this has influenced Jamil’s choices. As we can see Jamil has chosen Palestine as his five favorite countries – or to be exact he has chosen “Palestine” four times and then “Palestine 4 us” once. The last choice is interesting. “4 us” means “for us” and “Palestine 4 us” thus draws on the construction of a community with which Jamil demonstrates affiliation and aligns with by choosing this answer. I imagine that the specific formulation probably is to be understood as referring to Palestine's battle for independence, and it appears that Jamil is positioning himself as a supporter of this battle. So what we see is that Jamil uses semiotic resources, provided to him by Facebook, in order to construct himself as a member of a group/community with which he shares ancestral links (Edwards 1995). In doing so he performs an identification that draws traces to a Diaspora of Palestinians while at the same time aligning with his friend Isaam.

The next excerpt is taken from an interview with Jamil that I conducted in the summer of 2011. In the excerpt we talk about Jamil's take on the different subjects in school as well as about the different teachers.

Dishonest grades

Thomas:	hvad med øh hvem har I	*what about eh who else is*
	mere	*there*
Jamil:	[øh]	*[eh]*
Thomas:	[xxx] Inger	*[xxx] Inger*
Jamil:	[ja i ((fagets navn))]	*[yes in ((the class topic))]*
Thomas:	[kan du lide ((faget))]	*[do you like ((that class))]*
Jamil:	hun begynder sådan være	*she is becoming a little*
	sådan lidt jeg ved det ikke	*like I don't know*
	sådan før der var hun sådan	*like she used to be*
	mere ærlig	*more honest*
Thomas:	ja	*yes*
Jamil:	nu sådan i karakterer og	*now like with grades and*
	sådan noget	*stuff*
	jeg lægger mærke til sådan	*I notice that like*
	xxx sådan at hun giver	*xxx she gives out like*
	sådan mere til dem der bor	*higher grades to those who*
	her i Danmark de der dan-	*live here in Denmark those*
	skere og sådan hun giver	*Danes and like she gives*
	mere til dem og så dem	*more to them and then guys*
	sådan øh ja ligesom mig	*like eh yeah like me*
	jeg synes jeg betaler xxx	*I think I pay the price xxx*
	hun giver mig 4 4 og jeg	*she gives me 4 4 and I think*
	synes sådan jeg fortjener	*like I deserve*
	sådan 7 7 eller 7 4	*like 7 7 or 7 4*
	synes jeg	*I think*

In the excerpt Jamils explicitly divides the pupils in his class into two groups positioning himself on the one side and "the Danes" on the other. He mentions one of his teachers, Inger, who allegedly gives grades on the basis of what appears to be a sort of ethnic favoritism. According to Jamil she favors "those who live here in Denmark", "those Danes" (lines 16–18) while "guys (...) like me [Jamil]" (lines 19–20) pay the price by receiving lower – and unfair – grades. It is interesting that Jamil uses the term "honest" (line 10). A possible interpretation of "honest" is that he questions Inger's way of grading the pupils as well as the moral basis of it. If he had just described it as unjust, he would merely have indicated that he and Inger disagreed about the value of his academic efforts. However, "honest" appears as a stronger word as it implies that Inger is aware that Jamil deserves a better grade. Thereby Jamil's utterance works as a personal attack on Inger drawing up an image in which he is being deliberately disadvantaged. This positioning of himself, his fellow pupils and his teacher are central in his story which draws interesting parallels to the widespread macro-discursive image of Danish late modern classrooms (as outlined in the introduction to this chapter). I elaborate on this in the following.

Jamil uses another interesting wording in his explicit division of the pupils into those that Inger favors and those that are disfavored (the group to which he belongs). He characterizes the first group that is favored as "those who live here in Denmark" and "those Danes". By saying "those who live here in Denmark" Jamil performs a somehow paradoxical categorization. He refers to the group as "those guys" and thereby indicates that he is not a part of the group. He further characterizes "those guys" as living "here in Denmark". This is where it gets paradoxical. Jamil seems to speak from a perspective of living in Denmark but at the same time this is put forward as the one feature that separates him from "those guys". A possible interpretation of "those Danes" is that it functions as a self-correction relating to the previous utterance "those who live here in Denmark". Jamil's self-correction indicates that he is on shaky ground; in fact it could even be seen as reflecting the dubious character of the division altogether i.e. the difference between the "ethnic Danish" pupils and the pupils like Jamil who both has an Arabic family background, dark skin *and* was in born and raised in Denmark. Maybe this is why Jamil is having a hard time explaining who exactly constitute one group and who constitute the other. It could be argued that Jamil is actually drawing on the macro-discursive image of the contemporary Danish classroom in which "the Danes" are privileged and "the guys like Jamil" (the bilinguals) are not. As described in the introduction this image is very present in Danish public discourse and it seems that Jamil is using this image to position himself as mistreated and unprivileged while at the same time protesting against the unfairness involved in the division. So, apart from being one more example of Jamil using ethnicity as a resource in his identity work, the excerpt also shows that Jamil is aware of the macro-discursive image of social stratification in the Danish classroom.

The next example was taken from Jamil's facebook profile. Here he is asked by a random Facebook user to state who he thinks "is running the show" here in Denmark.

Jamil besvarede spørgsmålet Hvem styre her i dk ? med Palæstinenser

Mulige svar: palæstinenser, *styrer;), Mjølnerparken Styrer Lortet!, Mig! :D, Flot stavet!, 96'erne styrer sgu det hele!, Dansker, Årgang 95!!, Min mormors rolator bande!, MIG! :D

Jamil answered the question "Who runs the show here in DK?" with Palestinian

*Possible answers: Palestinian; *runs the show;); Mjølnerparken runs the got damn show!; Me! :D; Nice spelling!; The 96'ers is running the whole show!; Dane; class of 65!!; my grandmom's rollator gang!; ME! :D*

(Jamil's facebook profile, 20.06.11)

In this example both the question and the answer that Jamil gives are interesting. The formulation of the question includes a "here in dk". "Dk" means Denmark and the indexical adverb "here" suggests that the person asking the question is living or at least situated in Denmark and that the question addresses people who also live or find themselves (here) in Denmark. Bearing this in mind and adding the fact that Jamil's answer is "Palestinian", the Facebook update exemplifies identity formation in which Jamil identifies himself as a Palestinian (here) in Denmark. By doing so Jamil simultaneously draws on affiliations with Denmark and with the collective social identity category "Palestinians". The last excerpt of this chapter is a somewhat similar example. It comes from an interview in which Jamil tells about his work at the Danish supermarket Kvickly.

The only perker in Kvickly

01	Jamil:	jeg har lagt mærke til der	*I have noticed there are*
02		er nogle (1.0) sådan vi har	*some (1.0) like we have*
03		Amager og sådan nogle ting	*Amager and stuff like that*
04		så de andre så nogle af	*then the others then some of*
05		dem det har jeg set der	*them this I have seen who*
06		slet ikke sådan kender til	*does not at all like*

	det der jeg kender nogle	*know that stuff I know some*
	der bor øh sådan tæt ved	*people who live eh close to*
	Strandvejen derhenne	*Strandvejen over there*
	de kender slet ikke til det	*they do not at all know that*
	der ordet eow (!!) og sådan	*word eow (!!) and stuff like*
	noget da jeg arbejdede i	*that when I was working at*
	Kvickly der var jeg sådan	*Kvickly I was like the only*
	den eneste perker derhenne	*perker over there*
	i Kvickly (1.0) så da jeg	*at Kvickly (1.0) so when I*
	sagde sådan eow (!!) sådan	*said like eow (!!) like get*
	kom lige her og sådan	*over here and stuff like*
	noget hvad sker der *bree*	*that what's up bree*
	og sådan noget de forstod	*and stuff like that they did*
	slet ikke (!!)	*not at all understand (!!)*
	hvad jeg sagde jeg begyndte	*what I was saying I just*
	bare at lære dem alle de	*started teaching them all*
	der ord så nogle af dem de	*those words then some of*
	begyndte sådan lidt fortæl	*them they started like tell*
	det sådan sige det	*us they started saying it*
	lidt og sådan noget de kan	*a bit and stuff like that*
	slet ikke [det der]	*they can't do [it]*
Thomas:	[ja] nå de kendte det slet	*[yes] oh so they did not*
	ikke	*recognize it*
Jamil:	det er første gang	*it is the first time that*
	de hører det i	*they here this in*
	hele deres liv	*their entire lives*
Thomas:	nå okay	*oh okay*
Jamil:	de har aldrig hørt noget	*they have never heard any-*
	lignende	*thing like it*
Thomas:	nå hvordan kan det være	*oh okay how come that is*
Jamil:	jeg ved det ikke	*I don't know*
Thomas:	de xxx de kommer fra en	*they xxx they come from*
	anden xxx øh et andet	*another xxx eh another area*
	område måske [eller hvad]	*maybe [or what]*
Jamil:	[ja] også det er fordi de	*[yes] also because they*
	ikke er sammen med sådan	*don't hang out with like*
	nogle indvandrere de er kun	*immigrants they only hang*
	sammen med danskere	*out with Danes*

((eow, Kurdish origin = hey you)); ((bree, American origin = bro))

Jamil makes use of several identity categories in his story about his job experiences in Kvickly. He mentions the perker category (line 14) as he identifies himself explicitly as the only perker in Kvickly. He also introduces an immigrant category when he draws parallels between knowing words like "eow" and "bree" and hanging out with immigrants (lines 41–44). "Eow" is traditionally associated with Kurdish and it means something in line with "hey you!" ; "bree" is a variation of the American slang term "bro". Both "bro" and "bree" are typically associated by the participants with masculine urban youth environments where especially boys refer to each other as "brees" or "bros" to express affection and friendship. In the excerpt Jamil ascribes similar values to "eow" and "bree". He is drawing a clear line between the knowledge and use of specific linguistic resources and the specific ethnic identity categories "Dane", "perker" and "immigrant" exemplifying Gumperz' (2003: 110) claim that only few linguistic features are necessary in order to emphasize or index wide social connotations of different ways of speaking. Jamil never talks explicitly about his colleagues belonging to the Dane category but he does mention that they only hang out with Danes (line 43–44). He also talks about some people who live close to Strandvejen (line 6) in reference to Amager Strandvej (I asked him about this) and he draws parallels between them and his colleagues when he tells that none of them understands "eow" and "bree" (lines 19–21). By using these categories in his story Jamil positions himself as one who is different from his colleagues as they only hang out with Danes, as well as from those who live close to Strandvejen. At the same time he constructs oppositions with himself, the perker and the immigrant on one side, and the Dane on the other. He draws on this division in lines 2–3 where he says "we have Amager". This utterance is interesting from an ethnicity perspective because it plays on a link between individuals and territorial relationships. With the utterance Jamil constructs himself as a member of a group or community that claims what could be interpreted as a sort of ownership of this specific part of Copenhagen and after the remark about Amager he marks an important dichotomy when he mentions Strandvejen. Strandvejen is generally associated with wealth and "poshness" and this seems to play a significant part in Jamil's identification.

His division is based on several aspects. First of all it is based on whether or not a person has access to – or knowledge of – the words "eow" and "bree". Second it is based on the more explicit ascriptions "perker" and "immigrant" versus "people who only hang out with Danes". Finally it is constructed through the mentioning of the two places Amager and Strandvejen. On the basis of these facts it is evident that Jamil's story takes place in a very local territorial universe (Amager Strandvej is a 10 minutes' walk from where Jamil lives). So it is not Jamil's family's ancestral background, as immigrants from Palestine and Lebanon, that separates Jamil from the Danes and those who live close to Strandvejen; it is his background as an immigrant or "a foreigner" from a certain part of Amager as well as his knowledge of specific words carrying a certain "street smartness" value – which is then contrasted with the poshness of Strandvejen. Furthermore it is important to take note of the fact that neither "eow" nor "bree" is associated with Arabic. So in spite of using as self-identification an ethnicity aspect that separates him from the Danes and which draws parallels to his ancestral background as immigrants, Jamil is not drawing on a clear unambiguous Diaspora connection in the traditional sense. On the contrary it seems as if he constructs an ethnicity which he associates with a perker identity, one who belongs to a certain part of Amager and one who knows and has access to linguistics resources such as "eow" and "bree". In this way it seems that Jamil is drawing on both local and Diasporic relations in his story to position himself both locally – at Amager – and in relation to a macro-discursive image of late modern Denmark.

7 Concluding remarks

In this chapter I have shown how a young man living in contemporary Copenhagen positions himself in relation to specific ethnicities and how he brings into play aspects of belonging in his identity work. In his everyday social life Jamil is drawing on affiliations with Denmark, Lebanon and Palestine, and he is able to do so by employing a wide range of different semiotic resources. These resources are made available through, e.g. his family background, his being a part of a youth cultural environment (as well as *not* being part of another) at a certain part of Amager and Facebook. His ethnicity practices can be characterized as multifaceted in that he performs different ethnic identifications in different situations, in accordance with how he wishes to present or position himself in any given situation. This should not be understood, however, as a claim that Jamil "has" three ethnicities that he is able to draw on. As the analyses show, Jamil uses affiliations to for instance Palestine in his identity work in a number of ways. The Palestinian identifications furthermore contain different territorial anchorings. Even though they are connected to the same collective social identity category, namely Palestinians, they can both be anchored in Palestine (p. 211) and in Denmark (p. 214). Jamil will also, at times and if fitting, perform ethnic identifications and position himself in a perceived minority-majority dichotomy and thereby to some extent re-contextualize an image based in the ethnocentric discourse of school demography that is omnipresent in the Danish media. The overall image of Jamil's identifications is that he continuously re-contextualizes the different ethnic identity categories that he employs by linking them to very local settings at Amager as well as to larger social and cultural discourses and societal contexts.

Burton et. al. (2008) and Vertovec (2010a) claim that social and ethnic classification is a major problem for public institutions under current conditions of globalization, and the data and analyses presented in this chapter support this claim. Late modern cities like Copenhagen are characterized by diversity and the old binaries minority/majority, migrant/host etc. simply can no longer account for the divisions and alignments emerging in contemporary urban environments. They completely fail to account for individuals like Jamil whose self-image and social positionings clearly exceed the essentialistic and simplistic image of late modern reality which is presented daily in the Danish media. On the basis of these observations I align with the claims that we need new approaches to replace the orderly and inadequate model of multiculturalism (Blackledge and Creese 2010, Blommaert and Rampton 2011, Arnaut 2012) in order to obtain a comprehensive understanding of late modern social realities. Popular and prevalent efforts to outline and grasp diversity among youth in Denmark by dividing them into identity categories of bilinguals and ethnic Danes completely ignore the fact that the members of these "groups" differ in terms of migration processes, social positions, religious beliefs, linguistic, cultural and educational capital, etc., and all of these factors influence the social profiles of each individual. This leaves the traditionally used categories with poor (if any) explanatory power in themselves. This needs to be acknowledged and taken into account in order for us to be able to talk about cultural or ethnic diversity in a meaningful way under the conditions of demographic and socio-cultural (super)diversity. Only then can we start to consider the pedagogical and socio-political implications of the global flow of people and language that is characterizing today's societies and as a result qualify and nuance discussions about integration and the educational challenges of late modernity.

I certainly do not claim that my representation of Jamil's lived reality at Amager provides the reader with a complete insight into what it means to be a young man with minority background in late modern Copenhagen. I hope, however, to have shown that under today's societal conditions, grasping the meaning and significance of ethnicity requires a theoretical understanding of ethnicity as a social categorization process. And perhaps even more importantly, learning about what it means to be a young man in late modern Copenhagen requires empirical investigation. Clearly Jamil is not just a bilingual, he is not just non-Danish, and neither is he just Danish; Jamil Perkersen Nielsen Rasmussen is all of the above (and more).

Janus Spindler Møller

Discursive reactions to nationalism among adolescents in Copenhagen

1 Introduction

In Denmark a strong discourse circulates that constructs Danes with an ethnic minority background as persons who need to “integrate” where “integrate” means adjusting to the norms and expectations of majority Danes (Jaffe-Walter 2013, Møller forthcoming A & B, Madsen this volume). This understanding of integration is of course only one aspect of a complex debate (Madsen this volume), but it has been influential in political and public debates for several decades (Rennison 2009, Yilmaz 2006). It is spearheaded by nationalist politicians with the Danish People’s Party as one of the main exponents. The party is known for an anti-immigrant policy and for articulating strict demands for adaption aimed at immigrants and their descendants living in Denmark. This is illustrated in the following quote from the party’s former leader:

> If the Danish welfare society is to last economically, socially and without a risk of breaking down because of massive crime, the key is that we place demands on and have the courage to continue to place demands on immigrants and their descendants (Pia Kjærsgård’s weekly newsletter, 5th of February 2007, my translation)

In the quote “immigrants and their descendants” are constructed as a threat for society and therefore they need to “integrate” or, as Pia Kjærsgård formulates it, fulfill certain “demands” from a “we” which are opposed to the immigrants or their descendants who does not fulfill the demands. Being one of the founders and the leader of the party from 1995 to 2012 Pia Kjærsgård projected the party’s public image to a high degree. She is an iconic figure in Danish politics in a similar way to Le Pen in France and Geert Wilders in Holland, and the participants in our study often refer directly to her.

As this chapter will show the adolescents in our study are familiar with the nationalist discourse represented by Pia Kjærsgård. Especially the participants with an ethnic minority background experience to be targeted in the debates about immigration and integration and it is a subject that they are generally interested in. This was reflected in the subjects that the students chose during their obligatory project week in the 9th grade. Many of the student-groups chose to work on topics that more or less directly involved immigrants, ethnic minorities, etc. A group consisting of two boys chose the theme "New-Danes" and explained why in the introduction to their final report:

> In this project we have chosen the topic "New-Danes". This is a subject that pre-occupies the population a lot. We are interested in the subject, because we are New-Danes ourselves and therefore we have to relate to it constantly (Isaam & Bashaar, project week 2011, my translation)

"New-Dane" (*nydansker* in Danish) is generally regarded as a "politically correct" term for people in Denmark with a migration background. In the quote the boys label themselves "New-Danes" and describe how this label is something they "have to relate to". As part of the project-week the student-groups had to present their projects for the class. In connection to their presentation Isaam and Bashaar handed out Arabic candy and explained that the point of this was to show that immigrants can contribute positively to society. Of course this was ironic and the class reacted with laughter and applause. The act serves to illustrate in a very direct way how the group of adolescents on the one hand lives with diversity including a diversity of resources such as Arabic candy and on the other hand is familiar with the discourse that ascribe identities to them such as "immigrants", "second generation immigrants" and "Muslims" that need to "contribute" in order to be tolerated in "the Danish society".

The central piece of data in this chapter also involves the view of ethnic minorities from an outside nationalist perspective, when Israh – a student with Jordanian and Lebanese family background – parodies Pia Kjærsgård. This episode took place during a break between presentations on the same day as Isaam and Bashaar presented their project about "New-Danes". Israh's group consisted of herself and her classmate Yasmin, and the two girls also addressed issues involving immigrants and their descendants. Their project was entitled "children and adolescents taken into care" and they discussed how children and adolescents with an ethnic minority background were overrepresented in the Danish statistics concerning forced removal from the parents. In connection to this discussion they prepared a staged political debate where they pretended to be the politicians Pia Kjærsgård and Helle Thorning Schmidt (leader of the "Social Democrats") respectively. Israh performed the "Pia Kjærsgård" part. In the break before their presentation the two girls stood by the teacher's desk to prepare the classroom computer and rehearse bits of their talk. Israh had brought some glasses that she planned to use to dress up as Pia Kjærsgård. When she tried them on, she took the opportunity to tell her classmates several times that they were a bunch of ugly "*perkere*" and she asked them to leave the country. "Perker" as a category is associated with immigrants particularly from Middle Eastern countries and is stereotypically perceived as derogatory with racist connotations when used by Danes with majority background (see also Nørreby, this volume). Many of her classmates reacted by producing jocular counter arguments such as "we contribute" and "no immigrants – no transportation, we drive your buses". Other classmates participated by yelling offenses back or claiming that they belong in Denmark for one reason or the other. Israh, as well as other students, explicitly keyed the activity as a parody and the classroom atmosphere during the episode was humorous and full of irony.

During the activity many students used a range of different voices. These voices involved linguistic and discursive material that links up with discussions they had had during the project week, issues debated in mass media, and so forth. For instance, the students had discussed what it means to be Danish as well as general life conditions for minorities. They had met politicians and several of the students included political statements in their project presentations. In many ways the episode can be seen as a product of and a comment to discussions and insights gained during the project week about the Danish society.

Furthermore, the students involved in the episode drew on a range of linguistic resources they generally associated with registers such as "integrated" (Madsen, this volume) and speaking "typical Danish" (Stæhr 2014b) and I will argue that the use of these registers functioned as a tool to relate the outside perspectives from e.g. nationalist politicians to the conceptions and organizations of languages and stereotypes which had relevance in their own daily life.

On a more general level the students' production of voices that use a nationalist perspective to ascribe negative identities to themselves reflects the complexities of living in superdiverse (Vertovec 2006, 2007a, Blommaert 2013) surroundings and simultaneously experiencing a nationalist discourse in society at large. A closer study of the episode provides us with knowledge of how the students discursively grasp and position themselves in relation to societal phenomena such as racism and anti-immigrant politicians.

2 Theoretical key concepts

My methodological approach in this study lies within the field of linguistic ethnography (Blommaert & Dong 2010, Creese 2008, Rampton et al. 2014). I analyze key moments of the case described above against the backdrop of observations and recordings collected by the research team among the same group of participants over time. In the following section I introduce central theoretical concepts and exemplify them with data relevant for understanding the Pia Kjærsgård parody. Thereby the section has two aims: clarifying the parts of the theoretical framework that has not already been described in this book's introduction, and contributing to the investigation of the context for the case I will analyze in detail afterwards.

2.1 Identity performance, social categories, and "dissing contests"

Blommaert (2005) describes identities in interaction as "particular forms of semiotic potential, organized in a repertoire." (p. 207). In this understanding identities are different compositions of semiotic resources which may consist of linguistic resources in interplay with a range of other types of resources. The uptake of identity formation of course depends on the interlocutors' comprehension potential as well as their willingness to accept the proposed identities, and uptakes vary in different contexts. Furthermore several identities may be relevant within the same piece of interaction. As Blommaert formulates it:

> The performance of identity is not a matter of articulating *one* identity, but of the mobilisation of a whole *repertoire* of identity features converted into complex and subtle moment-to-moment speaking positions. (Blommaert 2005: 232)

In order to illustrate the dynamic nature of this perspective we can look at the visible and audible semiotic resources (of course not an exhaustive list) that Israh mobilizes as part of her Pia Kjærsgård parody. In the field diary the activity was described like this:

> Israh stands up behind the teacher's desk, wearing the Pia Kjærsgaard-glasses, and yells to the class: "Perker swine the whole bunch". An answer comes from the class. She continues: "You are all perker swines", and "go home to your country"". Someone from the class answers that she can go home to her own country herself. "I am in my country", "buzz of you ugly Pakistani", to Massima. There is a heartily exchange of similar "compliments" between a part of the students while they are waiting for the teachers to return. It takes place completely without malice. (Extract from field diary 2. February 2011 written by J. Normann Jørgensen, my translation)

In the description of the episode the field worker starts by pointing out some features with semiotic potential: the Pia Kjærsgaard-glasses, Israh's location (by the teacher's desk) and bodily position (standing), and Israh's way of addressing the whole class. It is normally the teacher's privilege to stand behind this desk and address the class as a whole, and thereby Israh's bodily and verbal behavior potentially indexes the power distribution in teacher-centered classroom activities (Scollon & Scollon 2004: 39). The speaking position associated with power which she constructs for herself is further enforced by the interactional pattern of what follows: Israh takes the initiatives and different classmates respond (see below for a more detailed analysis). In this way the field diary describes how Israh combines semiotic resources such as appearance (the glasses), bodily positioning and interactional behavior in her parodic construction of the Pia Kjærsgård persona. Furthermore, the description of the classmates' reactions with words such as "heartily exchange" and "completely without malice" indicate that the classmates align with Israh's creation of a fake Pia Kjærsgård persona and also that they accept Israh's situated identity as leading entertainer (cf. Zimmerman 1998). In addition, the field diary describes how Israh constructs the others as a group of "perkers" and summons them to leave the country. From a dynamic identity perspective Israh's parody may be understood as building up a position indexing power from which she can ascribe identities to her classmates.

Categorizing other people and ascribing them identities are fundamental practices in our social lives and as exemplified above they unfold on a range of societal levels from political statements to classroom interaction. From this follows a potential interest in what identities or group memberships other people may ascribe to us, just as we saw exemplified in Bashaar and Isaam's description of how debates about "New-Danes" influenced them. Their identification as "New-Danes" in this particular context may be viewed as a result of how families with a migration background are referred to and discussed in political debates, news media, etc. As Brubaker (2004: 15) reminds us "(...) a category is not a group. It is at best a potential basis for group-formation or "groupness"". In this perspective "groups" should be understood as results of identification processes rather than given in advance. Processes of identification necessarily involve our individual experiences and choices in combination with perceptions of other people's categorizations and evaluations. In this understanding, groups (including ethnic groups) and group membership must be viewed as social constructions that potentially may change from context to context (Brubaker 2004: 11). As we shall see in the micro analyses a range of different category labels occur in the exchange and the participants jump in and out of more or less serious identifications with social categories such as "Dane", "potato" (slang for majority Dane), etc.

In general the participants frequently use labels and categories associated with ethnicity in their everyday peer group interaction (Møller forthcoming A, Nørreby this volume, Nørreby & Møller 2015). In a field diary involving participants from Israh's class, the fieldworker notes how such categories are exploited in so-called "dissing contests":

> Shahid and Selma give it full power. They tease each other back and forth and it is funny how they themselves – and sometimes some of the other – approve their "diss". For example [by saying] "good diss", "totally bad diss". Selma tells Shahid that he has to practice his diss. She instructs him on how to tell his jokes well, that they need to be coherent and lead forward towards a point. It is rather fun to listen to. Selma keeps dissing Shahid with one more or less successful joke after the other concerning Pakistanis and chili. Among other things, she says to him: "you are not born with a silver spoon up your arse but with a chili up your arse". (Extract from field diary 11. February 2011 written by Astrid Ag, my translation)

Apart from illustrating the use of categories related to ethnicity, the extract provides information about the practice of dissing as it is performed by the participants. In the description we can see how it is framed as a platform event by the participants with performers and spectators (Goffman 1983: 7) and sometimes explicitly evaluated. The description of the dissing episode also shows that just because a situation involves aspects of ethnicity it does not necessarily mean that such aspects are particularly significant to the activity. In this case the quality of the dissing seems to be what is in focus. As we will see, the elements of "dissing contests" as well as explicit evaluations of the performance are also part of the activities in relation to Israh's Pia Kjærsgård parody.

2.2 Registers, stylisation and double-voicing

A central element in verbal activities such as parodies and dissing contests is the involved *ways of speaking* or *registers* in Agha's understanding of the term:

> [...] registers are cultural models of action that link diverse behavioral signs to enactable effects, including images of persona, interpersonal relationship and type of conduct (Agha 2007a: 145)

Fundamentally, the concept of registers concerns how speakers organize the bits and pieces of language they use and experience in their everyday languaging. Language is viewed as a social tool and in processes of enregisterment (Agha 2003, 2007a) speakers link recognizable formations of linguistic resources to interpersonal conduct, norms for situational use, and stereotypical images of persona. By viewing registers as cultural models of action Agha stresses that registers used in interaction always send signals to the interlocutors. How these signals are interpreted very much depends on how interlocutors view the relation between the speaker and the register. Does the register "belong" to the speaker, does it point to specific roles and personas, does the speaker signal or explicitly express a distance to the register, etc? Some concepts dealing with the relation between the speaker and the produced speech are *stylization, crossing* and *double-voicing*. Stylization and crossing are defined by Rampton (2009) as follows:

> Stylisation involves reflexive communicative action in which speakers produce specially marked and often exaggerated representations of languages, dialects and styles that lie outside their own habitual repertoire (at least as this is perceived within the situation at hand). Crossing is closely related, but it involves a stronger sense of social or ethnic boundary transgression (Rampton 2009: 149)

In stylization speakers use registers that are not generally thought to belong to them by the other participants. In crossing the sense of belonging is related to perceived social or ethnic boundaries. Rampton (1995) has described how e.g. a word in Panjabi used by speakers of Anglo or Afro-Caribbean descent is used to negotiate social relations and the more or less strong senses of boundaries between ethnic and social groups. In connection with the Pia Kjærsgård parody the participants with an ethnic minority background employ linguistic resources associated with registers thought to "belong" to people in Denmark with ethnic majority background.

One of these registers is described as "speaking integrated" by several of the participants (Madsen 2013, Møller & Jørgensen 2013). In interviews and essays concerning language use in their everyday the participants describe how they typically use it to address adults (particularly teachers) and generally associate this way of speaking with signalling respect. This is, however, only when they address adults as exemplified in the following extract from a student essay on the subject "What does language mean to me in my daily life":

> Other people also speak in different ways to me, my teachers speak integratedly to me, and my friends speak slang. But my sister does not speak to me in that slang-way. She speaks integratedly all the time to me, but I answer her in the slang-way. (Lamis, essay, 8th grade, my translation)

Lamis mentions the two linguistic registers "slang" and "integrated" and describes how the appropriate use of the registers depends on the context and the relation to the interlocutors. With friends she uses "slang" and she refuses to use "integrated" when talking to her sister. The example illustrates that it may be considered rude among the peers to address each other with language associated with "integrated". The label "integrated" further points to the macro-discourse in the Danish society described above according to which citizens with a minority background are asked to "integrate" (i.e., to "contribute" and adopt standard Danish cultural norms). In this sense the participants' use of the label "integrated" about this way of speaking is in itself evidence of the strong impact the "integration" discourse has. The performable signs the participants associate with speaking "integratedly" are "distinct pronunciation, abstract and academic vocabulary (long, fine words), high pitch, quiet and calm attitude, ritual politeness phrases" (Madsen 2013: 127). It is noteworthy that in some contexts it may be considered inappropriate (or impolite) to use politeness phrases. Israh uses several ritual politeness phrases when she imitates Pia Kjærsgård which potentially points to the way of speaking called "integrated" and the attached values of power on the one hand and distance-marking in relation to her peers on the other (c.f. Gumperz 1982 on *we*-codes and *they*-codes).

Another register which is thought to "belong" to ethnic majority Danes, Stæhr (2014b) describes as "performance of stereotypical Danishness". We have not described this register as well as the "integrated" register. It has primarily been observed in interactions involving Isaam and Bashar and the performable signs include old Danish proverbs, stereotypical Copenhagen working class pronunciation and Danish curses – particularly *for helvede* ("oh hell", functionally equivalent to "damn it"). In several instances, such as excerpt 2 below and a similar case described in Stæhr (2014b), the performable signs are explicitly linked to being Danish. This way of speaking does not index a powerful position like "integrated" potentially does. Rather it points to stereotypes of elderly men with an ethnic majority background living in the same area as the participants in the study. The way Isaam uses the linguistic material to construct persona is described by Stæhr:

> During fieldwork I have overheard Bashaar and his friend Isaam play with similar stereotypes several times, and one character made up by Isaam is called Claus. He is characterised as an elderly man who frequently visits the local pubs in Amager, and in Isaam's impersonation, Claus says 'for helvede' ('damn it') in ways that resemble Bashaar's pronunciation in excerpt 10 [fronting and prolongation of the vowels]. (Stæhr 2014b: 21)

Fronting and prolongation of vowels are significant features of a traditional low Copenhagen register stereotypically associated with working class (Brink & Lund 1975) and Claus is a typical male name among ethnic majority background Danes. According to Stæhr the phrase *for helvede* (damn it) is one of the central linguistic building blocks Isaam uses for styling the "Claus"-persona. As we shall see, Isaam plays a very active role in the Pia Kjærsgård parody and several times employ the oath *for helvede* in his contributions. In most cases (but not all) this particular way of speaking occurs in utterances where he parodies majority Danes. This resonates with Jaspers' (2011b) findings concerning the use of Antwerp dialect among school students with an ethnic minority background. On the one hand features associated with Antwerp dialect provided an excellent verbal resource for styling the "institutional other" (Jaspers 2011b: 510) and on the other hand the students seemed to exploit the "semiotic potency" of the "uncool, outmoded and white urban dialect" (Jaspers 2011b: 519–520).

Where the concept of stylization may be used specifically to address the relation between the speaker and the involved registers, the concept of double-voicing more directly aims at describing linguistic production that points back to another person's production. Double-voicing is described by Bakhtin as a particular type of discourse characterized as "discourse [...] directed both toward the referential object of speech, as in ordinary discourse, and toward *another's discourse*, toward *someone else's speech*" (Bakhtin 1984: 185, italics in the original). In this way double-voicing addresses the simultaneous, but different orientations of the one and same linguistic product to the producer as well as "someone else", i.e. to another person. Bakhtin distinguishes between uni-directional and vari-directional double-voicing. In uni-directional double-voicing the producer of the utterance shares the perspective of the discourse with the person the produced utterance orients to, and in vari-directional double-voicing the producer of the utterance takes a perspective different from the person oriented to. Israh's performance (as well as parody in a more general sense) is an example of vari-directional double-voicing in the sense that she explicitly claims to be Pia Kjærsgård and "dresses up" like her. When it comes to her actual verbal production it is not direct quotes of Pia Kjærsgård. Pia Kjærsgård has never used words such as *grimme perkere* (ugly perkers) in public appearances.

The following excerpt exemplifies vari-directional double-voicing and furthermore it shows how imitations of Pia Kjærsgård is a repeated activity. The episode takes place during a break in class in the project week on the day after Israh's and Yasmin's presentation. Michael is doing an imitation of a Spanish accent and at the same time denying Israh the access to the classroom computer, when she asks him to do a Pia Kjærsgård parody:

Excerpt 1: recorded 8. february 2011, break before presentation, Participants: Israh and Michael, translation to English in italics, transcription key in appendix,

```
1 Israh:    vær lidt Pia Kjærsgård i dag
            be a little bit Pia Kjærsgård today
2 Michael:  hvad
            what
3 Israh:    Pia Kjærsgård
            Pia Kjærsgård
4 Michael:  vi (.) her i det danske samfund
            we (.) here in the Danish society
            ((high pitch, distinct pronunciation))
```

```
5 Israh:    ((laughs))
6 Michael:      må stå sammen (.) om jer (.) dumme indvandrere
                must stand together (.) around [potentially also
                against] you (.) stupid immigrants
                ((high pitch, distinct pronunciation))
7 Israh:        du skal ikke kalde mig indvandrer
                don't call me an immigrant
                ((shouting and laughing))
```

Michael in line 4 and 6 speaks with a high pitch and a very distinct pronunciation. Furthermore, he uses pauses and intonation dramatically as if it were a political speech with a lot of the political points emphasized. Thereby Michael's linguistic production can be described as specially marked and it certainly lies outside of his habitual repertoire. Furthermore, Michael and Israh work together to explicitly frame the activity as imitating Pia Kjærsgård. In this sense the activity is an example of double-voicing. It illustrates how parodies are reoccurring practices (including parodies of Pia Kjærsgård), how these parodies may lead to staged verbal fights (or dissing contests) involving membership of social groups, and how these activities often involve social categories related to ethnic backgrounds and discourses of nationalism such as the one described in the introduction.

In this section I have described how I view the concepts of identity performance, social categories, registers, stylization, crossing and double-voicing and I have shown how these concepts can be used to describe linguistic activities such as speech parodies and dissing contests. Furthermore, I have introduced two enregistered ways of speaking among the adolescents ("integrated" and "performance of stereotypical Danishness") which point to ethnic majority Danes. The examples used (apart from the essay extract) are all taking place during the same week which is the project week in the 9th grade. Before the micro analysis I will now provide some more contextual information about the project week and briefly introduce the participants.

3 Data and analysis

3.1 The project week

Project weeks constitute an obligatory part of curriculum in the 9th grade in the Danish school system. Normal classroom teaching is suspended, the students engage in a project that lasts for at least a week, and the students are given grades for their work; they can choose to include these grades in their final certificate. In 2011 the overall topic for the project week in 9th grade was "Remarkable world" which of course may cover almost everything, and so rather than a constraint the topic should be viewed as an encouragement to be curious. A central idea in the project week is that the students must provide material from outside their classroom to shed light on their chosen subjects such as interviews, questionnaire surveys, and so on.

The students typically chose subjects which were relevant in relation to their everyday life, such as "social media", "eating disorders" and "being young in the nightlife". Thereby the students potentially gained new insights that were related to their own lives. This is of course a simplified account and some students learned more than others, but the engagement was generally high, and the grades given to them by the teachers after their presentations were generally also taken seriously. Their engagement was also reflected by the fact that some of the subjects dealt with in the projects were discussed during the breaks, that is, even when no teachers were present.

As I already mentioned several of the groups in one way or another included a focus on issues related to migration and ethnic minorities. It is reasonable to assume that this was partly due to the composition of the class. In Israh's class there were 19 students and when we asked them 15 of them reported to have another mother tongue than Danish. Eight students reported Arabic to be their mother tongue, four students said Urdu and/or Punjabi, and the languages Turkmen, Somali, and Farsi were represented by one student each. Some of the main participants in the event were Israh, Yasmin and Isaam. They were all born in Denmark. Israh's and Isaam's parents have Jordanese and Lebanese background, and Yasmin's parents had emigrated from Pakistan.

In the students' school everyday very few conflicts in the group of students were related to ethnicity. As we saw in the examples above the students frequently played with social categories and ethnicity and exploited the possibilities in staged activities. However, the participants were in general rather explicit in appointing activities as play (Møller forthcoming A) which is also the case in the Pia Kjærsgård parody.

3.2 Micro analysis

The following analysis is guided by three overall questions: Who use what voices and registers? How are these interactional inputs framed and reacted to? How do the activities relate to other activities, discourses, events, etc.? I will address these questions by analyzing sequentially how the participants react on each other's contributions, by drawing on knowledge gained through ethnographic observation, and by describing political statements, mediated events, etc. that the participants refer to and/or recycle.

The transcriptions below are all based on recordings from radio-microphones worn by Israh and Yasmin and a recorder standing on a closet near Isaam. As the recording was conducted in a school break with probably around 10–15 students in the classroom there is of course a range of things going on. Furthermore, the students are highly skilled in participating in more than one conversation at the same time and sometimes they jump back and forth between several simultaneous conversations. The transcriptions should be viewed in this light. My guideline was to transcribe everything I could hear that could be interpreted as a contribution to the Pia Kjærsgård performance. Several students participated and it is not always possible to distinguish who is saying what.

Israh and Yasmin were the fourth group to present on the day where Isaam and Bashaar were first. This means that the students had heard Isaam's and Bashaar's presentation about "New-Danes" and the ensuing discussion before this episode. The break before Israh and Yasmin's presentation lasted approximately 20 minutes, and Israh initiated the Pia Kjærsgård parody after around 10 minutes. Up until this point in the break Israh and Yasmin spent time preparing the different components in their presentation. They had a PowerPoint presentation, props for dressing up as politicians, and candles they were going to light when reading a poem written by a girl who was taken into care. From time to time they asked questions to the fieldworker concerning their presentation and informed him on what they were going to do. He had followed the class during two years at this point, so they knew him well. At some point Israh could not find the glasses she was going to use to dress up as Pia Kjærsgård. When she retrieved them, she put them on and initiated the parody:

Excerpt 2: recorded 7. february 2011, break before presentation

1 Israh: ved I hvad (1.4) I er nogle grimme perkere
you know what (.) you are a bunch of ugly perkers
((distinct pronunciation))

2 Isaam: hvorfor (.) hvem har sagt vi er perkere jeg er dansker for helvede mand [xxx](>)
why (.) who said we are perkers I'm a Dane god dammit xxx
((prolonged vowel in "for helvede"))

3 Israh: [Jeg er Pia Kjærsgård](<)
I'm Pia Kjærsgård
((laughs during and after))

Line 1 contains the first of several contributions where Israh addresses the classmates and classifies them as perkers (or other potentially derogative names for people with an ethnic minority background). As described above Israh's distinct pronunciation possibly points to the values associated with speaking "integratedly". The phrase *ved I hvad* (do you know what) is also more polite than a range of other possible calls for attention (Ag 2010, Møller forthcoming B) which Israh uses regularly to address her classmates. This for Israh unusual choice of expression may signal a distance to the verbal production and indicate that it is stylized.

Isaam objects to Israh's statement in line two and claims that he is a Dane, an identity he would not generally claim among his classmates (see e.g. Møller & Jørgensen 2013) which along with the use of the phrase *for helvede* (damn it) indicates that Isaam aligns with the frame of role playing suggested by Israh. Israh then specifically states that she parodies Pia Kjærsgård in line 3. Furthermore, she signals the playful character by laughing.

Thereby the frames are set up for the following activity of a playful parody (Goffman 1986, see also Lytra 2007 on play frames). Excerpt 3 unfolds about a minute after excerpt 2. In the meantime Israh has practiced her part of the presentation and asked the fieldworker for advice on how to start. In excerpt 3 she returns to harass her classmates:

Excerpt 3: recorded 7. february 2011, break before presentation

1 Israh: allesammen nogle dyr allesammen perkersvin
all of you are animals all of you perker swines
((perkersvin is said when there is silence in the class))
(1.0)
2 Yasmin: så [så så](>)
now [now now](>)
3 Israh: [nej nej](<) det er bare for sjov
[no no](<) it's just for fun ((laughs))
(.) ((several people laugh quietly))
4 ?: så så
now now
5 Isaam: så stopper du det racisme ikke (.) Pia K (.) jeg er så træt af dig (.) for helvede
now you stop that racism right (.) Pia K (.) I'm so tired of you (.) god dammit
((prolonged and raised vowel in "for helvede"))
6 Israh: ved du hvad du får en sko i hovedet (.) kom lige med den her nej ikke noget

you know what you get a shoe in your head (.) give that to me no nothing
(4.7)
((something happens that results in laughter and clapping - possibly Israh throwing a shoe after Isaam))

7 Isaam: hvad fanden skete der
what the hell happened

8 Yasmin: bare lad være kotch (0.8) [hun disser dig](>)
just leave it kotch [she is dissing you](>)
((I interpret kotch as a slangword for relax))

9 Anas: [du har lært noget af mig xxx](<)
[you learned something from me xxx](<)

10 Israh: ved I hvad (1.5) perkersvine hele bundtet
You know what (1.5) perker swines the whole bunch
((”svine” is a nonstandard plural form of swine))

11 Yasmin: [svine](>)
[swines](>)
((repeat Israh’s way of pronouncing “svine”))

12 ?: [undskyld for det](<) jeg har gjort [mand](>)
[sorry for what](<) I have done [man](>)

13 Israh: [hele bundtet](<) [undtagen](>)
[the whole bunch](<) [except](>)

14 Anas: [hvad med](<) hvad med mig [xxx](>)
[what about](<) what about me [xxx](>)

15 Israh [den (.) smukke kartoffel der](<)
[the (.) beautiful potato over there](<)

16 Yasmin: [Pia Kjærsgård kan ikke tale](<) sit eget sprog
[Pia Kjærsgård can’t speak](<) her own language
((low voice))

17 massima: og mig og mig og [mig](>)
and me and me and [me](>)

18 Israh: [og](<) (.) [den smukke kartoffel der](>)
[and](<) (.) [the beautiful potato over there](>)

19 Isaam: [hvis hvis hvis I ikke havde](<)
[if if if you didn’t have](<)

20 Israh: I er alle sammen nogle grimme [perkersvin (.) ud](>)
you’re all a bunch of ugly [perker swines (.) out](>)

21 Isaam: [hvis I ikke hvis I ikke havde perkere](<)
[if you didn’t if you didn’t have perkers](<)
(noise, Yasmin is laughing)

22 Isaam: hvis I ikke havde
if you didn't have

23 girl: dø med dig gå hjem til dit hjemland hvad er det du siger
you just die go to your home country what is it you are saying
((loud voice - followed by giggling))

24 ?: hvad
what

25 Israh: jeg er i mit hjemland
I am in my home country

26 boy: gå hjem til dit [hjemland](>)
go to your home [country](>)

27 Israh: [gå](<) hjem med jer [allesammen](>)
[go](<) home [altogether](>)

28 girl: [xxx](<)
[xxx](<)

29 Israh: ud med jer jeg sparker jer ud
you get out I kick you out

30 Isaam: hvis I ikke havde perkere så havde I ikke transport
if you didn't have perkers then you had no transportation

31 Israh: ved du hvad
you know what

32 Isaam: vi kører jeres busser og sådan noget
we drive your buses and such
((laughter and applause, fieldworker can be heard laughing))
(.)

33 boy: over for rødt
crossing the red light
(1.7) ((applause is continued))

34 Israh: ved du hvad I er bare slaskede til at køre hvor mange ulykker er der
you know what you are just shabby drivers how many accidents are there
((loud))

Israh's main activity in excerpt 3 is similar to what we observed in excerpt 2. Israh calls her classmates *perkersvin* (perker swines) and playfully threatens to throw them out of the country (lines 1, 10, 20, 27 and 29). As described above she draws on several semiotic resources indexing power in her parody. From the field notes (specifically referring to what Israh says in line 10) we know that Israh is standing by the teacher's desk during this episode and just as if she was a "real" teacher Israh takes the initiatives and the classmates react. As in excerpt 2 the first couple of contributions contain meta-comments on the situation when Israh says "it is just for fun" in line 3, and Isaam addresses her as Pia Kjærsgård in line 5. This time a larger group of students are involved and several react to her mock insults.

Isaam again uses linguistic resources associated with stereotypical Danishness in his request to "Pia Kjærsgård" to stop the racism in line 5. In this case it is not clear whether Isaam speaks from his own perspective or somebody else's. Israh reacts by threatening Isaam to throw a shoe at him. This is probably a reference to a specific episode taking place about two years earlier (December 2008) when an Iraqi journalist throws his shoes at George Bush (president in USA at the time) at a press conference in Baghdad. The episode is accessible on YouTube in several versions and has had millions of views (as observed in 2014). The link to this episode is further strengthened when Israh refers to it later in the Pia Kjærsgård parody. This happens when a boy tells her that she should have shoes thrown at her head and Israh replies by asking him if he thinks she is Bush. In this way an event on the international political scene symbolically indexing opposition against American activities in Iraq is exploited as a resource in the participants' role play and it is related to nationalist politicians on the political stage in Denmark.

In line 10, Israh returns to the activity of labelling her classmates as "perker swines". A boy instantly claims that he is sorry for what he has done (line 12) and thereby performs an identity that may be described as the guilty and suppressed "perker" who knows he did not do as he was supposed to. What follows is that first Anas and then Massima ask to be an exception and Israh grants them the social category of "potatoes" instead. *Kartoffel* (potato) is a widespread slang word among youth for ethnic majority Danes (c.f. Pharao et al. 2014). In this sense, when Massima (with Pakistani family background) asks for the "beautiful potato" identity in line 17 and gets it from Israh in line 18, the play with categories may be viewed as a destabilization of a Dane/Non-Dane dichotomy.

The "beautiful potato" exchange (lines 13–18) points to a very central aspect of the whole episode. In the parody Pia Kjærsgård is acted out as a politician who tells people which social category they belong to, i.e., Dane or a Non-Dane, and what they, accordingly, are worth. She is also in a position to ascribe an identity as acceptable and part of the group to people who live up to her demands. This part is of course played by Israh. Anas and Massima on the other hand perform the voices of the submissive people with immigrant background who want acceptance.

Yasmin (Israh's project partner) reacts to a non-standard pronunciation of "*svine*" (swine) in Israh's statement in line 10 and thereby also introduces an element of linguistic normativity into the activity. As described by Stæhr (this volume) commenting and correcting others' language is a frequent practice in playful interactions among the participants. Yasmin's term "her own language" reconstructs the ideological connection that "real" Danes of course speaks "real" Danish and points to the paradoxical fact that the nationalist politician does not speak "correct" Danish. Yasmin's comment may also be seen as a critique of Israh's performance, since Israh is the producer of the Pia Kjærsgård voice. In this sense Yasmin is exploiting the ambiguity of Israh's double-voicing by addressing both voices at once. However, Yasmin's contribution is produced in the middle of the "beautiful potato" exchange and it is not reacted to.

In line 20 Israh takes a further step up rhetorically when she moves from harassing minorities to throwing them out. This triggers a reaction from a girl, who loudly asks Israh to die and to return to her home country (line 23). Israh answers loud that she *is* in her home country. This part of the exchange adds another element to the nationalism discourse, namely the relation between human beings and "home countries". The concept of a "home country" is based on an essentialist ideology and here introduced as an argument for "kicking people out" of Denmark.

After several attempts Isaam finally in line 30 manages to take the floor during this loud and busy verbal exchange of the classroom to produce the statement that he seemingly initiated in line 19, 21, and 22. Isaam's contribution introduces the stereotypical immigrant worker and the power relations between a minority of "perkere" and a Danish majority by the use of "we" and "your buses". He constructs "perkere" as necessary for the well-functioning society, and thereby as contributing constructively to it, but at the same time he constructs them as taking low status jobs as bus drivers. In this sense he points to a distinction between majority and minority based in significant differences in access and power positions with respect to the labour market.

Isaam's production targets people with ethnic majority background who do not see the broader perspective, but also potentially targets people with ethnic minority background who accept and identify themselves with low status job such as bus driver and thereby maintain the unequal, societal power distributions. The punchline "we drive your buses" is received by the classmates with cheering and applause which goes on for some time just like a well-received statement produced in a public political debate.

Following excerpt 3 the boy Anas tries to convince Israh to enter a webpage of an amusement park on the classroom computer, but Israh denies, because the computer is already prepared for their presentation. From time to time Israh returns to the harassment of the classmates. The parody is taken up again when Israh manages to get Anas to participate instead of trying to get access to the computer. Except 4 occurs approximately half a minute after excerpt 3, and it begins when Israh in her Pia Kjærsgård role addresses Anas directly:

Excerpt 4: recorded 7. february 2011, break before presentation

1 Israh: perkersvin hele bundtet (.) og især dig
perker swine the whole bunch (.) and particularly you
2 Anas: hvad er du så (.) er du en perkerhund
what are you then (.) a perker dog
3 Israh: vent lidt
wait a minute
4 Anas: perkersvin du er [bare](>)
perker swine you are [just](>)
5 girl: [Israh](<) du kan ikke disse fætter
[Israh](<) you can't diss cousin
6 Israh: [jeg er ikke perker for helvede jeg er dansker] (>)
I'm not a perker god damn it I'm a Dane
7 Anas: [du er sort du er xxx perker](<)
you are black you are xxx perker
8 boy: kom så [xxx fætter](>)
come on [xxx cousin] (>)
9 Anas: [dit sorte svin dit dit](<)
[you black swine you you](<)
10 Massima: kom så fætter xxx jeg hepper på fætter
come on cousin xxx I cheer on cousin
(0.9) ((several people laughing and giggling))
11 Massima: det er min fætter
it is my cousin
12 Israh: hvad siger du din grimme perkersvin gå ud af landet
what are you saying you ugly perker swine walk out of the country
14 Yasmin: [Israh ti stille](>)
[Israh be quiet](>)
15 Anas: [jeg jeg bidrager](<)
[I I contribute](<)
16 Israh: ved du hvad
do you know what
17 Anas: var det ikke det vi sagde
wasn't that what we said

```
18 Yasmin:  [du er ikke sjov mere](>)
            [you are not funny anymore](>)
19 Israh:   [du går ud](<)
            [you move out](<)
20 Anas:    jeg bidrager
            I contribute
```

When Anas in line 2 reacts to Israh's use of "perker swine" in line 1 by suggesting that she is a "perker dog", this initiates a dissing contest similar to the one described above. It is striking how ritualized this activity seems to be with the explicit mentioning of "dissing" in line 5, cheering in line 8 and 10, and Massima explicitly pointing out who she is cheering for to the interlocutors (also line 10). In line 15 Anas changes strategy from calling Israh names to claim that he "contributes". Thereby Anas repeats a phrase that has been in focus earlier the same day in connection with Isaam's and Bashaar's presentation which was introduced above. In the discussion following the presentation, one of the teachers asked the boys the following question:

> You refer to Pia Kjærsgård and she says that they need to contribute to the Danish society or otherwise leave or that was your interpretation. Then I ask you – well isn't it okay if you don't want to (.) just want to sponge on our society isn't it okay then if one says out of the country if they cannot contribute (recording, 7th February 2011, teacher's question after presentation, my translation)

In his question the teacher maintains a perspective on the population emphasizing a division into a group with migration background called "them" and another group who could throw out people from the group with migration background if they do not "contribute". It should be noted that such incidents where teachers reproduce nationalist perspectives in classroom discourse are relatively rare. Bashaar answers hesitantly for the boys that in his opinion one can contribute just by being in the country and after a few clarifying questions they leave the subject. The point here is not to conduct a discourse analysis of the teachers' contributions. What I want to make probable is that Anas' use of the phrase "to contribute" recycles what happened earlier the same day, including this discussion. This interpretation is supported by the fact that Anas in line 17 specifically states that he refers to an earlier event. If this is the case Anas exploits the ongoing role play to distance himself from the group of "contributors". The meta-discursive question in line 17 "isn't that what we said" spells out that the "I contribute" phrase should be viewed as stylized and not as Anas' "own" voice. No matter whether Anas' production has any connection to what happened earlier or not it is still an example of how the participants reconstruct the patterns of identification suggested by a nationalist perspective and distance themselves from the offered identities by parodying them.

Following excerpt 4 Israh continues practicing more specific parts of the Pia Kjærsgård role in their upcoming presentation. She returns a few times to harass the classmates, but in particular her partner Yasmin urges her to stop the activity and argues that it is getting embarrassing. Two minutes after the episode in excerpt 4 Isaam addresses Israh by saying *"kære Pia Kjærsgård"* (dear Pia Kjærsgård) and afterwards Isaam pretends to be a journalist interviewing her about her statements. Excerpt 5 starts when Israh and Isaam are interrupted by someone calling out for Yasmin which causes them to change lanes and discuss why immigrants always have to disturb the debate:

Excerpt 5: recorded 7. february 2011, break before presentation

1 girl: Yasmin
(1.2)
2 Yasmin: hvad
what
3 Israh: shut up
shut up
4 Isaam: I forstyrrer debatten
you disturb the debate
5 Israh: vil I gerne lade være med at forstyrre debatten I er nogle grimme perkersvin
would you please stop disturbing the debate you are a bunch of ugly perker swines
6 Isaam: typisk perkere de skal altid forstyrre
typically perkers they always disturb
7 Israh: kan du se (.) altså
you see (.) really
8 Isaam: altså
really
9 Israh: ud af landet
out of the country
10 boy: nej nu holder I sgu kæft eller I styrer [jer mand](>)
no now you shut up or control [yourself man](>)
11 Isaam: [du spiser](<)
[you eat](<)
12 Isaam: du spiser vores kager for helvede du drikker [vores te](>)
you eat our cakes damn it you drink [our tea](>)

```
13 Israh:  [hvem er du] (<) (.) du tager vores mad du tager vores
           elektricitet
           [who are you](<) (.) you take our food and you take our
           electricity
14 Isaam:  du tager vores kager fra personalet for helvede
           you take our cakes from the staff damn it
15 Israh:  du stjæler penge
           you steal money
16 Isaam:  ja
           yes
17 Israh:  du er kriminel
           you are a criminal
18 Isaam:  ja (.) du er gået på førtidspension mens du har en
           grillbar i Libanon eller sådan noget
           yes (.) you went on early retirement while still having
           a fast-food place in Libanon
           ((Israh laughs))
19 Isaam:  for helvede
           damn it
20 Israh:  du taler om dig selv nu ((continues to laugh))
           now you talk about yourself
```

In this excerpt Israh and Isaam pretend to be "Danes" who are harassing people with a migration background and complaining about them to each other. Israh's use of a ritually polite form in line 5 contributes to this construction of this "Danishness" and so does Isaam's use of *for helvede* (damn it) in line 12, 14, and 19. In the first part of the excerpt (line 1–9) they address Yasmin and the girl who called her names and they use this activity to make the generalization that all "perkers" are always disturbing the debate. Israh uses some of the same formulations as in her recent Pia Kjærsgård parody ("ugly perkers", "out of the country", etc.) and thereby points to Pia Kjærsgård and her political agenda again.

When another boy interferes and asks them to stop in line 10 they direct their attention to him and Isaam accuses him of "eating our cakes and drinking our tea". This is a specific reference to an accusation made about two month earlier by the Danish People's Party. In their monthly magazine for members they postulated that "patients with an immigrant background brought the whole family to the [doctor's] waiting room and extensively used the free supplies [tea, coffee, and biscuits]" (Dansk Folkeblad (Danish People's Magazine), no 6, Nov. 2010). The accusation was denied by doctors all over the country and led to the establishment of a Facebook group called "Send a Lemon Moon [traditional Danish sponge cake] to the Danish People's Party" (my translation) which resulted in more than 200 cakes sent to their office in the parliament. The entire event received huge media attention. Isaam's reference to this shows that he parodies the Danish People's Party and furthermore it illustrates once more how colorful media stories about political issues are recycled in interaction by the participants. Israh does not respond specifically to Isaam's reference, but moves on to accuse the classmate for being a criminal. Isaam tops this by accusing him of social fraud because he receives early retirement benefit in Denmark and at the same time runs a fast-food shop in Lebanon. This makes Israh laugh and at the same time she leaves her role by claiming that Isaam is talking about himself.

Once again we can observe how registers are employed in stylizations which in turn are used to voice stereotyped images of people with an ethnic majority background who are biased against people with an ethnic minority background. This time Isaam specifically voice the Danish People's Party. If we compare this to his contributions in excerpt 3 we can see how Isaam switches between the voices of "Danes" who are either for or against the politics of the Danish People's Party and the voice of a contributing immigrant who knows his worth and his place (the "we drive your buses" persona). Isaam organize social categories through languaging and shows how he positions himself in relation to those categories. His languaging practices also communicates his views of identity positions and power distributions in society to his peers.

After excerpt 5 Israh and Isaam continue to pretend that Isaam is a serious journalist interviewing Pia Kjærsgård. Shortly after Israh and Yasmin present their project and they are very successful. Both the group consisting of Israh and Yasmin and the group consisting of Bashaar and Isaam receive the top grade for their projects.

The perhaps most central element of Israh's Pia Kjærsgård parody represented in excerpt 2–5 is the repeated instances of name-calling. Israh continuously addresses the classmates with derogatory expressions about ethnic minorities and urges them to leave the country. It is somehow puzzling that this repeated activity of name-calling followed by other types of harassment generates as many reactions as it does. Taken as a whole the activities are carried out enthusiastically by the participants and the intensity is high. For example, the 34 utterances in excerpt 3 are produced within about 50 seconds and the classmates almost line up to contribute. A possible explanation for this enthusiastic participation is that Israh's static name-calling reflects a more general experience shared by the participants with minority background, namely the experience of being targeted by nationalists who identify them as a problematic group who need to integrate (i.e. "become Danish", "contribute", etc.). In this sense the parody of nationalists and submissive immigrants can be viewed as driven by reflections over as well as needs to cope with the ascription of negative identities.

4 Conclusion

The most obvious but still important conclusion to make from the analysis of the Pia Kjærsgård parody and its context is that the adolescents are familiar with the ethnocentric version of integration and that it plays a role in their self-understanding and ways of organizing their world. The case reflects how the participants organize social categories and how they position themselves in relation to them. Nationalists are parodied as a group who ascribe negative identities to people with a minority background and link those identities to stereotypical behavior such as social fraud, exploitation of the welfare system, and so forth. Submissive immigrants are portrayed as people who "contribute", apologize, want to be "potatoes", drive buses for people with ethnic majority background, and so forth. Through their performances of the voices of nationalists and submissive people with ethnic minority backgrounds the participants distance themselves from both categories. At the same time they create a shared standpoint and thereby potentially a spirit of solidarity.

We have also observed how ritual types of interaction such as parodies and dissing contests play a role in the formations and organizations of these social groups and how these processes involve acts of stylization (Rampton 2009) and double-voicing (Bakhtin 1984). A central component in signaling how the participants relate to the voices they produce is the use of linguistic resources associated with registers such as speaking "integrated" and speaking "stereotypical Danish", both of which are associated with ethnic majority speakers. In this way the episode reflects how metalinguistic organizations are employed in the adolescents' organizations of social groups. Furthermore the episode involves metalinguistic enregisterment (Agha 2007a) in the sense that ways of speaking explicitly are connected to specific persons (such as Pia Kjærsgård) or social categories (such as "Dane").

The students combine enregistered ways of speaking with references to national and international media events in the Pia Kjærsgård parody. Furthermore, they draw on expressions that occured in earlier discussions in the project week (such as "we contribute"). This illustrates how experiences from the lived lives (including school life) of the adolescents are recycled in peer group activities for the sake of entertainment, but potentially also in order to share, systematize and evaluate their experiences with each other. In the role play activity the impressions from school life, media, and other sources are used to create and test voices representing social categories and provide an opportunity for the participants to position themselves in relation to these voices.

As mentioned in the introduction, the episode reflects the adolescents' everyday life as characterized by ethnic and linguistic diversity in their local environment on the one hand and the voices of nationalism placing demands on people with ethnic minority background on the other. In connection with this it is striking how much explicit meta-communication the participants include in their interactional activities, when they for example set the frames for dissing contests, proclaim that now they carry out a parody, encourage each other to perform, and explain to each other how "it is just for fun". Furthermore, the participants exploit meta-communication in their activities exemplified by Yasmin claiming that "Pia Kjærsgård can't speak her own language" and Israh and Isaam agreeing that immigrants always "disturb the debates". As mentioned above conflicts based in ethnic differences are very rare among these adolescents and one reason may be their frequent use of their meta-communicative skills (cf. Møller forthcoming A).

More generally I have focused on how the participants discursively deals with nationalism when they parody politicians, stylize the language of "majority Danes", engage in dissing contest, and recycle discussions from class as well as mediated political events on a national and international level. In this way the chapter is first and foremost an analysis of reactions among adolescents who are characterized by for example the Danish Peoples' Party as a group of people who need to "integrate" and "contribute" because they have a certain family background. But the different voices employed by the adolescents have another thing in common: they "belong" to or point to adults such as politicians, bus-drivers, teachers, journalists, etc. In this sense the parodying can also be explained as an activity related to being young, creating distance to the adult world by making fun of it, while at the same time examining possible identities in it, and defining their positions in relation to these identities. What this case shows us is that part of the adolescents' organization and understanding of this adult world in relation to ethnicity involves the opposed groups of demand-making nationalists and "contributing" immigrants.

Asif Agha

Growing up bilingual in Copenhagen

The accompanying articles present the result of a multi-year collaborative effort by a team of researchers to examine the social lives of Danish schoolchildren under conditions of increasing migration-based diversity. Children from more than 20 distinct ethnolinguistic backgrounds form multilingual cohorts in Copenhagen classrooms, just as their immigrant parents form a multi-ethnic workforce in Denmark. The authors of these articles observe students in school and leisure activities in order to understand the everyday lives of youth on their way to becoming adult citizens in Danish society. Along the way, these students – and the researchers who follow them – encounter public representations of Danish society that metasemiotically formulate the normal form that specific semiotic practices take (or have taken, or should take) in the nation state imaginary. Language use is one of these practices, and proficiency in one of its normal forms, Standard Danish, is emblematic of adult citizenship in the nation state, even if – and despite its emblematic pre-eminence – Standard Danish is simply one speech register among many in use among adult Danes today. Since protocols of public schooling comprise a State-sponsored instrument of socialization into adult society, Standard Danish is a salient norm for students too, even if children employ other speech registers as well, just as adults do.

Many of these articles explore processes of enregisterment in situations where more than one "language" – in the sense of a phono-lexico-grammatical system; hereafter, a PLG system – is available in discursive interaction. Under contemporary conditions of multilingualism, students often speak languages other than Danish at home. Although all students speak Danish at school, speech tokens from other languages readily occur as utterance segments in the course of speaking Danish. Many speech tokens exhibit partial fidelity to more than one PLG type, as they routinely do in multilingual speech everywhere around the world. An example from an 8th grade Copenhagen classroom is discussed in the passage quoted below (where italicized parenthetical comments are my own interpolations):

> "In the exchange in example 2, Michael asks for glue or paste. Esen answers with the construction "eine limesteife". The word "eine" is associated with German, and this is quite straightforward. However, the word "limesteife" [*pronounced as li:mestajfe; understood as 'gluestick'*] is not associated with any language or variety (that we know of). The element "lim" pronounced with a long high front vowel ([i:]) equals the Danish-associated word for "glue", and the middle -e- may also be associated with Danish, as many compounds associated with Danish have an -e attached to the first element as a compound marker. This

> is not the case of the word "lim", however. In addition, the element "steife" is not associated with Danish, and neither with German in any sense that would give an immediately accessible meaning here. It may sound like a German word to the Danish ear, but not to the German ear. This feature does not lend itself to being [*uniquely*] categorized in any [*one*] "language"." (Jørgensen, Karrebaek, Madsen and Møller 2011: 25)

The expression "eine limesteife" is uttered as a speech token by Esen in response to Michael's query, and is intelligible in relation to it. Yet the speech token does not exhibit unambiguous fidelity-to-type with respect to word-types from either Danish or German: Esen's utterance is fractionally congruent with both Danish and German along distinct dimensions of its phonological or morphoysntactic organization, and thus constitutes a blend of two distinct PLG systems.

I have argued elsewhere (Agha 2009) that bilingualism is a social practice that involves the transposition of speech tokens across geographic or social settings in ways that alter their "type"-level construal both at the level of grammar and social indexicality: Bilinguals reanalyze PLG blends not only as grammatical types but also as stereotypic indexicals of role and relationship, and hence reanalyze the register models used to interpret speech behaviors in social interaction. From the standpoint of its persona-indexing effects, any register constitutes a class of enregistered emblems (Agha 2007a, ch. 5) that enable social persons to perform or recognize stereotypic images of self and other in social interaction. Most of the accompanying articles describe the social-semiotic processes through which enregistered emblems of social differences are formulated under conditions of immigration-based multilingualism.

In contemporary Copenhagen youth speech, several features of speech behavior are grouped together as isopragmatic indexical signs (i.e., are treated as having comparable indexical values), and two such emblems, which are shown in the columns of Table 1, are sometimes described as "integrated" and "street" demeanors by those who deploy them. Danish scholars have documented the speech behaviors that express these emblems. The top half of Table 1 shows contrasts in the PLG organization of speech tokens; the bottom half shows contrastive social personae stereotypically indexed by speech contrasts.

Contrasts between "integrated" and "street" personae may be indexed by multiple diacritics of PLG organization, including contrasts of phonology, lexis and morphosyntax: Contrasts of pronunciation include presence versus absence of creaky voice, stress-timed versus syllable-timed prosody, longer versus shorter vowels (except before syllables with schwa). Morphosyntactically, "street" utterances can have SVO word order in environments where "integrated" utterances exhibit VSO inversion, and "common" gender marking where the latter exhibit neuter gender forms. A salient features of "street" demeanor is the use of lexical items sourced from languages other than Danish but tropically altered in form and significance, including cases where lexical items from Turkish, Arabic, Kurdish or Serbian acquire features of word-form or word-sense that are wholly or partly reanalyzed when they occur in Danish utterances as stereotypic indexicals of youth speech and demeanor.

Table 1: Enregistered emblems of "Integrated" vs. "Street" persona

	"Integrated" personae	**"Street" personae**
PLG diacritics	creaky voice syllables	absence of creaky voice
	stress-timed prosody	syllable-timed prosody
	longer vowels	shorter vowels
	standard word order, gender	non-standard word order & noun gender
	Danish PLG sourcing	non-Danish PLG sourcing ("polylingual" lexemes)
	polite phrases	swearing, slang
	high pitch	affricated-palatized /t/, fronted /s/, voiceless uvular /r/
	↓	↓
stereotypic personae	higher class (wealth)	toughness
	sophistication, authority	masculinity
	academic skill	academic non-prestige
	self-possession	absence of politeness
	Danish persona	panethnic "street" or ethnically "foreign" personae

Source: Madsen 2013a, Quist 2008

In any society, emblems associated with differences in perceivable behavior are variably known to members of that society, and are often variably deployed in behavior in a manner that is indexically selective for types of social interaction and setting. Although Table 1 provides a useful summary of emblematic contrasts, it is vital to understand that persons acquainted with these emblems need not deploy all of these diacritics in their own behaviors, and those who do deploy them, need not deploy all diacritics in all situations. Indeed, as with enregistered speech emblems in all other societies, Danish youth can display these social personae to fractional degrees, and, through interactionally cued forms of role dissonance, inhabit a variety of gradient, hybrid and out-group selves (Agha 2007a: 265–268) in social encounters with others.

Karrebæk (this volume) observes that whereas adolescent kids (age 13–16) effectively deploy the full range of diacritics of "street" demeanor, much younger kids, such as school starters (age 5–6), produce some phonetic tokens (perceived as "accented Danish") but very few of its lexical diacritics. Karrebæk's own article presents longitudinal data on the practices of a group of kids over a number of years (as students first in grade 0, and then through grades 1 and 2), and these data provide some evidence of the process of socialization through which they come to recognize and deploy these emblems in peer group interactions.

Excerpt 1 is an interaction between Danish majority kids who engage in playful banter that transgresses adult norms even as it establishes footings and alignments within the peer group itself. When Michelle, who is not of immigrant background, uses an English swear word (*fuck*, line 1, excerpt 1), Konrad immediately responds by asking "Are you an Arab?" This is not a non sequitur, by any means. The diacritics of the street emblem include the use of swear words, a practice associated with ethnically foreign (including Middle Eastern) identities (Table 1). Even though Michelle is visibly not of immigrant background and is using an English swear word, calling her "Arab" exhibits playful familiarity with a minority emblem by majority kids who are progressively becoming acquainted with it. When Michelle denies being Arab (line 21) and Konrad laughs (line 22), Tommy, who is also a non-immigrant and has already produced a more elaborate curse based on the same English lexeme (*fucking l:ort*, line 13), now steps in and fills the interactional slot vacated by Michelle's denial and readily accepts the role designator "Arab" as a contrastive description of himself ("I *am* an Arab", line 23), as Konrad continues to laugh (line 25) and Michelle to protest (line 26). Having formulated himself as "Arab", Tommy then proceeds to utter two quasi-Arabic lexical items in a loud voice (*KHABAKHALÆ*, line 29; *SHÆDA:M*, line 38). He can vouch for neither the exact lexical form nor the sense of these words. Yet the fidelity of his speech tokens to Arabic PLG types is irrelevant to this interaction since neither he nor his interlocutors speak Arabic. An emblem that stereotypically links swearing to Middle Eastern personae is nonetheless salient through its partials, and the interactional organization of the encounter remains tightly coherent for its participants.

Karrebæk discusses a series of other interactions between members of youth peer groups over the course of the next two years of schooling. It is worth emphasizing that all speakers in her data exhibit proficiency in Danish at every moment-interval of these interactions. However, at discontinuous moments of the speech stream, acts of producing speech tokens that exhibit non-fidelity to Standard Danish PLG types come to count as acts of inhabiting emblematic personae that contrast with the Danish persona they inhabit at other moment-intervals in surrounding discourse, and these moments of indexical non-congruence to co-text

(Agha 2007a: 24) become occasions for doing interpersonal work. Since the street emblem can both be inhabited and disavowed by kids from a variety of ethnic backgrounds (Danish, Somali, Eritrean, Palestinian, etc.), the ethnicity of specific individuals is not indexed by the acoustical speech tokens they produce (although it is often variably indexed by features of their visible demeanor). Moreover, the speech tokens they utter are sourced from a variety of PLG types across speaking turns (see, for instance, the sequence of *wallah, koran*_(Arabic), *fuck* (English), *jeg ME:NER* (Danish), *eow* (Kurdish), uttered in a sequence of moves and countermoves by distinct interlocutors across lines 1–8 of Example 9), so that no single PLG system is consistently at issue. The interactional game consists of performing utterance segments that differ from Standard Danish in a variety of ways, and of responding through some form of interpersonal alignment with the semiotic partials of a youth emblem and hence with each other – whether by producing or avoiding comparable diacritics, whether by inhabiting or disavowing corresponding role designations – during the course of peer-group interactions. Karrebæk's multi-year data suggest that kids are progressively socialized to the emblem over the course of time, and, through prolonged immersion in peer group culture over three years of schooling (grade 0, grade 1 and grade 2), come to recognize a wider range of its diacritics over time, while also continuing to differentiate themselves from each other by the degree to which they deploy them in their own behaviors.

Stæhr's article (this volume) draws attention to forms of metasemiotic activity that are characteristic of online platforms like Facebook. Since social interaction on Facebook is mediated by pixelated script-tokens of words and sentences that are produced by typing on keyboards, evaluations of word spelling themselves mediate interpersonal footings among youth linked to each other as Facebook users. Offline spelling conventions are implicitly or explicitly in play at every moment-interval of the interaction: They are implicitly in play whenever word-tokens exhibit type-fidelity to Standard spelling (which most tokens do). They become explicitly part of the interactional game when word-tokens do not conform to Standard spelling and give rise to interpersonal evaluations. Quite apart from their word-spelling, the speech tokens that mediate persona evaluations of interlocutors are category clusters of PLG category types whose phonological and morphosyntactic organization establishes multiple text-defaults on the form and construal of speech tokens, so that any given text token may be defective with respect to one categorical dimension while conforming to others (Agha 2007a: 103–6). When specific word-tokens appear defective as PLG types along one or another of these dimensions, they are readily evaluated as stereotypic indexicals of the interactant's social type. Thus in Excerpt 3, where Fatima keyboards the word-form *IIGÅÅS*, her Facebook interlocutor, Tahir, construes it as a casual speech contraction of the Standard expression *ikke også* 'right', and cites his own biology teacher as someone who speaks this way. By treating pronunciation (not spelling) as the relevant dimension of type-fidelity, he evaluates Fatima's defective (and pixelated) word-token as a canonical sample of a casual register of (oral) speech among majority Danish speakers, and thus as a speech sample which (since Tahir and Fatima are themselves minority Danes) indexes a social category distinct from their own. This case is an inverse of one discussed earlier: Just as in Karrebæk's earlier example (where Tommy says "I *am* an Arab") majority Danes negotiate interpersonal personae through stereotypes of minorities, here minority Danes negotiate their own personae by deploying stereotypes of majority speech.

Yet entitlements to produce the speech of social others are unevenly distributed as interactional norms. In Excerpt 4, Jamil types out a stylized sample of foreigner/minority speech (marked by subject-verb inversion), which, since he is a minority Dane, counts as a typification of the social category to which he himself belongs. His interlocutor is a majority Dane, Rasmus, who responds with a sample of the same minority register (marked by excessive use of definite articles) but then proceeds, a minute later, to produce a self-correction, perhaps because he realizes that his initial response, although produced during intimate banter as a way of aligning with his minority friend, Jamil, happens also to be a quasi-public post on Facebook, which can later be evaluated by any subsequent reader of the page as an act where a majority Dane is poking fun at minorities.

Similar issues of entitlement and ownership emerge when young people exhibit alignment to emblems in the cases discussed by Hyttel-Sørensen (this volume). Yet the classroom encounters in which these alignments are exhibited have little to do with peer group school culture. They involve students' responses to variants of the emblem that are metasemiotically formulated and disseminated by mediatized products – like video games and TV shows – across a national-scale imaginary. Hyttel-Sørensen locates contemporary TV representations of minority Danes in a larger history of mediatized practices. Across these cases, the diacritics that index "street" personae (such as the ones in Table 1) consistently recur in a variety of mediatized products, where, since these products have an audiovisual format, acoustical speech tokens are linked to a number of additional diacritics of social difference, including visible depictions of non-Nordic physiognomy and immigrant lifestyle. These mediatized representations thereby transform the enregistered emblem along every dimension of its social-semiotic existence (Agha 2007a: 169), including its *semiotic repertoires* (the behavioral signs that index its deployment), its *social range* (what these repertoires stereotypically index), and its *social domain* (those capable of recognizing such indexicals).

An early such product is an online computer game, *Mujaffaspillet* 'The Mujaffa game', produced initially in 2000 as an entertainment product for a national youth market. The game's content links minority youth repertoires to gangster personae, such as the game's main character, Mujaffa, an immigrant youth who, decked in gold necklaces, drives around Copenhagen in a BMW picking up blonde girls. Parodies of ethnic minorities are extended further in a 2007 Christmas season TV show, *Yallahrup Færgeby*, whose main characters, Ali and Hassan, are hand puppets who mingle with their puppet friends in gangster-ish activities (involving handguns, cocaine, etc.), while idolizing the American rapper Tupac, with whom they are sometimes arrayed as suspects in a police lineup. Insofar as they reach national markets, these products expand the social domain of those capable of recognizing the emblem substantially beyond the Copenhagen youth who comprise the social domain of its competent speakers. And insofar as they link audible speech repertoires to visible features of "gangster" activities and milieus, they transform the semiotic repertoires of the emblem by expanding the perceivable diacritics that signal its deployment: specific kinds of discursive tokens (such as affricated-t allophones and Arabic-sourced lexemes) are now bundled with ghetto-like settings, minority ethnicities, and illegal activities. And the social domain of Danish speakers who encounter this transformed emblem is much larger than the social domain of those who have directly encountered Copenhagen youth speech and its speakers in social interactions.

When the more recent TV show, *Det Slører Stadig* 'It still veils', begins to air in 2013 for an adult market, the show presuppose awareness by its national audience of a pejorative emblem whose discursive tokens have already been linked through ethnic parody to images of minorities and gangsters by a series of mediatized products during the preceding decade. The show attempts to make fun not of minorities but of ethnic parodies of minorities. Yet this effort remains controversial because it occupies delicate ground. In skits like "gangster talk on the phone", a dark haired girl portrays a minority character who switches rapidly between diacritics of "street" speech and demeanor (deployed when speaking to a presumed fellow "gangster" on the phone) and diacritics of "integrated" speech and demeanor plus a sprinkling of scientific lexicon (deployed when discussing her nuclear physics homework with a blonde school classmate). The dark haired character displays a wide register range and the selective ability to deploy distinct registers (and associated emblems of minority Dane rudeness vs. majority Dane academic finesse) in distinct participation frameworks (on vs. off the phone) in a single physical setting. The blonde haired character appears less academically skilled and less familiar with nuclear physics, and exhibits surprise at her interlocutor's ability to switch in and out of the academic persona that is appropriate to their homework discussion. Meanwhile, the dark haired girl displays competence in the PLG and prosodic features of each register and a proficient grasp of its indexical selectivity for the participation framework to which it is appropriate.

When the video skit is played in a classroom setting – where students comprise a kind of focus group, whose own evaluations of the show and its characters are then recorded – an awareness of emblematic links between speech and ethnicity is evident in all student responses, though handled differently in different ones. Students like Jamil who habitually display acoustical diacritics of the street emblem in their own behaviors (which all minorities don't) and who routinely encounter mock ethnic representations of the emblem in mediatized products (as other Danes also do) find the TV show insulting. They evaluate it as mocking them. The emblem they find insulting is not the one whose use and construal they negotiate in peer-groups and classroom settings every day, but the pejorative variant that has been rescaled to a nation-state imaginary through mediatized representations in the preceding decade. The two emblems overlap in acoustical tokens, to be sure, but the range of semiotic devices through which they are performed (by school peers vs. mediatized characters) and the social personae recognizable through such displays (to Copenhagen youth vs. national audiences) are very distinct. When the TV skit is played in class, the mediatized emblem intrudes into school culture by implying gangster-like identities that students neither seek for themselves nor ascribe to each other.

The articles by Madsen, Nørreby, and Møller discuss a variety of mediatized representations of immigrants that are formulated by national agencies (like government bureaucracies and political parties) and disseminated through specific discursive artifacts (like policy documents, curricular protocols, political speeches, etc.) to a relatively large (sometimes nationwide) audience. Each such project produces an "immigrant" formulation – or formulates the characteristics of "immigrants" in contrast to the rest of Danish society – through metasemiotic discourses that group disparate phenomena together, typifies their social significance and makes them known to a social domain of persons through its own dissemination. Discourses that seek to "integrate" minorities into Danish society (as discussed by Madsen), or link multilingualism to ethnicity (as discussed by Nørreby) or link minorities to crime (as discussed by Møller) disseminate distinct "immigrant"-formulations within the nation state imaginary to which actual minorities respond through their own activities. Mediatized representations of social kinds of persons are disseminated not merely by what is commonly called "the media" (which is simply a narrow special case of mediatization; see Agha 2011a, 2011b), but by any semiotic practice that links forms of communication and commoditization to each other in some specific way, as do practices of schooling, state bureaucracy, and the law (see Agha 2012). In the case of bureaucracies, such links are commonly established by the coordination of communicative tasks among personnel within a division of wage-labor, where task-allocated forms of co-authorship yield composite discursive artifacts like policy documents (which seem to represent society to itself), and which, when these policies are implemented through the State's funding protocols, enable specific intake groups of citizens to encounter representations of what they are (or have been, or should be like) as members of society in the very funded projects and initiatives in which they now find themselves to be positioned as participants. Yet since any form of mediatization is englobed by forms of semiotic mediation not anticipated by its design (Agha 2011a), these bureaucratic policies are readily altered by those who implement them, as Madsen shows.

Madsen (this volume) discusses policies and funding schemes formulated by the Ministry of Integration, that are designed to assimilate ethnic minorities into mainstream Danish society by promoting leisure activities. She observes that Ministry policies formulate an "ethnocentric" conception of Danish culture, where "Danish values and norms" are assumed (in principle) to be societally homogenous, yet viewed (in practice) as best exemplified by those who have authentic links to a Danish "birthplace and nation". Immigrant minorities are expected to mingle with majority Danes in leisure clubs, and to adopt more authentically Danish norms and values. Madsen finds that when Ministry policies of assimilation through leisure clubs are implemented in the creation of a rap music club, the club's convener, Ali Sufi, has a vision quite distinct from the Ministry that funds his club. He organizes the club's activities by linking different minority youth practices – rap music making, peer group sociality, doing school homework – to each other. As they participate in the music club, rap musicians also begin to do better at school. But they do so by responding to a vision distinct from the vision that funds and enables their participation. The Ministry, which views society in nation-centric terms, seeks to link outsiders to insiders. The club's organizer seeks to link disparate minority youth practices to each other. Rather than integrating minorities to majority culture, the club integrates minority practices better with each other. At the same time, the club also emphasizes the importance of making rap music that can reach a wider Danish audience. As a result the YouTube videos produced by the youth group come to contain more features of Danish majority speech and fewer features of street speech over time. Yet when they speak to each other within their peer community, rap music makers readily employ street speech as an emblem of in-group sociability. Rather than doing away with emblematic contrasts, the young rappers learn to deploy them in ways that are indexically selective for participation frameworks of effective and appropriate use: They use more Standard Danish in YouTube videos (in order to reach a wider national audience) and maintain the use of street register in in-group practices (in order to maintain peer group sociality).

Nørreby (this volume) describes an analogous case, where the display of emblems of self-positioning remains indexically selective for the participation frameworks in which they are displayed. The mediatized representations of society now at issue are those of the Ministry of Education and of the popular press. Nørreby observes that in these discourses the term "bilingual" has shifted from a more inclusive to a less inclusive sense: Whereas the term once denoted all schoolchildren with non-Danish mother tongues, it is now used more or less consistently only for children who have a non-Western ethnic background, and count as ethnic minorities. In this newer classification, samples of the category "bilingual" can no longer be identified by attending only to speech behavior: It is necessary instead to consider visible diacritics of ethnicity independent of speech in order to partition, within the set of people who audibly speak more than one language, just the ones who visibly count as "bilingual". Nørreby suggests that this difference between the explicit and implicit denotation of the term is a "covert and symbolic way of exercising discrimination".

How do the persons who count as samples of this category themselves display forms of belonging or non-belonging to Danish society? Nørreby describes the case of one student, Jamil, who is born and raised in Denmark and has family ties in Lebanon and Palestine. Jamil produces distinct self-formulations in narratives about his encounters with others. In describing family vacations to Lebanon, Jamil describes Lebanese practices and lifestyles as strange and unfamiliar, and, by distancing himself from them, formulates himself as Danish. When he describes encounters in Denmark with people outside his peer group, he describes himself as singled out as a minority and differentiated from majority Danes by teachers in his classes and by co-workers at his part-time job. But in his self-presentations on Facebook, which are directed to members of his peer-group, he is able to exhibit his affiliations with the country where he lives (by describing himself as Danish) and his country of heritage (by describing Palestine as his favorite country) and, through various forms of irony about himself (such as a fictive last name), to describe his hybrid position in Denmark without concern for any misunderstanding by friends in his peer group.

Møller (this volume) describes a case where adult society itself becomes an object of mockery in youth peer group settings. When a 9th grade class is asked to evaluate complex social problems for a school project, the anti-immigrant stance of nationalist politicians becomes the object of lampooning in a class presentation, where immigrant and non-immigrant students perform and evaluate the voiced speech of conservative politicians like Pia Kjærsgård, who use immigrant-phobic political rhetoric – that links immigrants to crime and to undue demands on the welfare state – in order to seek voter support in her own electoral constituency. One of the students, Israh, chooses to perform Pia Kjærsgård's anti-immigrant rhetoric and political persona for her class project. By calling herself Pia Kjærsgård and voicing her presentation as Kjærsgård's political oratory, an immigrant student thus recycles anti-immigrant mediatized personae (Agha 2010) into the classroom, and at the same time, through a hyperbolic exaggeration of the rhetoric she employs, effectively distances herself from the personae she performs. Meanwhile, by using ethnic slur terms to address her classmates – minority classmates as "Paki swine", white Danish classmates as "beautiful potatoes" – Israh is effectively able to elicit politically engaged responses from her own classmates, along with a good deal of cheering and applause. As students engage her and each other through their responses, they employ a variety of enregistered signs of speech and demeanor in the course of formulating themselves or their interlocutors as social categories of specific kinds (elderly Danish men, ethnic bus drivers, criminals, politicians) including social categories that may not correspond to actual persons in Danish society but nonetheless have a vivid half-life during the course of dissing sessions where immigrants and non-immigrant youth align with each other as peer groups in lampooning divisive figurements of Danes in adult society.

Viewed as a collection, the articles in this volume bring to light a number of features of the social lives of youth emblems and minority youths that are likely to recur across similar conditions in other locales. Differences in speech behavior do count as diacritics of social difference within these youth emblems, but since speech is never encountered in isolation from other perceivable behaviors, discursive and non-discursive diacritics of difference are grouped together into multi-channel semiotic arrays that link audible and visible differences to each other. Some features of these models are formulated by mediatized processes and made available to a national imaginary; others are formulated and negotiated by young people in peer group activities. As young Danes negotiate the semiotic partials of these emblems, whether in encounters with each other in peer groups, or in encounters with mediatized representations of themselves, they reanalyze the form and significance of their own behaviors and thus of youth emblems to incremental degrees in their daily lives. We can only study these increments through sociohistorical snapshots of a moment or phase of social history. But just as being young is a temporary feature of age-graded positionality in Danish society, emblems of social difference associated with youth are themselves undergoing change and reanalysis, as the accompanying articles show, in the lived experiences of young people growing up and into Danish society.

Transcription Conventions

[ggg]	overlap
[ggg](>)	brackets encloses overlapping speech, arrows (used in chapter 10)
[hhh](<):	indicate what is said simultaneously
>ggg<	segment quicker than surrounding talk
<ggg>	segment slower than surrounding talk
xxx	unintelligible speech
?ggg?	unsure speech
((ggg))	Comments
(2.0)	pause (2 sec)
(.)	very short pause
Uni:	unidentified speaker
°quiet°	segment quieter than surrounding talk
LOUD	segment louder than surrounding talk
↑	raising pitch
↓	faling pitch
G >	screen gaze
emphasis	emphasis
=	latching
:	prolongation of sound
☺	smile voice ☺
{raises head}	action, gesture and gaze simultaneous with speech
dashed underline	Arabic speech (used in chapter 6)
italics	Danish speech
bold	Swedish speech

References

Ag, Astrid & Jens Normann Jørgensen. 2013. Ideologies, norms, and practices in youth poly-languaging. *International Journal of Bilingualism* 17(4). 525–539.
Ag, Astrid. 2010. *Sprogbrug og identitetsarbejde hos senmoderne storbypiger* [Language use and identity work among latemodern urban girls] (Copenhagen Studies in Bilingualism 53). Copenhagen: University of Copenhagen, Faculty of Humanities.
Agergaard, Sine & Hans Bonde. 2013. *Integration gennem kroppen. Idræt, etnicitet og velfærd-spolitik* [Integration through the body. Sports, ethnicity and welfare politics]. Copenhagen: Museum Tusculanum.
Agergaard, Sine. 2008. *Unges idrætsdeltagelse og integration i idrætsforeninger i Århus Vest* [Youth's sports participation and integration in sports clubs in Århus West]. Copenhagen: Idrættens Analyseinstitut [Danish institute for sport studies].
Agergaard, Sine. 2013. Hvordan danske idrætsforeninger blev arenaer for etnisk integration. Udvikling og tilegnelse af integrationspolitk for idræt [How Danish sports clubs became arenas for ethnic integration. Development and acquisition of integration politics for sports]. In Agergaard, Sine & Hans Bonde. 2013. *Integration gennem kroppen. Idræt, etnicitet og velfærdspolitik* [Integration through the body. Sports, ethnicity and welfare politics]. Copenhagen: Museum Tusculanum, 63–84.
Agha, Asif & Stanton Wortham (eds.). 2005. Discourse across speech-events: Intertextuality and interdiscursivity in social life. [Special issue]. *Journal of Linguistic Anthropology* 15(1).
Agha, Asif. 2003. The social life of cultural value. *Language & Communication* 23(3–4). 231–273.
Agha, Asif. 2005a. Registers of language. In Alessandro Duranti (eds.), *A companion to linguistic anthropology,* 23–45. Oxford: Blackwell.
Agha, Asif. 2005b. Voice, footing, enregisterment. *Journal of Linguistic Anthropology* 15(1). 38–59.
Agha, Asif. 2007a. *Language and social relations. Studies in the social and cultural foundations of language.* Cambridge, UK & New York: Cambridge University Press.
Agha, Asif. 2007b. Recombinant selves in mass mediated spacetime. *Language & Communication* 27. 320–335. 2009. 'What Do Bilinguals Do? A Commentary.' In *Beyond Yellow English: Toward a Linguistic Anthropology of Asian Pacific America*, pp. 253–58, Angela Reyes and Adrienne Lo, eds. New York: Oxford University Press.
Agha, Asif. 2010. 'Recycling mediatized personae across participation frameworks.' *Pragmatics and Society* 1 (2): 311–319.
Agha, Asif. 2011. Commodity registers. *Journal of Linguistic Anthropology* 21(1). 22–53.
Agha, Asif. 2011a. 'Meet mediatization.' *Language and Communication* 31: 163–170
Agha, Asif. 2011b. 'Large and small scale forms of personhood.' *Language and Communication* 31: 171–180.
Agha, Asif. 2012. 'Mediatized projects at State peripheries.' *Language and Communication* 32 (2): 98–101.
Agha, Asif. Forthcoming. Tropes of slang. In Ivo Strecker & Stephen Tyler (eds.), *The rhetoric of social relations*. Oxford: Berghahn.
Alim, H. Samy, Awad Ibrahim & Alastair Pennycook. 2009. *Global linguistic flows. Hip hop cultures, youth identities and the politics of language*. New York: Routledge.

Alim, H. Samy. 2011. Global Ill-literacies: Hip hop cultures, youth identities and the politics of literacy. *Review of Research in Education* 35(1). 120–147.

Ambjörnsson, Fanny. 2003. *I en klass för sig – Genus, klass och sexualitet bland gymnasietjejer* [In a class of their own – Gender, class and sexuality among school girls]. Stockholm: Ordfront Forläg.

Andersen, Simon Calmar. 2010. *Mehmet og modkulturen: En undersøgelse af drenge med etnisk minoritetsbaggrund* [Mehmet and the counter culture: A study of boys with ethnic minority background]. Copenhagen: Rambøll Management Consulting.

Anderson, Benedict. 1991. *Imagined communities: Reflections on the origin and spread of nationalism*. London & New York: Verso.

Anderson, Sally. 2003. *Civilizing children: Children's sports and civil sociality in Copenhagen, Denmark*. Copenhagen: University of Copenhagen PhD dissertation.

Anderson, Sally. 2005. "Vi kender hinanden alle sammen hvor vi så end er fra". At leve lokalt gennem global sport i København ["We all know each other wherever we are from". To live locally through global sports in Copenhagen]. In Karen Fog Olwig, Laura Gilliam & Karen Valentin (eds.), *Lokale liv, fjerne forbindelser. Studier af børn, unge og migration* [Local lives, distant connections. Studies of children, youth and migration], 153–174. Copenhagen: Hans Reitzel.

Androutsopoulos, Jannis & Arno Scholz (eds.). 1998. *Jugendsprache – language des jeunes – youth language: Linguistische und soziolinguistische Perspektiven*. Frankfurt am Main: Peter Lang.

Androutsopoulos, Jannis & Arno Scholz. 2003. Spaghetti funk: appropriation of hip-hop culture and rap music in Europe. *Popular Music and Society* 26(4). 463–479.

Androutsopoulos, Jannis. 2001. "From the streets to the streets and back again": on the mediated diffusion of ethnolectal patterns in contemporary German. *LAUD Linguistic Agency* A522. 1–24.

Androutsopoulos, Jannis. 2008. Potentials and limitations of discourse-centered online ethnography. *Language@Internet* 5(9), 1–20.

Androutsopoulos, Jannis. 2011. Language change and digital media: A review of conceptions and evidence. In Tore Kristiansen & Nikolas Coupland (eds.), *Standard languages and language standards in a changing Europe*, 145–159. Oslo: Novus Press.

Androutsopoulos, Jannis. 2013. Online data collection. In Christine Mallinson, Becky Childs & Gerad Van Herk (eds.), *Data collection in sociolinguistics. Methods and applications*, 236–249. New York: Routledge.

Arnaut, Karel. 2012. Super-diversity: elements of en emerging perspective. In Karel Arnaut, Jan Blommaert, Ben Rampton & Massimiliano Spotti (eds.), Language and superdiversities II. [Special Issue]. *Diversities* 14(2). 1–16.

Auer, Peter. 1984. *Bilingual conversation*. Amsterdam: John Benjamins.

Auer, Peter. 1998. *Code-switching in conversation, language, interaction and identity*. London: Routledge.

Auer, Peter. 2003. 'Turkenslang': Ein jugendsprachlicher Ethnolekt des Deutschen und seine Transformationen. In Annelies Häcki Buhofer, Lorens Hofer, Hansjakob Schneider, Teresa Tschui & Eva L. Wyss (eds.), *Spracherwerb und Lebensalter*, 255–264. Basel & Tübingen: Francke.

Bakhtin, Mikhail Mikhajlovitj. 1981. Discourse in the novel. In Michael Holquist (ed.), *The dialogic imagination. Four essays by M.M. Bakhtin*, 169–422. Austin: University of Texas Press.

Bakhtin, Mikhail Mikhajlovitj. 1984. *Problems of Dostoevsky's poetics* (Theory and History of Literature 8). Minneapolis: University of Minnesota Press.

Baquedano-López, Patricia & Ariana Mangual Figueroa. 2011. Language socialization and immigration. In Alessandro Duranti, Elinor Ochs & Bambi Schieffelin (eds.), *Handbook of language socialization*, 536–563. Malden, MA: Wiley-Blackwell.

Baron, Naomi S. 2008. *Always on: Language in an online and mobile world*. Oxford: Oxford University Press.

Bartholdsson, Åsa. 2009. *Den venlige magtudøvelse. Normalitet og magt i skolen* [Friendly execution of power. Normality and power in school]. Stockholm: Akademisk Forlag.

Barton, David & Carmen Lee. 2013. *Language online: Investigating digital texts and practices*. Abingdon, UK: Routledge.

Bauman, Richard & Charles Leslie Briggs. 2003. *Voices of modernity: Language ideologies and the politics of inequality*. Cambridge: Cambridge University Press.

Bauman, Zygmunt. 1998. *Globalization*. Cambridge: Cambridge University Press.

Beck, Ulrich. 1992. *Risk society*. London: Sage.

Bhatia, Sunil. 2000. Language socialisation and the construction of socio-moral meanings. *Journal of Moral Education* 29(2). 149–166.

Billig, Michael. 1995. *Banal nationalism*. London: Sage.

Billig, Michael. 1999. *Freudian repression: Conversation creating the unconscious*. Cambridge: Cambridge University Press.

Blackledge, Adrian & Angela Creese. 2010. *Multilingualism: A critical perspective* (Advances in Sociolinguistics). London: Continuum.

Blackledge, Adrian. 2005. *Discourse and power in a multilingual world*. Amsterdam: John Benjamins Publishing.

Blommaert, Jan & Ad Backus. 2011. Repertoires revisited: 'Knowing language' in superdiversity. *Working Papers in Urban Language and Literacies* 67. London: King's College London. www.kcl.ac.uk/sspp/departments/education/research/ldc/publications/workingpapers/67.pdf (accessed 22-7-2014).

Blommaert, Jan & Ben Rampton. 2011. Language and super-diversity. In Jan Blommaert, Ben Rampton & Massimiliano Spotti (eds.), Language and superdiversities. [Special Issue]. *Diversities* 13(2). 1–20. http://www.mmg.mpg.de/fileadmin/user_upload/Subsites/Diversities/Journals_2011/2011_13-02_gesamt_web.pdf (accessed 21-7-2014).

Blommaert, Jan, Jim Collins & Stef Slembrouck. 2005. Polycentricity and interactional regimes in 'global neighborhoods'. *Ethnography* 6(2). 205–235.

Blommaert, Jan & Dong Jie. 2010. *Ethnographic fieldwork. A beginner's guide*. Bristol: Multilingual Matters.

Blommaert, Jan & Fie Velghe. 2013. Learning a supervernacular: Textspeak in a South African township. In Adrian Blackledge & Angela Creese (eds.), *Heteroglossia as practice and pedagogy*, 137–154. Dordrecht: Springer.

Blommaert, Jan & Jef Verschueren. 1998. *Debating diversity. Analysing the discourse of tolerance*. New York: Routledge.

Blommaert, Jan, Lies Creve & Evita Willaert. 2006. On being declared illiterate: Language-ideological disqualification in Dutch classes for immigrants in Belgium. *Language & Communication* 26(1). 34–54.

Blommaert, Jan. 2005. *Discourse. A critical introduction*. Cambridge: Cambridge University Press.

Blommaert, Jan. 2007. Commentary: On scope and depth in linguistic ethnography. *Journal of Sociolinguistics* 11(5). 682–688.

Blommaert, Jan. 2010. *The sociolinguistics of globalization*. Cambridge: Cambridge University Press.

Blommaert, Jan. 2013. *Ethnography, superdiversity and linguistic landscapes*. Bristol: Multilingual Matters.

Boeskov, Signe & Thomas Ilkjær. 2005. *Integration og det frivillige foreningsliv* [Integration and the voluntary association life]. Copenhagen: University of Copenhagen, Department of Nutrition, Exercise and Sports.

Borland, James H. 1997. The construct of giftedness. *Peabody Journal of Education* 72(3–4). 6–20.

Bourdieu, Pierre. 1991. *Language and symbolic power*. Cambridge: Polity Press.

Brink, Lars & Jørn Lund. 1975. *Dansk rigsmål. Lydudviklingen siden 1840 med særligt henblik på sociolekterne i København* [Danish standard language. The development of speech sounds since 1840 with special emphasis on the sociolects in Copenhagen]. Copenhagen: Gyldendal.

Brown, Penelope & Steven Levinson. 1987. *Politeness: Some universals in language use*. Cambridge: Cambridge University Press.

Brubaker, Rogers & Frederick Cooper. 2000. Beyond "identity". *Theory and Society* 29(1). 1–47.

Brubaker, Rogers. 2002. Ethnicity without groups. *European Journal of Sociology* 43(2). 163–189.

Brubaker, Rogers. 2004. *Ethnicity without groups*. Cambrige, MA: Harvard University Press.

Bucholtz, Mary & Kira Hall. 2004. Language and identity. In Duranti, Alessandro (ed.), *A companion to linguistic anthropology*, 369–395. Malden, MA: Blackwell Publishing Ltd.

Bucholtz, Mary & Kira Hall. 2005. Identity and Interaction: a Sociocultural Linguistic approach, *Discourse Studies* 7(4–5), 585–614.

Bucholtz, Mary. 2007. Shop talk: Branding, consumption, and gender in American middle-class youth interaction. In McElhinny, Bonnie (ed.), *Words, worlds and material girls: Language, gender, globalization* (Language, Power and Social Process 19), 371–402. Berlin & New York: Mouton de Gruyter.

Bucholtz, Mary. 2011. *White kids: Language, race and styles of youth identities*. Cambridge: Cambridge University Press.

Bucholtz, Mary, Barnwell, Brendan, Skapoulli, Elena, & Lee, Jung-Eun Janie. 2012. Itineraries of Identity in Undergraduate Science. *Anthropology & Education Quarterly* 43(2), 157–172.

Burton, Jonathan, Nandi, Alita & Lucinda Platt. 2008. Who are the UK's minority ethnic groups? Issues of identification and measurement in a longitudinal study. *ISER Working Paper Series*. 2008–2026. Essex: Institute for Social and Economic Research.

Cameron, Deborah.1995. *Verbal hygiene: The politics of language*. London: Routledge.

Capps, Lisa & Elinor Ochs. 1995. *Constructing panic: The discourse of agoraphobia*. Cambridge, MA: Harvard University Press.

Cazden, Courtney. 1988. *Classroom discourse. The language of teaching and learning*. Portsmouth, NH: Heinemann.

Christensen, Mette Vedsgaard. 2010. One of my kind? Language and ethnicity among Danish adolescents. In Pia Quist & Bente Ailin Svendsen (eds.), *Multilingual urban Scandinavia: New linguistic practices*, 207–224. Bristol: Multilingual Matters.

Coates, Jennifer. 1999. Changing femininities: The talk of teenage girls. In Mary Bucholtz, A. C. Liang & Laurel A. Sutton (eds.), *Reinventing identities: The gendered self in discourse*, 123–144. New York: Oxford University Press.
Collins, James. 2007. Migration & multilingualism: Implications for linguistic anthropology and education research. *Working Papers in Urban Language and Literacies* 47. London: King's College London. www.kcl.ac.uk/sspp/departments/education/research/ldc/publications/workingpapers/47.pdf (accessed 22-7-2014).
Collister, Lauren B. 2011. *-repair in online discourse. *Journal of Pragmatics* 43(3). 918–921.
Connell, John & Chris Gibson. 2003. *Sound tracks: Popular music, identity and place.* London: Routledge.
Coupland, Nikolas & Tore Kristiansen. 2011. SLICE: Critical perspectives on language (de) standardisation. In Tore Kristiansen & Nikolas Coupland (eds.), *Standard languages and language standards in a changing Europe*, 11–35. Oslo: Novus Press.
Coupland, Nikolas. 2003. Introduction: Sociolinguistics and globalisation. *Journal of Sociolinguistics* 7(4). 465–472.
Creese, Angela & Adrian Blackledge. 2010. Translanguaging in the bilingual classroom: A pedagogy for learning and teaching? *The Modern Language Journal* 94(1). 103–115.
Creese, Angela. 2008. Linguistic ethnography. In Kendall A. King & Nancy H. Hornberger (eds.), *Encyclopedia of language and education, 2nd Edition. Volume 10: Research Methods in Language and Education*, 229–241. New York: Springer. http://link.springer.com/content/pdf/10.1007%2F978-0-387-30424-3_257.pdf (accessed 21-7-2014)
Cutler, Cecilia. 1999. Yorkville crossing: a case study of hip-hop and the language of a White middle class teenager in New York City. *Journal of Sociolinguistics* 3(4). 428–442.
Dagkas, Symeon & Kathleen Armour (eds.). 2011. *Inclusion and exclusion through youth sports.* London: Routledge.
Daryai-Hansen, Petra. 2014. *Begegnungen mit fremden Sprachen: Ein Instrumentarium zur Analyse von Sprachhierarchien und Sprachrepräsentationen am Beispiel des dänischen und deutschen sprachenpolitischen Diskurses.* Tübingen: Narr Francke Attempto Verlag.
Davies, Bronwyn & Rom Harré. 1990. Positioning: The discursive production of selves. *Journal for the Theory of Social Behavior* 20(1). 43–63.
DR [Denmark's Radio]. 2013a. Det slører stadig. http://www.dr.dk/tv/se/det-sloerer-stadig/det-sloerer-stadig-1-15/ (accessed 28-11-2013).
DR [Denmark's Radio]. 2013b. Det slører stadig. Facebook. https://www.facebook.com/detslorerstadig (accessed 3-12-2013).
DR [Denmark's Radio]. 2013c. DR2. Om kanalen. http://www.dr.dk/tv/kanal/dr2/om_kanalen (accessed 28-11-2013).
Du Bois, John W. 2007. The stance triangle. In Robert Englebretson (ed.), *Stance in discourse: Subjectivity in interaction*, 139–182. Amsterdam: John Benjamins.
Duranti, Alessandro. 1994. From Grammar to Politics: Linguistic Anthropology in a Western Samoan Village. Berkeley & Los Angeles: University of California Press.
Durkheim, Emile. 2006, org. 1897. *On Suicide.* London: Penguin Classics.
Eckert, Penelope. 2008. Variation and the indexical field. *Journal of Sociolinguistics* 12(4). 453–476.
Eckert, Penelope. 2011. Language and power in the preadolescent heterosexual market. In *American Speech* 86(1). 85–97.
Eckert, Penelope. 1989. Jocks and burnouts: Social categories and identity in the high school. New York: Teachers College Press.

Eckert, Penelope. 2000. Linguistic variation as social practice. Oxford: Blackwell.
Edwards, John. 1995. *Multilingualism*. London: Penguin.
Egelund, Niels, Chantal Pohl Nielsen & Beatrice Schindler Rangvid. 2011. *PISA etnisk 2009. Etniske og danske unges resultater i PISA 2009* [PISA ethnic 2009. Ethnic and Danish youth's results in PISA 2009]. Copenhagen: Anvendt KommunalForskning. www.kora.dk/media/1290/udgivelser_2011_pdf_2861_pisa_etnisk.pdf (accessed 22-7-2014).
Ejrnæs, Morten. 2002. Etniske minoriteters tilpasning til livet i Danmark – forholdet mellem majoritetssamfund og etniske minoriteter [Ethnic minorities' adaption to life in Denmark – the relationship between the majority society and ethnic minorities]. *AMID Working Paper Series* 18.
Ellison, Nicole & danah boyd. 2013. Sociality through social network sites. In William H. Dutton (ed.), *The Oxford handbook of internet studies*, 151–172. Oxford: Oxford University Press.
Erickson, Ken & Donald Stull. 1998. *Doing team ethnography: Warnings and advice*. London: Sage.
Extra, Guus , Massimiliano Spotti & Piet van Avermaet (eds.). 2009. *Language testing, migration and citizenship: Cross national perspectives on integration regimes*. London: Continuum.
Fairclough, Norman. 1992. Discourse and Social Change. Cambridge: Polity Press
Faist, Thomas. 2009. Diversity – a new mode of incorporation?. *Ethnic and Racial Studies* 32(1). 171–190.
Fedorak, Shirley A. 2009. *Pop culture. The culture of everyday life*. Toronto: The University of Toronto Press.
Fleming, Luke & Michael Lempert. 2011. Introduction: Bad words. (Special issue on The unmentionable: Verbal taboo and the moral life of language.) Anthropological Quarterly 84: 5–14.
Foner, Nancy & Christophe Bertossi. 2011. Immigration, incorporation, and diversity in Western Europe and the United States: Comparative perspectives. *American Behavioral Scientist* 55(12). 1535–1540.
Frith, Simon. 1996. Music and identity. In Stuart Hall & Paul du Gay (eds.), *Questions of cultural identity*, 108–127. London & New York: Sage.
Gal, Susan & Judith T. Irvine. 1995. The boundaries of languages and disciplines: How ideologies construct difference. *Social Research* 62(4). 966–1001.
García, Ofelia & Li Wei. 2014. *Translanguaging, language, bilingualism and education*. Basingstoke: Palgrave Macmillan.
García, Ofelia. 2009. *Bilingual education in the 21st century: A global perspective*. Malden, MA: Wiley Blackwell.
Garrett, Paul B. & Patricia Baquedano-López. 2002. Language socialization: Reproduction and continuity, transformation and change. *Annual Review of Anthropology* 31. 339–361.
Garrett, Peter. 2010. *Attitudes to language*. Cambridge: Cambridge University Press.
Giddens, Anthony. 1984. *The constitution of society: Outline of a theory of structuration*. Cambridge: Polity Press.
Giddens, Anthony. 1991. *Modernity and self-identity, self and society in the late modern age*. Cambridge: Polity Press.
Goffman, Erving 1983. The interaction order. *American Sociological Review* 48. 1–17.
Goffman, Erving. 1955. On face-work: An analysis of ritual elements in social interaction. *Psychiatry: Journal for the Study of Interpersonal Processes* 18. 213–231.

Goffman, Erving. 1963. *Stigma: Notes on the management of spoiled identity*. New York: Simon & Schuster Inc.
Goffman, Erving. 1981. *Forms of talk*. Philadelphia & Oxford: University of Pennsylvania Press & Blackwell.
Goffman, Erving. 1986. *Frame analysis: An essay on the organization of experience*. Boston: Northeastern University Press.
Goodwin, Marjorie Harness & Amy Kyratzis. 2007. Children socializing children: Practices for negotiating the social order among peers. *Research on Language and Social Interaction* 40(4). 279–289.
Goodwin, Marjorie Harness & Amy Kyratzis. 2012. Peer language socialization. In Alessandro Duranti, Elinor Ochs & Bambi B. Schieffelin (eds.), *The handbook of language socialization*, 365–390. West Sussex: Wiley-Blackwell.
Goodwin, Marjorie Harness & Charles Goodwin. 1987. Children's arguing. In Susan Philips, Susan Steele & Christine Tanz (eds.), *Language, gender, and sex in comparative perspective*, 200–48. Cambridge: Cambridge University Press.
Goodwin, Marjorie Harness. 1990. *He-said-she-said: Talk as social organization among black children*. Bloomington: Indiana University Press.
Goodwin, Marjorie Harness. 2006a. Participation, affect, and trajectory in family directive/response sequences. *Text & Talk* 26(4/5). 513–541.
Goodwin, Marjorie Harness. 2006b. *The hidden life of girls: Games of stance, status, and exclusion*. Malden, MA: Blackwell Publishing Ltd.
Gordon, Cynthia. 2009. *Making meanings, creating families. Intertextuality and framing in family interaction*. Oxford: Oxford University Press.
Gramsci, Antonio. 1971. *Selections from the prison notebooks*. London: Lawrence and Wishart.
Gumperz, John Joseph. 1982. *Discourse strategies* (Studies in Interactional Sociolinguistics 1). Cambridge & New York: Cambridge University Press.
Hanks, William. 1996. Language form and communicative practices. In John Joseph Gumperz & Stephen Levinson (eds.), *Rethinking linguistic relativity*, 232–270. Cambridge: Cambridge University Press.
Hansen, Gert Foget & Nicolai Pharao. 2010. Prosody in the Copenhagen multiethnolect. In Pia Quist & Bente Ailin Svendsen (eds.), *Multilingual urban Scandinavia: New linguistic practices*, 79–94. Bristol: Multilingual Matters.
Harris, Roxy. 2006. *New ethnicities and language use*. Basingstoke: Palgrave Macmillan.
Harris, Roy. 1999. Integrational linguistics and the structuralist legacy. *Language & Communication* 19(1). 45–68.
Hatt, Beth. 2007. Street smarts vs. book smarts: The figured world of smartness in the lives of marginalized, urban youth. *The Urban Review* 39(2). 145–166.
Heath, Shirley Brice. 1983. *Ways with words: Language, life, and work in communities and classrooms*. Cambridge: Cambridge University Press.
Heller, Monica & Marilyn Martin-Jones. 2001. Introduction: Symbolic domination, education, and linguistic differences. In Monica Heller & Marilyn Martin-Jones (eds.), *Voices of authority: Education and linguistic difference*, 1–28. Westport, CT & London: Ablex Publishing.
Heller, Monica. 1992. The politics of codeswitching and language choice. In Carol M. Eastman (ed.), *Codeswitching*, 123–143. Avon: Multilingual Matters.
Heller, Monica. 2007. Bilingualism as ideology and practice. In Monica Heller (ed.), *Bilingualism: a social approach*, 1–22. Basingstoke: Palgrave Macmillan.

Hewitt, Roger. 1992. Language, youth and the destabilisation of ethnicity." In Cecilia Palmgren, Karin Lövgren & Göran Bolin (eds.) *Ethnicity in youth culture*, 27–41. Stockholm: Stockholm University.

Heyd-Metzuyanim, Einat. 2013. The co-construction of learning difficulties in mathematics – teacher-student interactions and their role in the development of a disabled mathematical identity. *Educational Studies in Mathematics* 83(3). 341–368.

Hill, Jane Hassler. 2008. *The everyday language of white racism* (Blackwell Studies in Discourse and Culture 3). Chichester, UK & Malden, MA: Wiley-Blackwell.

Hill, Marc Lamont. 2009. *Beats, rhymes and classroom life. Hip-hop pedagogy and the politics of identity*. New York: Teachers College Press.

Hirst, Elizabeth Wyshe. 2007. Identity construction in complex second language classrooms. *International Journal of Educational Research* 46(3). 159–171.

Hogan-Brun, Gabrielle, Clare Mar-Molinero & Patrick Stevenson. 2009. Discourses on Language and Integration. Critical Perspectives on Language Testing Regimes in Europe. Amsterdam: John Benjamins.

Holmen, Anne & Jens Normann Jørgensen. 2000. Har vi en dansk sprogpolitik? Om holdninger til sproglig mangfoldighed i Danmark [Do we have a Danish language policy? On attitudes to linguistic diversity in Denmark]. In Jens Normann Jørgensen & Anne Holmen (eds.), *Sprogs status i Danmark år 2011* [The status of language(s) in Denmark in 2011] (Copenhagen Studies in Bilingualism 32), 75–90. Copenhagen: University of Copenhagen.

Holmen, Anne & Jens Normann Jørgensen. 2010. Skærpede holdninger til sproglig mangfoldighed i Danmark [Aggravated attitudes to linguistic diversity in Denmark]. In Jens Normann Jørgensen & Anne Holmen (eds.), *Sprogs status i Danmark år 2021* [The status of language(s) in Denmark in 2021] (Copenhagen Studies in Bilingualism 58), 121–135. Copenhagen: University of Copenhagen.

Holmen, Anne. 2009. Multilingualism in education. In favour of a dynamic view of languages. In Ole Kolbjørn Kjørven, Bjørg-Karin Ringen & Antoinette Gagné (eds.), *Teacher diversity in diverse schools: Challenges and opportunities for teacher education*, 32–55. Vallset: Oplandske Bokforlag.

Howard, Kathryn M. 2010. Social relationships and language shift in Northern Thailand. *Journal of Sociolinguistics* 14(3). 313–340.

Hymes, Dell. 1972. On communicative competence. In J. B. Pride & Janet Holmes (eds.), *Sociolinguistics. Selected readings*, 269–293. Harmondsworth: Penguin.

Hyttel-Sørensen, Liva. 2009. *Dem de andre ikke vil lege med – en undersøgelse af børns sprogholdninger med fokus på dansk som andetsprog* [Those the others do not want to play with – a study of children's language attitudes focusing on Danish as a second language] (Copenhagen Studies in Bilingualism 49). Copenhagen: University of Copenhagen.

Hyttel-Sørensen, Liva. 2011. Children and language attitudes – a study of language attitudes among eight year old children in Denmark. In Janus Spindler Møller & Jens Normann Jørgensen (eds.), *Language enregisterment and attitudes*, 10–26. Copenhagen: University of Copenhagen.

Ibrahim, Awad. 1999. Becoming black: Rap and hip-hop, race gender, identity and the politics of ESL learning. *TESOL Quarterly* 15(3). 349–369.

Ibsen, Bjarne & Laila Ottesen. 1996. Youth sport in Europe – Denmark. In Paul de Knop, Lars-Magnus Engstrom, Berit Skirstad & Maureen R. Weiss (eds.), *Worldwide trends in youth sport*, 101–114. Champaign, IL: Human Kinetics.

Irvine, Judith T. & Susan Gal. 2000. Language ideology and linguistic differentiation. In Paul Kroskrity (ed.), *Regimes of language*, 35–83. Santa Fe: School of American Research Press.

Jacquemet, Marco. 2005. Transidiomatic practices: Language and power in the age of globalization. *Language & Communication* 25(3). 257–277.

Jaffe, Alexandra, Jannis Androutsopoulos, Mark Sebba & Sally Johnson (eds.). 2012. *Orthography as social action: Scripts, spelling, identity and power.* Berlin: Mouton De Gruyter.

Jaffe, Alexandra. 2011. Sociolinguistic diversity in mainstream media: Authenticity, authority and processes of mediation and mediatization. *Journal of Language & Politics* 10(4). 562–586.

Jaffe-Walter, Reva. 2013. "Who would they talk about if we weren't here?": Muslim youth, liberal schooling, and the politics of concern. *Harvard Educational Review* 83(4). 613–635.

Jaspers, Jürgen. 2005. Linguistic sabotage in a context of monolingualism and standardization. *Language & Communication* 25(3). 279–297.

Jaspers, Jürgen. 2008. Problematizing ethnolects: Naming linguistic practices in an Antwerp secondary school. *International Journal of Bilingualism* 12(1–2). 85–103.

Jaspers, Jürgen. 2011a. Talking like a 'zerolingual': Ambiguous linguistic caricatures at an urban secondary school. *Journal of Pragmatics* 43(5). 1264–1278.

Jaspers, Jürgen. 2011b. Strange bedfellows: Appropriations of a tainted urban dialect. *Journal of Sociolinguistics* 15 (4), 493–524

Johnstone, Barbara, Jennifer Andrus & Andrew E. Danielson. 2006. Mobility, indexicality and the enregisterment of "Pittsburghese". *Journal of English Linguistics* 34(2). 77–104.

Jørgensen, Jens Normann & Janus Spindler Møller. 2014. Polylingualism and languaging. In Constant Leung & Brian Street, *The Routledge companion to English studies* (eds.), 67–83. London: Routledge.

Jørgensen, Jens Normann, Martha Sif Karrebæk, Lian Malai Madsen & Janus Spindler Møller. 2011. Polylanguaging in superdiversity. In Jan Blommaert, Ben Rampton & Massimiliano Spotti (eds.), Language and superdiversities. [Special Issue]. *Diversities* 13(2). 23–37. http://www.mmg.mpg.de/fileadmin/user_upload/Subsites/Diversities/Journals_2011/2011_13-02_gesamt_web.pdf (accessed 21-7-2014).

Jørgensen, Jens Normann. 2003. Linguistic construction and negotiation of social relations among bilingual Turkish-speaking adolescents in North-Western Europe. *Journal of Multilingual and Multicultural Development* 24(1/2). 1–12.

Jørgensen, Jens Normann. 2004. Languaging and languagers. In Christine B. Dabelsteen & Jens Normann Jørgensen (eds.), *Languaging and language practice* (Copenhagen Studies in Bilingualism 36), 5–22. Copenhagen: University of Copenhagen.

Jørgensen, Jens Normann. 2008. Poly-lingual languaging around and among children and adolescents. *International Journal of Multilingualism* 5(3). 161–176.

Jørgensen, Jens Normann. 2010. *Languaging. Nine years of poly-lingual development of young Turkish-Danish grade school students, vol. I–II* (Copenhagen Studies in Bilingualism, The Køge Series K15–K16). Copenhagen: University of Copenhagen.

Jørgensen, Jens Normann. 2012. Ideologies and norms in language and education policies in Europe and their relationship with everyday language behaviours. *Language, Culture and Curriculum* 25(1). 57–71.

Just Jeppesen, Kirsten & Anne Nielsen. 2001. *Tosprogede småbørn i Danmark* [Bilingual toddlers in Denmark]. Copenhagen: Socialforskningsinstituttet [The Danish national centre for social research].

Karrebæk, Martha Sif & Narges Ghandchi. 2015. 'Pure' Farsi and political sensitivities: Language and ideologies in Farsi complementary language classrooms in Denmark. *Journal of Sociolinguistics* 19(1). 62–90

Karrebæk, Martha Sif, Andreas Stæhr, Anu Muhonen & Kasper Juffermans. Forthcoming. Negotiating norms on social network sites: Polycentric normativities in superdiversity. In Dorthe Duncker & Bettina Perregaard (eds.), *Creativity and continuity. Perspectives on the dynamics of language conventionalization.* Amsterdam: John Benjamins.

Karrebæk, Martha Sif, Ulla Lundqvist, Narges Ghandchi & Lamies Nassri. 2013. *Mother tongue education for linguistic minority pupils in the super-diverse metropolis of Copenhagen: Organizing and structuring the classrooms* (Project Report 1). Copenhagen: University of Copenhagen.

Karrebæk, Martha Sif. 2006. *Tosprogede børn i det danske samfund* [Bilingual children in the Danish society]. Copenhagen: Hans Reitzel.

Karrebæk, Martha Sif. 2011a. *At blive et børnehavebarn. En minoritetsdrengs sprog, interaktion og deltagelse i børnefællesskabet* [Becoming a child in day care. The language, interaction and participation of a minority boy in child community] (Copenhagen Studies in Bilingualism 62). Copenhagen: University of Copenhagen.

Karrebæk, Martha Sif. 2011b. It farts: The situated management of social organization in a kindergarten peer group. *Journal of Pragmatics* 43(12). 2911–2931.

Karrebæk, Martha Sif. 2012a. "What's in your lunch-box today?: Health, respectability, and ethnicity in the primary classroom. *Journal of Linguistic Anthropology* 22(1). 1–22.

Karrebæk, Martha Sif. 2012b. Authority relations: The mono-cultural educational agenda and classrooms characterized by diversity. *Naldic Quarterly* 10(1). 33–37.

Karrebæk, Martha Sif. 2013a. "Don't speak like that to her!" Linguistic minority children's socialization into an ideology of monolingualism. *Journal of Sociolinguistics* 17(3). 355–375.

Karrebæk, Martha Sif. 2013b. Fodboldkort i indskolingen: Literacy, populærkultur og polycentricitet i en minoritetsdrengs hverdagsliv [Football cards in primary school: Literacy, popular culture and polycentricity in the everyday life of a minority boy]. *Nordand* 8(2). 9–31.

Karrebæk, Martha Sif. 2013c. Lasagna for breakfast: The respectable child and cultural norms of eating practices in a Danish kindergarten classroom. *Food, Culture and Society* 16(1). 85–106.

Karrebæk, Martha Sif. Forthcoming. "I am lucky I can speak Arabic": A linguistic minority child's socialization into an ideology of double monolingualism in super-diversity. In Dorthe Duncker & Bettina Perregaard (eds.), *Creativity and continuity. Perspectives on the dynamics of language conventionalization.* Amsterdam: John Benjamins.

Kendall, Shari. 2007. Introduction: Family talk. In Deborah Tannen, Shari Kendall & Cynthia Gordon (eds.), *Family Talk. Discourse and identity in four American families*, 3–23. Oxford: Oxford University Press.

Knoop-Henriksen, Line. 2013. *"www.lærogstav.dk" – En sociolingvistisk undersøgelse af sproglige, sociale og kulturelle normer og praksisser i superdiversiteten* [www.learntospell.dk – A sociolinguistic study of linguistic, social and cultural norms and practices in superdiversity]. Copenhagen: University of Copenhagen. MA thesis.

Korp, Helena. 2011. What counts as being smart around here? The performance of smartness and masculinity in vocational upper secondary education. *Education, Citizenship and Social Justice* 6(1). 21–37.

Kotsinas, Ulla-Britt. 1988. Immigrant children's Swedish – a new variety? *Journal of Multilingual and Multicultural Development* 9(1). 129–140.
Kress, Gunther Rolf. 2005. *Literacy in the new media age.* New York: Routledge.
Kristiansen, Tore & Jens Normann Jørgensen. 2003. Introduction. The Sociolinguistics of Danish. In Tore Kristiansen & Jens Normann Jørgensen (eds.), The sociolinguistics of Danish. [Special Issue]. *International Journal of the Sociology of Language* 2003(159). 1–7.
Kristiansen, Tore. 2009. The macro-level social meanings of late-modern Danish accents. *Acta Linguistica Hafniensia* 41(1). 167–192.
Kristjánsdóttir, Bergthóra S. & Lene Timm. 2007. *Tvetunget uddannelsespolitik. Dokumentation af etnisk ulighed i folkeskolen* [Double-tounged education policy. Evidence of ethnic inequality in the Danish folkeskole]. Frederiksberg: Nyt fra Samfundvidenskaberne.
Kroskrity, Paul (ed.). 2000. *Regimes of language, ideologies, polities, and identities.* Santa Fe: School of American Research Press.
Kulick, Don & Bambi B. Schieffelin. 2004. Language socialization. In Alessandro Duranti (ed.), *A companion to linguistic anthropology*, 349–368. Oxford: Blackwell.
Kyratzis, Amy, Jennifer E. Reynolds & Ann-Carita Evaldsson (eds.). 2010. Heteroglossia and language ideologies in children's peer play. [Special Issue]. *Journal of Pragmatics* 20(4).
Kyratzis, Amy. 2004. Talk and interaction among children and the co-construction of peer groups and peer culture. *Anuual Review of Anthropology* 33. 625–649.
Lave, Jean & Etienne Wenger. 1998. *Communities of practice: Learning, meaning and identity.* Cambridge: Cambridge University Press.
Leaper, Campbell & Tara A. Smith. 2004. A meta-analytical review of gender variation in children's language use: Talkativeness, affiliative speech and assertive speech. *Developmental Psychology* 40(6). 993–1027.
Leaper, Campbell.1994. Exploring the consequences of gender segregation on social relationships. In Leaper, Campbell (ed.), *Childhood gender segregation: Causes and consequences* (New Directions for Child Development 65). 67–86. San Francisco: Jossey-Bass.
Maccoby, Eleanor E. 1998. *The two sexes: Growing up apart, coming together.* Cambridge, MA: Belknap Press/Harvard University Press.
Madsen, Lian Malai & Martha Sif Karrebæk. 2015. Urban classrooms, polycentricity and sociolinguistic resources. In Julia Snell, Sara Shaw & Fiona Copland (eds.), *Linguistic ethnography: Interdisciplinary explorations.* London: Palgrave.
Madsen, Lian Malai, Janus Spindler Møller & Jens Normann Jørgensen. 2010. "Street language" and "Integrated": Language use and enregisterment among late modern urban girls. In Lian Malai Madsen, Janus Spindler Møller & Jens Normann Jørgensen (eds.), *Ideological Constructions and Enregisterment of Youth Styles* (Copenhagen Studies in Bilingualism 55), 81–113. Copenhagen: University of Copenhagen.
Madsen, Lian Malai, Martha Sif Karrebæk & Janus Spindler Møller. 2013. The Amager project: The study of language and social life of minority children and youth. *Tilburg Working Papers in Culture Studies* 52.
Madsen, Lian Malai. 2008. Fighters and outsiders: Linguistic practices, social identities and social relationships among youth in a martial arts club. Copenhagen: University of Copenhagen. PhD dissertation.
Madsen, Lian Malai. 2011. Interactional renegotiations of educational discourses in recreational learning contexts. *Linguistics and Education* 22(1). 53–68.

Madsen, Lian Malai. 2012. Discourses on Integration and Interaction in a Martial Arts Club. In Barbara Segaert, Marc Theeboom, Christiane Timmerman & Bart Vanreusel (eds.) *Sports Governance, Development and Coporate Responsibility*. Routledge, 74–87.

Madsen, Lian Malai. 2013a. 'High' and 'low' in urban Danish speech styles. *Language in Society* 42(2). 115–138.

Madsen, Lian Malai. 2013b. Stylised, normal street language. Paper presented at Language and Super-diversity: Explorations and Interrogations, University of Jyväskylä, June 4–7.

Madsen, Lian Malai. 2013c. "Klubben, grupperne og sproget": Social praksis, sprogbrug og social integration i en københavnsk kampsportsklub ["The club, the groups and the language": Social practice, language use and social integration in a Copenhagen martial arts club]. In Sine Agergaard & Hans Bonde (eds.) *Integration gennem kroppen. Idræt, etnicitet og velfærdspolitik* [Integration through the body. Sports, ethnicity and welfare politics] Museum Tusculanum, 105–125.

Madsen, Lian Malai. 2014. Heteroglossia, voicing and social categorisation. In Adrian Blackledge & Angela Creese (eds.), *Heteroglossia as practice and pedagogy* (Educational Linguistics 20), 41–58. Dordrecht: Springer.

Madsen, Lian Malai. 2015. *Fighters, girls and other identities: Sociolinguistics in a martial arts club*. Bristol: Multilingual Matters.

Maegaard, Marie, Torben Juel Jensen, Tore Kristiansen & Jens Normann Jørgensen. 2013. Diffusion of language change: Accommodation to a moving target. *Journal of Sociolinguistics* 17(1). 3–36.

Maegaard, Marie. 2007. *Udtalevariation og -forandring i københavnsk – en etnografisk undersøgelse af sprogbrug, sociale kategorier og social praksis blandt unge på en københavnsk folkeskole* [Pronunciation variation and change in Copenhagen speech – an ethnographic study of language use, social categories and social practice among youth in a Copenhagen public school]. Copenhagen: University of Copenhagen. PhD dissertation.

Makoni, Sinfree & Alastair Pennycook. 2007. Disinventing and reconstituting languages. In Sinfree Makoni & Alastair Pennycook (eds.), *Disinventing and reconstituting languages*, 1–41. Clevedon: Multilingual Matters.

Makoni, Sinfree. 2012. A critique of language, languaging and supervernacular. *Muitas Vozes* 1(2). 189–199.

Maltz, Daniel N. & Ruth A. Borker. 1982. A cultural approach to male–female miscommunication. In John Gumperz (ed.), *Language and social identity*, 195–216. Cambridge: Cambridge University Press.

Martín Rojo, Luisa. 2010. *Constructing inequality in multilingual classrooms*. Berlin & New York: Mouton de Gruyter.

Maybin, Janet & Karin Tusting. 2011. Linguistic ethnography. In James Simpson (ed.). *The Routledge handbook of applied linguistics*. London: Routledge.

McDermott, Ray. 2006. What is not known about genious. In Shirley R. Steinberg & Joe Lyons Kincheloe (eds.), *What you don't know about schools*. New York: Palgrave Macmillan.

Mehan, Hugh. 1979. *Learning lessons: Social organization in the classroom*. Cambridge, MA: Harvard University Press.

Mehan, Hugh. 1996. The construction of an LD student: A case study in the politics of representation. In Michael Silverstein & Greg Urban (eds.), *Natural histories of discourse*. Chicago: University of Chicago Press.

Meredith, Joanne & Elizabeth Stokoe. 2014. Repair: Comparing Facebook 'chat' with spoken interaction. *Discourse & Communication* 8(2). 181–207.

Milani, Tomasso. 2010. What's in a name? Language ideology and social differentiation in a Swedish print-mediated debate. *Journal of Sociolinguistics* 14(1). 116–142.

Møller, Janus Spindler & Jens Normann Jørgensen. 2011a. Enregisterment among adolescents in superdiverse Copenhagen. In Janus Spindler Møller & Jens Normann Jørgensen (eds.), *Language enregisterment and attitudes* (Copenhagen Studies in Bilingualism 63), 99–122. Copenhagen: University of Copenhagen.

Møller, Janus Spindler & Jens Normann Jørgensen. 2011b. Linguistic norms and adult roles in play and serious frames. *Linguistics and Education* 22(1). 68–78.

Møller, Janus Spindler & Jens Normann Jørgensen. 2012. Enregisterment among adolescents in superdiverse Copenhagen. *Tilburg Working Papers in Culture Studies* 28. 1–15.

Møller, Janus Spindler & Jens Normann Jørgensen. 2013. Organizations of language among Adolescents in superdiverse Copenhagen. *International Electronic Journal of Elementary Education* 6(1). 23–42.

Møller, Janus Spindler, Jens Normann Jørgensen & Anne Holmen. 2014. Polylingual development among Turkish speakers in a Danish primary school – a critical view on the 4th grade slump. *International Journal of Bilingual Education and Bilingualism* 17(1). 32–54.

Møller, Janus Spindler. 2009. *Poly-lingual interaction across childhood, youth and adulthood.* Copenhagen: University of Copenhagen PhD dissertation.

Møller, Janus Spindler. Forthcoming a. "You black black": Polycentric norms for the use of terms associated with ethnicity. In Max Spotti, Karel Arnaut & Martha Sif Karrebæk (eds.), *Engaging super-diversity and the sociolinguistics of interstices.* Clevedon, Avon: Multilingual Matters.

Møller, Janus Spindler. Forthcoming b. The enregisterment of minority languages in a Danish classroom. In Asif Agha & Frog (eds.), *Registers of Communication* (Studia Fennica Linguistica). Helsinki: Finnish Literature Society.

Munk, Martin D. & Jakob B. Lind. 2004. *Idrættens kulturelle pol* [The cultural pole of sports]. Copenhagen: Museum Tusculanum.

Myers-Scotton, Carol. 1993. *Social motivations for codeswitching: Evidence from Africa.* Oxford: Clarendon.

Newell, Sasha. 2009. Enregistering modernity, bluffing criminality: How Nouchi speech reinvented (and fractured) the nation. *Journal of Linguistic Anthropology* 19(2). 157–84.

Nørreby, Thomas Rørbeck. 2012. *"Jamil Perkersen Nielsen Rasmussen" – en sociolingvistisk undersøgelse af identitet og etnicitet i superdiversiteten* ["Jamil Perkersen Nielsen Rasmussen" – a sociolinguistic study of identity and ethnicity in superdiversity] (Copenhagen Studies in Biligualism 67). Copenhagen: University of Copenhagen.

Nørreby, Thomas Rørbeck & Janus Spindler Møller. 2015. Ethnicity and social categorization in on- and offline interaction among Copenhagen adolescents. Discourse, Context and Media 8: 46–54.

Nožić, Dijana. 2013. *Ej blot til lyst – sprogpsykologisk kritisk diskursanalyse af fordomme, forståelse og mening inden for rammerne af det sociale og satiriske* [Not just for pleasure – a language psychology critical discourse analysis of prejudice, understanding and meaning in the context of the social and satirical]. Copenhagen: University of Copenhagen MA thesis.

Nusche, Deborah, Gregory Wurzburg & Breda Naughton. 2010. *OECD Reviews of Migrant education: Denmark.* http://www.oecd.org/denmark/44855206.pdf (accessed 21-3-2014).

Ochs, Elinor & Bambi B. Schieffelin. 2012. The theory of language socialization. In Alessandro Duranti, Elinor Ochs & Bambi B. Schieffelin (eds.), *The handbook of language socialization*, 1–21. Malden, MA: Wiley-Blackwell.
Ochs, Elinor & Bambi Schieffelin. 1994. Language acquisition and socialization: Three developmental stories and their implications. In Benjamin G. Blount (ed.), *Language, culture, and society: A book of readings*, 470–512. Prospect Heights, ILL: Waveland Press Inc.
Ochs, Elinor & Carolyn Taylor. 1996. The "father knows best" dynamic in family dinner narratives. In Kira Hall & Mary Bucholtz (eds.), *Gender articulated: Language and the socially constructed self*, 97–121. New York: Routledge.
Ochs, Elinor & Tamar Kremer-Sadlik. 2007. Introduction: morality as family practice. *Discourse & Society* 18(1). 5–10.
Ochs, Elinor, Carolyn Taylor, Dina Rudolph & Ruth Smith. 1992. Storytelling as a theory-building activity. *Discourse Processes* 15(1). 37–72.
Ochs, Elinor. 1988. *Culture and language development: Language acquisition and socialization in a Samoan village*. New York: Cambridge University Press.
Ochs, Elinor. 1992. Indexing gender. In Alessandro Duranti & Charles Goodwin (eds.), *Rethinking context: Language as an interactive phenomenon*, 335–358. Cambridge: Cambridge University Press.
Olwig, Karen Fog & Karsten Pærregaard (eds.). 2007. *Integration. Antropologiske perspektiver* [Integration. Anthropological perspectives]. Copenhagen: Museum Tusculanum
Olwig, Karen Fog & Kartens Pærregaard. 2011. The Question of Integration. Immigration, Exclusion and The Danish Welfare State. Newcastle: Cambridge Scholars Publishing.
Olwig, Karen Fog. 2010. 'Integration': Migrants and refugees between Scandinavian welfare societies and family relations. *Journal of Ethnic and Migrant Studies* 37 (2), 179–96.
Orman, Jon. 2012. Not so super: The ontology of "supervernaculars". *Language & Communication* 32(4). 349–357.
Otsuji, Emi & Alastair Pennycook. 2010. Metrolingualism: Fixity, fluidity and language in flux. *International Journal of Multilingualism* 7(3). 240–254.
Paugh, Amy & Carolina Izquierdo. 2009. Why is this a battle every night? Negotiating food and eating in American dinnertime interaction. *Journal of Linguistic Anthropology* 19(2). 185–204.
Paugh, Amy. 2005. Learning about work at dinnertime: Language socialization in dual-earner American families. *Discourse & Society* 16(1). 55–78.
Pedersen, Inge Lise. 2009. The social embedding of standard ideology through four hundred years of standardisation. In Marie Maegaard, Frans Gregersen, Pia Quist and Jens Normann Jørgensen (eds.), *Language attitudes, standardization and language change*, 51–58. Oslo: Novus Press.
Pennycook, Alastair & Emi Otsuji. 2015. *Metrolingualism: Language in the City*. London: Routledge.
Pennycook, Alastair & Emi Otsuji. 2014. Metrolingual multitasking and spatial repertoires: 'Pizza mo two minutes coming'. *Journal of Sociolinguistics* 18(2). 161–184.
Pennycook, Alastair. 2007. *Global Englishes and transcultural flows*. Abingdon: Routledge.
Perregaard, Bettina. 2010. 'Luckily it was only for 10 minutes': Ideology, discursive positions, and language socialization in family interaction. *Journal of Sociolinguistics* 14(3). 370–398.

Pharao, Nicolai & Gert Foget Hansen. 2005. Prosodiske træk i et- og tosprogede unges københavnsk [Prosodic features in mono- and bilingual youth's Copenhagen Danish]. *Danske Talesprog* 6. 1–50.
Pharao, Nicolai, Marie Maegaard, Janus Spindler Møller & Tore Kristiansen. 2014. Indexical meanings of [s+] among Copenhagen youth: Social perception of a phonetic variant in different prosodic contexts. *Language in Society* 43(1). 1–13.
Quist, Pia & Jens Normann Jørgensen. 2007. Crossing – negotiating social boundaries. In Peter Auer & Li Wei (eds.), *Handbook of multilingualism and multilingual communication*, 371–389. Berlin & New York: Mouton de Gruyter.
Quist, Pia & Bente Ailin Svendsen. 2010. New linguistic practices in multilingual urban Scandinavia: An introduction. In Pia Quist & Bente Ailin Svendsen (eds.), Multilingual Urban Scandinavia: New Linguistic Practices, xiii–xxiii. Clevedon: Multilingual Matters.
Quist, Pia. 2000. Ny københavnsk 'multietnolekt'. Om sprogbrug blandt unge i sprogligt og kulturelt heterogene miljøer [New Copenhagen 'multiethnolect'. On language use among youth in linguistically and culturally heterogeneous environments]. *Danske Talesprog* 1. 143–211.
Quist, Pia. 2005. *Stilistiske praksisser i storbyens heterogene skole – en etnografisk og sociolingvistisk undersøgelse af sproglig variation* [Stylistisc practices in the heterogeneous school in the big city – an ethnographic and sociolinguistic study of linguistic variation]. Copenhagen: Copenhagen University PhD dissertation.
Quist, Pia. 2008. Sociolinguistic approaches to multiethnolect: Language variety and stylistic practice. *International Journal of Bilingualism* 12(1–2). 43–61.
Rampton, Ben & Constadina Charalambous. 2010. Crossing: A review of research. *Working Papers in Language and Literacy 58.* http://www.kcl.ac.uk/innovation/groups/ldc/publications/workingpapers/58.pdf (accessed 25-7-2014).
Rampton, Ben, Janet Maybin & Celia Roberts. 2014. Methodological foundations in linguistic ethnography. *Working Papers in Urban Language & Literacies* 125.
Rampton, Ben, Karin Tusting, Janet Maybin, Richard Barwel, Angela Creese & Vally Lytra. 2004. UK linguistic ethnography: A discussion paper. http://www.lancaster.ac.uk/fss/organisations/lingethn/documents/discussion_paper_jan_05.pdf (accessed 24-7-2014).
Rampton, Ben. 1995. *Crossing: Language and ethnicity among adolescents*. London: Longman.
Rampton, Ben. 1999. Deutsch in inner London and the animation of instructed foreign languages. *Journal of Sociolinguistics* 3(4). 480–504.
Rampton, Ben. 2001. Language crossing, cross-talk and cross-disciplinarity in sociolinguistics. In Nikolas Coupland, Srikant Sarangi & Christopher Candlin (eds.), *Sociolinguistics and social theory*, 261–296. London: Longman.
Rampton, Ben. 2005 [1995]. *Crossing. Language and ethnicity among adolescents*, 2nd edn. Manchester: St. Jerome Publishing.
Rampton, Ben. 2006. *Language in late modernity: Interaction in an urban school*. Cambridge: Cambridge University Press.
Rampton, Ben. 2007. Neo-Hymesian linguistic ethnography in the United Kingdom. *Journal of Sociolinguistics* 11(5). 584–607.
Rampton, Ben. 2009. Interaction ritual and not just artful performance in crossing and stylization. *Language in Society* 38(2). 149–176.
Rampton, Ben. 2011. From 'multiethnic adolescent heteroglossia' to 'contemporary urban vernaculars'. *Language & Communication* 31(4). 276–294.

Rampton, Ben. 2014. Contemporary urban vernaculars. In Jacomine Nortier & Bente Ailin Svendsen (eds.), *Language, youth and identity in the 21st century. Linguistic practices across urban spaces*. Cambridge: Cambridge University Press.

Raviv, Amiram, David Bar-Tal, Alona Raviv, Braha Biran, & Zvia Sela. 2003. Teachers' epistemic authority: Perceptions of students and teachers. *Social Psychology of Education* 6(1). 17–42.

Rennison, Bettina Wolfgang. 2009. *Kampen om integrationen* [The fight over integration]. Copenhagen: Hans Reitzel.

Reyes, Angela. 2014. Linguistic Anthropology in 2013: Super-New-Big. *American Anthropologist* 116(2). 366–378)

Rymes, Betsy & Diana Pash. 2001. Questioning identity: The case of one second-language learner. *Anthropology and Education Quaterly* 32(3). 276–300.

Schegloff, Emanuel Abraham, Gail Jefferson & Harvey Sacks. 1977. The preference for self-correction in the organization of repair in conversation. *Language* 53(2). 361–382.

Schieffelin, Bambi B. & Elinor Ochs. 1986. *Language socialization across cultures*. Cambridge: Cambridge University Press.

Schieffelin, Bambi B. 1990. *The give and take of everyday life: Language socialization of Kaluli children*. Cambridge: Cambridge University Press.

Schönfedt, Juliane & Andrea Golato. 2003. Repair in chats: A conversation analytic approach. *Research on language and social interaction* 36(3). 241–284.

Scollon, Ron & Suzie Wong Scollon. 2004. *Nexus analysis. Discourse and the emerging internet*. London: Routledge.

Sebba, Mark. 1993. *London Jamaican, language systems in interaction*. London: Longman.

Sebba, Mark. 2009. Sociolinguistic approaches to writing systems research. *Writing Systems Research* 1(1). 35–49.

Sebba, Mark. 2012. Orthography as social action: Scripts, spelling, identity and power. In Alexandra Jaffe, Jannis Androutsopoulos, Mark Sebba & Sally Johnson (eds.), *Orthography as social action: scripts, spelling, identity and power*, 1–20. Berlin: Mouton De Gruyter

Sedgwick, Eva Kosofsky. 1985. *Between men. English literature and male homosocial desire*. New York: Columbia University Press.

Segaert, Barbara, Marc Theeboom, Christiane Timmerman & Bart Vanreusel (eds.) 2012. Sports Governance, Development and Coporate Responsibility. London: Routledge.

Seymor, Philip Herschel Kean, Mikko Aro & Jane M. Erskine. 2003. Foundation literacy acquisition in European orthographies. *British Journal of Psychology* 94. 143–174.

Shortis, Tim. 2009. Revoicing TXT: Spelling, vernacular orthography and 'unregimented writing'. In Steve Wheeler (ed.), *Connected minds, emerging cultures: Cybercultures in online learning*, 225–246. Charlotte: Information Age Publishing.

Silverstein, Michael & Greg Urban. 1996. The natural history of discourse. In Michael Silverstein & Greg Urban (eds.), *Natural histories of discourse*, 1–17. Chicago & London: University of Chicago Press.

Silverstein, Michael. 1985. Language and the culture of gender. In Elizabeth Mertz & Rick Parmentier (eds.), *Semiotic mediation*, 219–259. New York: Academic Press.

Silverstein, Michael. 1996. Monoglot "standard" in America: Standardization and metaphors of linguistic hegemony. In Donald Brenneis & Ronald K.S. Macaulay (eds.), *The matrix of language*, 284–306. Boulder, CO: Westview Press.

Silverstein, Michael. 1998. Contemporary transformations of local linguistic communities. Annual Review of Anthropology 27: 401-426.

Silverstein, Michael. 2003. Indexical order and the dialectics of sociolinguistic life. *Language & Communication* 23(3). 193–229.

Skeggs, Beverley. 2010. Class, culture and morality: Legacies and logics in the space for identification. In Margaret Wetherell & Chandra Talpade Mohanty (eds.), *The Sage handbook of identities*. London: Sage.

Spradley, James P. 1980. *Participant observation*. South Melbourne: Wadsworth Cengage Learning.

Stæhr, Andreas & Lian Malai Madsen. 2015. Standard language in urban rap: Social media, linguistic practice and ethnographic context. *Language and Communication* 40, 67–81.

Stæhr, Andreas. 2010. *'Rappen reddede os'. Et studie af senmoderne storbydrenges identitetsarbejde i fritids- og skolemiljøer København* ['The Rap saved us'. A study of late modern urban boys' identity work in leisure and school environments in Copenhagen] (Copenhagen Studies in Bilingualism 54). Copenhagen: University of Copenhagen.

Stæhr, Andreas. forthc. Languaging and normativity on Facebook. In Max Spotti, Karel Arnaut & Martha Sif Karrebæk (eds.), *Wasted language: Super- diversity and the sociolinguistics of the interstices*. Clevedon, Avon: Multilingual Matters.

Stæhr, Andreas. 2015 (in press). Reflexivity in Facebook interaction. Enregisterment across written and spoken language practices. In: Sirpa Leppänen, Janus S. Møller & Thomas R. Nørreby (eds.), Authenticity and normativity in social media. Discourse, Context and Media.

Stæhr, Andreas. 2014. Social media and everyday language use among Copenhagen youth. Copenhagen: University of Copenhagen PhD dissertation.

Sternberg, Robert J. 2007. Who are the bright children? The cultural context of being and acting intelligent. *Educational Researcher* 36(3). 148–155.

Storey, John. 2001. *Cultural theory and popular culture*. Harlow: Pearson.

Stroud, Christopher. 2004. Rinkeby Swedish and semilingualism in language ideological debates. A Bourdieuean perspective. *Journal of Sociolinguistics* 8(2). 196–214.

Styles, Ruth. 2013. I got braces because One Direction's Niall got them!: Inside the minds of the obsessive 1D superfans known as 'Directioners'. *Daily Mail*. http://www.dailymail.co.uk/femail/article-2394594/I-got-braces-One-Directions-Niall-got--Inside-minds-obsessive-1D-superfans-known-Directioners.html (accessed 5-8-2014).

Tannen, Deborah. 2007. Power maneuvers and connection maneuvers in family interaction. In Deborah Tannen, Shari Kendall & Cynthia Gordon (eds.), *Family talk. Discourse and identity in four American families*, 27–48. Oxford: Oxford University Press

Tannen, Deborah. 2013. The medium is the metamessages: Conversational style in new media interaction. In Deborah Tannen & Anna Trester (eds.), *Discource 2.0. Language and new media*, 99–117.Washington: Georgetown University Press.

Thorne, Barrie. 1993. *Gender play: Girls and boys in school*. New Brunswick, NJ: Rutgers University Press.

Thurlow, Crispin. 2006. From statistical panic to moral panic: The metadiscursive construction and popular exaggeration of new media language use in the print media. *Journal of Computer-Mediated Communication* 11(3). 667–701.

Urban, Greg. 2001. *Metaculture: How culture moves through the world*. Minneapolis, MN: University of Minnesota Press.

Varenne, Hervé & Ray McDermott. 1998. *Successful failure. The school America builds*. Colorado & London: Westview.

Vertovec, Steven. 2006. The emergence of super-diversity in Britain. *Oxford University Centre on Migration, Policy and Society Working Paper* 25. www.compas.ox.ac.uk/fileadmin/files/Publications/working_papers/WP_2006/WP0625_Vertovec.pdf (accessed 7-8-2014).

Vertovec, Steven. 2007a. New complexities of cohesion in Britain: Super-diversity, transnationalism and civil-integration. *Commision on Integration and Cohesion*. http://www.compas.ox.ac.uk/fileadmin/files/Publications/Reports/Vertovec%20%20new_complexities_of_cohesion_in_britain.pdf (accessed 22-7-2014).

Vertovec, Steven. 2007b. Super-diversity and its implications. *Ethnic and Racial Studies* 30(6). 1024–1054.

Vertovec, Steven. 2010a. Super-diversity and its implications. In Steven Vertovec (ed.), *Anthropology of migration and multiculturalism: New directions*, 65–96. London: Routledge.

Vertovec, Steven. 2010b. Towards post-multiculturalism? Changing conditions, communities and contexts of diversity. *International Social Science Journal* 61(199). 83–95.

Weber, Sandra & Claudia Mitchell. 2008. Imagining, keyboarding, and posting identities: Young people and new media technologies. In David Buckingham (ed.), *Youth, identity, and digital media*, 25–48. Cambridge, MA: The MIT Press.

Wood, Stephanie. 2013. One Direction world domination complete as their Comic Relief single hits number one spot in SIXTY-THREE countries. *Mirror*. http://www.mirror.co.uk/3am/celebrity-news/one-directions-comic-relief-single-1718681 (accessed 6-8-2014).

Wortham, Stanton. 2004. The interdependence of social identification and learning. *American Educational Research Journal* 41(3). 715–750.

Wortham, Stanton. 2005. Socialization beyond the speech event. *Journal of Linguistic Anthropology* 15(1). 95–112.

Wortham, Stanton. 2006. *Learning identity*. Cambridge: Cambridge University Press.

Wortham, Stanton. 2008. Linguistic anthropology of education. In *Encyclopedia of language and education* (pp. 849–859). Springer US.

Wortham, Stanton. 2012. Introduction to the special issue: Beyond macro and micro in the linguistic anthropology of education. In Stanton Wortham (ed.), Beyond macro and micro in the linguistic anthropology of education. [Special Issue]. *Anthropology & Education Quarterly* 42(2). 128–137.

Yilmaz, Ferruh. 1999. Konstruktionen af de etniske minoriteter: Eliten, medierne og "etnificeringen" af den danske debat [The construction of the ethnic minorities: The Elite, the media and the "ethnification" of the Danish debate]. *Politica* 31(2). 177–191. https://tidsskrift.dk/index.php/politica/article/viewFile/9035/17069 (accessed 24-7-2014).

Yilmaz, Ferruh. 2006. *Ethnicized ontologies: from foreign worker to Muslim immigrant: How Danish public discourse moved to the right through the question of immigration*. San Diego: University of California Electronic MA thesis.

Zimmerman, Don H. 1998. Identity, context and interaction. In Charles Antaki & Sue Widdicombe (eds.), *Identities in talk*, 87–106. London: Sage.

Index

www.ingramcontent.com/pod-product-compliance
Lightning Source LLC
Chambersburg PA
CBHW050856160426
43194CB00011B/2176
9781501516290